LONDON

THE MINI ROUGH GUIDE

There are more than one hundred and fifty Rough Guide travel, phrasebook, and music titles, covering destinations from Amsterdam to Zimbabwe, languages from Czech to Vietnamese, and musics from World to Opera and Jazz

Forthcoming titles include

Alaska • Copenhagen
Ibiza and Formentera • Iceland

Rough Guides on the Internet

www.roughguides.com

Rough Guide Credits

Text editor: Polly Thomas
Series editor: Mark Ellingham
Production: Michelle Draycott, Helen Ostick
Cartography: Maxine Repath

Publishing Information

This second edition published September 2000
by Rough Guides Ltd, 62–70 Shorts Gardens,
London WC2H 9AH

Distributed by the Penguin Group:
Penguin Books Ltd, 27 Wrights Lane, London W8 5TZ
Penguin Books USA Inc., 375 Hudson Street, New York 10014, USA
Penguin Books Australia Ltd, 487 Maroondah Highway,
PO Box 257, Ringwood, Victoria 3134, Australia
Penguin Books Canada Ltd, 10 Alcorn Avenue,
Toronto, Ontario, Canada M4V 1E4
Penguin Books (NZ) Ltd,
182–190 Wairau Road, Auckland 10, New Zealand

Typeset in Bembo and Helvetica to an original design by Henry Iles.
Printed in Spain by Graphy Cems.

400pp, includes index
A catalogue record for this book is available from the British Library.

ISBN 1-85828-775-8

LONDON

THE MINI ROUGH GUIDE

by Rob Humphreys

with additional contributions by
Sean Bidder, Charles Campion
and Mel Steel

We set out to do something different when the first Rough Guide was published in 1982. Mark Ellingham, just out of university, was traveling in Greece. He brought along the popular guides of the day, but found they were all lacking in some way. They were either strong on ruins and museums but went on for pages without mentioning a beach or taverna. Or they were so conscious of the need to save money that they lost sight of Greece's cultural and historical significance. Also, none of the books told him anything about Greece's contemporary life – its politics, its culture, its people and how they lived.

So with no job in prospect, Mark decided to write his own guidebook, one which aimed to provide practical information that was second to none, detailing the best beaches and the hottest clubs and restaurants, while also giving hard-hitting accounts of every sight, both famous and obscure, and providing up-to-the-minute information on contemporary culture. It was a guide that encouraged independent travellers to find the best of Greece, and was a great success, getting shortlisted for the Thomas Cook travel guide award, and encouraging Mark, along with three friends, to expand the series.

The Rough Guide list grew rapidly and the letters flooded in, indicating a much broader readership than had been anticipated, but one which uniformly appreciated the Rough Guide mix of practical detail and humour, irreverence and enthusiasm. Things haven't changed. The same four friends who began the series are still the caretakers of the Rough Guide mission today: to provide the most reliable, up-to-date and entertaining information to independent-minded travellers of all ages, on all budgets.

We now publish more than 100 titles and have offices in London and New York. The travel guides are written and researched by a dedicated team of more than 100 authors, based in Britain, Europe, the USA and Australia. We have also created a unique series of phrasebooks to accompany the travel series, along with an acclaimed series of music guides, and a best-selling pocket guide to the Internet and World Wide Web. We also publish comprehensive travel information on our Web site: **www.roughguides.com**

Help us update

We've gone to a lot of trouble to ensure that this second edition of the Mini Rough Guide to London is as up to date and accurate as possible. However, things do change, and any suggestions, comments and corrections are much appreciated, we'll send a copy of the next edition (or any other *Rough Guide* if you prefer) for the best letters.

Please mark letters
"**Rough Guide Mini London Update**" and send to:
Rough Guides, 62–70 Shorts Gardens, London WC2H 9AH, or
Rough Guides, 4th Floor, 345 Hudson St, New York, NY 10014.

Or send email to: **mail@roughguides.co.uk**
Online updates about this book can be found on
Rough Guides' Web site (see opposite)

Readers' Letters

Many thanks to the readers of the first edition who took the time to write in with their comments and suggestions:
Joan Craig, Bo Lundin, Donald B. McKay, Jo Pascoe, Karen Reber, Bernadine E. Sperling and José Valverde-Bastán.

Acknowledgements

The author would like to thank
Polly Thomas for her ruthless editing,
Helen Ostick for typesetting beyond the call of duty,
Russell Walton for proofing, and Maxine Repath for cartography.

The author

Rob Humphreys joined Rough Guides in 1989, having worked as a failed actor, taxi driver and male model. He has travelled extensively in central and Eastern Europe, writing guides to Prague, the Czech and Slovak Republics, and St Petersburg. He has lived in London since 1988.

CONTENTS

The Listings 167

Contexts 351

MAP LIST

Colour Maps at back of book

Introduction

With a population of just under eight million, London is Europe's largest city, spreading across an area of more than 620 square miles from its core on the River Thames. Ethnically it's also Europe's most diverse metropolis: around two hundred languages are spoken within its confines, and more than thirty percent of the population is made up of first, second- and third-generation immigrants. Despite Scottish, Welsh and Northern Irish devolution, London still dominates the national horizon, too: this is where the country's news and money are made, it's where the central government resides and, as far as its inhabitants are concerned, provincial life begins beyond the circuit of the city's orbital motorway. Londoners' sense of superiority causes enormous resentment in the regions, yet it's undeniable that the capital has a unique aura of excitement and success – in most walks of British life, if you want to get on you've got to do it in London.

For the visitor, too, London is a thrilling place – and since the beginning of the new millennium, the city has also been overtaken by an exceptionally buoyant mood. Thanks to the lottery and millennium-oriented funding frenzy of the last few years, virtually every one of London's world-class museums, galleries and institutions has been reinvented, from the Royal Opera House to the British

Museum. With the completion of the Tate Modern and the London Eye, the city can now boast the world's largest modern art gallery and Ferris wheel; there's also a new tube extension and the first new bridge to cross the Thames for over a hundred years. And after sixteen years of being the only major city in the world *not* to have its own governing body, London finally has its own elected mayor and assembly.

In the meantime, London's traditional sights – Big Ben, Westminster Abbey, Buckingham Palace, St Paul's Cathedral and the Tower of London – continue to draw in millions of tourists every year. Monuments from the capital's more glorious past are everywhere to be seen, from medieval banqueting halls and the great churches of Sir Christopher Wren to the eclectic Victorian architecture of the triumphalist British Empire. There is also much enjoyment to be had from the city's quiet Georgian squares, the narrow alleyways of the City of London, the riverside walks, and the quirks of what is still identifiably a collection of villages. And even London's traffic pollution – one of its worst problems – is offset by surprisingly large expanses of greenery: Hyde Park, Green Park and St James's Park are all within a few minutes' walk of the West End, while, further afield, you can enjoy the more expansive parklands of Hampstead Heath and Richmond Park.

You could spend days just shopping in London, too, hobnobbing with the upper classes in Harrods, or sampling the offbeat weekend markets of Portobello Road and Camden. The music, clubbing and gay/lesbian scenes are second to none, and mainstream arts are no less exciting, with regular opportunities to catch brilliant theatre companies, dance troupes, exhibitions and opera. Restaurants, these days, are an attraction, too. London has caught up with its European rivals, and offers a range from three-star Michelin establishments to low-cost, high-quality Indian curry houses.

Meanwhile, the city's pubs have heaps of atmosphere, especially away from the centre – and an exploration of the farther-flung communities is essential to get the complete picture of this dynamic metropolis.

When to go

Considering the temperateness of the English climate, it's amazing how much mileage the locals get out of the subject – a two-day cold snap is discussed as if it were the onset of a new Ice Age, and a week in the upper 70s starts rumours of drought. The fact is that English summers rarely get hot and the winters don't get very cold, though they're often wet. The bottom line is that it's impossible to say with any degree of certainty that the weather will be pleasant in any

	F°	C°	RAINFALL	
	AVERAGE DAILY	AVERAGE DAILY	AVERAGE MONTHLY	
			INCHES	MILLIMETRES
January	42	5	2.1	54
February	43	6	1.6	40
March	46	8	1.5	37
April	51	11	1.5	37
May	56	14	1.8	46
June	62	17	1.8	46
July	65	18	2.2	57
August	65	18	2.3	59
September	60	16	1.9	49
October	54	12	2.2	57
November	48	9	2.5	64
December	44	6	1.9	48

given month. May might be wet and grey one year and gloriously sunny the next, and the same goes for the autumnal months – November stands an equal chance of being crisp and clear or foggy and grim.

As far as crowds go, tourists stream into London pretty much all year round, with peak season from Easter to October, and the biggest crush in July and August, when you'll need to book your accommodation well in advance. Costs, however, are pretty uniform year-round.

THE GUIDE

Introducing the City

Stretching for more than thirty miles at its broadest point, **London** is by far the largest city in Europe. The majority of its sights are situated to the north of the River Thames, which loops through the city from west to east. However, there is no single predominant focus of interest, for London has grown not through centralized planning but by a process of agglomeration – villages and urban developments that once surrounded the core are now lost within the amorphous mass of Greater London.

One of the few areas that you can easily explore on foot is **Westminster and Whitehall**, the city's royal, political and ecclesiastical power base, where you'll find the National Gallery and a host of other London landmarks, from Buckingham Palace to Westminster Abbey and Big Ben. The grand streets and squares of **St James's**, **Mayfair and Marylebone**, to the north of Westminster, have been the playground of the rich since the Restoration, and now contain the city's busiest shopping zones.

East of Piccadilly Circus, **Soho and Covent Garden** are also easy to walk around and form the heart of the West End entertainment district, containing the largest concentration of theatres, cinemas, clubs, flashy shops, cafés and restaurants. To the north lies the university quarter of **Bloomsbury**, home to the ever-popular British Museum, and the secluded quadrangles of Holborn's Inns of Court, London's legal heartland.

The City – the City of London, to give it its full title – is at one and the same time the most ancient and the most modern part of London. Settled since Roman times, it is now one of the world's great financial centres, yet retains its share of historic sights, notably the Tower of London and a fine cache of Wren churches that includes St Paul's Cathedral. Despite creeping trendification, the **East End**, to the east of the City, is not conventional tourist territory, but to ignore it entirely is to miss out a crucial element of contemporary London. **Docklands** is the converse of the down-at-heel East End, with the Canary Wharf tower, the country's tallest building, epitomizing the pretensions of the Thatcherite dream.

Lambeth and Southwark comprise the small slice of central London that lies south of the Thames. The South Bank Centre, London's little-loved concrete culture bunker, is enjoying a new lease of life thanks to its proximity to the new Tate Gallery of Modern Art in Bankside, which is linked to the City by a new pedestrian bridge.

The largest segment of greenery in central London is Hyde Park, which separates wealthy **Kensington and Chelsea** from the city centre. The **museums** of South Kensington – the Victoria & Albert Museum, the Science Museum and the Natural History Museum – are a must; and if you have shopping on your agenda, you'll want to check out the hive of plush stores in the vicinity of Harrods.

The capital's most hectic weekend market takes place around Camden Lock in **North London**. Further out, in the literary suburbs of Hampstead and Highgate, there are unbeatable views across the city from half-wild Hampstead Heath, the favourite parkland of thousands of Londoners. The glory of **South London** is Greenwich, with its nautical associations, royal park and observatory (not to mention its Dome). Finally, there are plenty of rewarding day-trips along the Thames from **Chiswick to Windsor**, most notably Hampton Court Palace and Windsor Castle.

ARRIVAL

London's international airports are all less than an hour from the city centre, and the city's train and bus terminals are all pretty central, and have tube stations close at hand.

Airports

Flying into London, you'll arrive at one of the capital's five **international airports**: Heathrow, Gatwick, Stansted, Luton or City Airport.

Heathrow, twelve miles west of the city, has four terminals, and two train/tube stations: one for terminals 1, 2 and 3, and a separate one for terminal 4. The high-speed **Heathrow Express** trains travel non-stop to Paddington Station (every 15min; 15–20min) for £12 each way or £22 return. A much cheaper alternative is to take the slow Piccadilly **Underground** line into central London (every 2–5min; 50min) for £3.50. If you plan to make several sightseeing journeys on your arrival day, buy a multi-zone One-Day Travelcard for £4.70 (see p.5). There is also **Airbus** #2, which runs from outside all four Heathrow terminals to several destinations in the city (every 30min; 1hr) and costs £7 single, £12 return. From midnight, you'll have to take **night bus** #N97 to Trafalgar Square (every 30min; 1hr 10min) for a bargain £1.50. **Taxis** are plentiful, but cost at least £35 to central London, and take around an hour (longer in the rush hour).

Gatwick, thirty miles to the south, has two terminals, North and South, connected by a monorail. The non-stop

Gatwick Express train runs day and night between the South Terminal and Victoria Station (every 15–30min; 30min) for £9.50. Other options include the **Connex South Central** service to Victoria (every 30min; 40min) for £8.20, or **Thameslink** to King's Cross (every 15–30min; 50min) for £9.50. **Airbus** #5 runs from both terminals to Victoria Coach Station (hourly; 1hr 30min) and costs £8 single, £10 return. A taxi ride into central London will set you back £50 or more, and take at least an hour.

Stansted, London's swankiest international airport, lies 34 miles northeast of the capital, and is served by the **Stansted Express** to Liverpool Street (every 15–30min; 45min), which costs £12 single, £22 return. **Airbus** #6 or #7 also runs to Victoria Coach Station (hourly; 1hr 15min), and costs £8 single, £10 return. A taxi into central London will cost £50 or more, and take at least an hour.

Luton airport (Ⓣ01582/405100; Ⓦ*www.london-luton.com*) is roughly thirty miles north of the city centre, and mostly handles charter flights. Luton Airport Parkway station is connected by **rail** to King's Cross and other stations in central London, with **Thameslink** running trains every fifteen minutes, plus one or two throughout the night; the journey takes thirty to forty minutes; the single fare is £9.50, returns are £16.90. **Green Line** (Ⓣ0870/6087261) buses run approximately every hour from Luton to Victoria Station, taking around an hour and a half, and costing £7.50 single, £12 return. A **taxi** will cost in the region of £70 and take at least an hour from central London.

London's smallest airport, **City Airport**, is situated in Docklands, nine miles east of central London. It handles European flights only, and is connected by shuttle bus with Canning Town (every 5min; 5min), and Canary Wharf (every 10min; 10min) for £2, plus Liverpool Street (every 10min; 25–35min) for £5. A taxi into central London will cost around £15 and take half an hour or so.

Train and coach stations

Eurostar trains arrive at **Waterloo International**, south of the river. Trains from the Channel ports arrive at **Charing Cross** or **Victoria** train stations; boat trains from Harwich arrive at **Liverpool Street**. Arriving by train from elsewhere in Britain, you'll come into one of London's numerous main-line stations, all of which have adjacent Underground stations linking into the city centre's tube network. Coaches terminate at **Victoria Coach Station**, a couple of hundred yards south down Buckingham Palace Road from the train station and Underground.

INFORMATION

The **London Tourist Board** (LTB; Ⓦ*www.londontown.com*) has a desk in the arrivals section of Heathrow Terminal 3 (daily 6am–11pm), and another in the Underground station concourse for Heathrow Terminals 1, 2 and 3 (daily 8am–6pm), but the **main central office** is in the forecourt of Victoria Station (Easter–April Mon–Sat 8am–7pm, Sun 8am–6pm; May Mon–Sat 8am–8pm, Sun 8am–6pm; June–Sept Mon–Sat 8am–10pm, Sun 8am–7pm; Oct–Easter daily 8am–7pm). Other centrally located offices can be found near Piccadilly Circus in the **British Visitor Centre** (Ⓦ*www.visitbritain.com*), 1 Regent St (June–Oct Mon 9.30am–6.30pm, Tues–Fri 9am–6.30pm, Sat & Sun 9am–5pm; Nov–May same times except Sat & Sun 10am–4pm), in the arrivals hall of Waterloo International (daily 8.30am–10.30pm), and in Liverpool Street Underground station (Mon–Fri 8am–6pm, Sat & Sun 8.45am–5.30pm).

Individual boroughs also run tourist offices at various prime locations. The two most central ones are on the south side of St Paul's Cathedral (April–Sept daily 9.30am–5pm,

Oct–March Mon–Fri 9.30am–5pm, Sat 9.30am–12.30pm; Ⓣ020/7332 1456; Ⓦ*www.cityoflondon.gov.uk*), and at the south end of London Bridge (Mon–Sat 10am–6pm, Sun 10.30am–5.30pm; Ⓣ020/7403 8299; Ⓦ*www.southwark.gov.uk*). The above offices will answer **phone enquiries**; LTB can only offer Visitorcall (Ⓣ0839/123456), a spread of pre-recorded phone announcements – these are a very poor service, and the calls are charged at an exorbitant rate.

Most of the above offices hand out a useful reference **map** of central London, plus plans of the public transport systems, but to find your way around every cranny of the city you need to invest in either an *A–Z Atlas* or a *Nicholson Streetfinder*, both of which have a street index covering every street in the capital; you can get them at most bookshops and newsagents for under £5. The only comprehensive and critical weekly **listings** magazine is *Time Out*, which costs £1.95 and comes out every Tuesday afternoon. In it you'll find details of all the latest exhibitions, shows, films, music, sport, guided walks and events in and around the capital.

CITY TRANSPORT

London's transport network is among the most complex and expensive in the world. The London Transport (LT) **travel information office**, at Piccadilly Circus tube station (daily 9am–6pm), will provide free transport maps; there are other desks at Euston Station, Heathrow (terminals 1, 2 and 3), King's Cross, Liverpool Street, Paddington and Victoria stations. There's also a 24-hour phone line for transport information (Ⓣ020/7222 1234), and a Web site giving real-time travel news (Ⓦ*www.londontransport.co.uk*). If you can, avoid travelling during the **rush hour** (Mon–Fri 8–9.30am & 5–7pm) when tubes become unbearably crowded, and some buses become full to overflowing.

TRAVELCARDS

To get the best value out of the transport system, buy a **Travelcard**. Available from machines and booths at all tube and train stations, and at some newsagents (look for the sticker), these are valid for the bus, tube, Docklands Light Railway, and suburban rail networks.

One-Day Travelcards, valid on weekdays from 9.30am and all day at weekends, cost £3.90 (central zones 1 and 2), rising to £4.70 for all zones (1–6, including Heathrow); the respective **Weekend Travelcards**, for unlimited travel on Saturday and Sunday, cost £5.80 for zones 1–2, and £7 for zones 1–6. If you need to travel before 9.30am on a weekday, but don't need to use suburban trains, you can buy a **One-Day LT Card**, which costs from £5 (zones 1 and 2) to £7.50 (all zones). **Weekly Travelcards** are even more economical, beginning at £18.20 for zones 1 and 2; for these cards you need a **photocard**, available free of charge from tube and train stations on presentation of a passport-sized photo.

The tube

The eleven different London Underground – or **tube** – lines cross much of the metropolis, although London south of the river is not very well covered. Each line has its own colour and name – all you need to know is which direction you're travelling in: northbound, eastbound, southbound or westbound. Services operate from around 5.30am Monday to Saturday, and from 7.30am on Sundays, and end around midnight every day; you rarely have to wait more than five minutes for a train between central stations.

Tickets must be bought in advance from the machines or booths in station entrance halls; if you cannot produce a valid ticket, you will be charged an on-the-spot Penalty

Fare of £10. A single journey in the central zone costs an unbelievable £1.50; a **Carnet** of ten tickets costs £11. If you're intending to travel about a lot, however, a Travelcard is by far your best bet (see overleaf).

Buses

Tickets for all bus journeys within, to or from the central zone costs a flat fare of £1; journeys outside the central zone cost 70p. Normally you pay the driver on entering, but some routes are covered by older Routemaster buses, staffed by a conductor and with an open rear platform. Note that at request stops (easily recognizable by their red sign) you must stick your arm out to hail the bus you want. In addition to the Travelcards mentioned overleaf, a **One-Day Bus Pass** is also available and can be used before 9.30am; it costs £3 for zones 1 and 2.

Regular buses run between about 6am and midnight; **night buses** (prefixed with the letter "N") operate outside this period. Night bus routes radiate out from Trafalgar Square at hourly intervals, more frequently on some routes and on Friday and Saturday nights. Fares are a flat £1.50 from central London; only weekly, monthly or yearly Travelcards are valid on these.

Suburban trains

Large areas of London's suburbs are best reached by the **suburban train** network (Travelcards valid). Wherever a sight can only be reached by overground train, we've indicated the nearest train station and the central terminus from which you must depart. If you're planning to use the railway network a lot, you might want to purchase a **Network Railcard**, which is valid for a year, costs £20, and gives you up to 34 percent discount on fares to destinations in and

GUIDED TOURS

Sightseeing **bus tours** are run by several rival companies, their open-top double-deckers setting off every thirty minutes from Victoria Station, Trafalgar Square, Piccadilly, and other tourist spots. Tours take roughly ninety minutes (though you can hop on and off as often as you like) and cost around £12. Alternatively, you can hop aboard one of the bright yellow World War II amphibious vehicles used by Frog Tours (Ⓣ020/7928 3132; Ⓦ*www.frogtours.com*) for a combined **bus and boat tour**. After fifty minutes driving round the usual sights, you plunge into the river and go on a half-hour cruise. Tours set off every half-hour from behind County Hall, from 10am to dusk, with tickets costing £13. Another money-saving option is to skip the commentary by hopping on a real London bus – the #11 from Victoria will take you past Westminster Abbey, the Houses of Parliament, up Whitehall, round Trafalgar Square, along the Strand and on to St Paul's Cathedral.

Walking tours are infinitely more appealing, mixing solid historical facts with juicy anecdotes in the company of a local specialist. Walks on offer range from a literary pub crawl round Bloomsbury to a tour of places associated with the Beatles. Tours tend to cost £4–5 and usually take two hours. To find out what's on offer for the week, check in the "Around Town" section of *Time Out*. The widest range of walks on offer are run by Original London Walks (Ⓣ020/7624 3978).

around the southeast. To find out about a particular service, phone **National Rail Enquiries** on Ⓣ08457/484950.

Taxis

If you're in a group of three or more, London's metered **black cabs** can be an economical way of getting around

THE GOSEE CARD AND LONDON PASS

For the really serious museum addict, the **GoSee Card** gives you entry into around twenty museums and galleries, from the Design Museum and the Hayward Gallery to the National Maritime Museum and Shakespeare's Globe Museum. The three-day card costs £16 (though this gives you too little time to visit all the above); the seven-day card costs £26. Even better value is the Family Card, which covers two adults and up to four children and costs £32 for three days or £50 for seven. The cards are available from any of the above museums or galleries, and at LTB and LT offices; for more information, phone ⓣ020/7923 0807 or visit ⓦ*www.london-gosee.com*.

An alternative to the GoSee Card is the new **London Pass**, which not only gives you entry to a whole range of attractions from the London Aquarium and Buckingham Palace to St Paul's Cathedral and Windsor Castle, but also throws in an all-zone Travelcard, £5 worth of free phone calls and various other perks and incentives. The pass costs £22 for one day, £49 for three days, and £79 for six days. However, the London Pass is currently in its infancy, more sights need to be added to its portfolio if it's going to compete for value with the GoSee Card. The London Pass can be bought over the phone (ⓣ0870/242 9988) or on the Internet (ⓦ*www.londonpass.com*).

the centre – a ride from Euston to Victoria, for example, should cost around £10. A yellow light over the windscreen tells you if the cab is available – just stick your arm out to hail it. (If you want to book one in advance, call ⓣ020/7272 0272.)

Minicabs are less reliable than black cabs, but considerably cheaper, so you might want to take one back from a late-night club. Most minicabs are not metered, so always establish the fare beforehand. If you want to be certain of a woman driver, call Ladycabs (ⓣ020/7254 3501).

Boats

Boat services on the Thames still do not form part of an integrated public transport system, and Travelcards are not currently valid on the river. So for the moment at least, travelling by boat remains a leisure pastime and not really a commuting option. There are regular services between central London and Greenwich, and, in the summer, even as far upstream as Hampton Court. **Timetables and services** are complex, however; for a full list, pick up the Thames river services booklet from an LT travel information office, phone ⓣ020/7222 1234 or visit ⓦ*www.londontransport.co.uk*.

Westminster and Whitehall

Political, religious and regal power has emanated from **WESTMINSTER** and **WHITEHALL** for almost a millennium. It was Edward the Confessor who first established Westminster as London's royal and ecclesiastical power base, some three miles west of the City of London. The embryonic English parliament met in the abbey in the fourteenth century and eventually took over the old royal palace of Westminster. In the nineteenth century, Whitehall became the "heart of the Empire", its ministries ruling over a quarter of the world's population. Even now, though the UK's world status has diminished, the institutions that run the country inhabit roughly the same geographical area: Westminster for the politicians, Whitehall for the civil servants.

The monuments and buildings covered in this chapter also span the millennium, and include some of London's most famous landmarks – **Nelson's Column**, **Big Ben** and the **Houses of Parliament**, **Westminster Abbey** and **Buckingham Palace**, plus two of the city's finest permanent art collections, the **National Gallery** and the **Tate**

Britain Gallery. Since it's also one of the easiest parts of London to walk round, this is a well-trodden tourist circuit, with all the major sights within a mere half-mile of each other and linked by two of London's most triumphant avenues, **Whitehall** and **The Mall**.

TRAFALGAR SQUARE

Map 8, G1. ⊖ Leicester Square or Charing Cross.

Despite being little more than a glorified, sunken traffic island, infested with scruffy urban pigeons, **Trafalgar Square** is still one of London's grandest architectural set-pieces. John Nash designed the basic layout in the 1820s, but died long before the square took its present form. The Neoclassical National Gallery filled up the northern side of the square in 1838, followed five years later by the square's central focal point, **Nelson's Column**; the famous bronze lions didn't arrive until 1868, and the fountains – a real rarity in a London square – didn't take their present shape until the eve of World War II.

As one of the few large public squares in London, Trafalgar Square has been both a tourist attraction and a focus for political demonstrations since the Chartists assembled here in 1848 before marching to Kennington Common. On a more festive note, the square is graced each December with a giant Christmas tree, donated by Norway in thanks for liberation from the Nazis, and on **New Year's Eve**, thousands of inebriates sing in the New Year.

Stranded on a traffic island to the south of the column, and predating the entire square, is the **equestrian statue of Charles I**, erected shortly after the Restoration on the very spot where eight of those who had signed the king's death warrant were disembowelled. Charles's statue also marks the original site of the thirteenth-century **Charing**

Cross, from where all distances from the capital are measured – a Victorian imitation now stands outside Charing Cross train station.

The northeastern corner of the square is occupied by James Gibbs' church of **St Martin-in-the-Fields** (Ⓦ*www.stmartin-in-the-fields.org*), fronted by a magnificent Corinthian portico and topped by an elaborate, and distinctly unclassical, tower and steeple. Completed in 1726, the interior is purposefully simple, though the Italian plasterwork on the barrel vaulting is exceptionally rich; it's best appreciated while listening to one of the church's free lunchtime concerts. There's a licensed café in the roomy crypt, not to mention a shop, gallery and brass-rubbing centre (Mon–Sat 10am–6pm, Sun noon–6pm).

THE NATIONAL GALLERY

Map 8, G1. Daily 10am–6pm (Wed till 9pm); free; Ⓦ*www.nationalgallery.org.uk* ⊖Leicester Square or Charing Cross.

Unlike the Louvre or the Hermitage, the **National Gallery**, on the north side of Trafalgar Square, is not based on a royal collection, but was begun in 1824 when the government reluctantly agreed to purchase 38 paintings belonging to a Russian émigré banker, John Julius Angerstein. The gallery's canny acquisition policy has resulted in a collection of more than 2200 paintings, but the collection's virtue is not so much its size, but the range, depth and sheer quality of its contents.

To view the collection chronologically, begin with the **Sainsbury Wing**, the softly-softly, postmodern 1980s adjunct which playfully imitates elements of the original gallery's Neoclassicism. However, with more than a thousand paintings on permanent display in the main galleries, you'll need real stamina to see everything in one day, so if time is tight your best bet is to home in on your areas of special interest, having picked up a gallery plan at one of the information desks. A welcome innovation is the **Gallery Guide Soundtrack**, with a brief audio commentary on a large selection of the paintings on display. The Soundtrack is available free of charge, though you're asked for a "voluntary contribution". Another possibility is to join up with one of the gallery's **free guided tours** (daily 11.30am & 2.30pm, plus Wed 6.30pm), which set off from the Sainsbury Wing foyer.

Among the National's **Italian** masterpieces are Leonardo's melancholic *Virgin of the Rocks*, Uccello's *Battle of San Romano*, Botticelli's *Venus and Mars* (inspired by a Dante sonnet) and Piero della Francesca's beautifully composed *Baptism of Christ*, one of his earliest works. The fine collection of Venetian works includes Titian's colourful early masterpiece *Bacchus and Ariadne*, his very late, much gloomier *Death of Acteon*, and Veronese's lustrous *Family of Darius before Alexander*. Elsewhere, Bronzino's erotic *Venus, Cupid, Folly and Time*, and Raphael's trenchant *Pope Julius II* keep company with Michelangelo's unfinished *Entombment*. Later Italian works to look out for include a couple by Caravaggio, a few splendid examples of Tiepolo's airy draughtsmanship and glittering vistas of Venice by Canaletto and Guardi.

From **Spain** there are dazzling pieces by El Greco, Goya, Murillo and Velázquez, among them the provocative *Rokeby Venus*. From the **Low Countries**, standouts include van Eyck's *Arnolfini Marriage*, Memlinc's perfectly poised *Donne Triptych*, and a couple of typically serene Vermeers. There are numerous genre paintings, such as Frans Hals' *Family Group in a Landscape*, and some superlative landscapes, most notably Hobbema's *Avenue, Middleharnis*. An array of Rembrandt paintings that features some of his most searching portraits – two of them self-portraits – is followed by abundant examples of Rubens' expansive, fleshy canvases.

Holbein's masterful *Ambassadors* and several of van Dyck's portraits were painted for the English court, and there's home-grown **British** art, too, represented by important works such as Hogarth's satirical *Marriage à la Mode*, Gainsborough's translucent *Morning Walk*, Constable's ever popular *Hay Wain*, and Turner's *Fighting Téméraire*. Highlights of the **French** contingent include superb works by Poussin, Claude, Fragonard, Boucher and Watteau, and the only two paintings in the country by David.

Finally, there's a particularly strong showing of **Impressionists and Post-Impressionists** in rooms 43–46 of the East Wing. Among the most famous works are Manet's unfinished *Execution of Maximilian*, Renoir's *Umbrellas*, Monet's *Thames below Westminster*, Van Gogh's *Sunflowers*, Seurat's pointillist *Bathers at Asnières*, a Rousseau junglescape, Cézanne's proto-Cubist *Bathers* and Picasso's Blue Period *Child with a Dove*.

THE NATIONAL PORTRAIT GALLERY

Map 4, J7. Daily 10am–6pm (Thurs & Fri till 9pm); free; Ⓦ*www.npg.org.uk* ⊖Leicester Square or Charing Cross.

Around the east side of the National Gallery lurks the **National Portrait Gallery** (NPG), founded in 1856 to house uplifting depictions of the good and the great. Though it has some fine works in its collection, many of the studies are of less interest than their subjects, and the overall impression is of an overstuffed shrine to famous Brits rather than a museum offering any insight into the history of portraiture. However, it is fascinating to trace who has been deemed worthy of admiration at any moment: aristocrats and artists in previous centuries, warmongers and imperialists in the early decades of the twentieth century, writers and poets in the 1930s and 1940s, and, latterly, retired footballers, and film and pop stars.

The NPG's **new extension** opened in spring 2000, with a bigger Tudor gallery, and a new contemporary gallery to expand the section that's by far the most popular. There's also a new computer gallery, a lecture theatre and rooftop café/restaurant with a view over the cityscape. The NPG's **Sound Guide**, which gives useful biographical background information to some of the pictures, is provided free of charge, though you're strongly invited to give a "voluntary contribution".

THE MALL AND ST JAMES'S PARK

Map 8, E4. ⊖ St James's Park.

The tree-lined sweep of **The Mall** – London's nearest equivalent to a Parisian boulevard – was laid out in the first decade of the twentieth century as a memorial to Queen Victoria, and runs from Trafalgar Square to Buckingham Palace. The bombastic **Admiralty Arch**, recently used as a hostel for the homeless, was erected to mark the entrance at the Trafalgar Square end of The Mall, while at the other end stands the ludicrous **Victoria Memorial**, Edward VII's overblown tribute to his mother.

The best time to view The Mall is on a Sunday, when it's closed to traffic.

St James's Park, on the south side of The Mall, is the oldest of the royal parks, having been drained and enclosed for hunting purposes by Henry VIII. It was landscaped by Nash in the 1820s, and today its tree-lined lake is a favourite picnic spot for the civil servants of Whitehall. Pelicans can still be seen at the eastern end of the lake, and there are ducks, swans and geese aplenty. From the bridge across the lake there's also a fine view over to Westminster and the jumble of domes and pinnacles along Whitehall.

BUCKINGHAM PALACE

Map 8, B6. Aug & Sept daily 9.30am–4.15pm; £10; advance booking on ⓣ020/7321 2233; ⓦ*www.royal.gov.uk* ⊖ Green Park.

The graceless colossus of **Buckingham Palace**, popularly known as "Buck House", has served as the monarch's permanent London residence only since the accession of Victoria. Bought by George III in 1762, the building was overhauled by Nash in the late 1820s, and again by Aston Webb in time for George V's coronation in 1913, producing a palace that's about as bland as it's possible to be.

For two months of the year, the hallowed portals are grudgingly nudged open; timed tickets are sold from the marquee-like box office in Green Park at the western end of The Mall. The interior, however, is a bit of an anticlimax: of the palace's 660 rooms you're permitted to see around twenty, and there's little sign of life, as the Queen decamps to Scotland every summer. For the other ten months of the year there's little to do here, as the palace is closed to visitors – not that this deters the crowds who mill around the railings, and gather in some force to watch the **Changing of the Guard** (see p.22), in which a detachment of the Queen's Foot Guards marches to appropriate martial music from St James's Palace (unless it rains, that is).

From spring 2002, the public will also be able to view the best of the Royal Collection at the rebuilt, greatly expanded **Queen's Gallery**, on the south side of the palace. Among the highlights will be works by Michelangelo, Reynolds, Gainsborough, Vermeer, van Dyck, Rubens, Rembrandt and Canaletto, as well as the odd Fabergé egg and heaps of Sèvres china.

There's more pageantry on show at the Nash-built **Royal Mews** (Map 8, B7; Mon–Thurs: Aug & Sept 10.30am–4.30pm; Oct–July noon–4pm; £4), further along Buckingham Palace Road. The royal carriages, lined up

THE ROYAL FAMILY

Tourists may still flock to see London's royal palaces, but over the last decade the British public have become more critical of the huge tax bill that goes to support the **Royal Family** (Ⓦ*www.royal.gov.uk*) in the style to which they are accustomed. This creeping republicanism can be traced back to 1992, which the Queen herself, in one of her few memorable Christmas Day speeches, accurately described as her *annus horribilis*. This was the year that saw the marriage break-ups of Charles and Di, and Andrew and Fergie, and the second marriage of divorcee Princess Anne.

Matters came to a head, though, over who should pay the estimated £50 million costs of repairs after the fire at Windsor Castle (p.164). Misjudging the public mood, the Conservative government offered taxpayers' money to foot the entire bill. After a furore, it was agreed that some of the cost would be raised from the astronomical admission charges to the royal palaces. In addition, under pressure from the media, the Queen also reduced the number of royals paid out of the Civil List, and, for the first time in her life, agreed to pay taxes on her enormous personal fortune.

Given the mounting public resentment against the Royal Family, it was hardly surprising that public opinion tended to side with Princess Diana rather than Prince Charles during their various disputes. Diana's subsequent death, and the huge outpouring of grief that accompanied her funeral, further damaged the reputation of the royals, though her demise has also meant the loss of one of the Royal Family's most vociferous critics. Despite the Royal Family's low poll ratings, none of the political parties currently advocates abolishing the monarchy, and public appetite for stories about the adolescent princes (and their potential girlfriends), or trysts between Charles and Camilla, shows few signs of abating.

THE CHANGING OF THE GUARD

The Queen is colonel-in-chief of the seven **Household Regiments**: the Life Guards (who dress in red and white) and the Blues and Royals (who dress in blue and red) are the two Household Cavalry regiments; while the Grenadier, Coldstream, Scots, Irish and Welsh Guards make up the Foot Guards.

The Foot Guards can only be told apart by the plumes (or lack of them) in their busbies, and by the arrangement of their tunic buttons. The first three date back to the seventeenth century, and all these regiments still form part of the modern army as well as performing ceremonial functions such as the Changing of the Guard. If you're keen to find out more about the Foot Guards, pay a visit to the **Guards' Museum** (Map 8, D6; daily 10am–4pm; £2), in the Wellington Barracks on the south side of St James's Park.

The **Changing of the Guard** takes place at two separate locations in London: the two Household Cavalry regiments take it in turns to stand guard at Horse Guards on Whitehall (Map 8, H3; Mon–Sat 11am, Sun 10am), with inspection daily at 4pm, while the Foot Guards take care of Buckingham Palace (May–Aug daily 11.30am; Sept–April alternate days; no ceremony if it rains). A ceremony also takes place regularly in Windsor Castle (see p.165).

under a glass canopy in the courtyard, are the main attraction, in particular the Gold Carriage, made for George III in 1762, smothered in 22-carat gilding and weighing four tons, its axles supporting four life-size figures.

WHITEHALL

Map 8, H4 ⊖Charing Cross or Westminster.

Whitehall, the unusually broad avenue connecting Trafalgar Square to Parliament Square, is synonymous with the faceless, pin-striped bureaucracy charged with the day-to-day running of the country. Since the sixteenth century, nearly all the key governmental ministries and offices have migrated here, rehousing themselves on an ever-increasing scale. The statues dotted about Whitehall recall the days when this street stood at the centre of an empire on which the sun never set. Nowadays, with the Scots, Welsh and Northern Irish all with their own assemblies, Whitehall's remit is ever-decreasing.

During the sixteenth and seventeenth centuries Whitehall was also synonymous with royalty, since it was the permanent residence of the kings and queens of England. The original **Whitehall Palace** was the London seat of the Archbishop of York, confiscated and greatly extended by Henry VIII after a fire at Westminster forced him to find alternative accommodation; it was here that he celebrated his marriage to Anne Boleyn in 1533, and here that he died fourteen years later.

The chief section of the old palace to survive the fire of 1698, was the **Banqueting House** (Map 7, H3; Mon–Sat 10am–5pm; Ⓦ*www.hrp.org.uk*; £3.80), begun by Inigo Jones in 1619 and the first Palladian building to be built in England. The one room now open to the public has no original furnishings, but is well worth seeing for the superlative Rubens ceiling paintings glorifying the Stuart dynasty, commissioned by Charles I in the 1630s. Charles himself walked through the room for the last time in 1649 when he stepped onto the executioner's scaffold from one of its windows.

Across the road, two mounted sentries of the Queen's Household Cavalry and two horseless colleagues, all in ceremonial uniform, are posted daily from 10am to 4pm. Ostensibly they are protecting the **Horse Guards** building, originally built as the old palace guard house, but now guarding nothing in particular. The mounted guards are changed hourly; those standing every two hours. Try to coincide your visit with the Changing of the Guard (see p.22), when a squad of twelve mounted troops arrive in full livery. The main action takes place in the parade ground at the rear of the building overlooking Horse Guards' Parade.

Further down this west side of Whitehall is London's most famous address, **Number 10 Downing Street** (Map 8, H4; Ⓦ*www.number-10.gov.uk*), the seventeenth-century terraced house that has been the residence of the prime minister since it was presented to Sir Robert Walpole, Britain's first PM, by George II in 1732. Just beyond the Downing Street gates, in the middle of the road, stands Edwin Lutyens' **Cenotaph**, eschewing any kind of Christian imagery, and inscribed simply with the words "The Glorious Dead". The memorial remains the focus of the Remembrance Sunday ceremony in November.

In 1938, in anticipation of Nazi air raids, the basement of the civil service buildings on the south side of King Charles Street were converted into the **Cabinet War Rooms** (Map 8, G5; daily: April–Sept 9.30am–6pm; Oct–March 10am–6pm; £5; Ⓦ*www.iwm.org.uk*). It was here that Winston Churchill directed operations and held cabinet meetings for the duration of World War II. The rooms have been left pretty much as they were when they were finally abandoned on VJ Day 1945, and make for an atmospheric underground trot through wartime London. The museum's free acoustophone commentary helps bring the place to life and includes various eyewitness accounts by folk who worked there.

THE HOUSES OF PARLIAMENT

Map 8, I7. Ⓦ*www.parliament.uk* ⊖Westminster.

Clearly visible at the south end of Whitehall is one of London's best-known monuments, the Palace of

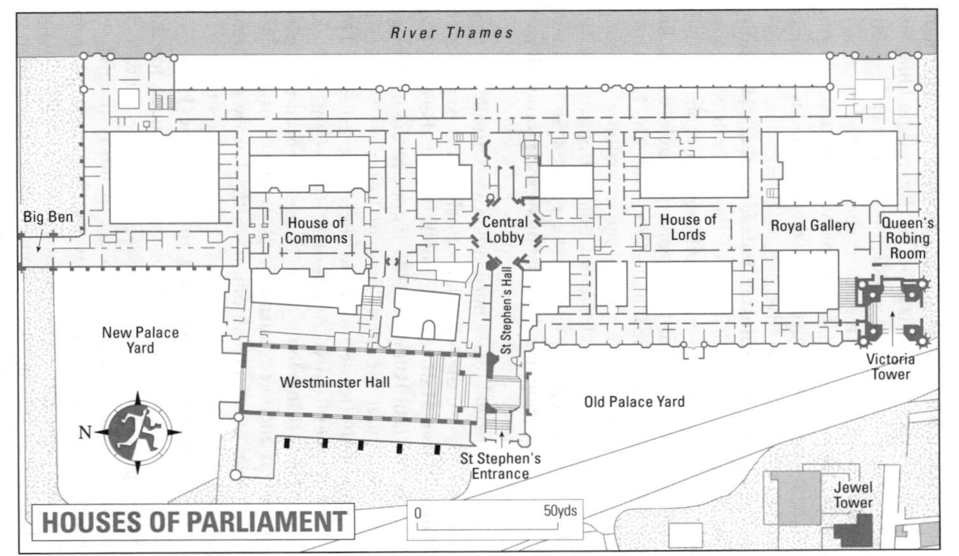
River Thames
Big Ben
House of Commons
Central Lobby
House of Lords
Royal Gallery
Queen's Robing Room
St Stephen's Hall
New Palace Yard
Westminster Hall
Victoria Tower
Old Palace Yard
N
St Stephen's Entrance
Jewel Tower
HOUSES OF PARLIAMENT
0
50yds

Westminster, better known as the **Houses of Parliament**. The city's finest Victorian Gothic Revival building and symbol of a nation once confident of its place at the centre of the world, it is distinguished above all by the ornate, gilded clock tower popularly known as **Big Ben**, after the thirteen-ton main bell that strikes the hour (and is broadcast across the world by the BBC).

The original **Westminster Palace** was built by Edward the Confessor in the first half of the eleventh century, so that he could watch over the building of his abbey. It then served as the seat of all the English monarchs until a fire forced Henry VIII to decamp to Whitehall. The Lords have always convened at the palace, but it was only following Henry's death that the House of Commons moved from the abbey's Chapter House into the palace's St Stephen's Chapel, thus beginning the building's associations with parliament.

In 1834 the old palace burned down – virtually the only relic of the medieval palace is the bare expanse of **Westminster Hall**, on the north side of the complex. Built by William Rufus in 1099, it's one of the most magnificent secular medieval halls in Europe – you get a glimpse of the hall en route to the public galleries. The **Jewel Tower** (daily: April–Oct 10am–6pm or dusk; Nov–March 10am–4pm; £1.50), across the road from parliament, is another remnant of the medieval palace, now housing an excellent exhibition on the history of parliament.

To watch the proceedings in either the House of Commons or the Lords, simply join the queue for the **public galleries** (known as Strangers' Galleries) outside St Stephen's Gate. The public are let in slowly from about 4.30pm onwards from Monday to Thursday, and from 10am on Fridays; the security checks are very tight, and the whole procedure can take an hour or more. If you want to avoid the queues, turn up an hour or more later, when the crowds have usually thinned. Recesses (holiday closures) of both Houses occur at Christmas, Easter, and from August to the middle of October; phone ⓣ020/7219 4272 for more information.

To see **Question Time** (Mon–Wed 2.30–3.30pm, Thurs 11.30am–12.30pm) you need to book a **ticket** several weeks in advance from your local MP (if you're a UK citizen) or your embassy in London (if you're not). To contact your MP, simply phone ⓣ020/7219 3000 and ask to be put through. It's also possible to tour the building on Monday and Thursday mornings and Friday afternoons; first off, however, you must obtain a **permit** from your MP and or embassy. The full price of a guided tour is £30, and while it used to be simple enough to join up with a group on a pre-booked **guided tour**, for around £3 per person, this has become much more difficult since security measures have been tightened up. For individuals, the only alternative is to guide yourself around the building once you've obtained your permit. Only those with a genuine specialist interest may visit **Big Ben**, either separately or before or after a tour; to find out more about access requirements, phone ⓣ020/7219 4862.

WESTMINSTER ABBEY

Map 8, H7. Mon–Fri 9.30am–4.45pm, Sat 9.30am–2.45pm, also Wed 6–7.45pm; £5; ⓦ*www.westminster-abbey.org* ⊖Westminster.

The Houses of Parliament dwarf their much older neighbour, **Westminster Abbey**, yet this single building embodies much of the history of England: it has been the venue for all but two coronations since the time of William the Conqueror, and the site of more or less every royal burial for some five hundred years between the reigns of Henry III and George II. Scores of the nation's most famous citi-

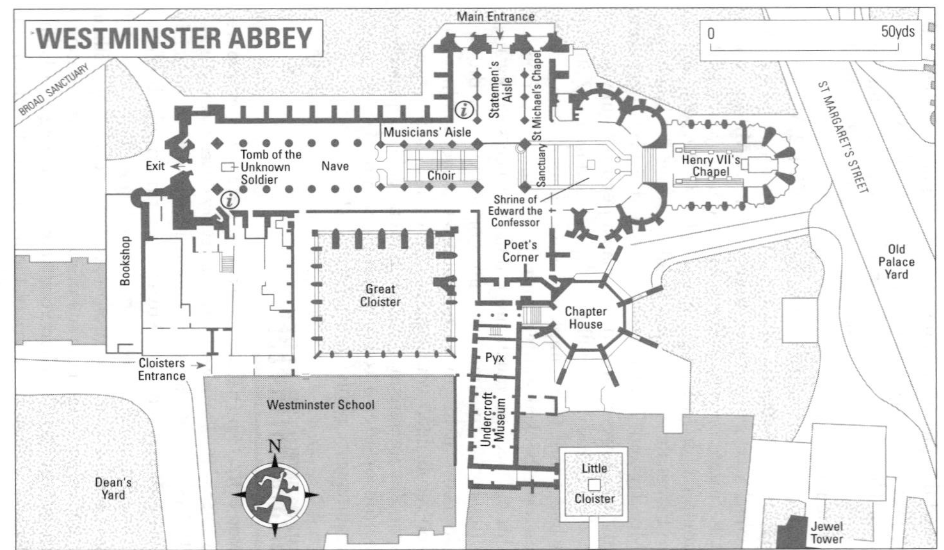
WESTMINSTER ABBEY
Main Entrance
0
50yds
BROAD SANCTUARY
Statemen's Aisle
St Michael's Chapel
Musicians' Aisle
Exit
Tomb of the Unknown Soldier
Nave
Choir
Sanctuary
Henry VII's Chapel
ST MARGARET'S STREET
Shrine of Edward the Confessor
Poet's Corner
Old Palace Yard
Bookshop
Great Cloister
Chapter House
Pyx
Cloisters Entrance
Westminster School
Undercroft Museum
N
Little Cloister
Dean's Yard
Jewel Tower

zens are honoured here, too (though many of the stones commemorate people buried elsewhere), and the interior is cluttered with hundreds of monuments, reliefs and statues.

Entry is currently via the north transept, cluttered with monuments to politicians and traditionally known as **Statesmen's Aisle**, shortly after which you come to the abbey's most dazzling architectural set-piece, the **Lady Chapel**, added by Henry VII in 1503 as his future resting place. With its intricately carved vaulting and fan-shaped gilded pendants, the chapel represents the final spectacular gasp of the English Perpendicular style. Unfortunately, the public are no longer admitted to the **Shrine of Edward the Confessor**, the sacred heart of the building, though you do get to inspect Edward I's **Coronation Chair**, a decrepit oak throne dating from around 1300 and still used for coronations.

Nowadays, the abbey's royal tombs are upstaged by **Poets' Corner**, in the south transept, though the first occupant, Geoffrey Chaucer, was in fact buried here not because he was a poet, but because he lived nearby. By the eighteenth century this zone had become an artistic pantheon, and since then the transept has been filled with tributes to all shades of talent. From the south transept, you can view the central sanctuary, site of the coronations, and the wonderful **Cosmati floor mosaic**, constructed in the thirteenth century by Italian craftsmen, and often covered by a carpet to protect it.

Doors in the south choir aisle lead to the **Great Cloisters** (daily 8am–6pm), rebuilt after a fire in 1298 and now home to a café. At the eastern end of the cloisters lies the octagonal **Chapter House** (daily: April–Oct 10am–5.30pm or dusk; Nov–March 10am–4pm; £2.50 or £1 with an abbey ticket), where the House of Commons met from 1257. The thirteenth-century decorative paving-tiles and wall-paintings have survived intact. Chapter House tickets include entry to some of the few surviving Norman sections of the abbey: the neighbouring **Pyx Chamber** (daily 10.30am–4pm), which displays the abbey's plate, and the **Undercroft Museum** (daily 10.30am–4pm), filled with generations of bald royal death masks and wax effigies.

It's only after exploring the cloisters that you get to see the **nave** itself: narrow, light and, at over a hundred feet in height, by far the tallest in the country. The most famous monument is the **Tomb of the Unknown Soldier**, by the west door, which now serves as the main exit.

TATE BRITAIN

Map 3, H8. Daily 10am–5.50pm; free; Ⓦ*www.tate.org.uk* ⊖Pimlico.

The Tate offers audioguides to the displays for £3.

Founded in 1897 with money from Sir Henry Tate, inventor of the sugar cube, the purpose-built Tate Gallery, half a mile south of parliament, is now devoted exclusively to British art. With the new Tate Modern now established in the disused Bankside Power Station (see p.109), the original building on Millbank has now been rechristened **Tate Britain**. As well as displaying British art from 1500 to 2000, plus a whole wing devoted to Turner, Tate Britain also showcases contemporary British artists and continues to sponsor the Turner Prize, the country's most prestigious modern-art prize.

The galleries are rehung more or less annually, but will always include a fair selection of works by British artists such as Hogarth, Constable, Gainsborough, Reynolds and Blake, plus foreign artists like van Dyck who spent much of their career over here. The ever-popular **Pre-Raphaelites** are always well represented, as are established twentieth-century greats such as Stanley Spencer and Francis Bacon alongside living artists such as David Hockney and Lucien Freud. Lastly, don't miss the Tate's outstanding **Turner collection**, displayed in the Clore Gallery.

WESTMINSTER CATHEDRAL

Map 3, G7. Mon–Fri & Sun 7am–7pm, Sat 8am–7pm; free; ⓦ*www.westminsterdiocese.org.uk* ⊖Victoria.

Halfway down Victoria Street from Westminster Abbey, you'll find one of London's most surprising churches, the stripy neo-Byzantine concoction of the Roman Catholic Westminster Cathedral. Begun in 1895, it is one of the last and wildest monuments to the Victorian era: constructed from more than twelve million terracotta-coloured bricks and decorated with hoops of Portland stone, it culminates in a magnificent tapered **campanile** which rises to 274 feet, served by a lift (daily 9am–5pm; £2). The **interior** is only half finished, so to get an idea of what the place will look like when it's finally completed, explore the series of **side chapels** whose rich, multicoloured décor makes use of over one hundred different marbles from around the world.

St James's, Piccadilly, Mayfair and Marylebone

ST JAMES'S, **MAYFAIR** and **MARYLEBONE** emerged in the late seventeenth century as London's first real suburbs, characterized by grid-plan streets feeding into grand, formal squares. This expansion set the westward trend for middle-class migration, and as London's wealthier consumers moved west, so too did the city's more upmarket shops and luxury hotels, which are still a feature of the area.

Aristocratic **St James's**, the rectangle of land to the north of St James's Park, was one of the first areas to be developed, and remains the preserve of the seriously rich. **Piccadilly**, which forms the border between St James's and Mayfair, is no longer the fashionable promenade it once was, but a whiff of exclusivity still pervades **Bond Street** and its tributaries. **Regent Street** was created as a new "Royal Mile", a tangible borderline to shore up these new fashionable suburbs against the chaotic maze of Soho and the City, where the working population still lived. Now, along with **Oxford Street**, it has become London's busiest shopping district – it's here that Londoners mean when they talk of "going shopping up the West End".

Marylebone, which lies to the north of Oxford Street, is another grid-plan Georgian development, a couple of social and real-estate leagues below Mayfair, but a wealthy area nevertheless. It boasts a very fine art gallery, the **Wallace Collection**, and, in its northern fringes, one of London's biggest tourist attractions, **Madame Tussaud's**, the oldest and largest wax museum in the world.

ST JAMES'S

Map 8, E2. ⊖ Piccadilly Circus or Green Park.

St James's, the exclusive little enclave sandwiched between The Mall and Piccadilly, was laid out in the 1670s close to St James's Palace. Royal and aristocratic residences predominate along its southern border, gentlemen's clubs cluster along Pall Mall and St James's Street, while jacket-and-tie restaurants and expense-account gentlemen's outfitters line Jermyn Street. Hardly surprising, then, that most Londoners rarely stray into this area.

St James's does, however, contain some interesting architectural set pieces, such as **Lower Regent Street** (Map 8, E1), which was the first stage in John Nash's ambitious plan to link George IV's magnificent Carlton House with Regent's Park. Like so many of Nash's grandiose schemes, it never quite came to fruition, as George IV, soon after ascending the throne, decided that Carlton House – the most expensive palace ever to have been built in London – wasn't quite luxurious enough, and had it pulled down. Instead, Lower Regent Street now opens up into **Waterloo Place** (Map 8, F2), at the centre of which stands the

Guards' Crimean Memorial, fashioned from captured Russian cannons and featuring a statue of Florence Nightingale. Clearly visible, beyond, is the "Grand Old" **Duke of York's Column** (Map 8, F2), erected in 1833, ten years before Nelson's more famous one.

Cutting across Waterloo Place, **Pall Mall** – named after the croquet-like game of *pallo a maglio* (ball to mallet) – leads west to **St James's Palace** (Map 8, D4), whose main red-brick gate-tower is pretty much all that remains of the Tudor palace erected here by Henry VIII. When Whitehall Palace burned down in 1698, St James's became the principal royal residence, and in keeping with tradition, an ambassador to the UK is still known as "Ambassador to the Court of St James", even though the court moved down the road to Buckingham Palace when Queen Victoria ascended the throne. The rambling complex now provides a bachelor pad for **Prince Charles** (Ⓦ*www.princeofwales.gov.uk*) and is off-limits to the public, with the exception of the **Chapel Royal** (Oct–Good Friday Sun 8.30am & 11.15am), situated within the palace, and the **Queen's Chapel** (Easter–July Sun 8.30am & 11.15am), on the other side of Marlborough Road; both are open for services only.

One palatial St James's residence you can visit, however, is the late Princess Diana's ancestral home, **Spencer House** (Map 8, C3; Feb–July & Sept–Dec Sun 11.30am–4.45pm; £6), a superb Palladian mansion erected in the 1750s. Inside, tour guides take you through nine of the state rooms, the most outrageous of which is Lord Spencer's Room, with its astonishing gilded palm-tree columns.

PICCADILLY CIRCUS

Map 4, E6. ⊖ Piccadilly Circus.

Anonymous and congested it may be, but **Piccadilly Circus**, is, for many Londoners, the nearest their city comes to having a centre. A much-altered product of Nash's grand 1812 Regent Street plan, and now a major traffic bottleneck, it may not be a picturesque place, but thanks to its celebrated aluminium statue, popularly known as **Eros**, it's prime tourist territory. The fountain's archer is one of the city's top attractions, a status that baffles all who live here. Despite the bow and arrow, it's not the god of love at all but the Angel of Christian Charity, erected to commemorate the Earl of Shaftesbury, a Bible-thumping social reformer who campaigned against child labour.

If Eros's fame remains a mystery, the regular queue outside the nearby **Rock Circus** (Map 4, F6; Mon, Wed, Thurs & Sun 10am–8pm, Tues 11am–8pm, Fri & Sat 10am–9pm; £8.25; Ⓦ*www.rock-circus.com*) is a good deal more perplexing. Billed as an all-singing extravaganza, it's little more than an array of Madame Tussaud's waxen rock legends accompanied by snippets of their hits. Next door is the equally tacky **Trocadero** (Mon–Fri 10.30am–midnight, Sat & Sun 10.30am–1am), Europe's largest indoor virtual-reality theme park. For all the hype, this is really just a glorified amusement arcade with a few virtual-reality rides thrown in.

REGENT STREET

Map 4, B4. ⊖ Piccadilly Circus or Oxford Circus.

Regent Street is London's only equivalent to Haussmann's Parisian boulevards. Drawn up by John Nash in 1812 as both a luxury shopping street and a triumphal way between George IV's Carlton House and Regent's Park, it was the city's first attempt at dealing with traffic congestion, and also the first stab at slum clearance and planned social segregation, which would later be perfected by the Victorians.

Despite the subsequent destruction of much of Nash's work in the 1920s, it's still possible to admire the stately intentions of his original Regent Street plan. The increase in the purchasing power of the city's middle classes in the nineteenth century brought the tone of the street "down" and heavyweight stores catering for the masses now predominate. Among the best known are **Hamley's**, the world's largest toy shop, and **Liberty**, the department store that popularized Arts and Crafts designs at the beginning of the twentieth century.

PICCADILLY

Map 4, E7. ⊖ Piccadilly Circus or Green Park.

Piccadilly apparently got its name from the ruffs or "pickadills" worn by the dandies who used to promenade here in the late seventeenth century. Despite its fashionable pedigree, it's no place for promenading in its current state, with traffic careering down it nose to tail most of the day and night. Infinitely more pleasant places to window-shop are the various **nineteenth-century arcades**, originally built to protect shoppers from the mud and horse-dung on the streets, but now equally useful for escaping exhaust fumes.

Piccadilly may not be the shopping heaven it once was, but there are still several old firms here that proudly display their royal warrants. One of the oldest institutions is the food emporium of **Fortnum & Mason** (Map 4, C8; Ⓦ*www.fortnumandmason.com*) at no. 181, established in the 1770s by one of George III's footmen, Charles Fortnum, and his partner Hugh Mason. In a kitsch addition dating from 1964, the figures of Fortnum and Mason bow to each other on the hour every day as the clock over the main entrance clanks out the Eton school anthem.

Further along Piccadilly, with its best rooms overlooking Green Park, stands the **Ritz Hotel** (Map 4, A9; Ⓦ*www.theritzhotel.co.uk*), a byword for decadence since it first wowed Edwardian society in 1906; the hotel's design, with its two-storey French-style mansard roof and long arcade, was based on the buildings of Paris's Rue de Rivoli. For a prolonged look inside, you'll need to be in good appetite (and book in advance) for the famous afternoon tea in the hotel's Palm Court.

The Royal Academy

Map 4, B7. Mon–Thurs & Sat 10am–6pm, Fri 10am–8.30pm; £6–8; guided tours of the permanent collection Tues–Fri 1pm; free; Ⓦ*www.royalacademy.org.uk* ⊖ Green Park or Piccadilly Circus.

Across the road from Fortnum & Mason, the **Royal Academy of Arts** (RA) occupies the enormous Burlington House, one of the few survivors from the ranks of aristocratic mansions that once lined the north side of Piccadilly. The Academy itself was the country's first-ever formal art school, founded in 1768 by a group of English painters including Thomas Gainsborough and Joshua Reynolds. Reynolds went on to become the academy's first president, and his statue now stands in the courtyard, palette in hand.

The Academy has always had a conservative reputation for its teaching and, until recently, most of its shows. The **Summer Exhibition**, which opens in June each year, remains a stop on the social calendar of upper middle-class England. Anyone can enter paintings in any style, and the lucky winners get hung, in rather close proximity, and sold. Supposed gravitas is added by the RA "Academicians", who are allowed to display six of their own works – no matter how awful. The result is a bewildering display, which gets annually panned by highbrow critics.

Burlington Arcade

Map 4, B7.

Running along the west side of the Royal Academy is the

Burlington Arcade, built in 1819 for Lord Cavendish, then owner of Burlington House, to prevent commoners throwing rubbish into his garden. It's Piccadilly's longest and most expensive nineteenth-century arcade, lined with mahogany-fronted jewellers, gentlemen's outfitters and the like. Upholding Regency decorum, it is still illegal to whistle, sing, hum, hurry or carry large packages or open umbrellas on this small stretch, and the arcade's beadles (known as Burlington Berties), in their Edwardian frock-coats and gold-braided top hats, take the prevention of such criminality very seriously.

BOND STREET AND AROUND

Map 3, G5. ⊖ Green Park or Bond Street.

While Oxford Street, Regent Street and Piccadilly have all gone downmarket, **Bond Street**, which runs parallel with Regent Street, has carefully maintained its exclusivity. It is, in fact, two streets rolled into one: the southern half, laid out in the 1680s, is known as Old Bond Street; its northern extension, which followed less than fifty years later, is known as New Bond Street. They are both pretty unassuming streets architecturally, being a mixture of modest Victorian and Georgian town houses. However, the shops that line them, and those of neighbouring Conduit Street and South Molton Street, are among the flashiest in London, dominated by perfumeries, **jewellers** and designer clothing stores like Versace, Gucci, Nicole Farhi, Saint-Laurent and so on.

In addition to fashion, Bond Street is also renowned for its **auction houses** and for its fine-art galleries. Sotheby's, 34–35 New Bond St (Ⓦ*www.sothebys.com*), is the oldest of the auction houses, and its viewing galleries are open free of charge. Bond Street's **art galleries** – exclusive mainstays of the street – are actually outnumbered by those on nearby

Cork Street. The main difference between the two locations is that the Bond Street dealers are basically heirloom offloaders, whereas Cork Street galleries sell largely contemporary art. Both have impeccably presented and somewhat intimidating staff, but if you're interested, walk in and look around. They're only shops, after all.

See p.297 for listings of the best shops in London.

Savile Row

Map 4, B6.

Running parallel with New Bond Street and Cork Street is another classic address in sartorial matters, **Savile Row**, still the place to go for made-to-measure suits, for those with the requisite £2000 or so to spare. The number of bespoke tailors may have declined, but several venerable businesses remain. Gieves & Hawkes, at no. 1, were the first tailors to establish themselves here back in 1785, with Nelson and Wellington among their first customers, and their wares are still an exhibition of upper-class taste.

Savile Row also has connections with the pop world at no. 3, where Apple, the record label set up by **The Beatles**, had their offices and recording studio from 1968 until 1972. In February 1969 The Beatles gave their last live gig on the roof here, stopping the traffic and eventually attracting the attentions of the local police – as captured on film in *Let It Be*.

OXFORD STREET

Map 4, B2. Ⓦ*www.oxfordstreet.co.uk* ⊖ Bond Street, Oxford Circus or Tottenham Court Road.

As wealthy Londoners began to move out of the City in the

eighteenth century in favour of the newly developed West End, so **Oxford Street** – the old Roman road to Oxford – gradually became London's main shopping street. Today, despite successive recessions and sky-high rents, this scruffy, two-mile hotchpotch of shops is still one of the world's busiest streets.

East of Oxford Circus, the street forms the northern border of Soho, and features two of the city's main record stores, HMV and Virgin Megastore, and the Borders mega-bookstore. West of Oxford Circus, the street is dominated by more upmarket stores, including one great landmark, **Selfridge's** (Map 3, E4; Ⓦ*www.selfridges.co.uk*), a huge Edwardian pile fronted by giant Ionic columns, with the Queen of Time riding the ship of commerce and supporting an Art Deco clock above the main entrance. The store was opened in 1909 by Chicago millionaire Gordon Selfridge, who flaunted its 130 departments under the slogan, "Why not spend a day at Selfridge's?", but was later pensioned off after running into trouble with the Inland Revenue.

THE WALLACE COLLECTION

Map 3, E4. Mon–Sat 10am–5pm, Sun 2–5pm; free; Ⓦ*www.wallace-collection.org.uk* ⊖ Bond Street.

Immediately north of Oxford Street, on Manchester Square, stands Hertford House, a miniature eighteenth-century French chateau which holds the splendid **Wallace Collection**, a museum-gallery best known for its eighteenth-century French paintings (especially Watteau), Franz Hals' *Laughing Cavalier*, Titian's *Perseus and Andromeda*, Velázquez's *Lady with a Fan* and Rembrandt's affectionate portrait of his teenage son, Titus. There's a modern café in the newly glassed-over courtyard, but at heart, the Wallace Collection remains an old-fashioned place, with exhibits piled high in glass cabinets, and paintings covering every inch of wall space. The fact that these exhibits are set amidst period fittings – and a bloody great armoury – makes the place even more remarkable. If you're here for the paintings, head for the Great Gallery on the first floor, where the best of the works are hung.

LANGHAM PLACE AND PORTLAND PLACE

Map 3, F3. ⊖ Oxford Circus.

Regent Street finally stops just north of Oxford Street at **Langham Place**, site of **All Souls**, Nash's simple and ingenious little Bath-stone church, built in the 1820s. The church's unusual circular Ionic portico and conical spire, which caused outrage in its day, were designed to provide a visual full stop to Regent Street and a pivot for the awkward twist in the triumphal route to Regent's Park. Behind lies the totalitarian-looking **Broadcasting House**, built as the BBC headquarters in 1931, and now home to the new interactive "BBC Experience" (see below). Opposite Broadcasting House stands the **Langham Hilton**, built in heavy Italianate style in the 1860s, badly bombed in the last war, but now back to its former glory.

The BBC Experience

Map 3, G3. Mon 11am–4.30pm, Tues–Sun 10am–4.30pm; £7.50; Ⓦ*www.bbc.co.uk/experience*.

Since 1997, the BBC has had its very own interactive museum, the **BBC Experience**. However, a word of warning is necessary to TV addicts, as the emphasis of the museum is on radio (Broadcasting House is the home of BBC radio, but not television). The museum is part guided-tour, part hands-on experience, so visits are carefully orchestrated, with tours setting off every thirty minutes (every fifteen at peak times). As well as the usual static displays and audiovisuals extolling the virtues of the "Beeb", you get to record a short radio play with your fellow visitors, and play around in the museum's interactive section, mixing records, fine-tuning your sports commentary and presenting the weather.

Portland Place

Map 3, F3.

After the chicane around All Souls, you enter **Portland Place**, laid out by the Adam brothers in the 1770s, and incorporated by Nash in his grand route. Once the widest street in London, it's still a majestic avenue, lined exclusively with Adam-style houses boasting wonderful fanlights and iron railings.

Arguably the finest of all the buildings on Portland Place, though, is the sleek **Royal Institute of British Architects** (RIBA; Ⓦ*www.architecture.com*), built in the 1930s. The highlight of the building is the interior, which you can view en route to the institute's excellent first-floor **café** (Mon, Wed, Fri & Sat 8am–6pm, Tues & Thurs 8am–9pm), or during one of the frequent exhibitions and Tuesday-evening lectures held here. The main staircase remains a wonderful period piece, with its etched glass balustrades and walnut veneer, and with two large black-marble columns rising up on either side.

MADAME TUSSAUD'S AND THE PLANETARIUM

Map 3, E3. Daily: June to mid-Sept 9am–5.30pm; mid-Sept to May 10am–5.30pm; £10.50 or £12.95 with Planetarium. ⊖ Baker Street.

Madame Tussaud's, just up Marylebone Road from Baker Street tube, has been pulling in the crowds ever since the good lady arrived in London from Paris in 1802 bearing the sculpted heads of guillotined aristocrats (she herself only just managed to escape the same fate – her uncle, who started the family business, was less fortunate). The entrance fee might be extortionate, the likenesses occasionally dubious and the automated dummies inept, but you can still rely on finding London's biggest queues here – to avoid queuing, book your ticket in advance over the phone or on the Internet.

You can buy tickets for Tussaud's and the Planetarium (or both) in advance at the slightly cheaper price of £9.25 or £11.50; call Ⓣ0870/400 3000 or visit Ⓦ*www.madame-tussauds.com*.

As well as the usual parade of wax figures, the tour of Tussaud's ends with a manic five-minute "ride" through the history of London in a miniaturized taxi cab. The adjoining and equally crowded London **Planetarium** (Mon–Fri 11.30am–5pm, Sat, Sun & school holidays 10am–5pm; £6.50) features a thirty-minute high-tech presentation, projected onto a giant dome; a standard romp through the basics of astronomy accompanied by a cosmic astro-babble commentary.

Soho and Covent Garden

SOHO and **COVENT GARDEN** are very much the heart of London – and the centre's most characterful areas. It's here you'll find the city's street fashion on display, its more oddball shops, its opera houses, theatres and mega-cinemas, and the widest variety of restaurants and cafés – where, whatever hour you wander through, there's invariably something going on. There always was a life to these neighbourhoods, of course, but their aspect today is very different to the recent past. Both neighbourhoods started out as wealthy residential developments, then sank into legendary squalor, until their revival over the past twenty years.

For Soho and Covent Garden's café, pub and restaurant listings – see Chapters 15, 16 and 17.

Soho retains a uniquely unorthodox and slightly raffish air, and gives you the best and worst of London. The porn joints that made the district notorious in the 1970s are still in evidence, especially to the west of Wardour Street, as are the yuppies who pushed up the rents in the 1980s. In the 1990s, Soho transformed itself again, this time into one of Europe's leading gay centres, with bars and cafés bursting out from the **Old Compton Street** area. Nevertheless, the area continues to boast a lively fruit and vegetable market on **Berwick Street**, and a nightlife scene that has attracted writers and ravers to the place since the eighteenth century. The big movie houses on **Leicester Square** always attract crowds of punters, and the tiny enclave of **Chinatown** continues to double as a focus for the Chinese community and a popular place for inexpensive Oriental restaurants.

Covent Garden's transformation from a fruit and vegetable market into a fashion-conscious *quartier* is one of the most miraculous and enduring developments of the 1980s. More sanitized and brazenly commercial than Soho, Covent Garden today is a far cry from its heyday when the piazza was the great playground (and red-light district) of eighteenth-century London. The buskers in front of St Paul's Church, the theatres round about, and the **Royal Opera House** on Bow Street are survivors in this tradition, and on a balmy summer evening, **Covent Garden Piazza** is still an undeniably lively place to be. Another positive side-effect of the market development has been the renovation of the run-down warehouses to the north of the piazza, especially around the Neal Street area, which now boasts some of the trendiest shops in the West End, selling everything from shoes to skateboards.

LEICESTER SQUARE

Map 4, H6. ⊖ Leicester Square.

By night, when the big cinemas and discos are doing good business, and the buskers are entertaining the crowds, **Leicester Square** is one of the most crowded places in London, particularly on a Friday or Saturday when huge numbers of tourists and half the youth of the suburbs seem to congregate here. By day, queues form for half-price deals at the Society of West End Theatres booth at the south end of the square, while touts haggle over the price of dodgy tickets for the top shows, and clubbers hand out flyers to likely looking punters.

For the lowdown on buying theatre tickets, see p.278.

It wasn't until the mid-nineteenth century that the square actually began to emerge as an entertainment zone, with accommodation houses (for prostitutes and their clients), and music halls such as the grandiose Empire and the Hippodrome (just off the square), edifices which survive today as cinemas and discos. Cinema moved in during the 1930s, a golden age evoked by the sleek black lines of the Odeon on the east side, and maintains its grip on the area. The Empire, at the top end of the square, is the favourite for the big royal premieres, and, in a rather half-hearted imitation of the Hollywood (and Cannes) tradition, there are even hand-prints visible in the pavement by the south-western corner of the square.

CHINATOWN

Map 4, H5. ⊖ Leicester Square.

Chinatown, hemmed in between Leicester Square and Shaftesbury Avenue, is a self-contained jumble of shops, cafés and restaurants that makes up one of London's most distinct and popular ethnic enclaves. **Gerrard Street**, Chinatown's main drag, has been endowed with ersatz touches – telephone kiosks rigged out as pagodas and fake oriental gates – but few of London's 60,000 Chinese actually live in the three small blocks of Chinatown. Nonetheless, it remains a focus for the community, a place to do business or the weekly shopping, celebrate a wedding, or just meet up for meals, particularly on Sundays, when the restaurants overflow with Chinese families tucking into dim sum.

The **Chinese New Year** celebrations, instigated here in 1973, draw in thousands of Chinese for the Sunday nearest to New Year's Day (late January or early February). Huge papier-maché lions dance through the streets to a cacophony of firecrackers, devouring cabbages hung from the upper floors by strings pinned with money. The noise is deafening, and if you want to see anything, you'll need to position yourself close to one of the cabbages around noon and stand your ground.

For restaurant listings, see p.206.

For the rest of the year, most Londoners come to Chinatown simply to eat – easy and inexpensive enough to do, though the choice is somewhat overwhelming, especially on Gerrard Street itself. Cantonese cuisine predominates, and you're unlikely to be disappointed wherever you go.

CHARING CROSS ROAD AND SHAFTESBURY AVENUE

Map 4, I4. ⊖ Leicester Square or Tottenham Court Road.

Charing Cross Road, Soho's eastern border and a thoroughfare from Trafalgar Square to Oxford Street, boasts the highest concentration of **bookshops** anywhere in London. One of the first to open here was the chaotic, antiquated Foyles at no. 119, which now struggles to compete with the nearby heavyweight chain bookshops such as Books Etc, Borders, Blackwell's and Waterstones. The street retains more of its original character south of Cambridge Circus, where you'll find the capital's main feminist bookshop,

Silver Moon, along with a cluster of ramshackle secondhand bookshops, such as Quinto.

One of the nicest places for secondhand book browsing is **Cecil Court** (Map 4, J6), the southernmost alleyway between Charing Cross Road and St Martin's Lane. This short, paved street boasts specialist bookshops devoted to dance, Italy, New Age philosophies and the like, plus various antiquarian dealers. Another place you shouldn't miss, just off Charing Cross Road, is the **Photographers' Gallery** (Map 4, J5; Mon–Sat 11am–6pm, Sun noon–6pm; free; ⓦ*www.photonet.org.uk*) at 5 and 8 Great Newport St, which hosts free temporary exhibitions that are invariably worth a browse.

Sweeping northeast towards Bloomsbury from Piccadilly Circus, and separating Soho proper from Chinatown, the gentle curve of **Shaftesbury Avenue** is the heart of mainstream theatreland, with five theatres and two cinemas along its length. Like Charing Cross Road, it was conceived in the late 1870s, ostensibly to relieve traffic congestion but with the dual purpose of destroying the slums that lay in its path. Ironically, it was then named after Lord Shaftesbury, whose life had been spent trying to help the likes of those dispossessed by the road scheme.

OLD COMPTON STREET AND CENTRAL SOHO

Map 4, H4. ⊖ Leicester Square or Piccadilly Circus.

If Soho has a main drag, it has to be **Old Compton Street**, which runs parallel with Shaftesbury Avenue. The corner shops, peep shows, boutiques and trendy cafés here are typical of the area and a good barometer of the latest Soho fads. Soho was a permanent fixture on the **gay scene** for much of the twentieth century, but the approach is much more upfront nowadays, with gay bars, clubs and cafés jostling for position on Old Compton Street, and round the corner in Wardour Street. And it doesn't stop there: there's now a gay travel agency, a gay financial adviser and a gay taxi service.

For gay and lesbian listings, see p.251.

The streets off Old Compton Street are lined with Soho institutions past and present. One of the best known is London's longest-running jazz club, *Ronnie Scott's* (Map 4, H3; Ⓦ*www.ronniescotts.co.uk*), on **Frith Street**, founded in 1958 and still capable of pulling in the big names. Opposite is the *Bar Italia*, an Italian café with a big screen for satellite TV transmissions of Italian football games, and late-night hours popular with Soho's clubbers. It was in this building, appropriately enough for such a media-saturated area, that John Logie Baird made the world's first public television-transmission in 1926.

If you're finding it difficult to imagine Soho ever having been an aristocratic haunt, pay a visit to the **House of St Barnabas-in-Soho** (Map 4, H2; Wed 2.30–4.30pm, Thurs 11am–12.30pm; donation), a Georgian mansion at the top of Greek Street. Built in the 1740s, the house retains some exquisite Rococo plasterwork on the main staircase and in the Council Chamber, which has a lovely view onto Soho Square. Since 1861 the building has been a Christian charity house for the destitute, so the rest of the interior is much altered and closed off.

Wardour Street and beyond

Map 4, F4.

At the western end of Old Compton Street runs **Wardour Street**, a kind of dividing line between the trendier, eastern half of Soho and the seedier western zone. The street itself is largely given over to the film industry – Warner Brothers is based here, along with numerous smaller companies.

Immediately west of Wardour Street, the sex and prostitution rackets still have the area well staked out. However, straight prostitution in fact makes up a small proportion of what gets sold here, and has been since Paul Raymond – now Britain's richest man – set up his Folies-Bergère style *Revue Bar* (Map 4, F4) in the late 1950s, now complemented by the transvestite floor show next door at *Madame Jo-Jo's*. These last two are paragons of virtue compared with the dodgy videos, short con outfits and rip-off joints that operate in the neighbouring streets.

In amongst the video shops and triple-X-rated cinemas is the unlikely sight of **Berwick Street Market** (Map 4, F4), one of the capital's finest (and cheapest) fruit and vegetable markets. The street itself is no beauty spot, but the market's barrow displays are works of art in themselves, while, on either side of the marketholders, are some of London's best specialist record shops.

Carnaby Street

Map 4, C4.

Until the 1950s, **Carnaby Street** was a backstreet on Soho's western fringe, occupied, for the most part, by sweatshop tailors who used to make up the suits for nearby Savile Row. Then, sometime in the mid-1950s, several trendy boutiques opened catering for the new market in flamboyant men's clothing. In 1964 – the year of the official birth of the Carnaby Street myth – Mods, West Indian Rude Boys and other "switched-on people", as the *Daily Telegraph* noted, began to hang out here. The area quickly became the epicentre of Swinging Sixties' London, and its street sign London's most popular postcard. A victim of its own hype, Carnaby Street declined equally quickly into an avenue of overpriced tack. More recently, things have started to pick up again, especially in neighbouring

Newburgh Street, and the whole area is currently enjoying a new lease of life.

COVENT GARDEN PIAZZA

Map 4, M5. ⊖ Covent Garden.

London's oldest planned square, laid out in the 1630s by Inigo Jones, **Covent Garden Piazza** was initially a great success, its novelty value alone attracting a rich and aristocratic clientele. Over the next century, though, the tone of the place fell as the fruit and vegetable market expanded, and theatres and coffee houses began to take over the peripheral buildings. When the flower market closed in 1974, the piazza narrowly survived being turned into an office development. Instead, the elegant Victorian market hall and its environs were restored to house shops, restaurants and arts-and-crafts stalls. Boosted by buskers and street entertainers, the piazza has now become one of London's major tourist attractions, its success prompting a wholesale gentrification of the streets to the north of the market.

St Paul's Church

Map 4, L5.

Of Jones's original piazza, the only remaining parts are the two rebuilt sections of north-side arcading, and **St Paul's Church**, facing the west side of the market building. The proximity of so many theatres has earned it the nickname of the "Actors' Church", and it's filled with memorials to international thespians from Boris Karloff to Gracie Fields. The space in front of the church's Tuscan portico – where Eliza Doolittle was discovered selling violets by Henry Higgins in George Bernard Shaw's *Pygmalion* – is now a legalized venue for buskers and street performers, who must audition for a slot months in advance.

The piazza's history of entertainment goes back to May 1662, when the first recorded performance of Punch and Judy in England was staged by Italian puppeteer Pietro Gimonde, and witnessed by Samuel Pepys. This historic event is commemorated every second Sunday in May by a **Punch and Judy Festival**, held in the gardens behind the church; for the rest of the year, the churchyard provides a tranquil respite from the activity outside (access is from King Street, Henrietta Street or Bedford Street).

The London Transport Museum

Map 4, N5. Mon–Thurs, Sat & Sun 10am–6pm, Fri 11am–6pm; £5.50; Ⓦ*www.ltmuseum.co.uk*.

A former flower-market shed on the piazza's east side is now home to the **London Transport Museum**. A herd of old buses, trains and trams make up the bulk of the exhibits, though there's enough interactive fun – touch-screen computers and the odd costumed conductor and vehicles to climb on – to keep most children amused. There's usually a good smattering of London Transport's stylish maps and posters on display, too, and you can buy reproductions, plus countless other LT paraphernalia, at the shop on the way out.

The Theatre Museum

Map 4, N4. Tues–Sun 10am–6pm; £4.50; Ⓦ*www.theatremuseum.org*.

The rest of the old flower market now houses the Theatre Museum, displaying three centuries of memorabilia from every conceivable area of the performing arts in the West (the entrance is on Russell Street). The corridors of glass cases cluttered with props, programmes and costumes are not especially exciting, but the long-term "temporary" shows such as "The Wind in the Willows", tend to be a lot more fun, and usually have a workshop or hands-on element to them. The museum also runs a booking service for West End shows and has an unusually good selection of cards and posters.

BOW STREET

Map 4, M3. ⊖ Covent Garden.

Bow Street, to the east of the Piazza, is famous for its magistrates' court, first opened in 1748. Here, Henry Fielding, author of *Tom Jones*, and his blind half-brother John set about creating the city's first police force, the **Bow Street Runners**. Never numbering more than a dozen, they were employed primarily to combat prostitution. Before it was finally closed in 1989, Bow Street police station also had the honour of incarcerating Oscar Wilde after he was arrested for "committing indecent acts" in 1895 – he was eventually sentenced to two years' hard labour. And in 1928, Radclyffe Hall's lesbian novel, *Well of Loneliness*, was deemed obscene by Bow Street magistrates and remained banned in this country until 1949.

The Royal Opera House

Map 4, M3. Backstage tours Mon–Sat 10.30am, 12.30 & 2.30pm; £6; Ⓦ*www.royaloperahouse.org* ⊖ Covent Garden.

The Corinthian portico opposite Bow Street magistrates' court belongs to the **Royal Opera House** (ROH), whose main building dates from 1811, but which has recently undergone a £220 million redevelopment. Part and parcel of the rebuilding has been the construction of arcading in the northeast side of the piazza, from which there's now a passageway through to Bow Street. The public can also gain access to the spectacular wrought-iron **Floral Hall** (daily 10am–3pm), on the first floor, which now serves as the opera house's main foyer, and the *Amphitheatre* bar/restaurant, which has a glorious terrace overlooking the piazza.

NORTH OF THE PIAZZA

Map 4, L3. ⊖ Covent Garden.

The area to the north of Covent Garden Piazza is, on the whole, more interesting in terms of its shops, pubs and eating places than is the piazza itself. Floral Street, Long Acre, Shelton Street and especially Neal Street are all good shopping locales.

Looking east down the gentle curve of Long Acre, it's difficult to miss the austere, Pharaonic mass of the **Freemasons' Hall** (Map 4, N2; Mon–Fri 10am–5pm; free; Ⓦ*www.grand-lodge.org*), built as a memorial to all the masons who died in World War I. Whatever you may think of this reactionary, male-only, secretive organization, the interior is worth a peek for the Grand Temple alone, whose pompous, bombastic décor is laden with heavy symbolism. To see the Grand Temple, turn up for one of the free hourly **guided tours** (Mon–Fri 11am–4pm).

North from Long Acre runs **Neal Street**, one of the most sought-after commercial addresses in Covent Garden, which features some fine Victorian warehouses, complete with stair towers for loading and shifting goods between floors. Neal Street is now dominated by trendy fashion stores like Mango, Diesel and, on nearby Shorts Gardens, About Time. A decade or so ago, the feel of the street was a lot less moneyed and more alternative, but that ambience only really survives in **Neal's Yard**, a wholefood haven set in a tiny little courtyard off Shorts Gardens, prettily festooned with flower boxes and ivy.

West of Neal Street is **Seven Dials** (Map 4, J3), the meeting point of seven streets which make up a little circus centred on a slender column topped by six tiny blue sundials (the seventh dial is formed by the column itself and the surrounding road). **Earlham Street**, which runs west from Seven Dials, harbours an ironmongers and a local butchers alongside clubbers' shops. It was once a flourishing market street, and of the handful of stalls that remain is one of London's very best flower stalls – a visual treat at any time of year.

Bloomsbury

BLOOMSBURY gets its name from its medieval landowners, the Blemunds, though nothing was built here until the 1660s. Through marriage, the Russell family (the earls and later dukes of Bedford) acquired much of the area, and established the many formal, bourgeois squares which are the main distinguishing feature of Bloomsbury today. The Russells named the grid-plan streets after their various titles and estates, and kept the pubs and shops to a minimum to maintain the tone of the neighbourhood.

In the twentieth century, Bloomsbury acquired a reputation as the city's most learned quarter, dominated by the dual institutions of the **British Museum** and **London University**, and home to many of London's chief book publishers, but perhaps best known for its literary inhabitants. Today, the British Museum is clearly the star attraction, but there are other sights, such as the **Dickens House Museum**, that are high on many people's itineraries.

In its northern fringes, the character of the area changes dramatically, becoming steadily more seedy as you near the two big main-line train stations of **Euston** and **King's Cross**, where cheap B&Bs and run-down council estates provide fertile territory for prostitutes and drug dealers, and an unlikely location for the new **British Library**.

THE BLOOMSBURY GROUP

The **Bloomsbury Group** were essentially a bevy of upper middle-class friends, who lived in and around Bloomsbury. The Group revolved around Virginia, Vanessa, Thoby and Adrian Stephen, who moved into 46 Gordon Square in 1904. Thoby's Thursday evening gatherings and Vanessa's Friday Club for painters attracted a whole host of Cambridge-educated snobs who subscribed to Oscar Wilde's theory that "aesthetics are higher than ethics". Their diet of "human intercourse and the enjoyment of beautiful things" was hardly revolutionary, but their behaviour, particularly that of the two sisters (unmarried, unchaperoned, intellectual and artistic), succeeded in shocking London society, especially through their louche sexual practices (most of the group swung both ways).

All this, though interesting, would be forgotten were it not for their individual work. In 1922 Virginia declared, without too much exaggeration, "Everyone in Gordon Square has become famous": Lytton Strachey had been the first to make his name with *Eminent Victorians*, a series of unprecedentedly frank biographies; Vanessa, now married to the art critic Clive Bell, had become involved in Roger Fry's prolific design firm, Omega Workshop; and the economist John Maynard Keynes had become an adviser to the Treasury (he later went on to become the leading economic theorist of his day). The Group's most celebrated figure, Virginia, now married to Leonard Woolf and living in Tavistock Square, had become an established novelist; she and Leonard had also founded the Hogarth Press, which published T.S. Eliot's *The Waste Land* in 1922. Whatever their limitations, the Bloomsbury Group were Britain's most influential intellectual coterie of the interwar years, and their appeal shows little sign of waning.

THE BRITISH MUSEUM

Map 3, H3. Mon–Sat 10am–5pm, Sun noon–6pm; free; ⓦ*www.british-museum.ac.uk* ⊖ Tottenham Court Road or Russell Square.

One of the great museums of the world, the **British Museum** is Britain's most popular tourist attraction after Blackpool, drawing more than six million visitors a year. With over four million exhibits ranged over two and a half miles of galleries, the BM contains one of the most comprehensive collections of antiquities, prints, drawings and books to be housed under one roof.

The building itself, begun in 1823, is the grandest of London's Greek Revival edifices, dominated by the giant Ionian colonnade and portico that forms the main entrance. The British Library's departure to St Pancras (see p.61) has allowed the museum to open up and redevelop the building's **Great Court**, which now features a remarkable, curving glass-and-steel roof, designed by Norman Foster. At the centre stands the copper-domed former **Round Reading Room**, built in the 1850s to house the British Library. It was here, at desk O7, beneath one of the largest domes in the world, that Karl Marx penned *Das Kapital*. The building is now a public study area, and features a multimedia guide to the museum's collections.

The BM's collection of **Roman and Greek antiquities** is unparalleled, and is perhaps most famous for the Parthenon sculptures, better known as the **Elgin Marbles**, after the British aristocrat who walked off with the reliefs in 1801. Amidst the plethora of Greek and Roman statuary and vases, the only other single item with a similarly high profile is the **Portland Vase**, made from cobalt-blue blown glass around the beginning of the first century, and decorated with opaque white cameos.

The museum's **Egyptian collection** is easily the most

significant outside Egypt, and ranges from monumental sculptures, such the colossal granite head of Amenophis III, to the ever-popular mummies and their ornate outer caskets. Also on display is the Rosetta Stone, which finally unlocked the secret of Egyptian hieroglyphs. Close by the Egyptian Hall, you'll find a splendid series of **Assyrian reliefs** from Nineveh, depicting events such as the royal lion hunts of Ashurbanipal, in which the king slaughters one of the cats with his bare hands. Among the most extraordinary artefacts from **Mesopotamia** are the enigmatic Ram in the Thicket (a lapis lazuli and shell statuette of a goat), an equally mysterious box known as the Standard of Ur, and the remarkable hoard of goldwork known as the Oxus Treasure.

The leathery half-corpse of the 2000-year-old **Lindow Man**, discovered in a Cheshire bog, and the Anglo-Saxon treasure from the **Sutton Hoo** ship burial, are among one of the highlights of the Prehistoric and Romano-British collection. The medieval and modern collections, meanwhile, range from the twelfth-century Lewis chessmen, carved from walrus ivory, to twentieth-century exhibits such as a copper vase by Frank Lloyd Wright. It's also worth seeking out the museum's **Money Gallery**, which begins with the use of grain in Mesopotamia around 2000 BC, ends with a 1990s five hundred thousand million Yugoslav dinar note, and includes coins from all over the world.

The dramatically-lit Mexican Gallery, and the North American Gallery, mark the beginning of the return of the museum's **ethnographic collection**, but lack of space means that only a fraction of the BM's enormous collection of prints and drawings can be displayed at any one time. In addition, there are fabulous **Oriental treasures** in the north wing of the museum, closest to the back entrance on Montague Place. The displays include ancient Chinese porcelain, ornate snuffboxes, miniature landscapes, a bewildering array of Buddhist and Hindu gods, and – the showpiece of the collection – dazzling limestone reliefs from the second-century stupa of Amaravati in south India.

DICKENS' HOUSE

Map 3, J3. Mon–Sat 10am–5pm; £4; Ⓦ*www.dickensmuseum.com* ⊖ Russell Square.

Despite the plethora of blue plaques marking the residences of local luminaries, **Dickens' House**, at 48 Doughty St, in Bloomsbury's eastern fringes, is the area's only literary museum. Dickens moved here in 1837 shortly after his marriage to Catherine Hogarth, and they lived here for two years, during which time he wrote *Nicholas Nickleby* and *Oliver Twist*. This is the only one of Dickens' fifteen London addresses to survive intact, but only the drawing room, in which Dickens entertained his literary friends, has been restored to its original Regency style. Letters, manuscripts and lots of memorabilia, including first editions, the earliest known portrait and the annotated books he used during extensive lecture tours, are the rewards for those with more than a passing interest in the novelist.

THE UNIVERSITY

Map 3, H3. Ⓦ*www.lon.ac.uk* ⊖ Russell Square or Goodge Street.

London has more students than any other city in the world (over half a million at the last count), which isn't bad going for a city that only organized its own **University** in 1826, more than six hundred years after the likes of Oxford and Cambridge. The university started life in Bloomsbury, but it wasn't until after World War I that the institution really began to take over the area.

However, the university's piecemeal development has left

the place with no real focus other than a couple of landmarks in the form of the 1930s **Senate House** skyscraper, behind the British Museum, and the Neoclassical **University College** (UCL; *www.ucl.ac.uk*), near the top of Gower Street. UCL is home to London's most famous art school, the **Slade**, which puts on temporary exhibitions in the **Strang Print Room**, in the south cloister of the main quadrangle (term-time Wed–Fri 1–5pm; free). Also on display in the south cloisters is the fully-clothed skeleton of philosopher **Jeremy Bentham** (1748–1832), one of the university's founders, topped by a wax head and wide-brimmed hat.

The university also runs a couple of specialist museums. On the first floor of the Watson building, down Malet Place, the **Petrie Museum of Egyptian Archeology** (Tues–Fri 1–5pm, Sat 10am–1pm; free) has a couple of rooms jam-packed with antiquities, including the world's oldest dress. Tucked away in the southeast corner of Gordon Square, at no. 53, the **Percival David Foundation of Chinese Art** (Mon–Fri 10.30am–5pm; free) houses two floors of top-notch Chinese ceramics.

THE BRITISH LIBRARY

Map 3, H2. Mon & Wed–Fri 9.30am–6pm, Tues 9.30am–8pm, Sat 9.30am–5pm, Sun 11am–5pm; free; *www.bl.uk* ⊖ King's Cross or Euston.

After fifteen years of hassle, and £500 million of public money, the new **British Library**, located on the busy Euston Road on the northern fringes of Bloomsbury, finally opened to the public in 1998. As the country's most expensive public building, it's hardly surprising that the place has come under fierce criticism from all sides. Architecturally, the charge has been led, predictably enough, by Prince Charles, who compared it to an academy for secret policemen. Yet while it's true that the building's red-brick brutalism is horribly out of fashion, and compares unfavourably with its cathedralesque Victorian neighbour, the former *Midland Grand Hotel*, the interior of the library has met with general approval, and the new high-tech exhibition galleries are superb.

With the exception of the reading rooms, the library is open to the general public. The three exhibition galleries are to the left as you enter; straight ahead is the spiritual heart of the BL, a multistorey glass-walled tower housing the vast **King's Library**, collected by George III, and donated to the museum by George IV in 1823; to the side of the King's Library are the pull-out draws of the **philatelic collection**. If you want to explore the parts of the building not normally open to the public, you must sign up for a **guided tour** (Mon, Wed, Fri & Sun 3pm, Sat 10.30am & 3pm; £4; or Tues 6.30pm & Sun 11.30am & 3pm if you want to see the reading rooms; £5).

The first of the three exhibition galleries to head for is the dimly-lit **John Ritblat Gallery**, where a superlative selection of the BL's ancient manuscripts, maps, documents and precious books, including the richly illustrated Lindisfarne Gospels, are displayed. One of the most appealing innovations is "**Turning the Pages**", a small room off the main gallery, where you can turn the pages of selected texts "virtually" on a computer terminal. The **Workshop of Words, Sounds and Images** is a hands-on exhibition of more universal appeal, where you can design your own literary publication, while the **Pearson Gallery of Living Words** puts on excellent temporary exhibitions, for which there is sometimes an admission charge.

Strand, Holborn and Clerkenwell

The area covered in this chapter – **STRAND**, **HOLBORN** and **CLERKENWELL** – lies on the periphery of the entertainment zone of the West End and the financial district of the City. The **Strand**, as its name suggests, once lay along the riverbank: it achieved its present-day form when the Victorians shored up the banks of the Thames to create the Embankment. **Holborn** (pronounced "Ho-burn"), to the northeast, has long been associated with the law, and its **Inns of Court** make for an interesting stroll, their archaic, cobbled precincts exuding the rarefied atmosphere of an Oxbridge college, and sheltering one of the city's oldest churches, the twelfth-century **Temple Church**. Close by the Inns, in Lincoln's Inn Fields, is the **Sir John Soane's Museum**, one of the most memorable and enjoyable of London's small museums, packed with architectural illusions and an eclectic array of curios.

Clerkenwell, further to the northeast, is off the tourist trail, but has a host of unusual sights, including vestiges of two pre-Fire of London priories, an old prison house and the **Marx Memorial Library**, where the exiled Lenin plotted revolution.

STRAND

Map 4, L7. ⊖ Charing Cross or Temple (Mon–Sat only).

Once famous for its riverside mansions, and later its music halls, the **Strand** – the main road connecting Westminster to the City – is a shadow of its former self. Nowadays, it's best known for the young homeless who shelter in the shop doorways at night.

One such doorway, at no. 440, belongs to what was once London's largest private bank, **Coutts & Co** (Ⓦ*www.coutts.com*), whose customers include the Queen herself. Founded in 1692 by the Scottish goldsmith, John Campbell, a mock-up of whose original premises stands behind a screen in the bank's current concrete and marble atrium. Today's male employees still sport anachronistic tail-coated suits, but the horse-drawn carriage which used to convey royal correspondence was taken out of service in 1993.

The eastern stretch of the Strand, beyond Aldwych, is covered on p.66.

Some way further east on the opposite side of the Strand, the blind side street of Savoy Court – the only street in the country where the traffic drives on the right – leads to **The Savoy**, London's grandest hotel, built in 1889 on the site of the medieval Savoy Palace. César Ritz was the original manager, Guccio Gucci started out as a dishwasher here, and the list of illustrious guests is endless: Monet painted the Thames from one of the south-facing rooms, Sarah Bernhardt nearly died here, and Strauss the Younger arrived with his own orchestra.

VICTORIA EMBANKMENT

Map 4, N8. ⊖ Embankment.

The **Victoria Embankment**, built between 1868 and 1874, was the inspiration of French engineer Joseph Bazalgette, whose project simultaneously relieved congestion along the Strand, provided an extension to the underground railway and sewage systems, and created a new stretch of parkland with a riverside walk – no longer much fun due to the volume of traffic. The 1626 **York Watergate**, in the Victoria Embankment Gardens to the east of Villiers Street, gives you an idea of where the banks of the Thames used to be; the steps through the gateway once led down to the river.

London's oldest monument, **Cleopatra's Needle**, languishes little-noticed on the Thames side of the busy Victoria Embankment, guarded by two Victorian sphinxes. The 60-foot-high, 180-ton stick of granite in fact has nothing to do with Cleopatra – it's one of a pair erected in Heliopolis in 1475 BC (the other one is in New York's Central Park) and taken to Alexandria by the Emperor Augustus fifteen years after Cleopatra's suicide. This obelisk was presented to Britain in 1819 by the Turkish viceroy of Egypt, but nearly sixty years passed before it finally made its way to London.

The **Benjamin Franklin House** (Map 4, L8; Ⓦ*www.rsa.org.uk/franklin*), on the other side of Charing Cross Station at 36 Craven St, will probably attract more visitors than Cleopatra's Needle. Restored with help of, among others, the nearby Royal Society of Arts, the museum should be open some time in 2001; entry fees and times of opening were not available when this book went to press but you can call for more information on Ⓣ020/7930 9121. The tenth son of a candlemaker, Franklin (1706–1790) had "genteel lodgings" here more or less continuously from 1757 to

1775. Whilst Franklin was espousing the cause of the British colonies (as the US then was), the house served as the first de facto American Embassy; eventually, he returned to America to help draft the Declaration of Independence, negotiate the peace treaty with Britain and frame the Constitution.

THE ALDWYCH AREA

Map 5, A5. ⊖ Holborn or Temple (Mon–Sat only).

The wide crescent of **Aldwych**, forming a neat "D" with the eastern part of the Strand, was driven through the slums of this zone in the last throes of the Victorian era. A confident ensemble occupies the centre, with the enormous **Australia House** and **India House** sandwiching **Bush House**, home of the BBC's World Service (Ⓦ*www.bbc.co.uk/worldservice*) since 1940. Despite its thoroughly British associations, Bush House was actually built by the American speculator Irving T. Bush, whose planned trade-centre flopped in the 1930s. The giant figures on the north facade and the inscription, "To the Eternal Friendship of English-speaking Nations", thus refer to the friendship between the US and Britain, and are not, as many people assume, the declaratory manifesto of the current occupants.

Somerset House

Map 5, A6. Courtyard and terrace: daily 7.30am–11pm; free. Interior: Mon–Sat 10am–6pm; free; Ⓦ*www.somerset-house.org.uk* Gilbert collection and Courtauld galleries: Mon–Sat 10am–6pm, Sun noon–6pm; both £4; joint tickets £7. ⊖ Temple (Mon–Sat only) or Covent Garden.

Opposite the south side of Bush House stands **Somerset House**, sole survivor of the grandiose edifices which once lined this stretch of the riverfront, its four wings enclosing a large courtyard rather like a Parisian hôtel. The present building was begun in 1776 by William Chambers as a purpose-built governmental office development. The south wing, overlooking the Thames, now houses the Hermitage Rooms, featuring changing displays drawn from the Hermitage Museum in St Petersburg, and the magnificent **Gilbert Collection** (Ⓦ*www.gilbert-collection.org.uk*), a new museum of decorative arts displaying European silver and gold, micro-mosaics, clocks, portrait miniatures and snuffboxes.

Part of the north wing is now home to the **Courtauld Institute galleries** (Ⓦ*www.courtauld.ac.uk*), chiefly known for its dazzling collection of Impressionist and Post-Impressionist paintings, whose virtue is quality rather than quantity. Among the most celebrated works are a small-scale version of Manet's *Déjeuner sur l'herbe*, Renoir's *La Loge*, and Degas's *Two Dancers*, plus a whole heap of Cézanne's canvases, including one of his series of *Card Players*. The Courtauld also boasts a fine selection of works by the likes of Rubens, van Dyck, Tiepolo and Cranach the Elder.

St Mary-le-Strand and St Clement Danes

Map 5, B5. ⊖ Temple (Mon–Sat only) or Covent Garden.

Two historic churches survived the Aldwych development, and are now stranded amid the traffic of the Strand. The first is James Gibbs' **St Mary-le-Strand** (Mon–Fri 11am–3.30pm), his first commission, completed in 1724 in Baroque style and topped by a delicately tiered tower. Even in the eighteenth century, parishioners complained of the noise from the roads, and it's incredible that recitals are still given here (Wed 1pm). The entrance is flanked by two lovely magnolia trees, and the interior has a particularly rich plastered ceiling in white and gold.

In allusion to his own St Mary's, Gibbs placed a 115ft tower on top of Christopher Wren's nearby **St Clement**

Danes (Map 5, C5; daily 8.30am–4.30pm), whose bells play out the tune of the nursery rhyme "Oranges and Lemons" each day at 9am, noon, 3pm and 6pm. Reduced to a smouldering shell during the Blitz, St Clement Danes was handed over to the RAF in the 1950s and is now a very well-kept memorial to those killed in the air battles of the last war, the nave and aisles studded with more than 800 squadron and unit badges.

In front of the church are statues of the two wartime air chiefs: to the right, **Lord Dowding**, the man who oversaw the Battle of Britain; to the left, **Sir Arthur Harris** (better known as "Bomber Harris"), architect of the saturation bombing of Germany that resulted in the slaughter of thousands of civilians. Although Churchill was ultimately responsible, most of the opprobrium was left to fall on Harris, who was denied the peerage all the other service chiefs received, while his forces were refused a campaign medal.

TEMPLE AND THE LAW COURTS

Map 5, D5. ⊖ Temple (Mon–Sat only) or Covent Garden.

Temple is the largest and most complex of the Inns of Court, where every barrister in England must study before being called to the Bar. Temple itself is comprised of two Inns – **Middle Temple** (Ⓦ*www.middletemple.org.uk*) and **Inner Temple** (Ⓦ*www.innertemple.org.uk*) – both of which lie to the south of the Strand, and, strictly speaking, just within the boundaries of the City of London. A few very old buildings survive here, but the overall scene is dominated by the soulless neo-Georgian reconstructions that followed the devastation of the Blitz. Still, the maze of courtyards and passageways is fun to explore – especially after dark, when Temple is gas-lit.

There are several points of access, simplest of which is Devereux Court. Medieval students ate, attended lectures and slept in the **Middle Temple Hall** (Mon–Fri 10am–noon & 3–4pm), across the courtyard, still the Inn's main dining room. The present building was constructed in the 1560s and provided the setting for many great Elizabethan masques and plays – probably including Shakespeare's *Twelfth Night*, which is believed to have been premiered here in 1602. The hall is worth a visit for its fine hammerbeam roof, wooden panelling and decorative Elizabethan screen.

The two Temple Inns share use of the complex's oldest building, **Temple Church** (Wed–Sun 11am–4pm), built in 1185 by the Knights Templar. An oblong chancel was added in the thirteenth century, and the whole building was damaged in the Blitz, but the original round church – modelled on the Church of the Holy Sepulchre in Jerusalem – still stands, with its striking Purbeck-marble piers, recumbent marble effigies of knights and tortured grotesques grimacing in the spandrels of the blind arcading.

Temple Bar and the Royal Courts of Justice

Map 5, C5.

If you walk to the top of Middle Temple Lane, you'll hit the Strand right at **Temple Bar**, a plinth topped by a winged dragon, the latest in a long line of structures marking the boundary between Westminster and the City of London.

Occupying the north side of the last stretch of the Strand before it hits Temple Bar are the **Royal Courts of Justice** (Map 5, C4; Mon–Fri 8.30am–4.30pm), home to the Court of Appeal and the High Court, where the most important civil cases are tried. Appeals and libel suits are heard here – it was from here that the Guildford Four and Birmingham Six walked to freedom, and it is where countless pop and soap stars have battled it out with the tabloids. The fifty-odd courtrooms are open to the public, though you have to go through stringent security checks first (strictly no cameras allowed).

LINCOLN'S INN FIELDS

Map 5, B2. ⊖ Holborn.

North of the Law Courts lies **Lincoln's Inn Fields**, London's largest square, laid out in the early 1640s with **Lincoln's Inn** (Mon–Fri 9am–6pm; Ⓦ*www.lincolnsinn.org.uk*), the first – and in many ways the prettiest – of the Inns of Court on its east side. The Inn's fifteenth-century **Old Hall** is open by appointment only (Ⓣ020/7405 1393), but you can view the early seventeenth-century **chapel** (Mon–Fri noon–2pm), with its unusual fan-vaulted open undercroft and, on the first floor, its late Gothic nave, hit by a Zeppelin in World War I and much restored since.

The south side of Lincoln's Inn Fields is occupied by the gigantic **Royal College of Surgeons** (Map 5, B3; Ⓦ*www.rcseng.ac.uk*), home to the **Hunterian Museum** (Mon–Fri 10am–5pm; free), a fascinating collection of pickled bits and bobs. Also on view are the skeletons of the Irish giant, O'Brien (1761–83), who was seven feet ten inches tall, and the Sicilian midget Caroline Crachami (1815–24), who was just one foot ten and a half inches when she died at the age of nine. To the southwest is one of London's few surviving timber-framed buildings, the seventeenth-century **Old Curiosity Shop** (Map 5, A3) in Portsmouth Street, which claims to be the inspiration for Dickens' cloyingly sentimental tale of the same name. This seems unlikely, but it is certainly London's oldest shop building.

Sir John Soane's Museum

Map 5, A2. Tues–Sat 10am–5pm; first Tues of the month also 6–9pm; free; ⓦ*www.soane.org*

A group of buildings on the north side of Lincoln's Inn Fields house **Sir John Soane's Museum**, one of London's best-kept secrets. The chief architect of the Bank of England, Soane (1753–1837) was an avid collector who designed this house not only as a home and office, but also as a place to stash his large collection of art and antiquities. Arranged much as it was in his lifetime, the ingeniously planned house has an informal, treasure-hunt atmosphere, with surprises in every alcove. At 2.30pm every Saturday, a fascinating, hour-long **free guided tour** takes you round the museum and the enormous research library, next door, containing architectural drawings, books and exquisitely detailed cork and wood models.

CHANCERY LANE AND GRAY'S INN

Map 5, C2. ⊖ Holborn or Chancery Lane (Mon–Sat only).

Running along the eastern edge of Lincoln's Inn is legal London's main thoroughfare, **Chancery Lane**, home of the Law Society (the solicitors' regulatory body) and lined with shops where barristers, solicitors and clerks can buy their wigs, gowns, legal tomes, stationery and champagne. Halfway up the street are the **London Silver Vaults** (Map 5, C2; Mon–Fri 9am–5.30pm, Sat 9am–1pm; free), which began life as safe-deposit vaults, but now house a claustrophobic lair of subterranean shops selling every kind of silverware – occasionally antique, mostly tasteless.

The last of the four Inns of Court, **Gray's Inn** (Map 3, J3; Mon–Fri 10am–4pm; ⓦ*www.graysinn.org.uk*), lies hidden to the north of High Holborn, at the top of Chancery Lane; the entrance is through an anonymous cream-coloured building next door to the venerable *Cittie of Yorke* pub. Established in the fourteenth century, most of what you see today was rebuilt after the Blitz, with the exception of the **hall** (by appointment only; ⓣ020/7458 7800), with its fabulous Tudor screen and stained glass, where the premiere of Shakespeare's *Comedy of Errors* is thought to have taken place in 1594.

Heading east along High Holborn, it's worth pausing to admire **Staple Inn** (Map 5, D1) on the right, not one of the Inns of Court, but one of the now defunct Inns of Chancery, which used to provide a sort of foundation course for those aspiring to the Bar. Its overhanging half-timbered facade and gables date from the sixteenth century and are the most extensive in the whole of London; they survived the Great Fire, which stopped just short of Holborn Circus, but had to be extensively rebuilt after the Blitz.

CLERKENWELL

Map 3, K3. ⊖ Farringdon.

Poverty and overcrowding were the main features of nineteenth-century Clerkenwell, and **Clerkenwell Green** became known in the press as "the headquarters of republicanism, revolution and ultra-non-conformity". The Green's connections with **radical politics** have continued into this century, and its oldest building, built as a Welsh Charity School in 1737, is now home to the **Marx Memorial Library** (Mon 1–6pm, Tues–Thurs 1–8pm, Sat 10am–1pm; ⓦ*www.marxmemoriallibrary.sageweb.co.uk*), at no. 37a. One-time headquarters of the Social Democratic Federation press, this is where **Lenin** edited seventeen editions of the Bolshevik paper *Iskra* in 1902–03. The poky little back room where he worked is maintained as it was then, as a kind of shrine – you can view it along with the workerist Hastings Mural from 1935.

House of Detention

Map 3, K2. Daily 10am–5.15pm; £4. ⊖Farringdon.

Long before Clerkenwell became known for its "thieves' houses", it had been blessed with no fewer than four prison houses to take the overspill from the City jails. All have since been torn down, but the basement of the **House of Detention**, built in 1846 on Clerkenwell Close, just north of the Green, and demolished in 1890, has been opened as a museum. The place has been left authentically dark and dank, and tours are enhanced by a theatrical use of sound and light. The prison's greatest claim to fame was as the target of Britain's first-ever Irish Fenian bomb attack of 1867, which killed six people, marking the beginning of modern terrorism in the capital.

St John's Gate

Map 3, K3. Mon–Fri 10am–5pm, Sat 10am–4pm; free. ⊖Farringdon.

Of Clerkenwell's three medieval religious establishments, remnants of two survive, hidden away to the southeast of Clerkenwell Green. The oldest is the priory of the Order of St John of Jerusalem; the sixteenth-century **St John's Gate**, on the south side of Clerkenwell Road, is the most visible survivor of the foundation. Today, the gatehouse forms part of a **museum**, which traces the development of the order before its dissolution in this country by Henry VIII, and its reestablishment in the nineteenth century. In 1877, the St John Ambulance (Ⓦ*www.st-john-ambulance.org.uk*) was founded, to provide a voluntary first-aid service to the public. It's in this field that the order is now best known in Britain, and a splendid new interactive gallery is now devoted to the history of the service.

To get to see the rest of the gatehouse, and to visit the

Norman crypt of the Grand Priory Church over the road, you must take a **guided tour** (Tues, Fri & Sat 11am & 2.30pm; £4).

Charterhouse

Map 3, L3. Guided tours only April–July Wed 2.15pm; £3.
⊖ Barbican.

A little to the southeast of St John's, on the edge of Smithfield, lies **Charterhouse**, founded in 1371 as a Carthusian monastery. The public school, with which the foundation is now most closely associated, moved out to Surrey in 1872, but forty-odd pensioners – known, in the monastic tradition, as "brothers" – continue to be cared for here. The only way to visit the site is to join one of the exhaustive two-hour **guided tours**, which start at the gatehouse on Charterhouse Square. Very little remains of the original monastic buildings, but there's plenty of Tudor architecture to admire, dating from after the Dissolution when Charterhouse was rebuilt as a private residence.

The City

THE CITY is where London began. Long established as the financial district, it stretches from Temple Bar in the west to the Tower of London in the east – administrative boundaries that are only slightly larger than those marked by the Roman walls and their medieval successors. However, in this Square Mile (as the City is sometimes called), you'll find few leftovers of London's early days, since four-fifths of the area burned down in the Great Fire of 1666. Rebuilt in brick and stone, the City gradually lost its centrality as London swelled westwards, though it has maintained its position as Britain's financial heartland. What you see now is mostly the product of three fairly recent phases: the Victorian construction boom of the late nineteenth century; the postwar reconstruction following the Blitz; and the money-grabbing frenzy of the Thatcherite 1980s, in which nearly fifty percent of the City's office space was rebuilt.

When you consider what has happened here, it's amazing that so much has survived to pay witness to the City's two-thousand-year history. Wren's spires still punctuate the skyline here and there, and his masterpiece, **St Paul's Cathedral**, remains one of London's geographical pivots. At the eastern edge of the City, the **Tower of London** still stands protected by some of the best-preserved medieval fortifications in Europe. Other relics, such as the City's few surviving medieval alleyways, Wren's **Monument** to the Great Fire, and London's oldest synagogue and church, are less conspicuous, and even locals have problems finding the more modern attractions of the **Museum of London** and the **Barbican** arts complex.

Perhaps the biggest change of all, though, has been in the City's population. Up until the eighteenth century the majority of Londoners lived and worked in or around the City; nowadays 300,000 commuters spend the best part of **Monday to Friday** here, but only 5000 people remain at night and at weekends. The result of this demographic shift is that the City is fully alive only during office hours. This means that by far the best time to visit is during the week, since many pubs, restaurants and even some tube stations and tourist sights close down at the weekend.

THE CORPORATION OF LONDON

The one unchanging aspect of the City is its special status, conferred on it by William the Conqueror and extended and reaffirmed by successive monarchs and governments ever since. Nowadays, with its Lord Mayor, its Beadles, Sheriffs and Aldermen, its separate police force and its select electorate of freemen and liverymen, the City is an anachronism of the worst kind. **The Corporation** (Ⓦ*www.corpoflondon.gov.uk*), which runs the City like a one-party mini-state, is an unreconstructed old boys' network whose medievalist pageantry camouflages the very real power and wealth which it holds – the Corporation owns nearly a third of the Square Mile (and several tracts of land elsewhere in and around London). Its anomalous status is all the more baffling when you consider that the City was once the cradle of British democracy: it was the City that traditionally stood up to bullying sovereigns.

FLEET STREET

Map 5, E4. ⊖ Temple (Mon–Sat only) or Blackfriars.

In 1500 a certain Wynkyn de Worde, a pupil of William Caxton, moved the Caxton presses from Westminster to **Fleet Street**, to be close to the lawyers of the Inns of Court and to the clergy of St Paul's. However, the street really boomed two hundred years later, when in 1702, the now defunct *Daily Courant*, Britain's first daily newspaper, was published from here. By the nineteenth century, all the major national and provincial dailies had their offices and printing presses in the Fleet Street district, a situation that prevailed until the 1980s, when the press barons relocated their operations elsewhere.

The best source of information about the old-style Fleet Street is the so-called "journalists' and printers' cathedral", the church of **St Bride's** (Map 5, F4; Mon–Sat 9am–5pm), which boasts Wren's tallest and most exquisite spire (said to be the inspiration for the tiered wedding cake). The crypt contains a little museum of Fleet Street history, with information on the *Daily Courant* and the *Universal Daily Register*, which later became *The Times*, claiming to be "the faithful recorder of every species of intelligence . . . circulated for a particular set of readers only".

The western section of Fleet Street was spared the Great Fire, which stopped just short of **Prince Henry's Room** (Mon–Sat 11am–2pm; free), a fine Jacobean house with timber-framed bay windows. The first-floor room now contains material relating to the diarist **Samuel Pepys**, who was born nearby in Salisbury Court in 1633 and baptized in St Bride's. Even if you've no interest in Pepys, the wooden-panelled room is worth a look – it contains one of the finest Jacobean plasterwork ceilings in London, and a lot of original stained glass.

Numerous narrow alleyways lead off the north side of

Fleet Street, two of which – Bolt Court and Hind Court – eventually open out into Gough Square, on which stands **Dr Johnson's House** (Map 5, E3; Ⓦ*www.drjh.dircon.co.uk*; May–Sept Mon–Sat 11am–5.30pm; Oct–April Mon–Sat 11am–5pm; £3). The great savant, writer and lexicographer lived here from 1747 to 1759, whilst compiling the 41,000 entries for the first dictionary of the English language, two first editions of which can be seen in the grey-panelled rooms of the house. You can also view the open-plan attic, in which Johnson and his six helpers put together the dictionary.

ST PAUL'S CATHEDRAL

Map 5, I4. Mon–Sat 8.30am–4pm; £5; Ⓦ*www.stpauls.co.uk*
⊖ St Paul's.

St Paul's Cathedral, topped by an enormous lead-covered dome that's second in size only to St Peter's in Rome, has been a London icon since the Blitz, when it stood defiantly unscathed amid the carnage (or so it appeared on wartime propaganda photos). It remains a dominating presence in the City, despite the encroaching tower blocks – its show-piece west facade is particularly magnificent, and is at its most impressive at night when bathed in sea-green arc lights. Westminster Abbey has the edge, however, when it comes to celebrity corpses, pre-Reformation sculpture, royal connections and sheer atmosphere. St Paul's, by contrast, is a soulless but perfectly calculated architectural set piece, a burial place for captains rather than kings, though it does contain more artists than Westminster Abbey.

The cathedral's services, featuring the renowned St Paul's choir, are held Mon–Sat 5pm, Sun 10.15am, 11.30am & 3.15pm.

The best place from which to appreciate the glory of St Paul's is beneath the **dome**, decorated (against Wren's wishes) by Thornhill's trompe l'oeil frescoes. The most richly decorated section of the cathedral, however, is the Quire or **chancel**, where the mosaics of birds, fish, animals and greenery, dating from the 1890s, are particularly spectacular. The intricately carved oak and limewood **choir stalls**, and the imposing organ case, are the work of Wren's master carver, Grinling Gibbons. Meanwhile, in the south-choir aisle, is the only complete effigy to have survived from Old St Paul's (see overleaf), the upstanding shroud of **John Donne**, poet, preacher and one-time dean of St Paul's.

A series of stairs, beginning in the south aisle, lead to the dome's three **galleries**, the first of which is the internal **Whispering Gallery**, so called because of its acoustic properties – words whispered to the wall on one side are distinctly audible over one hundred feet away on the other, though the place is often so busy you can't hear very much above the hubbub. The other two galleries are exterior: the wide **Stone Gallery**, around the balustrade at the base of the dome, and ultimately the tiny **Golden Gallery**, below the golden ball and cross which top the cathedral.

The City of London tourist office, to the south of St Paul's, is open April–Sept daily 9.30am–5pm; Oct–March Mon–Fri 9.30am–5pm, Sat 9.30am–12.30pm.

Although the nave is crammed full of overblown monuments to military types, burials in St Paul's are confined to the **crypt**, reputedly the largest in Europe. The whitewashed walls and bright lighting, however, make this one of the least atmospheric mausoleums you could imagine. Immediately to your right you'll find **Artists' Corner**, which boasts as many painters and architects as Westminster

THE BLITZ

The **Blitz** bombing of London in World War II began on September 7, 1940, and continued for 57 consecutive nights, then intermittently until the final and most devastating attack on the night of May 10, 1941, when 550 Luftwaffe planes dropped over 100,000 incendiaries and hundreds of explosive bombs in a matter of hours. The death toll that night was over 1400, bringing the total killed during the Blitz to between 20,000 and 30,000, with some 230,000 homes wrecked. Along with the East End, the City was particularly badly hit: in a single raid on December 29 (dubbed the "Second Fire of London"), 1400 fires broke out across the Square Mile.

The authorities were ready to build mass graves, but unable to provide adequate air-raid shelters. Around 180,000 made use of the tube, despite initial government reluctance, by simply buying a ticket and staying below ground. The cheery photos of singing and dancing in the Underground which the censors allowed to be published tell nothing of the stale air, rats and lice that folk had to contend with. And even the tube stations couldn't withstand a direct hit, as occurred at Bank, when over 100 died. In the end, the vast majority of Londoners – some sixty percent – simply stayed at home in their back-garden shelters or hid under the sheets and prayed.

Abbey has poets, including Christopher Wren himself, who was commissioned to build the cathedral after its Gothic predecessor, Old St Paul's, was destroyed in the Great Fire. The crypt's two other star tombs are those of **Nelson** and **Wellington**, both occupying centre stage and both with more fanciful monuments upstairs.

PATERNOSTER SQUARE TO SMITHFIELD

Map 5, H3. ⊖ St Paul's.

The Blitz destroyed the area immediately to the north of St Paul's. In its place, the City authorities built the brazenly modernist **Paternoster Square**, a grim pedestrianized piazza that has recently been demolished to make way for a new, more restrained masterplan courtesy of Sir William Whitfield, who is seen as a compromise choice in the modernism-versus-classicism debate.

To the west along Newgate Street, you'll find the Central Criminal Court, more popularly known as the **Old Bailey**. Built on the site of the notoriously harsh Newgate Prison, where folk used to come to watch public hangings, the Old Bailey is now the venue for all the country's most serious criminal court cases; you can watch the proceedings from the visitors gallery (Mon–Fri 10.30am–1pm & 2–4pm), but note that bags and cameras are not allowed in, and there is no cloakroom.

St Bartholomew's hospital and church

Map 5, H1. ⊖ St Paul's or Farringdon.

North of the Old Bailey lies **St Bartholomew's Hospital**, affectionately known to Londoners as Bart's. It's the oldest hospital in London, founded in 1123 by Rahere, court jester to Henry I, on the orders of Saint Bartholomew, who appeared to him in a vision while he was in malarial delirium on a pilgrimage to Rome. You can visit the hospital's church, and the nearby **museum** (Tues–Fri 10am–4pm; free), which has a short video on the history of Bart's. This also gives you a chance to glimpse the mid-eighteenth-century interior, which features murals by Hogarth. To see and learn more, you need to go on a **guided tour** (April–Nov Fri 2pm; £4), which also takes in Smithfield and the surrounding area.

St Bartholomew-the-Great (Map 7, A1; Mon–Fri 8.30am–5pm, Sat 10.30am–1.30pm, Sun 8am–1pm & 2–8pm), hidden away to the north of the hospital, is London's oldest and most exquisite parish church. Begun in 1123, it was partly demolished in the Reformation, and afterwards fell into ruins. Restoration didn't begin until 1887, though by no means the whole church was rebuilt. To get an idea of the scale of the original, approach through the half-timbered Tudor **gatehouse** on Little Britain Street, which incorporates the thirteenth-century arch that once formed the entrance to the nave. One side of the medieval cloisters survives to the south, as does the **chancel**, where stout Norman pillars separate the main body of the church from the ambulatory. There are various pre-Fire monuments to admire, the most prominent being Rahere's tomb, which shelters under a fifteenth-century canopy north of the main altar.

Smithfield

Map 5, F1. ⊖ Farringdon.

Smithfield, to the north of Bart's, was for a long time a popular venue for **public executions** – in particular burnings, which reached a peak during the reign of "Bloody" Mary, when hundreds of Protestants were burned at the stake for their beliefs. These days, Smithfield is synonymous with its **meat market**; if you want to see it in action, you'll need to get here early – the activity starts around 4am and is all over by 9am or 10am. The compensation for getting up at this ungodly hour are the early licensing laws, which mean you can get a hearty breakfast and an early morning pint from the local pubs.

MUSEUM OF LONDON

Map 7, C1. Mon–Sat 10am–5.50pm, Sun noon–5.50pm; £5 (tickets valid for one year) or free after 4.30pm; ⓦ*www.museumoflondon.org.uk* ⊖ St Paul's or Barbican.

Despite London's long pedigree, very few of its ancient structures are now standing. However, numerous Roman, Saxon and Elizabethan remains have been discovered during the City's various rebuildings, and many of these finds are now displayed at the **Museum of London**, hidden above the western end of London Wall (the highway driven through the Blitz bomb-sites north of the city), in the south-western corner of the Barbican complex. The museum's permanent exhibition is basically an educational trot through London's past from prehistory to the present day, hence the large number of school groups who pass through. Highlights include the Bucklersbury Roman mosaic, the Lord Mayor's heavily gilded coach (still used for state occasions), a diorama of the Great Fire and one of the original Art Deco lifts from Selfridge's (see p.40). The real strength of the museum, though, lies in the excellent temporary exhibitions, lectures, walks and videos it organizes throughout the year.

THE BARBICAN

Map 7, D1. ⊖ Barbican or Moorgate.

The City's only large residential complex is the **Barbican**, a phenomenally ugly and expensive concrete ghetto built on the heavily bombed Cripplegate area. The zone's solitary prewar building is the heavily restored sixteenth-century church of **St Giles Cripplegate** (Map 7, C1; Mon–Fri 9.30am–5.15pm, Sat 9am–noon), situated across from the infamously user-repellent **Barbican Arts Centre** (ⓦ*www.barbican.org.uk*), London's supposed answer to Paris's Pompidou Centre, which was formally opened in 1982. The complex does, however, serve as home to the London Symphony Orchestra and the London chapter of the Royal Shakespeare Company, and holds free gigs in the foyer area.

BUNHILL FIELDS AND WESLEY'S CHAPEL

Map 3, M2. ⊖ Old Street.

Some way to the northeast of the Barbican lies **Bunhill Fields**, the main burial ground for Dissenters or Nonconformists (practising Christians who were not members of the Church of England). The three most famous graves have been relocated in the central paved area: William Blake's simple tombstone stands next to a replica of Daniel Defoe's, while opposite lies John Bunyan's recumbent statue.

Directly opposite Bunhill Fields on City Road stands the Georgian ensemble of **Wesley's Chapel and House** (Mon–Sat 10am–4pm, Sun noon–2pm; £4). A place of pilgrimage for Methodists, the uncharacteristically ornate chapel, built in 1777, heralded the coming of age of Wesley's sect. Predictably enough, the **Museum of Methodism** in the basement has only a passing reference mention to the insanely jealous forty-year-old widow Wesley married, and who eventually left him. Wesley himself spent his last two years in the delightful Georgian house to the right of the main gates, and inside you can see his death bed, plus an early shock-therapy machine he was particularly keen on.

GUILDHALL

Map 7, D2. May–Sept daily 10am–5pm; Oct–April Mon–Sat 10am–5pm; free; Ⓦ*www.corpoflondon.gov.uk* ⊖ St Paul's or Bank.

Situated at the geographical centre of the City, **Guildhall** has been the ancient seat of the City administration for over eight hundred years. It remains the headquarters of the Corporation of London, and is still used for many of the City's formal civic occasions. Architecturally, however, it is not quite the beauty it once was, having been badly damaged in both the Great Fire and the Blitz, and scarred by the addition of a grotesque 1970s concrete cloister and wing.

Nonetheless, the **Great Hall**, basically a postwar reconstruction of the fifteenth-century original, is worth a brief look, as is the **Guildhall Clock Museum** (Mon–Sat 10am–5pm, Sun noon–4pm; free), a collection of over six hundred timepieces, including one of the clocks that won John Harrison the Longitude prize (see p.151). Also worth a visit is the new, purpose-built **Guildhall Art Gallery** (Mon–Sat 10am–5pm, Sun noon–5pm; £2.50), which contains one or two exceptional works, such as Rossetti's *La Ghirlandata*, and Holman Hunt's *The Eve of St Agnes*, plus a massive painting depicting the 1782 Siege of Gibraltar, commissioned by the Corporation.

BANK AND AROUND

Map 7, F4. ⊖ Bank.

Bank is the finest architectural arena in the City. Heart of the finance sector and the busy meeting point of eight streets, it's overlooked by a handsome collection of Neoclassical buildings – among them, the Bank of England, the Royal Exchange and Mansion House (the Lord Mayor's official residence) – each one faced in Portland stone.

Sadly, only the **Bank of England** (Map 7, F3; Ⓦ*www.bankofengland.co.uk*), which stores the nation's vast gold reserves in its vaults, actually encourages visitors. Established in 1694 by William III to raise funds for the war against France, the so-called "Grand Old Lady of Threadneedle Street" wasn't erected on its present site until 1734. All that remains of the building on which Sir John Soane spent the best part of his career from 1788 onwards is the windowless, outer curtain wall, which wraps itself round the 3.5-acre island site. However, you can view a reconstruction of Soane's Bank Stock Office, with its characteristic domed skylight, in the **museum** (Mon–Fri 10am–5pm; free), which has its entrance on Bartholomew Lane.

Three churches worth exploring are situated to the south of Bank. On Walbrook, behind Mansion House, stands the church of **St Stephen Walbrook** (Map 7, E4; Mon–Thurs 10am–4pm, Fri 10am–3pm), Wren's most spectacular after St Paul's, with dark-wood furnishings by Grinling Gibbons. Hidden a short distance down King William Street is **St Mary Woolnoth** (Map 7, F4; Mon–Fri 8am–5pm), a typically idiosyncratic creation of Nicholas Hawksmoor, one of Wren's pupils, featuring a striking altar canopy held up by barley-sugar columns. A complete contrast to Hawksmoor's church is provided by Wren's **St Mary Abchurch** (Map 7, F5; Mon–Thurs 10.30am–3pm, Fri 10.30am–noon), on Abchurch Lane, off King William Street. The interior is dominated by a vast dome fresco painted by a local parishioner and lit by oval lunettes, while the lime-wood reredos is again by Gibbons.

LLOYD'S AND AROUND

Map 7, H4. ⊖ Bank or Monument.

East of Bank, beyond Bishopsgate, stands Richard Rogers' glitzy **Lloyd's Building**, completed in 1984. A startling array of glass and blue steel pipes – a vertical version of Rogers' own Pompidou Centre – this is easily the most popular of the new City buildings, at least with the general public. It remains to be seen whether Norman Foster's "upside-down ice-cream cone" building for **Swiss Re**, to be constructed on the site of the old Baltic Exchange, will upstage Lloyd's.

Just south of the Lloyd's building, you'll find the picturesque **Leadenhall Market**, whose cobbles and richly painted, graceful Victorian cast-ironwork dates from 1881. Inside, the traders cater mostly for the lunchtime City crowd, their barrows laden with exotic seafood and game, fine wines, champagne and caviar.

Bevis Marks Synagogue

Map 7, J3. Guided tours Mon, Wed, Fri & Sun noon, Tues 11.30am; £1. ⊖ Aldgate or Liverpool Street.

Hidden away behind a modern red-brick office block in a little courtyard off Bevis Marks, north up St Mary Axe from the Lloyd's building, the **Bevis Marks Synagogue** was built in 1701 by Sephardic Jews who had fled the Inquisition in Spain and Portugal. This is the country's oldest surviving synagogue, and its roomy, rich interior gives an idea of just how wealthy the congregation was at the time. Nowadays, the Sephardic community has dispersed across London and the congregation has dwindled, though the magnificent array of chandeliers makes it popular for candle-lit Jewish weddings.

LONDON BRIDGE AND THE MONUMENT

Map 7, F7. ⊖ Monument.

Until 1750, **London Bridge** was the only bridge across the Thames. The Romans were the first to build a permanent crossing here, but it was the medieval bridge that achieved world fame: built of stone and crowded with timber-framed houses, it became one of the great attractions of London (there's a model in the nearby church of St Magnus the Martyr). The houses were finally removed in the mid-eighteenth century, and a new stone bridge erected in 1831; that one now stands in the middle of the Arizona desert, having been bought for $2.4 million in the late 1960s by a gentleman who, so the story goes, was under the impression he had purchased Tower Bridge. The present concrete structure, without doubt the ugliest yet, dates from 1972.

The only reason to go anywhere near London Bridge is to see the **Monument** (Map 7, G6; daily 10am–6pm; £1.50), which was designed by Wren to commemorate the Great Fire of 1666. Crowned with spiky gilded flames, this plain Doric column stands 202 feet high, making it the tallest isolated stone column in the world; if it were laid out flat it would touch the bakery where the Fire started, east of Monument. The bas-relief on the base, now in very bad shape, depicts Charles II and the Duke of York in Roman garb conducting the emergency relief operation. The 311 steps to the viewing gallery once guaranteed an incredible view; nowadays it is somewhat dwarfed by the buildings around it.

THE GREAT FIRE

In the early hours of September 2, 1666, the **Great Fire** broke out at Farriner's, the king's bakery in Pudding Lane. The Lord Mayor refused to lose any sleep over it, dismissing it with the line "Pish! A woman might piss it out". Four days and four nights later, the Lord Mayor was found crying "like a fainting woman": the Fire had destroyed some four-fifths of London, including 87 churches, 44 livery halls and 13,200 houses. The medieval city was no more.

Miraculously, there were only nine recorded fatalities, but 100,000 people were made homeless. "The hand of God upon us, a great wind and a season so very dry" was the verdict of the parliamentary report on the Fire; Londoners preferred to blame Catholics and foreigners. The poor baker eventually "confessed" to being an agent of the pope and was executed, after which the following words, "but Popish frenzy, which wrought such horrors, is not yet quenched", were added to the Latin inscription on the Monument. (The lines were erased in 1831.)

THE TOWER OF LONDON

Map 7, K7. March–Oct Mon–Sat 9am–6pm, Sun 10am–6pm; Nov–Feb Mon & Sun 10am–5pm, Tues–Sat 9am–5pm; £11; Ⓦ*www.hrp.org.uk* ⊖ Tower Hill.

One of Britain's main tourist attractions, the **Tower of London** overlooks the river at the eastern boundary of the old city walls. Despite all the hype and heritage claptrap, it remains one of London's most remarkable buildings, site of

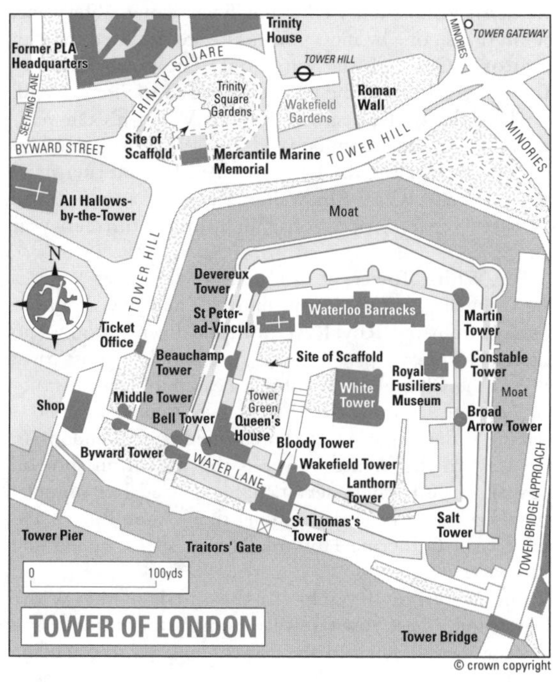

© crown copyright

some of the goriest events in the nation's history and somewhere all visitors and Londoners should explore at least once. Chiefly famous as a place of imprisonment and death, it has variously been used as a royal residence, armoury, mint, menagerie, observatory and – a function it still serves – a safe-deposit box for the Crown Jewels.

Before you set off to explore the Tower complex, it's a good idea to get your bearings by taking one of the free **guided tours**, given every thirty minutes by one of the forty-odd **Beefeaters** (officially known as Yeoman Warders). Visitors today enter the Tower along Water Lane, but in times gone by most prisoners were delivered through **Traitors' Gate**, on the waterfront. The nearby **Bloody Tower**, which forms the main entrance to the Inner Ward, is where the twelve-year-old Edward V and his ten-year-old brother were accommodated "for their own safety" in 1483 by their uncle, the future Richard III, and later murdered. It's also where **Sir Walter Ralegh** was imprisoned on three separate occasions, including a thirteen-year stretch.

The **White Tower**, at the centre of the Inner Ward, is the original "Tower", begun in 1076, and now home to displays from the **Royal Armouries**. Even if you've no interest in military paraphernalia, you should at least pay a visit to the **Chapel of St John**, a beautiful Norman structure on the second floor that was completed in 1080 – making it the oldest intact church building in London. To the west of the White Tower is the execution spot on **Tower Green** where seven highly-placed but unlucky individuals were beheaded, among them Anne Boleyn and her cousin Catherine Howard (Henry VIII's second and fifth wives).

The Waterloo Barracks, to the north of the White Tower, hold the **Crown Jewels**, perhaps the major reason so many people flock to the Tower; however, the moving walkways are disappointingly swift, allowing you just 28 seconds' viewing during peak periods. The oldest piece of regalia is the twelfth-century **Anointing Spoon**, but the vast majority of exhibits postdate the Commonwealth (1649–60), when many of the royal riches were melted down for coinage or sold off. Among the jewels are the three largest cut diamonds in the world, including the legendary **Koh-i-Noor**, set into the Queen Mother's Crown in 1937.

TOWER BRIDGE

Map 7, K8. Daily: April–Oct 10am–6.30pm; Nov–March 9.30am–6pm. Guided tour £6.25; Ⓦ*www.towerbridge.org.uk* ⊖ Tower Hill.

Tower Bridge is just over one hundred years old, yet it ranks with Big Ben as the most famous of all London landmarks. Completed in 1894, its neo-Gothic towers are clad in Cornish granite and Portland stone, but conceal a steel frame, which, at the time, represented a considerable engineering achievement, allowing a road crossing that could be raised to give tall ships access to the upper reaches of the Thames; the raising of the bascules (from the French for "see-saw") remains an impressive sight. The elevated walkways linking the summits of the towers (intended for public use) were closed from 1909 to 1982 due to their popularity with prostitutes and the suicidal. You can only visit them now on an overpriced **guided tour**, dubbed the "Tower Bridge Experience", that employs videos and an animatronic chirpy Cockney to describe the history of the bridge.

The East End and Docklands

Few places in London have engendered as many myths as the **EAST END**, a catch-all title which covers just about everywhere east of the City, but has its heart closest to the latter. Its name is synonymous with slums, sweatshops and crime, as epitomized by antiheroes such as Jack the Ripper and the Kray Twins, but also with the rags-to-riches careers of the likes of Harold Pinter and Vidal Sassoon, and whole generations of Jews who were born in the most notorious of London's cholera-ridden quarters and have now moved to wealthier pastures. Old East Enders will tell you that the area's not what it was – and it's true, as it always has been. The East End is constantly changing as newly arrived immigrants assimilate and move out.

The East End's first immigrants were French Protestant **Huguenots**, fleeing religious persecution in the late seventeenth century. Within three generations the Huguenots were entirely assimilated, and the **Irish** became the new immigrant population, but it was the influx of **Jews** escaping pogroms in eastern Europe and Russia that defined the character of the East End in the second half of the nineteenth

EAST END SUNDAY MARKETS

Most visitors to the East End come here for the **Sunday markets**. Approaching from Liverpool Street, the first one you come to is **Petticoat Lane** (Map 7, J2; Sun 9am–2pm; ⊖ Liverpool Street or Aldgate East), not one of London's prettiest streets, but one of its longest-running Sunday markets, specializing in cheap (and often pretty tacky) clothing. The authorities renamed the street Middlesex Street in 1830 to avoid the mention of ladies' underwear, but the original name has stuck.

To the north lies **Spitalfields Market** (Map 2, J4; organic market Fri & Sun 10am–5pm; general market Mon–Fri 11am–3pm & Sun 10am–5pm; ⊖ Liverpool Street), once the capital's premier wholesale fruit and vegetable market, now specializing in organic food, plus clothes, crafts and jewellery. Further east lies **Brick Lane** (Map 7, M1; Sun 8am–1pm; ⊖ Aldgate East, Shoreditch or Liverpool Street), heart of the Bengali community, famous for its bric-a-brac Sunday market, wonderful curry houses and non-stop bagel bakery, and now also something of a magnet for young designers. From Brick Lane's northernmost end, it's a short walk to **Columbia Road** (Map 2, J4; Sun 8am–1pm; bus #26 from Aldwych or Liverpool Street tube), the city's best market for flowers and plants.

The Vibe Bar, in the old Truman Brewery on Brick Lane, is just one of a number of trendy bars that have opened up here and in the neighbouring districts of Shoreditch and Hoxton, which have become something of an arty enclave on the edge of the City.

century. The area's Jewish population has now dispersed throughout London, though the East End remains at the bottom of the pile; even the millions poured into the

DOCKLANDS development have failed to make much impression on local unemployment and housing problems. Unfortunately, racism is still rife, and is directed, for the most part, against the extensive **Bengali** community, who came here from the poor rural area of Sylhet in Bangladesh in the 1960s and 1970s.

As the area is not an obvious place for sightseeing, and certainly no beauty spot – Victorian slum clearances, Hitler's bombs and postwar tower blocks have all left their mark – most visitors to the East End come for its famous **Sunday markets**. However, there's plenty more to get out of a visit, including a trio of **Hawksmoor churches**, and the vast **Canary Wharf** redevelopment, which has to be seen to be believed.

WHITECHAPEL AND SPITALFIELDS

Map 2, J4. ⊖ Liverpool Street or Aldgate East.

The districts of **Whitechapel**, and in particular **Spitalfields**, within sight of the sleek tower blocks of the financial sector, represent the old heart of the East End, where the French Huguenots settled in the seventeenth century, where the Jewish community was at its strongest in the late nineteenth century, and where today's Bengali community eats, sleeps, works and prays. If you visit just one area in the East End, it should be this zone, which preserves mementos from each wave of immigration.

The easiest approach is from Liverpool Street Station, a short stroll west of **Spitalfields Market**, the strange-looking red-brick and green-gabled market hall, built in 1893 and extended in the 1920s, which forms the centrepiece of the area. The dominant architectural presence in Spitalfields, however, is **Christ Church** (Mon–Fri noon–2.30pm), built in 1714–29 to a characteristically bold design by Nicholas Hawksmoor, and now facing the market hall. Best viewed from Brushfield Street, the church's main features are its huge 225-foot-high spire and a giant Tuscan portico, raised on steps and shaped like a Venetian window (a central arched opening flanked by two smaller rectangles), a motif repeated in the tower and doors.

Whitechapel Road

Map 7, N2. ⊖ Aldgate or Aldgate East.

Whitechapel Road – as Whitechapel High Street and the Mile End Road are collectively known – is still the East End's main street, shared by all the many races who live in the borough of Tower Hamlets. The East End institution that draws in more outsiders than any other here is the **Whitechapel Art Gallery** (Tues & Thurs–Sun 11am–5pm, Wed 11am–8pm; free; Ⓦ*www.whitechapel.org*), housed in a beautiful crenellated 1899 Arts and Crafts building by Charles Harrison Townsend, architect of the similarly audacious Horniman Museum (p.143). The gallery stages some of London's most innovative exhibitions of contemporary art, as well as hosting the biennial Whitechapel Open, a chance for local artists to get their work shown to a wider audience.

The most visible symbol of the new Muslim presence in the East End is the Saudi-financed **East London Mosque** (Map 2, J4), an enormous red-brick building that's a short walk up Whitechapel Road from the art gallery; it stands in marked contrast to the tiny **Great Synagogue**, dating from 1899, behind the mosque in Fieldgate Street. Neither of these buildings is open to the public, but you can pay a visit to the small exhibition in the nearby **Whitechapel Bell Foundry** (Map 2, J4; Mon–Fri 8am–5pm; guided tours Sat 10am; £7; book in advance on Ⓣ020/7247 2599), on the corner of Fieldgate Street. Big Ben, the Liberty Bell, the Bow Bells and numerous English church bells (including

THE WHITECHAPEL MURDERS

In the space of just eight weeks between August and November 1888, five prostitutes were stabbed to death in and around Whitechapel; all were found with their innards removed. Few of the letters received by the press and police, which purported to come from the murderer, are thought to have been genuine, including the one which coined the nickname **Jack the Ripper**, and to this day the murderer's identity remains a mystery. At the time, it was assumed by many that he was a Jew, probably a *shochet* (a ritual slaughterman), since the mutilations were obviously carried out with some skill. The theory gained ground when the fourth victim was discovered outside the predominantly Jewish Working Men's Club in Berner Street, and for a while it was dangerous for Jews to walk the streets at night for fear of reprisals.

Ripperologists have trawled through the little evidence there is to produce numerous other suspects, none of whom can be positively proven guilty. The man who usually tops the lists, however, was a cricket-playing barrister named Druitt, whose body was found floating in the Thames some weeks after the last murder, though there is no firm evidence linking him with any of the killings.

The one positive outcome of the murders was that they focused the attention of the rest of London on the squalour of the East End. Philanthropist Samuel Barnett, for one, used the media attention to press for improved housing, street lighting and policing to combat crime and poverty in the area. Today, the murders continue to be exploited in gory, misogynistic detail by the likes of Madame Tussaud's and the London Dungeon, while guided walks (listed each week in *Time Out*) retracing the Ripper's steps set off every week throughout the year (see p.11).

those of Westminster Abbey) all hail from the foundry, established here in 1738.

It was on the Mile End Road – the extension of Whitechapel Road – that Joseph Merrick, better known as the "**Elephant Man**", was discovered in a freak show by Dr Treves, and subsequently admitted as a patient to the **Royal London Hospital** (Map 2, J4) on Whitechapel Road. He remained there, on show as a medical freak, until his death in 1890 at the age of just 27. There's a small section on Merrick in the **Hospital Museum** (Mon–Fri 10am–4.30pm; free), housed beside the red-brick church (now the medical college library) on Newark Street.

Just before the point where Whitechapel Road turns into Mile End Road stands the gabled entrance to the former Albion Brewery, where the first bottled brown ale was produced in 1899. Next door lies the **Blind Beggar**, the East End's most famous pub since March 8, 1966, when Ronnie Kray walked into the crowded bar and shot gangland rival George Cornell for calling him a "fat poof". This murder spelled the end of the infamous Kray Twins, Ronnie and Reggie, both of whom were sentenced to life imprisonment, though their well-publicized gifts to local charities created a Robin Hood image that still persists in these parts of town.

EAST END MUSEUMS

The East End boasts a trio of fascinating museums dispersed across a wide area, all of them open to the public free of charge. The easiest one to get to is the **Bethnal Green Museum of Childhood** (Map 2, J4; daily 10am–5.50pm, closed Fri; free; Ⓦ*www.vam.ac.uk*), situated opposite Bethnal Green tube station. The open-plan, wrought-iron hall, originally part of (and still a branch of) the V&A museum (see p.121), was transported here in the 1860s to bring art to the East End. The variety of exhibits means that there's something here for everyone from three to ninety-three, but the museum's most frequent visitors are children – that said, the displays are not very hands-on. The ground floor is best known for its unique collection of antique dolls' houses dating back to 1673. You'll need a pile of 20p pieces with you to work the automata – Wallace the Lion gobbling up Albert is always a favourite. Elsewhere, there are puppets, a jumble of toys, a vast doll collection and excellent temporary exhibitions.

To the south of the Mile End Road, on Copperfield Road, the **Ragged School Museum** (Map 2, K4; Wed & Thurs 10am–5pm, first Sun of month 2–5pm; free; Ⓦ*www.ics-london.co.uk/rsm*; tube ⊖ Mile End) occupies a Victorian canalside warehouse. From 1877 to 1908, this was the largest of London's numerous Ragged Schools established by **Dr Thomas Barnardo**, and provided free education and two meals daily to kids from the local slums. Upstairs, there's a reconstructed Victorian schoolroom, where period-dressed teachers, cane in hand, take today's schoolkids through the rigours of a Victorian lesson; on the top floor you can learn to make a rag rug and take part in wash day.

The **Geffrye Museum** (Map 3, N1; Tues–Sat 10am–5pm, Sun noon–5pm; free; Ⓦ*www.geffrye-museum.org.uk*), set back from Kingsland Road in a peaceful little enclave of eighteenth-century ironmongers' almshouses, is essentially a furniture museum. A series of period living rooms, ranging from the oak-panelled seventeenth century through refined Georgian and cluttered Victorian, leads to the state-of-the-art New Gallery Extension, housing the excellent twentieth-century section and a pleasant café/restaurant. To get to the museum, take bus #149 or #242 from Liverpool Street tube.

DOCKLANDS

The architectural embodiment of Thatcherism, a symbol of 1980s smash-and-grab culture according to its critics, or a blueprint for inner-city regeneration to its free-market supporters – the **Docklands** redevelopment provokes extreme reactions. Despite its catch-all name, however, Docklands is far from homogeneous. Canary Wharf, with its Manhattan-style skyscraper, is only its most visible landmark; industrial-estate sheds and riverside flats of dubious architectural merit are more indicative of the area. **Wapping**, the westernmost district, has retained much of its old Victorian warehouse architecture, while the **Royal Docks**, further east, are only just beginning to be transformed from an industrial wasteland.

DOCKLANDS TRANSPORT

Although Canary Wharf is now on the Jubilee line, the best way to view Docklands is either from one of the boats that course up and down the Thames, or from the driverless, overhead **Docklands Light Railway** (DLR; Ⓦ*www.dlr.co.uk*), which sets off from Bank, or from Tower Gateway, close to Tower Hill tube. Travelcards are valid on the DLR, or you can get an off-peak Docklander ticket for £3.10, giving you unlimited travel on the network after 9.30am Monday to Friday and all day on the weekend. Tour guides give a free running commentary on DLR trains that set off on the hour from Tower Gateway (daily 10am–2pm), and Bank (Mon–Fri 11am–2pm, Sat & Sun 10am–2pm) as far as Crossharbour. If you're heading for Greenwich, and fancy taking a boat back into town, it might be worth considering a Sail & Rail ticket (£7.80), which gives you an off-peak Docklander ticket, plus a boat trip between Greenwich and Westminster piers.

The docks were originally built from 1802 onwards to relieve congestion on the Thames quays, and eventually became the largest enclosed cargo-dock system in the world. However, competition from the railways, and later, the development of container ships, signalled the closure of the docks in the 1960s. Then, at the height of the recession in the 1980s, regeneration began in earnest. No one thought the old docks could ever be rejuvenated, and twenty years on, more has been achieved than many thought possible (and less than some had hoped).

Travelling through on the overhead railway, Docklands comes over as an intriguing open-air design museum, not a place one would choose to live or work – most people stationed here still see it as a bleak business-oriented outpost – but a spectacular sight nevertheless.

Wapping to Limehouse

Map 2, K4.

From the DLR overhead railway, you get a good view of Hawksmoor's two other landmark East End churches; the first one is **St George-in-the-East**, built in 1726 and visible to the south just before you reach Shadwell station. It's easy to spot thanks to its four domed corner towers and distinctive west-end tower topped by an octagonal lantern. You're missing nothing by staying on the train, though, as the interior was devastated in the Blitz. As the DLR leaves Limehouse station and skirts Limehouse Basin marina, Hawksmoor's **St Anne's Church** is visible to the north. Begun in 1714 and dominated again by a gargantuan west tower, the church is topped by an octagonal lantern and adorned with the highest church clock in London. Again, the interior isn't worth the effort as it was badly damaged by fire in 1850.

An alternative to the DLR is to walk from Wapping to

Limehouse, along the Thames Path, which sticks to, or close to, the riverbank. You begin at **St Katharine's Dock** (Map 7, M7), immediately east of the Tower of London, and the first of the old docks to be renovated way back in the 1970s. St Katharine's redeeming qualities are the old swing bridges and the boats themselves, many of which are beautiful old sailing ships. Continue along desolate **Wapping High Street**, lined with tall brick-built warehouses, most now tastefully converted into yuppie flats, and you will eventually find yourself in Limehouse, beyond which lies the Isle of Dogs. The fairly well-signposted walk is about two miles in length, and will bring you eventually to Westferry Circus – for details of riverside pubs along the way, see p.228.

The Isle of Dogs

Map 2, L5.

The Thames begins a dramatic horseshoe bend at Limehouse, thus creating the **Isle of Dogs**, currently the geographical and ideological heart of the new Docklands. The area reaches its apotheosis in **Canary Wharf** (Ⓦ*www.canarywharf.com*), the strip of land in the middle of the former West India Docks, previously a destination for rum and mahogany, later tomatoes and bananas (from the Canary Islands – hence the name).

The only really busy bit of the new Docklands, Canary Wharf is best known as the home of Britain's tallest building. Cesar Pelli's landmark tower is officially known as **One Canada Square**, and at 800ft, it's the highest building in Europe after Frankfurt's Messerturm. The world's first skyscraper to be clad in stainless steel, it's an undeniably impressive sight, both from a distance (its flashing pinnacle is a feature of the horizon at numerous points in London) and close up. Unless you work here, however, there is no access except to the ground-floor marble atrium.

The warehouses to the north of Canary Wharf are currently being converted into flats, bars, restaurants and a **Docklands Museum** (scheduled to open in autumn 2001; for more information call ⓣ020/7515 1162), and will include a thirty-storey tower block and a multiplex cinema. Unless you're keen to visit the museum, there's little point in getting off the DLR as it cuts right through the middle of the Canary Wharf office buildings under a parabolic steel-and-glass canopy.

The rest of the Isle of Dogs remains surreally lifeless, an uneasy mix of drab high-rises, council estates, warehouses converted into expensive apartments, and a lot of new architecture – some of it startling, some of it crass, much of it empty. If you're heading for Greenwich (see p.144), you have a choice: either get off at **Island Gardens**, Christopher Wren's favourite spot from which to contemplate his masterpieces across the river (the Royal Naval College and Royal Observatory), and walk through the 1902 foot-tunnel to Greenwich; alternatively, you can stay on the DLR, which now tunnels underneath the Thames, and alight at Cutty Sark station.

Lambeth and Southwark

Until well into the seventeenth century, the only reason for north-bank residents to cross the Thames, to what is now **LAMBETH** and **SOUTHWARK**, was to visit the disreputable Bankside entertainment district around the south end of London Bridge, which lay outside the jurisdiction of the City. South London (a catch-all term for everything south of the river) still has a reputation, among north Londoners at least, as a boring, sprawling, residential district devoid of any local culture or life.

As it turns out, this is not too far from the truth: both boroughs are, for the most part, residential. However, **Lambeth**'s riverbank harbours several important cultural institutions, collectively known as the **South Bank Centre**. Although a mess architecturally, these galleries, theatres and concert halls, plus the nearby **Imperial War Museum**, draw large numbers across the river.

There are even more sights further east along **Southwark**'s riverfront, most notably a reconstruction of Shakespeare's **Globe Theatre**, and the new **Tate Modern**, housed in a converted power station. Another rash of popular museums can be found along Clink Street and Tooley Street, while further east still, **Butler's Wharf** is a thriving little warehouse development centred on the excellent **Design Museum**.

THE SOUTH BANK

Map 6, B3. ⊖ Waterloo.

In 1951, the South Bank Exhibition, held on derelict land south of the Thames, formed the centrepiece of the **Festival of Britain**, an attempt to revive postwar morale by celebrating the centenary of the Great Exhibition (when Britain really did rule over half the world). The most striking features of the site were the Royal Festival Hall (which still stands), the ferris wheel (which has been reincarnated as the London Eye), the saucer-shaped Dome of Discovery (inspiration for the Millennium Dome), and the cigar-shaped Skylon tower.

The festival's success provided the impetus for the eventual creation of the **South Bank Centre** (Ⓦ*www.sbc.org.uk*), home to institutions such as the National Theatre, the National Film Theatre, and the British Film Institute's new IMAX cinema. Sadly, the South Bank has become London's much unloved culture bunker, a mess of "weather-stained concrete, rain-swept walkways and urine-soaked stairs", as one critic aptly put it. On the plus side, the South Bank is currently under inspired artistic direction and stands at the heart of the capital's arts scene. Its unprepossessing appearance is softened, too, by its riverside location, its avenue of trees, its fluttering banners, excellent signposting, and its occasional buskers and skateboarders.

London Eye

Map 6, A5. Daily: April–Sept 9am–late evening; Oct–March 9am–5.30pm; £7.45; Ⓣ0870/500 0600; Ⓦ*www.ba-londoneye.com*
⊖ Waterloo or Westminster.

South of the South Bank Centre proper, beside County Hall, is London's most prominent new landmark, the Millennium Wheel or **London Eye**, British Airways' magnificently graceful observation wheel which spins slowly and silently over the Thames. Standing 443ft high, the wheel is the largest ever built, and it's constantly in slow motion – a full-circle "flight" in one of its 32 pods takes around thirty minutes, and lifts you high above the city. It's one of the few places (apart from a plane window) from which London looks a manageable size, as you can see right out to where the suburbs slip into the countryside. Queues can be bad at the weekend, so book in advance over the phone.

COUNTY HALL

Map 6, A6. ⊖ Westminster or Waterloo.

The colonnaded crescent of **County Hall** is the only truly monumental building in this part of town. Designed to house the London County Council, it was completed in 1933 and enjoyed its greatest moment of fame as the headquarters of the GLC (Greater London Council), abolished by Margaret Thatcher in 1986, leaving London as the only European city without an elected authority. Since May 2000, London has had its own elected mayor, the former GLC leader Ken Livingstone, as well as a GLA (Greater London Authority), which will eventually be housed in a new building near Tower Bridge. County Hall, meanwhile, is now in the hands of a Japanese property company, and currently houses hotels, restaurants, an amusement arcade, the London Aquarium and the FA Premier League Hall of Fame.

The London Aquarium

Daily 10am–6pm or later; £8.50; ⓦ*www.londonaquarium.co.uk*

⊖ Waterloo or Westminster.

So far, the most popular attraction in County Hall is the **London Aquarium**, laid out across three floors of the basement. With some super-large tanks, and everything from dog-face puffers to piranhas, this is somewhere that's pretty much guaranteed to please younger kids. The "**Beach**", where children can actually stroke the (non-sting) rays, is particularly popular. Though impressive in scale, the aquarium is fairly conservative in design, however, with no walk-through tanks and only the very briefest of information on any of the fish.

Dalí Universe

Map 3, I6. Daily 10am–6pm (later in the summer); £7; Ⓦ*www.daliuniverse.com*. ⊖ Westminster or Waterloo.

Three giant surrealist sculptures on the river-facing side of County Hall advertise the building's latest attraction, **Dalí Universe**. There's no denying Dalí was an accomplished and prolific artist, but you'll be disappointed if you're expecting to see his "greatest hits" – those are scattered across the globe. Most of the works here are little-known bronze and glass sculptures, and various drawings from the many illustrated books which he published, ranging from Ovid to the Marquis de Sade. Aside from these, there's one of the numerous Lobster Telephones, which Edward James commissioned for his London home, a copy of his famous Mae West lips sofa, and the oil painting from the dream sequence in Hitchcock's movie *Spellbound*.

FA Premier League Hall of Fame

Daily 10am–6pm; £9.95; Ⓦ*www.hall-of-fame.co.uk*
⊖ Westminster or Waterloo.

The latest string to County Hall's bow is the **FA Premier**

League Hall of Fame, whose entrance is on the south side of the building. If it weren't for the outrageous entrance fee, the museum would be an inoffensive enough trot through the history of football. Acres of text are interspersed with several historical mock-ups and a few predictable snippets of old footage. There's also the odd prize artefact, such as Roger Hunt's 1966 World Cup shirt, touch-screen computers that reel off Premiership statistics, and a saccharine twenty-minute film in which a schoolboy's dream of playing in the Premiership comes true. The eponymous Hall of Fame itself features life-sized wax models of Premiership idols, but the only hands-on fun in the is the final room of video football games.

LAMBETH

South of Westminter Bridge, you leave the South Bank proper, but there are a few minor sights worth considering, such as the **Florence Nightingale Museum**; this stretch of the riverbank also affords the best views of the Houses of Parliament. Inland lies London's most even-handed military museum, the **Imperial War Museum**, housed in a former lunatic asylum.

Florence Nightingale Museum

Map 3, I6. Mon–Fri 10am–5pm, Sat & Sun 11.30am–4.30pm; £4.80; Ⓦ*www.florence-nightingale.co.uk* ⊖ Westminster.

On the south side of Westminster Bridge, on Lambeth Palace Road and in the midst of St Thomas's Hospital, the **Florence Nightingale Museum** celebrates the woman who revolutionized the nursing profession by establishing the first school of nursing at St Thomas's in 1859. The exhibition hits just the right note, putting the two years she spent in the Crimea in the context of a lifetime of tireless social campaigning. Exhibits include the white lantern that earned her the nickname "The Lady with the Lamp", and a reconstruction of a Crimean military hospital ward.

Museum of Garden History

Map 3, I7. March to mid-Dec daily except Sat 10.30am–5pm; free. ⊖ Westminster.

A short walk south of St Thomas's is the Kentish ragstone church of St Mary-at-Lambeth, which now contains a café and an unpretentious little **Museum of Garden History** (March to mid-Dec Sun–Fri 10.30am–5pm; free). The graveyard has been transformed into a small seventeenth-century garden, where two interesting sarcophagi lurk among the foliage: one belongs to Captain Bligh, the commander of the *Bounty* in 1787; the other is a memorial to John Tradescant, gardener to James I and Charles I.

The Imperial War Museum

Map 3, K7. Daily 10am–6pm; £5.50; free after 4.30pm; Ⓦ*www.iwm.org.uk* ⊖ Lambeth North or Elephant & Castle.

The domed building at the east end of Lambeth Road, formerly the infamous lunatic asylum "Bedlam" is now the **Imperial War Museum**, by far the best military museum in the capital. The treatment of the subject is impressively

LONDON BY BALLOON

If the London Eye hasn't given you enough of a lift, you can go even higher, to over 500ft (weather permitting) in the **hot-air balloon** situated behind Vauxhall tube station in Spring Gardens. Though the Skyview Balloon (daily 10am–dusk; £9.95; Ⓦ*www.skyviewballooning.com*) is the largest tethered helium balloon in the world, it remains to be seen whether it can withstand the competition from the wheel.

wide-ranging and fairly sober, with the main hall's militaristic display, offset by the lower-ground-floor array of documents and images attesting to the human damage of war. The museum also has a harrowing new **Holocaust Exhibition** (not recommended for children under 14), which you enter from the third floor, and for which you must obtain a separate timed ticket from the ground floor box office either on arrival, or by booking ahead over the phone (Ⓣ020/7416 5439; last entry 5pm). The exhibition pulls few punches, and has made a valiant attempt to avoid depicting the victims of the Holocaust as nameless masses by focusing on individual cases, and interspersing the archive footage with eyewitness accounts from contemporary survivors.

BANKSIDE: THE GLOBE AND THE TATE

⊖ Southwark or Blackfriars.

Bankside, which lies between Blackfriars and Southwark Bridge, was the most nefarious area in London in Elizabethan times, thanks to its brothels, bearpits and theatres. Four hundred years on, and Bankside is once more a magnet for visitors and Londoners alike, thanks to the newly rebuilt **Globe Theatre** (where most of Shakespeare's plays had their first performances), and the new **Tate Modern** art gallery housed in the old Bankside power station. In addition, the area is now linked to St Paul's and the City by the fabulous new Norman Foster-designed **Millennium Bridge**, the first to cross the Thames for over a century, and London's first pedestrian-only bridge.

Tate Modern

Map 7, A7. Daily 10am–6pm; Fri & Sat open until 10pm; free; Ⓣ020/7887 8000; Ⓦ*www.tate.org.uk* ⊖ Southwark or Blackfriars.

Bankside is dominated by the austere power station of the same name, now transformed by the Swiss duo Herzog & de Meuron into the **Tate Modern**. The masterful conversion, completed in May 2000, has left plenty of the original, industrial feel, while providing wonderfully light and spacious galleries in which to show off the Tate's vast international twentieth-century art collection. The best way to enter is down the ramp from the west, so you get the full effect of the stupendously large turbine hall. It's easy enough to find your way around the galleries, with levels 3 and 5 displaying the permanent collection, level 4 used for fee-paying temporary exhibitions, and level 7 home to a rooftop café with a great view over the Thames – eventually visitors are to be given access to a viewing platform at the top of the central chimney.

Given that Tate Modern is the largest modern art gallery in the world, you need to spend the best part of a day here to do justice to the place. Pick up a plan (and, for an extra £1, an audioguide), and take the escalator to level 3. As at Tate Britain, the curators have eschewed the usual chronological approach through the "isms", prefering to group works together thematically: Landscape/Matter/Environment, Still Life/Object/Real Life, History/Memory/Society and Nude/Action/Body. On the whole this works very well, though the early twentieth-century canvases, in their gilded frames. do struggle when made to compete with contemporary installations.

Although the displays change every six months or so, you're still pretty much guaranteed to see at least some works by **Monet** and Bonnard, Cubist pioneers **Picasso** and Braque, Surrealists such as **Dalí**, abstract artists like **Mondrian**, Bridget Riley and Pollock, and Pop supremos **Warhol** and Lichtenstein. There are seminal works such as a replica of **Duchamp**'s urinal, entitled *Fountain* and signed "R. Mutt", Yves Klein's totally blue paintings and Carl André's trademark piles of bricks. And such is the space here that several artists get whole rooms to themselves, among them the painter Francis Bacon, Joseph Beuys and his shamanistic wax and furs, and **Mark Rothko**, whose abstract "Seagram Murals", originally destined for a posh restaurant in New York, have their own shrine-like room in the heart of the collection.

For more on attending performances at the Globe, see p.282.

Shakespeare's Globe Theatre

Map 7, B7. Box office Ⓣ020/7401 9919; Ⓦ*www.shakespeares-globe.org* ⊖ Southwark or Blackfriars.

Seriously dwarfed by the Tate Modern is the equally spectacular **Shakespeare's Globe Theatre**, a reconstruction of the polygonal playhouse where most of the Bard's later works were first performed, and which was originally erected on nearby Park Street in 1598. To find out more about Shakespeare and the history of Bankside, the Globe's pricey but stylish new **exhibition** (daily: May–Sept 9am–noon; Oct–April 10am–5pm; £7.50) is well worth a visit. It begins by detailing the long campaign by American actor Sam Wanamaker to have the Globe rebuilt, but it's the imaginative hands-on exhibits that really hit the spot. You can have a virtual play on medieval instruments such as the crumhorn or sackbut, prepare your own edition of Shakespeare, and feel the thatch, hazelnut-shell and daub used to build the theatre. Visitors also get taken on an informative **guided tour** round the theatre itself, except in the afternoons during the summer season, when you can only visit the exhibition (for a reduced entrance fee).

You can view the archeological remains of another Elizabethan playhouse, the **Rose Theatre**, nearby at 56 Park St; daily 10am–5pm; £3; Ⓦ*www.rdg.ac.uk/rose*

CLINK STREET, SOUTHWARK CATHEDRAL AND AROUND

Map 7, D7. ⊖ London Bridge.

East of Bankside, beyond Southwark Bridge, the latest big-money venture to hit this up-and-coming area is **Vinopolis** (daily 10am–5.30pm (closing times often vary in the summer); £11.50; Ⓦ*www.evinopolis.com*), discreetly housed in former wine vaults under the railway arches on Clink Street. The focus of the complex is the "**Wine Odyssey**", a light-hearted trot through the world's wine regions, equipped with a CD audioguide. There are plenty of visual gags – you get to tour round the Italian vineyards on a Vespa – but the most appealing and educative aspect of the tour is the **wine-tasting**. Visitors get five generous samples – from champagne to vintage port – with the option of buying another five for a mere £2.50 extra.

Further down the suitably gloomy confines of dark and narrow Clink Street is the **Clink Prison Museum** (Map 7, D8; daily 10am–6pm; £4; Ⓦ*www.clink.co.uk*), built on the site of the former Clink Prison, origin of the expression "in the clink". The prison began as a dungeon for disobedient clerics, built under the Bishop of Winchester's Palace – the rose window of the palace's Great Hall survives just east of the museum – and later became a dumping ground for heretics, prostitutes and a motley assortment of Bankside lowlife. Today's exhibition features a handful of prison life tableaux, and dwells on the torture and grim conditions within, but, given the rich history of the place, this is a disappointingly lacklustre museum.

An exact replica of the **Golden Hinde** (Map 7, E8; daily 10am–dusk; £3; Ⓦ*www.goldenhinde.co.uk*), the galleon in which Sir Francis Drake sailed around the world from 1577 to 1580, nestles in St Mary Overie Dock, at the eastern end of Clink Street. The ship is surprisingly small, and its original crew of eighty-plus must have been cramped to say the least. There's a refreshing lack of interpretive panels, so it's worth paying the little bit extra and getting a guided tour from one of the folk in period garb – ring ahead to check a group hasn't booked the place up (Ⓣ0870/011 8700).

Southwark Cathedral

Map 7, E8. Daily 8am–6pm; free. ⊖London Bridge.

Close by the *Golden Hinde* stands **Southwark Cathedral**, built as the medieval Augustinian priory church of St Mary Overie, and given cathedral status only in 1905. Of the original thirteenth-century church, only the choir and retrochoir now remain, separated by a tall and beautiful stone Tudor screen, making them probably the oldest Gothic structures left in London. The nave was entirely rebuilt in the nineteenth century, but the cathedral contains numerous interesting monuments, from a thirteenth-century oak effigy of a knight to an early twentieth-century memorial to Shakespeare.

The Old Operating Theatre

Map 7, F9. Daily 10am–4pm; £3.25;
users.aol.com/museumweb/chr.htm ⊖ London Bridge.

The most educational and strangest of Southwark's museums, the **Old Operating Theatre Museum** and **Herb Garret** is located to the east of the cathedral on St Thomas Street, on the other side of Borough High Street. Built in 1821 at the top of a church tower, where the hospital apothecary's herbs were stored, this women's operating theatre dates from the pre-anaesthetic era. Despite being entirely gore-free, the museum is as stomach-churning as the London Dungeon (see below). The surgeons who used this room would have concentrated on speed and accuracy (most amputations took less than a minute), but there was still a thirty percent mortality rate, with many patients simply dying of shock, and many more from bacterial infection, about which very little was known.

TOOLEY STREET AND AROUND

Map 7, G8. ⊖ London Bridge.

The vaults beneath the railway arches of London Bridge train station, on the south side of **Tooley Street**, are now occupied by two museums. Young teenagers and the credulous probably get the most out of the ever-popular **London Dungeon** (daily: April–Sept 10am–6pm; Oct–March 10.30am–5.30pm; £9.50; Ⓦ*www.thedungeons.com*) – to avoid the inevitable queue, buy your ticket from the Southwark tourist office (see below). The life-sized waxwork tableaux inside include a man being hung, drawn and quartered and one being boiled alive, the general hysteria being boosted by actors, dressed as top-hatted Victorian vampires, pouncing out of the darkness. Visitors are then herded into a court room, condemned to the "River of Death" boat ride, and forced to endure the "Jack the Ripper Experience", an exploitative trawl through post-mortem photos and wax mock-ups of the victims, followed by the "Great Fire of London", in which you experience the heat and the smell of the plague-ridden city, before walking through a revolving tunnel of flames.

Southwark **tourist office** is at 6 Tooley St (Easter–Oct Mon–Sat 10am–6pm, Sun 10.30am–5.30pm; Nov–Easter Mon–Sat 10am–4pm, Sun 11am–4pm; Ⓣ020/7403 8299; Ⓦ*www.southwark.gov.uk/tourism*).

A little further east along Tooley Street is **Winston Churchill's Britain at War** (Map 7, H9; daily: April–Sept 10am–5.30pm; Oct–March 10am–4.30pm; £5.95; ⓦ*www.britainatwar.co.uk*), an illuminating insight into the stiff-upper-lip London mentality during the Blitz. The museum contains hundreds of wartime artefacts, including an Anderson shelter, where you can hear the chilling sound of the V1 "doodlebugs" and tune in to contemporary radio broadcasts. The grand finale is a walk through the chaos of a just-bombed street.

On the other side of Tooley Street is **Hay's Galleria** (Map 7, H8), a shopping precinct built over what used to be Hay's Dock. The idea of filling in the curvaceous dock and covering it with glass and steel barrel-vaulting, while retaining the old Victorian warehouses on three sides, is an effective one. The pastiche of phoney market barrows, gravel underfoot and red phone boxes and the gimmicky kinetic sculpture at the centre, however, is less successful.

Permanently moored just along the riverfront from Hay's Galleria is the **HMS Belfast** (Map 7, I8; daily: March–Oct 10am–6pm; Nov–Feb closes 5pm; £4.70; ⓦ*www.iwm.org.uk*), a World War II cruiser. Armed with six torpedoes, and six-inch guns with a range of over fourteen miles, the *Belfast* spent over two years of the war in the Royal Naval shipyards, after being hit by a mine in the Firth of Forth at the beginning of hostilities. It later saw action in the Barents Sea during World War II, and during the Korean War, before being decommissioned. To find out more about the *Belfast*, head for the exhibition on level 5; otherwise the ship is a bit short on info, but the maze of cabins is fun to explore.

A ferry service runs April–Sept daily every 15min from HMS *Belfast* to the Tower of London.

BUTLER'S WHARF: THE DESIGN MUSEUM

Map 7, L9. ⊖ Tower Hill, London Bridge or Bermondsey.

In contrast to the brash offices on Tooley Street, **Butler's Wharf**, east of Tower Bridge, has retained its historical character. **Shad Thames**, the narrow street at the back of Butler's Wharf, has kept the wrought-iron overhead gangways by which the porters used to transport goods from the wharves to the warehouses further back from the river, and is one of the area's most atmospheric alleyways. The eight-storey Butler's Wharf warehouse itself, with its shops and restaurants, forms part of Terence Conran's commercial empire and caters for a moneyed clientele, but the wide promenade on the riverfront is open to the public.

The chief attraction of Butler's Wharf is Conran's superb riverside **Design Museum** (Mon–Fri 11.30am–6pm, Sat & Sun 10.30am–6pm; £5.50; Ⓦ*www.designmuseum.org*), a stylish, Bauhaus-like conversion of a 1950s warehouse at the eastern end of Shad Thames. The excellent temporary **exhibitions** on important designers, movements or single products are staged on the first floor, while the Collection and Review **galleries**, on the top floor, offer a brief overview of mass-produced industrial design from TVs to Tupperware. The small coffee bar in the foyer is a great place to relax, and there's a pricey Conran restaurant on the top floor.

The **Bramah Tea and Coffee Museum** (daily 10am–6pm; £4; Ⓦ*www.bramahmuseum.co.uk*), housed in an old tea warehouse, Tamarind House, on Maguire Street behind the Design Museum, is not quite in the same league as its neighbour. Still, it's fun, and well worth a visit. Founded in 1992 by Edward Bramah, who began his career on an African tea garden in 1950, the museum's emphasis is firmly on tea. There's an impressive array of teapots from Wedgwood to novelty, and coffee machines spanning the twentieth century, from huge percolator siphons to espresso machines.

Hyde Park, Kensington, Chelsea and Notting Hill

HYDE PARK, together with its westerly extension, Kensington Gardens, covers a distance of two miles from Speakers' Corner in the northeast to Kensington Palace in the southwest. At the end of your journey, you've made it to one of London's most exclusive districts, the Royal Borough of **KENSINGTON** and **CHELSEA**, which makes up the bulk of this chapter. Other districts go in and out of fashion, but this area has been in vogue ever since royalty moved into **Kensington Palace** in the late seventeenth century.

Aside from the shops around Harrods in Knightsbridge, however, the popular tourist attractions lie in **South Kensington**, where three of London's top **museums** – the Victoria and Albert, Natural History and Science museums – stand on land bought with the proceeds of the Great Exhibition of 1851. Chelsea's character is slightly more bohemian. In the 1960s, the **King's Road** carved out its reputation as London's catwalk, while in the late 1970s it was the epicentre of the punk explosion. Nothing so risqué goes on in Chelsea now, though its residents like to think of themselves as rather more artistic and intellectual than the purely moneyed types of Kensington.

Once slummy, now swanky, **Bayswater** and **NOTTING HILL**, to the north of Hyde Park, were the bad boys of the borough for many years, dens of vice and crime comparable to Soho. Despite gentrification over the last twenty-five years, they remain the borough's most cosmopolitan districts, with a strong Arab presence and vestiges of the black community who initiated and still run the city's (and Europe's) largest street **carnival**, which takes place every August Bank Holiday.

HYDE PARK AND KENSINGTON GARDENS

Map 3, D5. ⊖ Marble Arch, Hyde Park Corner or Lancaster Gate.

Seized from the Church by Henry VIII to satisfy his desire for yet more hunting grounds, **Hyde Park** (Ⓦ*www.royalparks.co.uk*) was first opened to the public by James I, and soon became a fashionable gathering place for the beau monde, who rode round the circular drive known as the Ring, pausing to gossip and admire each other's *equipage*. Hangings, muggings and duels, the Great Exhibition of 1851 and numerous public events have all taken place in Hyde Park – and it's still a popular gathering point or destination for political demonstrations. For most of the time, however, the park is simply a leisure ground – a wonderful open space which allows you to lose all sight of the city beyond a few persistent tower blocks.

Located at the treeless northeastern corner of the park, **Marble Arch** (Map 3, D4) was originally erected in 1828 as a triumphal entry to Buckingham Palace, but is now stranded on a ferociously busy traffic island at the west end of Oxford Street. This is the most historically charged spot in Hyde Park, as it marks the site of **Tyburn gallows**, the city's main public execution spot until 1783. It's also the location of **Speakers' Corner**, once an entertaining and peculiarly English Sunday tradition, featuring an assembly of characterful speakers and hecklers – now, sadly, a forum for soap-box religious extremists.

A better place to enter the park is at **Hyde Park Corner** (Map 3, F6), the southeast corner, where the **Wellington Arch** stands in the midst of another of London's busiest traffic interchanges. Erected in 1828 to commemorate Wellington's victories in the Napoleonic Wars, the arch originally served as the northern gate into Buckingham Palace grounds. Close by stands **Apsley House** (Map 3, F6; Tues–Sun 11am–5pm; £4.50; Ⓦ*www.vam.ac.uk*), Wellington's London residence and now a museum to the "Iron Duke". Unless you're a keen fan of the Duke (or the architect, Benjamin Wyatt), the highlight of the museum is the **art collection**, much of which used to belong to the King of Spain. Among the best pieces, displayed in the Waterloo Gallery on the first floor, are works by de Hooch, van Dyck, Velázquez, Goya, Rubens and Murillo. The famous, more than twice life-size nude statue of Napoleon by Antonio Canova stands at the foot of the main staircase.

Hyde Park is divided in two by the **Serpentine Lake**, which has a popular **Lido** (June–Sept daily 10am–6pm; £2.50) on its south bank. By far the prettiest section of the lake, though, is the upper section known as the **Long Water**, which narrows until it reaches a group of four fountains, laid out symmetrically in front of an Italianate summerhouse designed by Wren.

The western half of the park is officially known as **Kensington Gardens**, and is, strictly speaking, a separate entity, though you hardly notice the change. Its two most popular attractions are the **Serpentine Gallery** (Map 3, C6; daily 10am–6pm; free; Ⓦ*www.serpentinegallery.org*), which has a reputation for lively, and often controversial, contemporary art exhibitions, and the richly decorated, High Gothic **Albert Memorial** (Map 3, B6), clearly visible to the west. Erected in 1876, the monument is as much a hymn to the glorious achievements of Britain as to its subject, Queen Victoria's husband (who died of typhoid in 1861). Recently restored to his former gilded glory, Albert occupies the central canopy, clutching a catalogue for the 1851 Great Exhibition that he helped to organize.

The Exhibition's most famous feature, the gargantuan glasshouse of the Crystal Palace, no longer exists, but the profits were used to buy a large tract of land south of the park, now home to South Kensington's remarkable cluster of museums and colleges, plus the vast **Royal Albert Hall**, a splendid iron-and-glass-domed concert hall, with an exterior of red brick, terracotta and marble that became the hallmark of South Ken architecture. The hall is venue for Europe's most democratic music festival, the Henry Wood Promenade Concerts, better known as the **Proms**, which take place from July to September, with standing-room tickets for as little as £3.

KENSINGTON PALACE

Map 3, A6. May–Sept daily 10am–6pm; Oct–April Wed–Sun 10am–5pm; £9.50; Ⓦ*www.hrp.org.uk* ⊖ High Street Kensington or Queensway.

On the western edge of Kensington Gardens stands **Kensington Palace**, a modestly proportioned Jacobean brick mansion bought by William and Mary in 1689, and the chief royal residence for the next fifty years. KP, as it's fondly known in royal circles, is best known today as the place where **Princess Diana** lived until her death in 1997. It was, in fact, the official London residence of both Charles and Di until the couple formally separated. In the weeks following Diana's death, literally millions of flowers, mementos, poems and gifts were deposited at the gates to the south of the palace.

Visitors don't get to see Diana's apartments, which were on the west side of the palace, where various minor royals still live. Instead, they are given an audioguide which takes them round the Royal Ceremonial Dress Collection, where they get to view some of the Queen's frocks, and then the sparsely furnished state apartments. The highlights are the trompe l'oeil ceiling paintings by William Kent, in particular the Cupola Room, and the oil paintings in the King's Gallery. En route, you also get to see the tastelessly decorated rooms in which the future Queen Victoria spent her unhappy childhood. To recover from the above, take tea in the exquisite **Orangery** (daily: Easter–Sept 10am–6pm; Oct–Easter 10am–4pm), to the north of the palace.

THE VICTORIA AND ALBERT MUSEUM

Map 3, C7. Daily 10am–5.45pm (Wed also 6.30–9.30pm); £5; free after 4.30pm; Ⓦ*www.vam.ac.uk* ⊖South Kensington.

In terms of sheer variety and scale, the **Victoria and Albert Museum** (popularly known as the V&A), on Cromwell Road, is the greatest museum of applied arts in the world. The range of exhibits on display here means that, whatever your taste, there is almost bound to be something to grab your attention.

The most celebrated of the V&A's numerous exhibits are the **Raphael Cartoons**, seven vast biblical paintings that served as designs for a set of tapestries destined for the Sistine Chapel. Close by, you can view highlights from the country's largest dress collection, and the world's largest collection of Indian art outside India. In addition, there are galleries devoted to Chinese, Islamic, Japanese and Korean art, as well as costume jewellery, glassware, metalwork and photography. Wading through the huge collection of European sculpture, you come to the surreal **Plaster Casts** gallery, filled with copies of European art's greatest hits, from Michelangelo's *David* to Trajan's Column (sawn in half to make it fit). There's even a gallery of twentieth-century objets d'art – everything from Bauhaus furniture to Swatch watches – to rival that of the Design Museum.

Over in the **Henry Cole Wing**, meanwhile, you'll find an entire office interior by Frank Lloyd Wright, a collection of sixteenth-century portrait miniatures, more Constable paintings than the Tate, and a goodly collection of sculptures by Rodin. As if all this were not enough, the V&A's temporary shows are among the best in Britain, ranging over vast areas of art, craft and technology.

Beautifully but haphazardly displayed across a seven-mile, four-storey maze of halls and corridors, the V&A's treasures are impossible to survey in a single visit. Floor plans from the information desks can help you decide on which areas to concentrate. If you're flagging, there's *Millburns* restaurant in the basement of the Henry Cole Wing, or a more edifying café in the museum's period-piece **Poynter, Morris and Gamble** refreshment rooms.

MUSEUM SEASON TICKETS

If you can see yourself making more than one visit in the coming year to the Natural History, Science or V&A museums, it's worth buying a **South Kensington Museums Pass**, which costs £29 and provides unlimited access for a year to all three sights; for more details call ⓣ020/7942 4455.

Like all London's major museums, the V&A has big plans for the future, with a £75 million multifaceted extension, known as the "**Spiral**" and designed by controversial Polish-born architect Daniel Libeskind, due to open in 2004.

THE SCIENCE MUSEUM

Map 3, C7. Daily: 10am–6pm; £6.95; free after 4.30pm; Ⓦ*www.nmsi.ac.uk* ⊖ South Kensington.

The **Science Museum**, on Exhibition Road, is undeniably impressive, filling seven floors with items drawn from every conceivable area of science, including space travel, telecommunications, time measurement, chemistry, computing, photography and medicine. Keen to dispel the enduring image of museums devoted to its subject as boring and full of dusty glass cabinets, the Science Museum has been busy updating its galleries with more interactive displays, and puts on daily demonstrations to show that not all science teaching has to be deathly dry.

Once you've paid your entrance fee, head for the **information desk** in the Power Hall and find out what events and demonstrations are taking place; you can also sign up for a guided tour on a specific subject. The **Launch Pad**, aimed at kids, was one of the first hands-on displays and remains as popular and enjoyable as ever, as do the **Garden** and **Things** galleries all of which are in the basement. The new **Materials** gallery is aimed more at adults, and is an extremely stylish exhibition covering the use of materials ranging from aluminium to zerodur (used for making laser gyroscopes). The biggest revamp of all has been the new **Wellcome Wing**, which aims to keep its displays up-to-date with the latest in computer technology.

THE NATURAL HISTORY MUSEUM

Map 3, C7. Mon–Sat 10am–5.50pm, Sun 11am–5.50pm; £7.50; free Mon–Fri after 4.30pm, Sat & Sun after 5pm; ⓦ*www.nhm.ac.uk* ⊖ South Kensington.

Alfred Waterhouse's purpose-built mock-Romanesque colossus ensures the **Natural History Museum**'s status as London's most handsome museum. Caught up, without huge public funds, in the current enthusiasm for museum redesign and accessibility, the contents are a mishmash of truly imaginative exhibits peppered amongst others little changed since the museum's opening in 1881. The museum is caught in a genuine conundrum, for its collections are important resources for serious zoologists, while its collection of real dinosaurs is a big hit with the kids.

The **main entrance** is in the middle of the museum's 675-foot terracotta facade, which leads to what are now known as the **Life Galleries**. Just off the vast Central Hall, dominated by an 85ft-long plaster cast of a Diplodocus skeleton, you'll find the Dinosaur gallery, where a team of animatronic deinonychi feast on a half-dead tenontosaurus. Other popular sections include the Creepy-Crawlies Room and the Ecology Gallery, plus the somewhat ancient displays of stuffed creatures.

If the queues for the museum are long (as they can be at weekends and during school holidays), you're better off heading for the side entrance on Exhibition Road, which leads into the former Geology Museum, now known as the **Earth Galleries**, an expensively revamped and visually exciting romp through the earth's evolution. The most popular sections are the slightly tasteless Kobe earthquake simulator, and the spectacular display of gems and crystals in the Earth's Treasury.

KENSINGTON HIGH STREET AND AROUND

Map 3, A7. ⊖High Street Kensington.

Shopper-thronged **Kensington High Street** is dominated architecturally by the twin presences of Sir George Gilbert Scott's neo-Gothic church of St Mary Abbots, whose 250-foot spire makes it London's tallest parish church, and the Art Deco colossus of Barkers department store, remodelled in the 1930s.

Kensington's sights are mostly hidden away in the back-streets, the one exception being the **Commonwealth Institute** (Map 2, F5; Ⓦ*www.commonwealth.org.uk*), housed in a bold 1960s building set back from the High Street. The whole place has recently undergone a massive restoration and refurbishment programme. Gone is the permanent collection with a section on each of the member states; instead, the Institute aims to put on more up-to-date, interactive temporary exhibitions focusing on a particular Commonwealth country.

Two paths along the side of the Commonwealth Institute lead to densely wooded **Holland Park**, the former grounds of a Jacobean mansion (only the east wing still stands). Theatrical and musical performances are staged here throughout the summer, and several **formal gardens** surround the house, most notably the Japanese-style Kyoto Gardens, while the rest of the park is dotted with a newly-installed series of abstract sculptures.

A number of wealthy Victorian artists rather self-consciously founded an artists' colony in the streets that lie between the High Street and Holland Park. It's now possible to visit one of the most remarkable of these artist pads, **Leighton House** (Wed–Mon 11am–5.30pm; free), 12 Holland Park Rd. "It will be opulence, it will be sincerity", Lord Leighton opined before starting work on the house in the 1860s – he later became President of the Royal

Academy and was ennobled on his deathbed. The big attraction is the domed Arab Hall, decorated with Saracen tiles, gilded mosaics and woodwork drawn from all over the Islamic world. The other rooms are less spectacular but, in compensation, are hung with paintings by Lord Leighton and his Pre-Raphaelite chums.

KNIGHTSBRIDGE

Map 3, D7. ⊖ Knightsbridge.

Knightsbridge is irredeemably snobbish, revelling in its reputation as the swankiest shopping area in London, a status epitomized by **Harrods** (Mon, Tues & Sat 10am–6pm, Wed–Fri 10am–7pm; ⓦ*www.harrods.com*) on Brompton Road. London's most famous department store started out as a family-run grocery store in 1849, with a staff of two. The current 1905 terracotta building is owned by the Egyptian Mohammed Al Fayed and employs in excess of 3000 staff. Tourists flock to Harrods – it's thought to be one of the city's top-ranking tourist attractions – though if you can do without the Harrods carrier bag, you can buy most of what the shop stocks more cheaply elsewhere.

The store does, however, have a few sections that are architectural sights in their own right: the Food Hall, with its exquisite Arts and Crafts tiling, and the Egyptian Hall, with its pseudo-hieroglyphs and sphinxes, are particularly striking. Now that a fountain dedicated to Di and Dodi is in place, the Egyptian-style escalators are an added attraction, but don't bother taking them to the first floor "washrooms", unless you want to pay £1 for the privilege of relieving yourself. Note, too, that the store has a draconian dress code: no shorts, no ripped jeans, no vest T-shirts and no backpacks.

CHELSEA

Map 3, E8. ⊖ Sloane Square.

It wasn't until the latter part of the nineteenth century that **Chelsea** began to earn its reputation as London's very own Left Bank. Its household fame, however, came through **King's Road**'s role as the unofficial catwalk of the "Swinging Sixties". The road remained a fashion parade for hippies, too, and in the Jubilee Year of 1977 it witnessed the birth of punk, masterminded from a shop called Sex, run by Vivienne Westwood and Malcolm McLaren. The posey cafés and boutiques still persist, but these days, the area has a more subdued feel, with high rents and house prices keeping things pretty staid, and chain stores and interior design shops rather than avant-garde fashion the order of the day.

The area's other aspect, oddly enough considering its boho reputation, is a military one. For among the most nattily attired of all those parading down the King's Road are the scarlet or navy-blue clad Chelsea Pensioners, army veterans from the nearby **Royal Hospital** (Map 3, E8; Mon–Fri 9am–noon & 2–4.30pm, Sat & Sun closes 3pm; free), founded by Charles II in 1681. The hospital's majestic red-brick wings and grassy courtyards became a blueprint for institutional and collegiate architecture all over the English-speaking world. The public are allowed to view the austere hospital chapel, and the equally grand, wood-panelled dining hall, opposite, which has a vast allegorical mural of Charles II.

The concrete bunker next door to the Royal Hospital, on Royal Hospital Road, houses the **National Army Museum** (daily 10am–5.30pm; free; Ⓦ*www.national-army-museum.ac.uk*). The militarily obsessed are unlikely to be disappointed by the succession of uniforms and medals, but there is very little here for non-enthusiasts. The temporary exhibitions staged on the ground floor are the museum's strong point, but it's rather disappointing overall – you're better off visiting the infinitely superior Imperial War Museum (see p.108).

Cheyne Walk and Cheyne Row

Map 3, D9. Any bus heading down King's Road from Sloane Square ⊖.

The quiet riverside locale of **Cheyne Walk** (Map 3, D9; pronounced "chainy") drew artists and writers in great numbers during the nineteenth century. Since the building of the Embankment and the increase in the volume of traffic, however, the character of this peaceful haven has been lost. Novelist Henry James, who lived at no. 21, used to take "beguiling drives" in his wheelchair along the Embankment; today, he'd be hospitalized in the process.

The chief reason to come here nowadays is to visit the **Chelsea Physic Garden** (April–Oct Wed noon–5pm, Sun 2–6pm; £4; Ⓦ*www.cpgarden.demon.co.uk*), which marks the beginning of Cheyne Walk. Founded in 1673, this small walled garden is the second oldest botanical garden in the country. At the entrance (on Swan Walk) you can pick up a map of the garden with a list of the month's most interesting flowers and shrubs, whose labels are slightly more forthcoming than the usual terse Latinate tags. The garden also has an excellent teahouse, where you can get delicious home-made cakes.

It's also worth popping into the nearby **Chelsea Old Church** (daily 9.30am–1pm & 2–4.30pm), halfway down Cheyne Walk, where Thomas More built his own private chapel in the south aisle. The church was badly bombed in World War II, but an impressive number of monuments were retrieved from the rubble and continue to adorn the church's interior.

A short distance inland from Cheyne Walk, at 24 Cheyne Row, is **Carlyle's House** (Map 3, D9; April–Oct Wed–Sun 11am–5pm; £3.30), where the historian Thomas Carlyle set up home, having moved down from his native Scotland in 1834. Now a National Trust property, the house became a museum just fifteen years after Carlyle's death and is a typically dour Victorian abode, kept much as the Carlyles would have had it: his hat still hanging in the hall, and his socks in the chest of drawers. The top floor contains the garret study where Carlyle tried in vain to escape the din of the neighbours' noisy roosters in order to complete his final magnum opus on Frederick the Great.

NOTTING HILL

Map 3, A5. ⊖ Notting Hill.

Epicentre of the country's first race riots, when bus-loads of whites attacked West Indian homes in the area, **Notting Hill** is now more famous for the eponymous 1998 film, and for its annual Carnival (Ⓦ*www.nottinghillcarnival.net.uk*; see p.332), which began life in direct response to the riots. These days, it's the world's biggest street festival outside Rio, with an estimated two million revellers turning up on the last weekend of August for the two-day extravaganza of parades, steel bands and deafening sound systems.

The rest of the year, Notting Hill is a lot quieter, though its cafés and restaurants are cool enough places to pull in folk from all over. On Saturdays, big crowds of Londoners and tourists alike descend on the mile-long **Portobello Road Market**, which is lined with stalls selling everything from antiques to cheap secondhand clothes and fruit and vegetables.

Within easy walking distance of Portobello Road, on the other side of the railway tracks, gasworks and canal, is **Kensal Green Cemetery** (daily: April–Sept 8am–6pm;

Oct–March 9am–5pm; ⊖ Kensal Rise), opened in 1833 and still a functioning burial ground. Graves of the more famous incumbents – Thackeray, Trollope and Brunel – are less interesting architecturally than those arranged on either side of the Centre Avenue, which leads from the easternmost entrance on Harrow Road.

North London

The area of the city covered in this **NORTH LONDON** chapter concentrates on just a handful of the capital's satellite villages, now subsumed into the general mass of London. Almost all the northern suburbs are easily accessible by tube from the centre; in fact, it was the expansion of the tube which encouraged the forward march of bricks and mortar into many of these suburbs.

The first section covers one of London's finest parks, **Regent's Park**, framed by Nash-designed architecture and home of London Zoo. Close by is **Camden Town**, where the weekend market is one of the city's big attractions – a warren of stalls selling street fashion, books, records and ethnic goods.

The real highlights of north London, though, for visitors and residents alike, are **Hampstead** and **Highgate**, elegant, largely eighteenth-century developments which still reflect their village origins. They have the added advantage of proximity to one of London's wildest patches of greenery, **Hampstead Heath**, where you can enjoy stupendous views, kite-flying and nude bathing, as well as outdoor concerts and high art in the setting of **Kenwood House**.

Also covered are a handful of sights in more far-flung northern suburbs. They include the **RAF Museum** at

Hendon and the **Shri Swaminarayan Mandir**, the largest Hindu temple outside India.

REGENT'S PARK

Map 3, E2. Daily 5am–dusk; ⓦ*www.royalparks.co.uk* ⊖ Regent's Park, Baker Street or Great Portland Street.

As with almost all of London's royal parks, Londoners have Henry VIII to thank for **Regent's Park**, which he confiscated from the Church for yet more hunting grounds. However, it wasn't until the reign of the Prince Regent (later George IV) that the park began to take its current form. According to the masterplan, devised by John Nash in 1811, the park was to be girded by a continuous belt of terraces, and sprinkled with a total of 56 villas, including a magnificent pleasure palace for the Prince himself, which would be linked by Regent Street to Carlton House in St James's. The plan was never fully realized, due to lack of funds, but enough was built to create something of the idealized garden city that Nash and the Prince Regent envisaged.

To appreciate the special quality of Regent's Park, take a closer look at the architecture, starting with the Nash terraces, which form a near-unbroken horseshoe of cream-coloured stucco around the Outer Circle. Within the Inner Circle is the **Open Air Theatre**, which puts on summer performances of Shakespeare, opera and ballet, and **Queen Mary's Gardens**, by far the prettiest section of the park. A large slice of the gardens is taken up with a glorious rose garden, featuring some 400 varieties, surrounded by a ring of ramblers.

Clearly visible on the western edge of the park is the shiny copper dome and minaret of the **London Central Mosque**, an entirely appropriate addition given the Prince Regent's taste for the Orient. Non-Muslim visitors are wel-

come to look in at the information centre, and glimpse inside the hall of worship, which is packed out with a diversity of communities for the lunchtime Friday prayers.

London Zoo

Map 3, E1. Daily: March–Oct 10am–5.30pm; Nov–Feb 10am–4pm; £9; Ⓦ*www.londonzoo.co.uk* ⊖ Camden Town.

The northeastern corner of the park is occupied by **London Zoo**, founded in 1826. It may not be the most uplifting place for animal lovers, but kids will love the place – most are particularly taken by the children's enclosure, where they can actually handle the animals, and the regular "Animals in Action" live shows. The zoo boasts some striking architectural features, too, most notably the modernist,

REGENT'S CANAL BY BOAT

Three companies run **boat services** on the Regent's Canal between Camden (⊖ Camden Town) and Little Venice (⊖ Warwick Avenue), stopping off at London Zoo on the way and passing through the Maida Hill tunnel en route. The narrowboat *Jenny Wren* (Ⓣ020/7485 4433) starts off at Camden, while Jason's narrowboats (Ⓣ020/7286 3428) start off at Little Venice; the London Waterbus Company (Ⓣ020/7482 2660) – the only one to run all year round – sets off from both places. Whichever you choose, you can board at either end; **tickets** cost around £5–6 return and journey time is 35–45 minutes one-way.

Those interested in the history of the canal should head off to the **London Canal Museum** (Map 3, I1; Tues–Sun 10am–4.30pm; £2.50; Ⓦ*www.canalmuseum.org.uk*), on the other side of York Way, down New Wharf Road, ten minutes' walk from King's Cross Station.

spiral-ramped 1930s concrete penguin pool (where Penguin Books' original colophon was sketched); it was designed by the Tecton partnership, led by Russian émigré Berthold Lubetkin. Other zoo landmarks include the colossal tetrahedral aluminium-framed tent of the Snowdon Aviary, and the new, eco-conscious invertebrate-filled Web of Life.

CAMDEN TOWN

Map 2, H3. ⊖ Camden Town.

For all the gentrification of the last twenty years, **Camden Town** retains a seedy air, compounded by the various railway lines that plough through the area, the canal, and Europe's largest dosshouse. The market, however, gives the area a positive lift on the weekends, and is now the district's best-known attribute.

Having started out as a tiny crafts market in the cobbled courtyard by the lock, **Camden Market** has since mushroomed out of all proportion. More than 100,000 shoppers turn up here each weekend, and parts of the market now stay open week-long, alongside a similarly-oriented crop of shops, cafés and bistros. The market's overabundance of cheap leather, DM shoes and naff jewellery is compensated for by the sheer variety of what's on offer: from bootleg tapes to furniture, along with a mass of street fashion that may or may not make the transition to mainstream stores. To avoid the crowds, which can be overpowering on a summer Sunday afternoon, you'll need to get here by 10am – by 4pm many of the stalls will be packing up to go.

Despite having no significant Jewish associations, Camden is home to London's **Jewish Museum** (Mon–Thurs & Sun 10am–4pm; £3; Ⓦ*www.jewmusm.ort.org*), at 129 Albert St, just off Parkway. The purpose-built premises are smartly designed, but the conventional style and contents of the museum are disappointing: apart from the usual displays of

Judaica, there's a video and exhibition explaining Jewish religious practices and the history of the Jewish community in Britain. More challenging temporary exhibitions are held in the museum's Finchley branch on East End Road, N3 (Map 2, F1; ⓣ020/8349 1143).

HAMPSTEAD

Map 2, G2. ⊖ Hampstead.

Perched on a hill above Camden Town, **Hampstead** village developed into a fashionable spa in the eighteenth century, after a celebrated physician declared the waters of its spring as being of great medicinal value. Its sloping site, which deterred Victorian property speculators and put off the railway companies, saved much of the Georgian village from destruction, and it's little altered to this day. Later, it became one of the city's most celebrated literary *quartiers* and even now it retains its reputation as a bolt hole of the high-profile intelligentsia. You can get some idea of its tone from the fact that the local Labour MP is currently the actress-turned-politician Glenda Jackson.

The steeply inclined High Street, lined with trendy clothes shops and arty cafés, flaunts the area's ever-increasing wealth without completely losing its picturesqueness. There are several small house museums to explore, but proximity to the Heath is the real joy of Hampstead, for this mixture of woodland, smooth pasture and landscaped garden is quite simply the most exhilarating patch of greenery in London.

Fenton House

Map 2, G2. April–Oct Wed–Fri 2–5pm, Sat & Sun 11am–5pm; £4.20. ⊖ Hampstead.

Whichever route you take north of Hampstead tube, you'll

probably end up at the small triangular green on Holly Bush Hill, on the north side of which stands the late seventeenth-century **Fenton House**. As well as housing a collection of European and Oriental ceramics, this National Trust house contains the superb Benton-Fletcher collection of early musical instruments, chiefly displayed on the top floor. Among the many spinets, virginals and clavichords are the earliest extant English grand piano, and an Unverdorben lute from 1580 (one of only three in the world).

The Freud Museum

Map 2, G3. Wed–Sun noon–5pm; £3; Ⓦ*www.freud.org.uk*
⊖ Swiss Cottage.

One of the most poignant of London's house museums is the **Freud Museum**, hidden away in the leafy streets of south Hampstead at 20 Maresfield Gardens. Having lived in Vienna for his entire adult life, Freud, by now a semi-invalid with only a year to live, was forced to flee the Nazis, arriving in London in the summer of 1938. The ground-floor study and library look exactly as they did when Freud lived here; the collection of erotic antiquities and the famous couch, sumptuously draped in Persian carpets, were all brought here from Vienna. Upstairs, home movies of family life in Vienna are shown continually, and a small room is dedicated to his daughter, Anna, herself an influential child analyst, who lived in the house until her death in 1982.

Burgh House – the Hampstead Museum

Map 2, G3. Wed–Sun noon–5pm; free. ⊖Hampstead.

The Queen Anne mansion of **Burgh House**, on New End Square, dates from the halcyon spa days of Hampstead Wells

– as Hampstead was briefly known – and was at one time occupied by Dr Gibbons, the physician who discovered the spring's medicinal qualities. Surrounded by council housing, it now serves as the **Hampstead Museum**, an exhibition space and a modest local museum, with special emphasis on such notable locals as Constable and Keats; there's also a nice tearoom in the basement.

2 Willow Road

Map 2, G3. Tours April–Oct Thurs–Sat noon–5pm every 45min; Ⓣ020/7435 6166; £4.20. ⊖Hampstead.

Hampstead's newest attraction is **2 Willow Road**, a modernist, red-brick terraced house built in the 1930s by the Hungarian-born architect Ernö Goldfinger. When Goldfinger moved in, this was a state-of-the-art pad, and as he changed little in the house in the following sixty years, what you see is a 1930s avant-garde dwelling preserved in aspic, a house at once both modern and old-fashioned. An added bonus is that the rooms are packed with works of art by the likes of Max Ernst, Duchamp, Henry Moore and Man Ray. There are a limited number of tickets for the **guided tours**, so it's worth booking ahead. Incidentally, James Bond's adversary is indeed named after Ernö – Ian Fleming lived close by and had a deep personal dislike of both Goldfinger and his modernist abode.

Keats' House

Map 2, G3. April–Nov Tues–Sun noon–5pm; £3. ⊖ Hampstead.

Hampstead's most lustrous figure is celebrated at **Keats' House**, an elegant, whitewashed Regency double villa on Keats Grove, a short walk south of Willow Road. Inspired by the peacefulness of Hampstead and by his passion for girl-next-door Fanny Brawne (whose house is also part of the museum), Keats wrote some of his most famous works here before leaving for Rome, where he died from consumption in 1821. The neat, rather staid interior contains books and letters, Fanny's engagement ring and the four-poster bed in which the poet first coughed up blood, confiding to his companion, Charles Brown, "that drop of blood is my death warrant".

Hampstead Heath

Map 2, G2. No set hours.
North London's "green lung", **Hampstead Heath** is the city's most enjoyable public park. It may not have much of its original heathland left, but it packs a wonderful variety of bucolic scenery into its 800 acres. At its southern end are the rolling green pastures of **Parliament Hill**, north London's premier spot for kite-flying. On either side are numerous ponds, three of which – one for men, one for women and one mixed – you can swim in. The thickest woodland is to be found in the **West Heath**, beyond Whitestone Pond, also the site of the most formal section, **Hill Garden**, a secretive and romantic little gem with eccentric balustraded terraces and a ruined pergola. Beyond lies **Golders Hill Park**, where you can gaze at pygmy goats and fallow deer, and inspect the impeccably maintained aviaries, home to flamingos, cranes and other exotic birds.

Finally, don't miss the landscaped grounds of Kenwood, in the north of the Heath, which are focused on the whitewashed, Neoclassical mansion of **Kenwood House** (daily: April–Sept 10am–6pm; Oct 10am–5pm; Nov–March 10am–4pm; free). The house is now home to the **Iveagh Bequest**, a collection of seventeenth- and eighteenth-century art, including a handful of real masterpieces by the likes of Vermeer, Rembrandt, Boucher, Gainsborough and

Reynolds. Of the house's period interiors, the most spectacular is Robert Adam's sky-blue and gold **library**, its book-filled apses separated from the central entertaining area by paired columns. To the south of the house, a grassy amphitheatre slopes down to a lake where outdoor classical concerts are held on summer evenings.

HIGHGATE

Map 2, H2. ⊖ Highgate or bus #210 from Archway ⊖.

Northeast of the Heath, and fractionally lower than Hampstead (appearances notwithstanding), **Highgate** lacks the literary cachet of its neighbour, but makes up for it with London's most famous cemetery, resting place of Karl Marx. It also retains more of its village origins, especially around **The Grove**, Highgate's finest row of houses, the oldest dating as far back as 1685.

To get to the cemetery, head south down Highgate High Street and **Highgate Hill**, with its amazing views towards the City. When you get to the copper dome of "Holy Joe", the Roman Catholic Church which stands on Highgate Hill, pop into the pleasantly landscaped **Waterlow Park**, next door, with its fine café and restaurant.

The park provides a through route to **Highgate Cemetery** (Map 2, H2), which is ranged on both sides of Swain's Lane. Highgate's most famous corpse, that of **Karl Marx**, lies in the **East Cemetery** (daily: April–Sept 10am–5pm; Oct–March 10am–4pm; £1). Marx himself asked for a simple grave topped by a headstone, but by 1954 the Communist movement decided to move his grave to a more prominent position and erect the vulgar bronze bust that now surmounts a granite plinth. Close by lies the much simpler grave of the author George Eliot.

What the East Cemetery lacks in atmosphere is in part compensated for by the fact that you can wander at will through its maze of circuitous paths, whereas to visit the more atmospheric and overgrown **West Cemetery**, with its spooky Egyptian Avenue and terraced catacombs, you must go round with a guided tour (Mon–Fri noon, 2pm & 4pm, Sat & Sun hourly 11am–4pm; £3). Among the prominent graves usually visited are those of artist Dante Gabriel Rossetti, and lesbian novelist Radclyffe Hall.

HENDON: THE RAF MUSEUM

Map 2, E1. Daily 10am–6pm; £7.50; Ⓦ*www.rafmuseum.org.uk* ⊖ Colindale.

A world-class assembly of historic military aircraft can be seen at the **RAF Museum**, located in a godforsaken part of north London beside the M1 motorway. Enthusiasts won't be disappointed, but those looking for a balanced account of modern aerial warfare will – the overall tone is unashamedly militaristic, not to say jingoistic. Those with children should head for the hands-on Fun 'n' Flight gallery; those without might prefer to explore the often overlooked display galleries, ranged around the edge of the Main Aircraft Hall, which contain an art gallery and an exhibition on the history of flight, accompanied by replicas of some of the death-traps of early aviation.

NEASDEN: THE SHRI SWAMINARAYAN TEMPLE

Map 2, D3. Daily 9am–7.30pm; free; Ⓦ*www.swaminarayan-babs.org* ⊖ Stonebridge Park or Neasden.

Perhaps the most remarkable building in the whole of London lies just off the North Circular, in the glum suburb of **Neasden**. Here, rising majestically above the surrounding semi-detached houses like a mirage, is the **Shri Swaminarayan Mandir**, a traditional Hindu temple topped with domes and shikharas, erected in 1995 in a style and scale unseen outside of India for more than a millennium. To reach the temple, you must enter through the adjacent Haveli, or cultural complex, with its carved wooden portico and balcony. After taking off your shoes, you can proceed to the **Mandir** (temple) itself, carved entirely out of Carrara marble, with every possible surface transformed into a honeycomb of arabesques, flowers and seated gods. Beneath the Mandir, an **exhibition** (Mon–Fri 9am–6pm, Sat & Sun 7am–7pm; £2) explains the basic tenets of Hinduism and details the life of Lord Swaminarayan, and includes a video about the history of the building.

South London

Now largely built-up into a patchwork of Victorian terraces, one area of **SOUTH LONDON** stands head and shoulders above all the others in terms of sightseeing, and that is **Greenwich**. At its heart is the outstanding ensemble of the Royal Naval College and the Queen's House, courtesy of Christopher Wren and Inigo Jones respectively. Most visitors, however, come to see the *Cutty Sark*, the National Maritime Museum and the Royal Observatory, though Greenwich also pulls in an ever-increasing volume of Londoners in search of bargains at its Sunday **market**.

Greenwich is, of course, also famous as the "home of time", thanks to its status as the **Prime Meridian of the World**, from where time all over the globe is measured. It's partly for this reason that Greenwich was chosen as the centrepiece of the country's millennium celebrations, though the **Dome** is, in fact, situated in the reclaimed industrial wasteland of North Greenwich, a mile or so northeast of Greenwich town centre.

The only other suburban sights that stand out are the **Dulwich Picture Gallery**, a public art gallery even older than the National Gallery, and the eclectic **Horniman Museum**, in neighbouring Forest Hill.

DULWICH PICTURE GALLERY

Map 2, J7. Tues–Fri 10am–5pm, Sat & Sun 11am–5pm; £4; free all day Fri; Ⓦ*www.dulwichpicturegallery.org.uk*. West Dulwich train station, from Victoria.

Recently refurbished, **Dulwich Picture Gallery**, on College Road, is the nation's oldest public art gallery, designed by Sir John Soane and opened in 1817. Soane created a beautifully spacious building, awash with natural light and crammed with superb paintings – elegiac landscapes by Cuyp, one of the world's finest Poussin series, and splendid works by Hogarth, Gainsborough, van Dyck, Canaletto and Rubens. Rembrandt's *Portrait of a Young Man* is probably the most valuable picture in the gallery, and has been stolen no fewer than four times. At the centre of the museum is a tiny mausoleum designed by Soane for the sarcophagi of the gallery's founders.

THE HORNIMAN MUSEUM

Map 2, J7. Mon–Sat 10.30am–5.30pm, Sun 2–5.30pm; free; Ⓦ*www.horniman.ac.uk*. Forest Hill train station, from Victoria or London Bridge.

To the southeast of Dulwich Park, on the busy South Circular road, is the wacky **Horniman Museum**, purpose-built in 1901 by Frederick Horniman, a tea trader with a passion for collecting. The museum is principally a monument to its creator's freewheeling eclecticism: in addition to its small aquarium and its large collection of stuffed creatures, there's a wide-ranging anthropology section, and a musical department with more than 1500 instruments from Chinese gongs to electric guitars. However, the latter, and the new "centre for understanding the environment", are both undergoing massive rebuilding programmes, and won't be open to the public until 2002.

GREENWICH

Greenwich is one of London's most beguiling spots, and the one place in southeast London that draws large numbers of visitors. At its heart stands one of the capital's finest architectural set pieces, the former Royal Naval College overlooking the Thames. To the west lies Greenwich town centre, while to the south, you'll find Greenwich's two prime tourist sights, the National Maritime Museum and the Royal Observatory. If you're heading straight for either of the latter pair from central London, the quickest way to get there is to take the **train** from Charing Cross (every 30min) to Maze Hill, on the eastern edge of Greenwich Park. Those wanting to start with the town or the *Cutty Sark* should alight at Greenwich station.

A more scenic way of getting to Greenwich is to take a **boat** from one of the piers in central London (see p.13). A third possible option is to take the **Docklands Light Railway** (DLR) to the Cutty Sark station. For the best view of the Wren buildings, though, get out at Island Gardens, and then take the Greenwich Foot Tunnel under the Thames.

GREENWICH PASSPORTS

If you're planning to visit the National Maritime Museum, the Royal Observatory and the *Cutty Sark*, it's worth buying a **Greenwich Passport**, which costs £12 and is valid for two days, and includes a repeat visit to each sight within a year. Alternatively, you can buy a simple combined ticket for the National Maritime Museum and the Royal Observatory for £10.50.

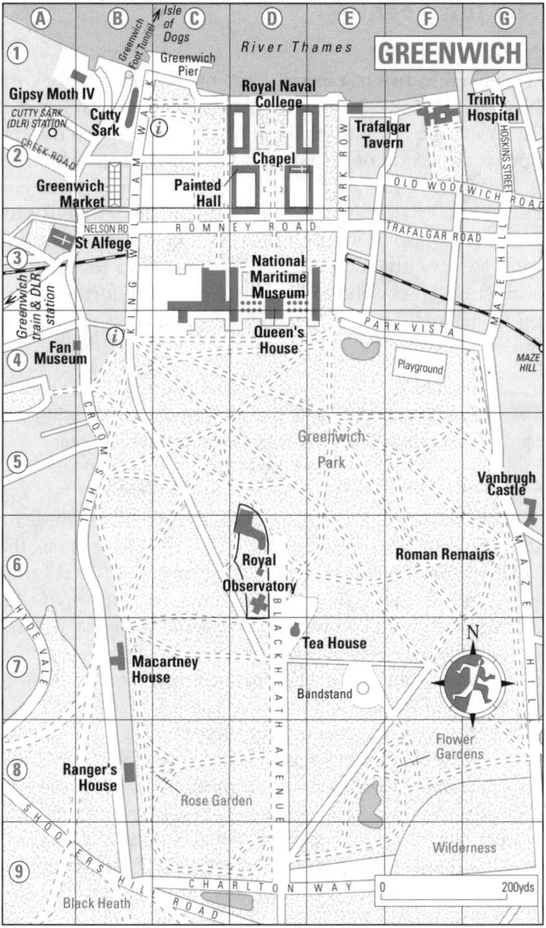

GREENWICH

A B C D E F G
1 2 3 4 5 6 7 8 9

River Thames
Isle of Dogs
Greenwich Foot Tunnel
Greenwich Pier
Gipsy Moth IV
CUTTY SARK (DLR) STATION
Cutty Sark
CREEK ROAD
Greenwich Market
Royal Naval College
Chapel
Painted Hall
Trafalgar Tavern
Trinity Hospital
HOSKINS STREET
OLD WOOLWICH ROAD
KING WILLIAM WALK
PARK ROW
NELSON RD
ROMNEY ROAD
TRAFALGAR ROAD
St Alfege
Greenwich train & DLR station
National Maritime Museum
Queen's House
PARK VISTA
MAZE HILL
Playground
Fan Museum
CROOMS HILL
Greenwich Park
Vanbrugh Castle
Royal Observatory
Roman Remains
HYDE VALE
Tea House
BLACKHEATH AVENUE
Macartney House
Bandstand
N
Flower Gardens
Ranger's House
Rose Garden
Wilderness
SHOOTERS HILL ROAD
CHARLTON WAY
0 200yds
Black Heath

GREENWICH

The town centre

See map on p.0145, B2.

Greenwich town centre, laid out in the 1820s with Nash-style terraces, is nowadays plagued with heavy traffic. To escape the busy streets, head for the old covered market, now at the centre of the weekend **Greenwich Market** (Sat & Sun 9am–5pm), a lively place full of antiques, crafts and clothes stalls that have spilled out up the High Road, Stockwell Road and Royal Hill. The best sections are the indoor secondhand book markets, flanking the Central Market on Stockwell Road; the antiques hall, further down on Greenwich High Road; and the flea market on Thames Street.

Greenwich **tourist office** is at 46 Greenwich Church St (daily: April–Oct 10am–5pm; Nov–March 11am–4pm; Ⓣ0870/608 2000).

A short distance in from the old covered market, on the opposite side of Greenwich Church Street, rises the Doric portico and broken pediment of Nicholas Hawksmoor's **St Alfege's Church** (see map on p.145, A3. Mon–Sat 10am–4pm, Sun 1–4pm; Ⓦ*www.longitude0.co.uk/st-alfege*). Built in 1712–18, the church was flattened in the Blitz, but it has been magnificently restored to its former glory.

Wedged in a dry dock by the Greenwich Foot Tunnel is the majestic **Cutty Sark** (see map on p.145, B2; April–Sept Mon–Sat 10am–6pm, Sun noon–6pm; Oct–March closes 5pm; £3.50; Ⓦ*www.cuttysark.org.uk*), the world's last surviving tea clipper, built in 1869. The *Cutty Sark* lasted just eight years in the China tea trade, and it was as a wool clipper that it actually made its name, returning from Australia in just 72 days. Inside, there's little to see beyond an exhibition in the main hold which tells the ship's story, from its inception to its arrival in Greenwich in 1954.

A mast's length from the *Cutty Sark*, and dwarfed by the bulk of its neighbour, is the tiny **Gipsy Moth**, the 54-foot boat in which, at the age of 66, Francis Chichester became the first person to sail solo around the world, in 1965–66 – he was later knighted for his efforts. The public are not allowed on board, but from the outside, you can glimpse the spartan, cramped interior.

Royal Naval College

See map on p.145, D2. Mon–Sat 10am–5pm, Sun 12.30–5pm; £3; free after 3.30pm & all day Sun.

It's entirely appropriate that the one London building that makes the most of its riverbank location should be the former **Royal Naval College**, Wren's beautifully symmetrical Baroque ensemble, initially built as a royal palace, but eventually converted into a hospital for disabled seamen. From 1873 until 1998 it was home to the Royal Naval College, but now houses the University of Greenwich and the Trinity College of Music.

The two grandest rooms, situated underneath Wren's twin domes, are open to the public and well worth visiting. The entrance to the college is on King William Walk, and visitors are ushered first into the **RNC Chapel** in the east wing. The exquisite pastel-shaded plasterwork and spectacular, decorative detailing on the ceiling were designed by James "Athenian" Stuart after a fire in 1799 destroyed the original interior. From the chapel, you can take the underground Chalk Walk to gain access to the magnificent **Painted Hall** in the west wing, which is dominated by James Thornhill's gargantuan allegorical ceiling painting, and his trompe l'oeil fluted pilasters.

National Maritime Museum

See map on p.145, C3. Daily 10am–5pm; £7.50; ⓦ*www.nmm.ac.uk*

The **National Maritime Museum**, which occupies the old Naval Asylum, has recently undergone a lengthy £20 million redevelopment programme. The main entrance is now on Romney Road, and brings you out into the spectacular glass-roofed central courtyard, which houses the museum's largest artefacts, among them the splendid 63ft-long gilded **Royal Barge**, designed in Rococo style by William Kent for Prince Frederick, the much unloved eldest son of George II.

The various themed galleries are superbly designed to appeal to visitors of all ages, In "Explorers", on Level 1, you get to view some of the museum's most highly prized relics, such as **Captain Cook**'s sextant and K1 marine clock, Shackleton's compass, and **Captain Scott**'s furry sleeping bag and sledging goggles. Sponsors P&O get to display their wares in "Passengers", which traces the history of modern passenger liners, and "Cargoes", which concentrates on containerization. On Level 2, there's a large maritime **art gallery**, an eco-conscious section on the future of the sea and biodiversity, and a gallery devoted to the legacy of the British Empire, warts and all.

Level 3 boasts two **hands-on galleries**: "The Bridge", where you can attempt to navigate a catamaran, a paddle steamer and a rowing boat to shore; and "All Hands", where children can have a go at radio transmission, loading miniature cargo, firing a cannon and so forth. Finally, you reach the **Nelson Gallery**, which contains the museum's vast collection of Nelson-related memorabilia, including Turner's *Battle of Trafalgar, 21st October, 1805*, his largest work and only royal commission.

Inigo Jones's **Queen's House**, originally built amidst a rambling Tudor royal palace, is now the focal point of the

Greenwich ensemble, and is an integral part of the Maritime Museum. As royal residences go, it's an unassuming country house, but as the first Neoclassical building in the country, it has enormous architectural significance. The interior is currently used for temporary exhibitions. Nevertheless, one or two features survive (or have been reinstated) from Stuart times. Off the Great Hall, a perfect cube, lies the beautiful Tulip Staircase, Britain's earliest cantilevered spiral staircase – its name derives from the floral patterning in the wrought-iron balustrade.

THE MILLENNIUM DOME

London's controversial **Millennium Dome** is clearly visible from the riverside at Greenwich and from the upper parts of Greenwich Park. Built at a cost approaching £800 million, and designed by Richard Rogers (of Lloyd's Building and Pompidou Centre fame), it is by far the world's largest dome – over half a mile in circumference and 160ft in height – held up by a dozen, 300ft-tall yellow steel masts. In 2000, for one year only, it housed the nation's chief millennium extravaganza: an array of high-tech themed zones set around a stage, on which a circus-style performance took place twice a day.

Like most grand projects, the Dome had a rough ride from the press right from the beginning. The hiccups and headaches continued into the year 2000, with bad reviews and over-optimistic estimates of visitor numbers costing the first Dome chief her job. Nevertheless, millions paid up £20 each to visit the Dome, and millions went away happy. Nobody quite knows what the future holds for the Dome, which has its very own, very large, very fancy Jubilee line tube station, also designed by Norman Foster. Various organizations, including Charlton Athletic football club, have put in bids to take over the site, but no decision had been made as the book went to print.

The Royal Observatory

See map on p.145, D6. Daily 10am–5pm; £6;
www.rog.nmm.ac.uk

Crowning the highest hill in Greenwich Park, behind the National Maritime Museum, the **Royal Observatory** was established in 1675 by Charles II to house the first Astronomer Royal, John Flamsteed. Flamsteed's chief task was to study the night sky in order to discover an astronomical method of finding the longitude of a ship at sea, the lack of which was causing enormous problems for the emerging British Empire. Astrologers continued to work here at Greenwich until the postwar smog forced them to decamp to Herstmonceux Castle and the clearer skies of Sussex (they've since moved to the Pacific); the old observatory, meanwhile, is now a very popular museum.

Greenwich's greatest claim to fame is of course as the home of **Greenwich Mean Time** (GMT) and the Prime Meridian. Since 1884, Greenwich has occupied zero longitude, which means the entire world sets its clocks by GMT. What the Royal Observatory don't tell you is that the meridian has, in fact, moved. Nowadays, longitude is calculated by a differential Global Positioning Receiver, served by several US military satellites, which places the meridian 336ft to the east of the brass strip in the courtyard that marks the Greenwich Meridian.

The oldest part of the observatory is the Wren-built **Flamsteed House**, whose northeastern turret sports a bright red time-ball that climbs the mast at 12.58pm and drops at 1pm GMT precisely; it was added in 1833 to allow ships on the Thames to set their clocks. Passing quickly through Flamsteed's restored apartments and the Octagon Room, where the king used to show off to his guests, you reach the Chronometer Gallery, which focuses on the search for the precise measurement of longitude, and displays four of the clocks designed by John Harrison, including "H4", which helped win the Longitude Prize in 1763.

Flamsteed's own meridian line is a brass strip in the floor of the Meridian Building. Edmond Halley, Flamsteed's successor, who charted the comings and goings of the famous comet, worked out his own meridian, and the Bradley Meridian Room reveals yet another, standard from 1750 to 1850 and still used for Ordnance Survey maps. Finally, you reach a room that's spliced in two by the present-day Greenwich Meridian, fixed by the cross-hairs in Airy's "Transit Circle", the astrological instrument that dominates the room.

The exhibition ends on a soothing note in the Telescope Dome of the octagonal **Great Equatorial Building**, home to Britain's largest telescope. In addition, there are half-hourly presentations in the Planetarium (Mon–Fri 2.30pm; £2), housed in the adjoining South Building.

The Ranger's House

See map on p.145, B8. April–Sept daily 10am–6pm; Oct–March Wed–Sun 10am–4pm; £2.50.

Southwest of the observatory, and backing onto Greenwich park's rose garden, is the **Ranger's House**, a red-brick Georgian villa that houses a collection of paintings donated by the 19th Countess of Suffolk, whose portrait, by John Singer Sargent, hangs in the foyer. The high points of the art collection are undoubtedly William Larkin's full-length portraits of a Jacobean wedding party. The commercial art gallery on the first floor is worth skipping, though, in favour of the Architectural Study Centre across the stable yard, filled with all manner of bits and bobs salvaged from London's buildings. Entrance to the house is either from Croom's Hill, or from the doorway in the wall by the park's Rose Garden. However, the house is likely to be closed until 2002, so phone ahead before you set out.

The Fan Museum

See map on p.145, A4. Tues–Sat 11am–5pm, Sun noon–5pm; £3.50; Ⓦ*www.fan-museum.org*

Croom's Hill boasts some of Greenwich's finest Georgian buildings, one of which houses the **Fan Museum** at no. 12. It's a fascinating little place (and an extremely beautiful house), revealing the importance of the fan as a social and political document. The permanent exhibition on the ground floor traces the history of the materials employed, from peacock feathers to straw, while temporary exhibitions on the first floor explore such subjects as techniques of production and changing fashion.

Chiswick to Windsor

Most people experience west London en route to or from Heathrow airport, either from the confines of the train or tube (which runs overground most of the way) or the motorway. The city and its satellites seem to continue unabated, with only fleeting glimpses of the countryside. However, in the five-mile stretch from Chiswick to Osterley there are several former country retreats, now surrounded by suburbia, which are definitely worth digging out.

The Palladian villa of **Chiswick House** is perhaps the best known of these attractions, though it draws nothing like as many visitors as **Syon House**, most of whom come for the gardening centre rather than for the house itself, a showcase for the talents of Robert Adam, who also worked at **Osterley House**, another Elizabethan conversion, now owned by the National Trust.

Running through much of the chapter is the **River Thames**, once known as the "Great Highway of London" and still the most pleasant way to travel in these parts during the summer. Boats plough up the Thames all the way

RIVER TRANSPORT

Westminster Passenger Services (Ⓣ020/7930 4721; Ⓦ*www.wpsa.co.uk*) run two to three **boats** between Westminster and Hampton Court daily from April to September, calling at Kew and Richmond; the full trip takes 3–4hr one-way, and costs £10 single, £14 return.

from central London, via the **botanical gardens of Kew** and the picturesque riverside at **Richmond**, as far as **Hampton Court**, home of the country's largest and most impressive royal residence (and the famous maze). To reach the heavily touristed royal outpost of **Windsor Castle**, however, you really need to take the train.

CHISWICK HOUSE

Map 2, E6. April–Sept daily 10am–6pm; first three weeks of Oct daily 10am–5pm; late-Oct to March Wed–Sun 10am–4pm; £3.30. Chiswick train station, from Waterloo.

Chiswick House is a perfect little Neoclassical villa, designed by the third Earl of Burlington in the 1720s, and set in one of the most beautifully landscaped gardens in London. Like its Palladian prototype, the house was purpose-built as a "temple to the arts" – here, amid his fine art collection, Lord Burlington could entertain artistic friends such as Swift, Handel and Pope. Visitors enter via the lower floor, where you can pick up an audioguide, before heading up to the upper floor, a series of cleverly interconnecting rooms, each enjoying a wonderful view out onto the gardens – all, that is, except the Tribunal, the central octagonal hall, where the earl's finest paintings and sculptures would have been displayed.

To do a quick circuit of the gardens, head across the

smooth carpet of grass, punctuated by urns and sphinxes, that sit under the shadow of two giant cedars of Lebanon. A great place from which to admire the northwest side of the house is from the stone benches of the exedra, a set of yew-hedge niches harbouring lions and copies of Roman statuary, situated beyond the cedars. Elsewhere, there's an Italian garden, a maze of high-hedge alleyways, a lake and a grassy amphitheatre, centred on an obelisk in a pond and overlooked by an Ionic temple.

HOGARTH'S HOUSE

Map 2, E5. April–Oct Tues–Fri 1–5pm, Sat & Sun 1–6pm; Nov–March Tues–Fri 1–4pm, Sat & Sun 1–5pm; closed Jan; free.

If you leave Chiswick House gardens by the northernmost exit, beyond the Italian garden, it's just a short walk along the thunderous A4 road to **Hogarth's House**, where the artist spent each summer from 1749 until his death in 1764. Nowadays it's difficult to believe Hogarth came here for "peace and quiet", but in the eighteenth century the house was almost entirely surrounded by countryside. Amongst the scores of Hogarth's engravings, you can see copies of his satirical series – *An Election, Marriage à la Mode, A Rake's Progress* and *A Harlot's Progress* – and compare the modern view from the parlour with the more idyllic scene in *Mr Ranby's House.*

KEW BRIDGE STEAM MUSEUM

Map 2, D5. Daily 11am–5pm; Mon–Fri £3; Sat & Sun £4; ⓦ*www.kbsm.org.uk*. Kew Bridge train station, from Waterloo; or bus #237 or #267 from ⊖ Gunnersbury.

Difficult to miss thanks to its stylish Italianate standpipe tower, **Kew Bridge Steam Museum** occupies a former pumping station, on the corner of Kew Bridge Road and Green Dragon Lane, 100m west of the bridge itself. At the heart of the museum is the Steam Hall, which contains a triple expansion steam engine and four gigantic nineteenth-century Cornish beam engines, while two adjoining rooms house the pumping station's original beam engines, one of which is the largest in the world.

The steam engines may be things of great beauty, but they are primarily of interest to enthusiasts. Not so the museum's new state-of-the-art "Water for Life" gallery in the basement, devoted to the history of the capital's water supply. The best time to visit is at weekends, when each of the museum's industrial dinosaurs is put through its paces, and the small narrow-gauge steam railway runs back and forth round the yard.

THE MUSICAL MUSEUM

Map 2, D5. April–Oct Sat & Sun 2–5pm; July & Aug also Wed 2–4pm; £3.50. Kew Bridge train station, from Waterloo; or bus #237 or #267 from ⊖ Gunnersbury.

Five minutes' walk west of the Steam Museum along Kew Bridge Road and Brentford High Street is the superb **Musical Museum**, a converted church packed with musical automata and run by wildly enthusiastic and engaging volunteers. During the noisy ninety-minute demonstrations, you get to hear every kind of mechanical music-making machine, from cleverly crafted music boxes to the huge orchestrions that were once a feature of London's swish cafés. The museum also boasts one of the world's finest collections of player-pianos, and an enormous Art Deco Wurlitzer cinema organ.

SYON HOUSE

Map 2, C6. Mid-March to Oct Wed, Thurs & Sun 11am–5pm; £6, including gardens Ⓦ*www.syonpark.co.uk* Bus #237 or #267 from ⊖ Gunnersbury or Kew Bridge train station.

Syon, seat of the Dukes of Northumberland since Elizabethan times, is now more of a working commercial concern than a family home, embracing a garden centre, a wholefood shop, a trout fishery, an aquatic centre stocked with tropical fish, a mini-zoo and a butterfly house, as well as the old aristocratic mansion and its gardens.

From its rather plain, castellated exterior, you'd never guess that **Syon House** contains the most opulent eighteenth-century interiors in the whole of London. The splendour of Robert Adam's refurbishment is immediately revealed, however, in the pristine Great Hall, an apsed double cube with a screen of Doric columns at one end and classical statuary dotted around the edges. There are several more Adam-designed rooms to admire in the house, plus a smattering of works by van Dyck, Lely, Gainsborough and Reynolds.

While Adam beautified Syon House, Capability Brown laid out its **gardens** (daily 10am–5pm; £3) around an artificial lake, surrounding the water with oaks, beeches, limes and cedars. The gardens' chief focus now, however, is the crescent-shaped **Great Conservatory**, an early nineteenth-century addition which is said to have inspired Joseph Paxton, architect of the Crystal Palace. Those with young children will be compelled to make use of the **miniature steam train** which runs through the park at weekends from April to October, and on Wednesdays during the school holidays.

Another plus-point for kids is Syon's **Butterfly House** (daily: May–Sept 10am–5.30pm; Oct–April 10am–3.30pm; £3.30; Ⓦ*www.butterflies.org.uk*), a small, mesh-covered hothouse, where you can walk amid hundreds of exotic butterflies from all over the world, as they flit about the foliage. An adjoining room houses a collection of iguanas, millipedes, tarantulas and giant hissing Tanzanian cockroaches.

If your kids show more enthusiasm for life-threatening reptiles than delicate insects, then you could skip the butterflies and go instead for the adjacent **London Aquatic Experience** (daily: April–Sept 10am–6pm; Oct–March 10am–5pm; £3.50; *www.aquatic-experience.org*), a purpose-built centre with a mixed range of aquatic creatures from the mysterious basilisk, which can walk on water, to the perennially popular piranhas.

OSTERLEY

Map 2, B5. Park: daily 9am–7.30pm or dusk; free. House: April–Oct Wed–Sun 1–4.30pm; £4.20. ⊖ Osterley.

Robert Adam redesigned another colossal Elizabethan mansion three miles northwest of Syon at **Osterley Park**, which maintains the impression of being in the middle of the countryside, despite the presence of the M4 to the north of the house. The park itself is well worth exploring, and there's a great café in the Tudor stables, but anyone with a passing interest in Adam's work should pay a visit to **Osterley House** itself. If you arrive by public transport, you get a £1 reduction off the price of your ticket.

From the outside, Osterley bears some similarity to Syon, the big difference being Adam's grand entrance portico, with its tall, Ionic colonnade. From here, you enter a characteristically cool Entrance Hall, followed by the so-called State Rooms of the south wing. Highlights include the Drawing Room, with Reynolds portraits on the damask walls and a coffered ceiling centred on a giant marigold, and the Etruscan Dressing Room, in which every surface is covered in delicate painted trelliswork, sphinxes and urns, a style that Adam (and Wedgwood) dubbed "Etruscan", though it is in fact derived from Greek vases found at Pompeii.

KEW GARDENS

Map 2, C6. Daily 9.30am–7.30pm or dusk; £5; Ⓦ*www.kew.org*
⊖ Kew Gardens.

Established in 1759, the **Royal Botanical Gardens** have grown from their original eight acres into a 300-acre site in which more than 33,000 species are grown in plantations and glasshouses, a display that attracts over a million visitors every year, most of them with no specialist interest at all. There's always something to see, whatever the season, but to get the most out of the place, come sometime between spring and autumn, bring a picnic and stay for the day. The only drawbacks to Kew are the high entry fee, and the fact that it lies on the main (and very noisy) flight path to Heathrow.

There are four entry points to the gardens, but the majority of people arrive at Kew Gardens tube and train station, a few minutes' walk east of the **Victoria Gate**. Of all the glasshouses, by far the most celebrated is the **Palm House**, a curvaceous mound of glass and wrought-iron designed by Decimus Burton in the 1840s. Its drippingly humid atmosphere nurtures most of the known palm species, while there's a small but excellent tropical aquarium in the basement. South of here is the largest of the glasshouses, the **Temperate House**, which contains plants from every continent, including one of the largest indoor palms in the world, the sixty-foot Chilean Wine Palm.

Kew's origins as an eighteenth-century royal pleasure garden are evident in the numerous follies dotted about the gardens, the most conspicuous of which is the ten-storey, 163-foot-high **Pagoda**, visible to the south of the Temperate House. The three-storey red-brick mansion of **Kew Palace**, to the northwest of the Palm House, bought by George II as a nursery for his umpteen children, has recently been restored and is worth a peek (there is a separate entrance charge). A sure way to lose the crowds is to head for the thickly wooded, southwestern section of the park around **Queen Charlotte's Cottage** (April–Sept Sat & Sun 10.30am–4pm; free), a tiny thatched summerhouse built in the 1770s as a royal picnic spot for George III's queen.

RICHMOND

Map 2, D7. ⊖ Richmond.

On emerging from the station at **Richmond**, you'd be forgiven for wondering why you're here, but the procession of chain stores spread out along the one-way system is only half the story. To see the area's more interesting side, take one of the narrow pedestrianized alleyways off busy George Street, which bring you to the wide open space of **Richmond Green**, one of the finest village greens in London, and no doubt one of the most peaceful before it found itself on the main flight path into Heathrow. Handsome seventeenth- and eighteenth-century houses line the south side of the Green, where the medieval royal palace of Richmond once stood, though only the unspectacular **Tudor Gateway** survives today.

The other place to head for in Richmond is the **Riverside**, pedestrianized, terraced and redeveloped in ersatz classical style in the 1980s. The real joy of the waterfront, however, is **Richmond Bridge**, London's oldest extant bridge, an elegant span of five arches made from Purbeck stone in 1777. The old town hall, set back from the new development, houses the **tourist office** (Mon–Sat 10am–5pm; Easter–Sept also Sun 10.15am–1.30pm; ⓣ020/8940 9125), and, on the second floor, the **Richmond Museum** (Tues–Sat 11am–5pm; May–Oct also Sun 1–4pm; £2), but most folk prefer to ensconce themselves in the riverside pubs, or head for the numerous boat- and bike-hire outlets.

Richmond's greatest attraction, though, is the enormous **Richmond Park** (daily March–Sept 7am–dusk; Oct–Feb 7.30am–dusk; free; Ⓦ*www.royalparks.co.uk*), at the top of Richmond Hill – 2500 acres of undulating grassland and bracken, dotted with coppiced woodland and as wild as anything in London. Eight miles across at its widest point, this is Europe's largest city park, famed for its red and fallow deer, which roam freely, and for its ancient oaks. For the most part untamed, the park does have a couple of deliberately landscaped plantations which feature splendid springtime azaleas and rhododendrons, in particular the **Isabella Plantation**.

HAM HOUSE

Map 2, C7. March, Nov & Dec Sat & Sun 11am–4.30pm; April–Oct Mon–Wed, Sat & Sun 11am–5.30pm; £5, including gardens. Bus #371 or walk from ⊖ Richmond.

Continuing along the towpath beyond Richmond Bridge, you'll arrive at **Ham House** after a mile or so, home to the Earls of Dysart for nearly three hundred years. Expensively furnished in the seventeenth century, and little altered since then, the house boasts one of the finest Stuart interiors in the country, from the stupendously ornate Great Staircase to the Long Gallery, featuring six "Court Beauties" by Peter Lely. Elsewhere, there are several fine ceiling paintings, some exquisite parquet flooring, and works by van Dyck and Reynolds. Another bonus are the formal seventeenth-century **gardens** (open all year Mon–Wed, Sat & Sun 10.30am–6pm; £1.50), especially the Cherry Garden, laid out with a pungent lavender parterre, and surrounded by yew hedges and pleached hornbeam arbours. The Orangery, overlooking the original kitchen garden, serves as a tearoom.

HAMPTON COURT PALACE

Map 2, B9. Mid-March to mid-Oct Mon 10.15am–6pm, Tues–Sun 9.30am–6pm; mid-Oct to mid-March closes 4.30pm; £10.50; Ⓦ*www.hrp.org.uk*. Hampton Court train station, from Waterloo.

Hampton Court Palace, a sprawling red-brick ensemble on the banks of the Thames, thirteen miles southwest of London, is the finest of England's royal abodes. Built in 1516 by the upwardly mobile **Cardinal Wolsey**, Henry VIII's Lord Chancellor, it was purloined by Henry himself after Wolsey fell from favour. Charles II laid out the gardens, inspired by what he had seen at Versailles, while William and Mary had large sections of the palace remodelled by Wren.

The **Royal Apartments** are divided into six thematic walking tours. There's not a lot of information in any of the rooms, but guided tours, each lasting 45 minutes, are available at no extra charge for Henry VIII's and the King's apartments; all are led by period-costumed historians, who do a fine job of bringing the place to life. If your energy is lacking – and Hampton Court is huge – the most rewarding sections are: **Henry VIII's State Apartments**, which feature the glorious double hammerbeamed Great Hall; the **King's Apartments** (remodelled by William III); and the vast **Tudor Kitchens**. The last two are also served by audio tours.

Tickets to the Royal Apartments cover entry to the rest of the sites in the grounds. Those who don't wish to visit the apartments are free to wander around the gardens, but will have to pay extra to visit the curious **Royal Tennis Courts** (50p), the palace's famously tricky hedge **Maze** (£2.30), and the **South Gardens** (£2.10), where you can view Andrea Mantegna's colourful, heroic canvases, *The Triumphs of Caesar*, housed in the Lower Orangery, and the celebrated **Great Vine**, whose grapes are sold at the palace each year in September.

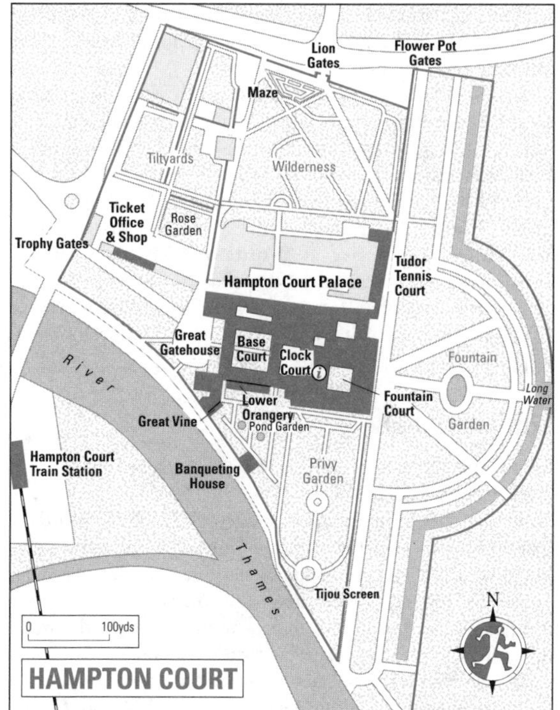

WINDSOR AND ETON

Every weekend, trains from Waterloo and Paddington are packed with people heading for **Windsor**, the royal enclave 21 miles west of London, where they join the human conveyor belt round Windsor Castle. Though almost as famous as Windsor, **Eton** (across the river from the castle) receives a mere fraction of the tourists, yet the guided tours of the school give an eye-opening glimpse of life as lived by the offspring of Britain's upper classes.

Windsor has two **train stations**, both very close to the centre. Direct trains from Waterloo (Mon–Sat every 30min, Sun hourly; journey time 50min) arrive at **Windsor & Eton Riverside**, five minutes' walk from the centre; trains from Paddington require a change at Slough (Mon–Fri every 20min; Sat & Sun every 30min; journey time 30–40min), and arrive at **Windsor & Eton Central**, directly opposite the castle. Note that you must arrive and depart from the same station, as tickets are not interchangeable. The **tourist office** (daily 10am–4pm; longer hours in summer; ⓣ01753/743900) is at 24 High St.

Windsor Castle

Daily: March–Oct 9.45am–5.15pm; Nov–Feb 9.45am–4.15pm; £10.50; ⓦ*www.royal.gov.uk*

Towering above the town on a steep chalk bluff, **Windsor Castle** is an undeniably awesome sight, its chilly grey walls, punctuated by mighty medieval bastions, continuing as far as the eye can see. Once there, the small selection of state rooms open to the public are unexciting, though the magnificent St George's Chapel and the chance to see another small selection of the Queen's private art collection make the trip worthwhile. On a fine day, it pays to put aside some time for exploring Windsor Great Park, which stretches for several miles to the south of the castle.

Once inside the castle, it's best to head straight for **St George's Chapel** (Mon–Sat 10am–4pm), a glorious Perpendicular structure ranking with Henry VII's chapel in Westminster Abbey, and the second most important resting place for royal corpses after the Abbey. Entry is via the south door and a one-way system operates, which brings you out by the **Albert Memorial Chapel**, built by Henry VII as a burial place for Henry VI, completed by Cardinal Wolsey for his own burial, but eventually converted for Queen Victoria into a High Victorian memorial to her husband, Prince Albert.

The Changing of the Guard takes place at Windsor April–June Mon–Sat at 11am; alternate days the rest of the year.

Before entering the State Apartments, pay a quick visit to **Queen Mary's Dolls' House**, a palatial micro-residence designed for the wife of George V, and the **Gallery**, where special exhibitions culled from the Royal Collection are staged. Most visitors just gape in awe at the gilded grandeur of the **State Apartments**, while the real highlights – the paintings from the Royal Collection that line the walls – are rarely given a second glance. The **King's Dressing Room**, for example, despite its small size, contains a feast of art treasures, including a dapper Rubens self-portrait, van Dyck's famous triple portrait of Charles I, and *The Artist's Mother*, a perfectly observed portrait of old age by Rembrandt.

You'd hardly know that Windsor suffered the most devastating **fire** in its history in 1992, so thorough (and uninspired) has the restoration been in rooms such as **St George's Hall**. By contrast, the octagonal **Lantern Lobby**, beyond, is clearly an entirely new room, a safe neo-Gothic design replacing the old chapel. At this point, those visiting during the winter season (Oct–March) are given the privilege of seeing four **Semi-State Rooms**, created in the 1820s by George IV, and still used in the summer months by the Royal Family.

Most tourists are put off going to **Windsor Great Park** due to its sheer scale. With the Home Park – including

Victoria and Albert's mausoleum of Frogmore – off limits to the public, except for a very few days in each year, visitors can only enter the park via the three-mile Long Walk. Another mile or so to the south is **Savill Garden** (daily: March–Oct 10am–6pm; Nov–Feb 10am–4pm; £4), a 35-acre patch of woodland that has one of the finest floral displays in and around London.

Eton College

College and chapel: Easter, July & Aug daily 10.30am–4.30pm; after Easter to June & Sept daily 2–4.30pm; £2.70; guided tours daily 2.15pm & 3.15pm; £4; ⓦ*www.etoncollege.com*

Crossing the bridge at the end of Thames Avenue in Windsor town brings you to **Eton**, a one-street village lined with bookshops and antique dealers, but famous all over the world for **Eton College**, a ten-minute walk from the river. When the school was founded in 1440, its aim was to give free education to seventy poor scholars and choristers; how times have changed. The original fifteenth-century **schoolroom**, gnarled with centuries of graffiti, survives, but the real highlight is the **College Chapel**, completed in 1482, a wonderful example of English Perpendicular architecture. The self-congratulatory **Museum of Eton Life**, where you're deposited at the end of the tour, is well worth missing unless you have a fascination with flogging, fagging and bragging about the school's facilities and alumni.

LISTINGS

Accommodation

There's no getting away from the fact that **accommodation** in London is expensive. Compared with most European cities, you pay over the odds in every category. The city's hostels are among the most expensive in the world, while venerable institutions such as the *Ritz*, the *Dorchester* and the *Savoy* charge guests the very top international prices – up to £300 or more per luxurious night.

The cheapest places to stay are the dorm beds of the city's numerous independent **hostels**, followed closely behind by the official YHA hostels. Even the most basic **B&Bs** struggle to bring their tariffs down to £40 for a double with shared facilities, and you're more likely to find yourself paying £50 or more.

When choosing your **area**, bear in mind that the West End – Soho, Covent Garden, St James's, Mayfair and Marylebone – and the western districts of Knightsbridge and Kensington, are dominated by expensive, upmarket hotels. For cheaper rooms, the widest choice is close to the main train termini of Victoria and Paddington, and the budget B&Bs of Earl's Court. Those close to King's Cross cater for those on welfare, or charge by the hour, although neighbouring Bloomsbury is both inexpensive and very central.

If you want to avoid the hassle of contacting individual

hotels and B&Bs, you could turn to one of the various **accommodation agencies**. All London tourist offices operate a room-booking service, which costs £5 (they also take the first night's fee in advance); with a credit card, you can also book over the phone or online (Ⓣ020/7604 2890; Ⓦ*www.londontown.com*).

In addition, **Thomas Cook** has accommodation desks at Charing Cross (Ⓣ020/7976 1171), Euston (Ⓣ020/7388 7435), Gatwick Airport (Ⓣ01293/529372), King's Cross (Ⓣ020/7837 5681), Paddington (Ⓣ020/7837 5681) and Victoria (Ⓣ020/7828 4646) train stations, plus Earl's Court (Ⓣ020/7244 0908) and South Kensington (Ⓣ020/7581 9766) tubes. Most open daily from 7am till 11pm, and will book anything from youth hostels through to five-star hotels (£5 fee). There's also a Thomas Cook desk at the British Visitor Centre on Lower Regent Street (see p.7).

The **British Hotel Reservation Centre** (BHRC; Ⓦ*www.bhrc.co.uk*) has desks at Heathrow arrivals, as well as at both Heathrow underground stations (Ⓣ020/8564 8808 or 8564 8211), and both terminals of Gatwick Airport (Ⓣ01293/502433). There are also four desks in and around Victoria: at the train station (Ⓣ020/7828 1027), coach station (Ⓣ020/7824 8232), underground (Ⓣ020/7828 2262) and at 13 Grosvenor Gardens (Ⓣ020/7828 2425). Most offices are open daily from 6am till midnight and most charge a £5 fee. The Victoria coach station and Heathrow underground offices offer their services free of charge, and you can book for free over the phone.

You can also book hotels and B&Bs online via **Web sites** such as Ⓦ*www.lastminute.com*, who almost always offer discounts, or through Ⓦ*www.hotelsengland.com*.

HOSTELS

London's official **Youth Hostel Association (YHA) hos-**

tels are generally the cleanest, most efficiently run hostels in the capital. There's no age limit, and if you're not already a member, you can join on the spot. You can book a bed over the phone with a credit card by ringing individual hostels, or by contacting the **YHA central reservations** (Ⓣ020/7373 3400; Ⓦ*www.yha.org.uk*). **Independent hostels** are cheaper and more relaxed, but can be less reliable in terms of facilities. Typical of this hippyish brand of hostel is the Astor chain of five hostels, run exclusively for the 18-30 age group.

YHA HOSTELS

Oxford Street

Map 3, G4. 14 Noel St, W1
Ⓣ020/7734 1618
Ⓦ*www.yha.org.uk*
⊖ Oxford Circus or Tottenham Court Road
Its unbeatable West End location and modest size (75 beds in rooms of 2, 3 and 4 beds) mean that this hostel tends to be full even out of high season. No children under 6, no groups, no café, but a large kitchen. £20.55 per person in a double room, or £21.80 per person in a twin room.

St Pancras

Map 3, H2. 79–81 Euston Rd, NW1
Ⓣ020/7388 9998
Ⓦ*www.yha.org.uk*
⊖ King's Cross or Euston
Big hostel situated opposite the new British Library, on the busy Euston Road. Beds cost £22.95 per person, and rooms are very clean, bright, triple-glazed and air-conditioned – some even have en-suite facilities. There are a few en-suite doubles and family rooms available with TVs for £50. No groups.

City of London

Map 5, H4. 36 Carter Lane, EC4
Ⓣ020/7236 4965
Ⓦ*www.yha.org.uk*
⊖ St Paul's
200-bed hostel in great situation opposite St Paul's Cathedral; some twins at £50 a room, but mostly 4- and

5-bed dorms for £22.95 per person, or triple bunks in larger dorms for £20.50 per person. No groups.

Holland House

Map 2, F5. Holland Walk, W8
Ⓣ 020/7937 0748
Ⓦ *www.yha.org.uk*
⊖ Holland Park or High Street Kensington
Idyllically situated in the wooded expanse of Holland Park and fairly convenient for the centre of town, this extensive hostel offers a decent kitchen and an inexpensive café. Popular with school groups. Dorms only at £19.95 per person.

Hampstead Heath

Map 2, G2. 4 Wellgarth Rd, NW11
Ⓣ 020/8458 9054
Ⓦ *www.yha.org.uk*
⊖ Golders Green
One of London's biggest and best-appointed YHA hostels, with its own garden and the wilds of Hampstead Heath nearby. Rooms with 3–6 beds cost £19.70; family rooms with 2–5 beds are also available, starting at £35 for one adult and one child or £45 for two adults.

Earl's Court

Map 3, A8. 38 Bolton Gardens, SW5
Ⓣ 020/7373 7083
Ⓦ *www.yha.org.uk*
⊖ Earl's Court
Better than a lot of accommodation in Earl's Court, but only offering dorms of mostly 10 beds – the triple-bunks take some getting used to. Kitchen, café and patio garden. No groups. £19.95 per person.

PRIVATE HOSTELS

Generator

Map 3, H2. Compton Place, off Tavistock Place, WC1
Ⓣ 020/7388 7666
Ⓦ *www.the-generator.co.uk*
⊖ Russell Square or Euston
The neon- and UV-lighting and post-industrial décor may not be to everyone's tastes, but the youthful clientele certainly enjoy the cheap bar that's open daily until 2am. Over 800 beds, and prices that vary from £38 for a

single to £26 each for a double, £22 each for a triple, £20 for a bed in a shared room and £15 for a dorm bed.

Leinster Hostel

Map 3, A5. 7–12 Leinster Square, W2
Ⓣ 020/7229 9641
Ⓦ *www.scoot.co.uk/astorhostels*
⊖ Queensway or Notting Hill Gate
The biggest and liveliest of the Astor hostels, with a party atmosphere, and two bars open until the small hours. Dorm beds (3–7 per room) £14–17, singles £30, doubles £40.

Museum Hostel

Map 3, I3. 27 Montague St, W1
Ⓣ 020/7580 5360
Ⓦ *www.scoot.co.uk/astorhostels*
⊖ Russell Square
In a lovely Georgian house by the British Museum, this is the quietest of the Astor hostels. There's no bar, but it's still a sociable, laid-back place, and well situated. Dorms with 4–10 beds per room from £14–17, including breakfast. Small kitchen, TV lounge, and baths as well as showers.

St Christopher's Village

Map 8, E9. 161–165 Borough High St, SE1
Ⓣ 020/7407 1856
Ⓦ *www.st-christophers.co.uk*
⊖ London Bridge
A new chain of independent hostels, with no fewer than three properties on Borough High Street (and more branches in Camden and Greenwich). The décor is upbeat and cheerful, the place is efficiently run and there's a party-animal ambience, fuelled by the neighbouring bar and the rooftop sauna and pool.

Tonbridge Club

Map 3, I2. 120 Cromer St, WC1
Ⓣ 020/7837 4406
⊖ King's Cross
This is a real last resort, but if you're desperate (and a non-British passport holder), you can sleep on a mattress on the floor for £5 per person. Hot showers, TV room. Check-in 9pm–midnight.

HOTELS AND B&BS

Most B&Bs and hotels are housed in former residential properties, which means that rooms tend to be on the small side, and that only the more upmarket properties have lifts. That said, most rooms have TVs, tea- and coffee-making facilities and telephones, and breakfast is nearly always included in the price.

The recommendations below cover every category from budget to luxury, though the bulk cost between £50–90 per double. Bear in mind that many of the plush hotels listed slash their advertised rates at the weekend when the business types have gone home.

Most places take all major **credit cards**, particularly Visa and Access/MasterCard, so in the listings we've simply noted those that don't.

ACCOMMODATION PRICE CODES

All hotel accommodation has been graded on a scale of ①–⑨ to the minimum nightly charge you can expect to pay for a double room in high season (breakfast is generally included in the price). The prices signified by these categories are as follows:

① under £40	④ £60–70	⑦ £110–150
② £40–50	⑤ £70–90	⑧ £150–200
③ £50–60	⑥ £90–110	⑨ over £200

ST JAMES'S, MAYFAIR AND MARYLEBONE

Edward Lear Hotel

Map 3, E4. 28–30 Seymour St, W1
Ⓣ 020/7402 5401
Ⓦ *www.edlear.com*
⊖ Marble Arch

Former home of the famous poet and artist, decorated with lovely flower boxes, and boasting a plush foyer and a great location close to Oxford Street and Hyde Park. The rooms themselves are less remarkable, but the low prices reflect both this and the fact that most only have shared facilities. Kids free at weekends. ❹.

Hotel La Place

Map 3, E3. 17 Nottingham Place, W1
Ⓣ 020/7486 2323
Ⓦ *www.hotellaplace.com*
⊖ Baker Street

Just off the busy Marylebone Road, this is a small, good-value place; rooms are all en suite, equipped with all the gadgets usually found in grander establishments, and comfortably furnished. ❻.

The Metropolitan

Map 3, F6. Old Park Lane, W1
Ⓣ 020/7447 1000
Ⓦ *www.metropolitan.co.uk*
⊖ Green Park or Hyde Park Corner

Run by Christina Ong, this terrifyingly trendy hotel near the *Hilton* adheres to the 1990s fad for pared-down minimalism. The staff are kitted out in DKNY clothes, the Japanese restaurant is outstanding, and the *Met* bar is members and residents only in the evenings. Double rooms start at £270. ❾.

The Ritz

Map 7, B2. 150 Piccadilly, W1
Ⓣ 020/7493 8181
Ⓦ *www.theritzhotel.co.uk*
⊖ Green Park

In a class of its own among London's hotels, with its extravagant Louis XVI interiors and overall air of decadent luxury. Rooms, which start at around £350 for a double, maintain the opulent French theme, with the west-facing accommodation, overlooking Green Park, in greatest demand. Ask about the special weekend packages, including breakfast and champagne, available throughout the year. ❾.

Wigmore Court Hotel

Map 3, E4. 23 Gloucester Place, W1
Ⓣ 020/7935 0928
Ⓦ *www.wigmore-court-hotel.co.uk*
⊖ Marble Arch or Baker Street

The relentlessly pink décor may not be to everyone's taste, but this Georgian town house is a better than average B&B, boasting a high tally of returning clients. Comfortable rooms with en-suite facilities, plus two doubles with shared facilities for just £70. Unusually, there's also a laundry and basic kitchen for guests' use. ❺.

SOHO, COVENT GARDEN AND THE STRAND

The Fielding Hotel

Map 4, M3. 4 Broad Court, Bow St, WC2
Ⓣ 020/7836 8305
Ⓦ *www.the-fielding-hotel.co.uk*
⊖ Covent Garden

Quietly and perfectly situated on a traffic-free and gas-lit court, this excellent hotel is one of Covent Garden's hidden gems. Its en-suite rooms are a firm favourite with visiting performers, since it's just a few yards from the Royal Opera House. Breakfast is extra. ❻.

Hazlitt's

Map 4, G3. 6 Frith St, W1
Ⓣ 020/7434 1771
Ⓔ *reservations@hazlitts.co.uk*
⊖ Tottenham Court Road

Located off the south side of Soho Square, this early-eighteenth-century building is a hotel of real character and charm, offering en-suite rooms decorated and furnished as close to period style as convenience and comfort allow. There is no dining room, but some of London's best restaurants are a stone's throw away; continental breakfast (served in the rooms) is available, but isn't included in the rates. ❾.

Manzi's

Map 4, H6. 1–2 Leicester St, WC2
Ⓣ 020/7734 0224
Ⓔ *manzis@netscapeonline.co.uk*
⊖ Leicester Square

Set over the Italian and seafood restaurant of the same name, *Manzi's* is one of very few central hotels in this price range. It's certainly right in the thick of the West End, just off Leicester Square, although noise might prove to be a nuisance. Continental breakfast is included in the price. ❺.

One Aldwych

Map 5, 6A. 1 Aldwych, WC2
Ⓣ 020/7300 1000
Ⓦ *www.onealdwych.co.uk*
⊖ Covent Garden or Temple

On the outside, this is one of London's few vaguely Art Nouveau buildings, built in 1907 for the *Morning Post* newspaper. However, little survives from those days, as the interior of this desperately fashionable luxury hotel firmly follows the 1990s minimalist trend. The draws now are the underwater music in the hotel's vast pool, the oodles of modern art about the place, and the TVs in the bathrooms of the £300-plus rooms. ❾.

St Martin's Lane

Map 4, K6. 45 St Martin's Lane, WC2
Ⓣ 020/7300 5500 or 0800/634 5500
Ⓔ *stmartinslane@compuserve.com*
⊖ Leicester Square

So cool you wouldn't know it was a hotel, this self-consciously chic "boutique hotel" from the New York-based Ian Schrager chain has proved an immediate hit with the media crowd. From the fluorescent yellow-and-white minimalist lobby to the large Portuguese limestone bathrooms, the interior has been designed throughout by the mischievous Philippe Starck. The *Light Bar* and the sushi *Sea Bar* are the most startling of the hotel's numerous eating and drinking outlets. Rooms currently start at around £250 a double, but rates come down at the weekend. ❾.

Sanderson

Map 3, G4. 50 Berners St, W1
Ⓣ 020/7300 1400
Ⓔ *sanderson.isuk@virginnet.co.uk*
⊖ Tottenham Court Road or Oxford Circus

This second collaboration by Schrager and Starck, set in an unlikely-looking block of 1960s offices just off Oxford Street, is a listed building, so new spaces and partitions have all had to be created by curtains. The usual assemblage of objets d'art peppers the white and magnolia lobby, where the black-clad staff flit about like silhouettes. The *Long Bar* (open to non-residents) is all transluscent backlit onyx, with a lovely outdoor courtyard. 3D "space" lifts take you to the equally bright white rooms (starting at around £250 a double), decked out with light wooden floors and billowing curtains. There's a large gym, steam room, sauna and health club on site. ❾.

The Savoy

Map 4, N6. Strand, WC2
Ⓣ 020/7836 4343
Ⓦ *www.savoy-group.co.uk*
⊖ Charing Cross

The *Savoy* is a byword for luxury and service, though in some respects, the charisma of the place is what keeps it ahead of many of its rivals. Rooms, which start at around £400 a double (weekend rates are considerably less) are decorated in the Deco style of the hotel's heyday or in a more classical vein. Guests have the use of gym and small pool on the third floor. The *Grill* is justly famed for its excellent cuisine, while the *American Bar* features jazz most evenings. Breakfast is served on the *Thames Foyer*, which peers through trees onto the river. ❾.

Strand Continental Hotel

Map 5, A6. 143 Strand, WC2
Ⓣ 020/7836 4880
Ⓕ 020/7379 6105
⊖ Temple or Covent Garden

This tiny Indian-run hotel near Aldwych offers very basic rooms with shared facilities, plus continental breakfast. Rooms have had a lick of paint in the not too distant past, but nothing too drastic, making this an unbeatable central London bargain. Cash only. ❷.

BLOOMSBURY

Hotel Cavendish

Map 3, H3. 75 Gower St, WC1
Ⓣ 020/7636 9079
Ⓦ *www.hotelcavendish.com*
⊖ Goodge Street
Gower Street is very busy with traffic, but get a room at the back of the property and you'll have a peaceful night, and a real bargain, too, with lovely owners, two beautiful overrun gardens and some quite well-preserved original features. All rooms have shared facilities, and there are some good-value family rooms, too. ❸.

Crescent Hotel

Map 3, H2. 49–50 Cartwright Gardens, WC1
Ⓣ 020/7387 1515
Ⓦ *www.crescenthoteloflondon.com*
⊖ Euston or Russell Square
Very comfortable and tastefully decorated Regency B&B – definitely a cut above the rest, with a lovely blacked-up range in the breakfast room. All doubles are en suite and have TVs, but there are a few bargain singles with shared facilities; guests also have use of tennis courts in the nearby gardens. ❺.

Jenkins Hotel

Map 3, H2. 45 Cartwright Gardens, WC1
Ⓣ 020/7387 2067
Ⓦ *www.jenkinshotel.demon.co.uk*
⊖ Euston or Russell Square
Smartly kept, family-run place in this fine Regency crescent, with just fourteen fairly small but well-equipped and very clean rooms, some en-suite, some with shared facilities. The lovely in-house black labrador is a big hit with visitors, and a full English breakfast is included in the price. ④.

myhotel

Map 3, H3. 11–13 Bayley St, WC1
Ⓣ 020/7667 6000
Ⓦ *www.myhotels.co.uk*
⊖ Tottenham Court Road
The aquarium in the lobby is

the tell-tale sign that this is a feng shui hotel. Despite the positive vibes, and Conran-designed look, the double-glazed, air-conditioned rooms are on the small side for the price. Still, there's a gym, a very pleasant library, a restaurant attached and the location is great for the West End. ❽.

Ridgemount Hotel

Map 3, H3. 65–67 Gower St, WC1
Ⓣ 020/7636 1141
Ⓕ 020/7636 2558
⊖ Goodge Street

Old fashioned, family-run place, with small rooms, mostly with shared facilities, a garden, free hot-drinks machine and a laundry room. Cash only, but a reliable, basic bargain for Bloomsbury. ❷.

Hotel Russell

Map 3 H3. Russell Square, WC1
Ⓣ 020/7837 6470
Ⓦ *www.principalhotels.co.uk*
⊖ Russell Square

From its grand 1898 exterior to its opulent interiors of marble, wood and crystal, this late-Victorian landmark fully retains its period atmosphere in all its public areas. The rooms have less character, but all are well appointed and decorated in a homely manner. Expensive, but various deals are available subject to availability. Breakfast is not included. ❽.

CLERKWENWELL AND THE CITY

City Hotel

Map 7, M2. 12 Osborn St, E1
Ⓣ 020/7247 3313
Ⓔ *info@cityhotellondon.co.uk*
⊖ Aldgate East

Spacious, clean and modern inside, this hotel stands on the eastern edge of the City, and in the heart of the Bengali East End at the bottom of Brick Lane. The plainly-decorated rooms are all en suite, and many have kitchens, too; four-person rooms are a bargain if you're in a small group. ❼.

Great Eastern Hotel

Map 7, I1. Liverpool Street, EC2

Ⓣ 020/7618 5000
Ⓦ *www.great-eastern-hotel.co.uk*
⊖ Liverpool Street
Without doubt, *the* place to stay if you need or wish to be near the City. This venerable late-nineteenth-century station hotel has had a complete Conran makeover, yet manages to retain much of its clubby flavour. The *George* pub boasts a superb mock-Tudor ceiling; the fabulous old lobby is now the *Aurora* restaurant, and the rooms themselves are impeccably well-appointed and tastefully furnished – to maximize your natural light, get a room facing out. Doubles start from around £250, but rates are cut at the weekend. ❾.

Jurys Inn

Map 3, J1. 60 Pentonville Rd, N1
Ⓣ 020/7282 5500
Ⓦ *www.jurys.com*
⊖ Angel
This modern Irish chain hotel is not a pretty sight on the busy Pentonville Road, but it's close to the tube, and equally convenient for the City and for Islington and Clerkenwell's trendy bars and restaurants. Service is very friendly, and the fixed room-rate is a bargain for three adults sharing or for those with kids. ❺.

The Rookery

Map 3, K3. Peter's Lane, Cowcross St, EC1
Ⓣ 020/7336 0931
⊖ Farringdon
Rambling Georgian town house on the edge of the City in trendy Clerkenwell that makes a fantastically discreet little hideaway. The rooms start at around £225 a double; each one has been individually designed in a sort of camp, modern take on the Baroque period, and all have super bathrooms with lots of character. ❽.

SOUTHWARK

London County Hall Travel Inn

Map 6, A6. Belvedere Rd, SE1
Ⓣ 020/7902 1619
Ⓦ *www.travelinn.co.uk*

⊖ Waterloo or Westminster.
Don't expect river views at these prices, but the location in County Hall itself is pretty good if you're up for a bit of sightseeing. Décor and ambience is functional, but for those with kids, the flat-rate rooms are a bargain. ❹.

Mad Hatter

Map 6, F2. 3–7 Stamford St, SE1
Ⓣ 020/7401 9222
Ⓔ *madhatter@fullers.co.uk*
⊖ Southwark or Blackfriars
Situated above a Fuller's pub on the corner of Blackfriars Road, and run by the Fuller's brewery. Breakfast is extra, and is served in the pub, but this is a great location, a short walk from the Tate Modern and the South Bank. Ask about the weekend deals. ❺.

VICTORIA

Elizabeth Hotel

Map 3, G7. 37 Eccleston Square, SW1
Ⓣ 020/7828 6812
Ⓦ *www.elizabeth-hotel.com*
⊖ Victoria
Comfortable and elegantly furnished hotel, very close to the train and coach stations and providing en-suite and more basic rooms at a decent price. Large TV lounge, and the gardens and tennis courts of Eccleston Square can be used by hotel residents. ❹.

The Goring

Map 3, F7. 15 Beeston Place, SW1
Ⓣ 020/7396 9000
Ⓦ *www.goringhotel.co.uk*
⊖ Victoria
Owned and run by the Goring family for three generations, this Edwardian hotel succeeds in creating an atmosphere of elegance and tranquillity, despite its position amid busy roads. Afternoon tea is served on the delightful private garden-terrace in fine weather; doubles start at £210 (breakfast not included). ❾.

Melbourne House Hotel

Map 3, G8. 79 Belgrave Rd, SW1
Ⓣ 020/7828 3516
Ⓕ 020/7828 7120
⊖ Victoria or Pimlico
One of the best B&Bs along

Belgrave Road: family run, well furnished, offering clean and bright rooms, excellent communal areas and friendly service. All doubles have en-suite facilities, but there are a couple of very cheap singles without. ❺.

Oxford House Hotel

Map 3, F8. 92–94 Cambridge St, SW1
Ⓣ 020/7834 6467
Ⓕ 020/7834 0225
⊖ Victoria

Probably the best-value rooms you can get in the vicinity of Victoria station. Showers and toilets are shared, but kept pristine. Full English breakfast is included in the price. ❷.

Sanctuary House

Map 7, F7. 33 Tothill St, SW1
Ⓣ 020/7799 4044
Ⓔ *sanctuary@fullers.demon.co.uk*
⊖ St James's Park

Run by Fuller's Brewery, situated above a Fuller's pub, and decked out like one, too, in smart, pseudo-Victoriana. Breakfast is extra, and is served in the pub, but the location right by St James's Park is very central. Ask about the weekend deals. ❻.

Topham's Hotel

Map 3, F7. 26 Ebury St, SW1
Ⓣ 020/7730 8147
Ⓦ *www.tophams.co.uk*
⊖ Victoria

Charming family-owned hotel in the English country-house style, just a couple of minutes' walk from Victoria station. Sumptuously furnished en-suite twins or doubles from £120, including full English breakfast. ❼.

Windermere Hotel

Map 3, F8. 42–144 Warwick Way, SW1
Ⓣ 020/7834 5163
Ⓦ *www.windermere-hotel.co.uk*
⊖ Sloane Square, Pimlico or Victoria

Situated at the western end of Warwick Way, this is a tastefully decorated and quietly stylish place, with a couple of good-value doubles with shared facilities, and en-suite doubles for considerably more. There's a tasty restaurant downstairs, too. ❹–❼.

Woodville House and Morgan House

Map 3, F7. 107 and 120 Ebury St, SW1
Ⓣ 020/7730 1048 or 7730 2384
Ⓦ *www.woodvillehouse.co.uk*
⊖ Victoria
Two above-average B&Bs, run by the same vivacious couple, with great breakfasts, patio gardens, and an iron and fridge for guests to use. All rooms at *Woodville* are with shared facilities; some at *Morgan* are en suite. ❹.

PADDINGTON, BAYSWATER AND NOTTING HILL

The Columbia

Map 3, C5. 95–99 Lancaster Gate, W2
Ⓣ 020/7402 0021
Ⓦ *www.columbiahotel.co.uk*
⊖ Lancaster Gate
The spacious public lounge, well-worn décor and useful 24-hour bar make this large white stucco hotel a rock-band favourite. The en-suite rooms themselves are actually very sober, and retain some original Victorian fittings. ❺.

Garden Court Hotel

Map 3, A4. 30–31 Kensington Garden Square, W2
Ⓣ 020/7229 2553
Ⓦ *www.gardencourthotel.co.uk*
⊖ Bayswater or Queensway
Presentable, family-run B&B on a quiet square close to Portobello market; half the rooms are with shared facilities, half are en-suite. Full English breakfast included. ❷.

The Gresham Hotel

Map 3, C4. 116 Sussex Gardens, W2
Ⓣ 020/7402 2920
Ⓦ *www.the-gresham-hotel.co.uk*
⊖ Paddington
B&B with a touch more class than many on Sussex Gardens. Rooms are small but tastefully kitted out, and all have TV. Continental breakfast included. ❺.

Inverness Court Hotel

Map 3, A5. 1 Inverness Terrace, W2
Ⓣ 020/7229 1444
Ⓕ 020/7229 3666
⊖ Bayswater or Queensway
Late-Victorian facade, reception area, bar and lounges lend a charming

ambience, even if most of the en-suite bedrooms are in an undistinguished modern style. Continental breakfast included. ❻.

Pavilion Hotel

Map 3, C4. 34–36 Sussex Gardens, W2
Ⓣ 020/7262 0905
Ⓦ *www.eol.net.mt/pavilion*
⊖ Paddington
The successful rock star's home-from-home, a self-styled "groovy crash pad" with outrageously over-the-top, kitsch bric-a-brac décor and every room individually themed from 1970s "Honky Tonk Afro" to Moorish "Casablanca Nights". ❻.

Pembridge Court Hotel

Map 3, A5. 34 Pembridge Gardens, W11
Ⓣ 020/7229 9977
Ⓦ *www.pemct.co.uk*
⊖ Notting Hill Gate or Holland Park
Attractively converted grandiose Victorian town house close to Portobello market, with spacious, fully equipped rooms. Two resident cats add to the homely feel, as does the lively *Caps Restaurant and Bar.* ❽.

KNIGHTSBRIDGE, KENSINGTON AND CHELSEA

Abbey House

Map 3, A6. 11 Vicarage Gate, W8
Ⓣ 020/7727 2594
⊖ High Street Kensington or Notting Hill
Inexpensive Victorian B&B in a quiet street just north of Kensington High Street, maintained to a very high standard by its attentive owners. Rooms are large and bright – prices are kept down by sharing facilities rather than fitting the usual cramped bathroom unit. Full English breakfast, with free tea and coffee available all day. Cash only. ❺.

Aster House

Map 3, C8. 3 Sumner Place, SW7
Ⓣ 020/7581 5888
Ⓦ *www.welcome2london.com*
⊖ South Kensington
Pleasant, non-smoking B&B

in a luxurious white-stuccoed South Ken street; there's a lovely garden at the back and a large conservatory, where breakfast is served. Singles with shared facilities start at a bargain £70 a night. ❽.

Blakes

Map 3, B8. 33 Roland Gardens, SW7
Ⓣ 020/7370 6701
Ⓔ *blakes@easynet.co.uk*
⊖ Gloucester Road

Blakes' dramatic interior – designed by Anouska Hempel – and glamorous suites have long attracted visiting celebs. A faintly Rafflesesque flavour pervades, with bamboo furniture and old travelling trunks mixing with unusual objets d'art, tapestries and prints. Doubles from £220 are smart but small; fully equipped suites are spectacular, as they should be for £495. The restaurant and bar are excellent, and service is of a very high standard. ❾.

Five Sumner Place

Map 3, C8. 5 Sumner Place, SW7
Ⓣ 020/7584 7586
Ⓦ *www.sumnerplace.com*
⊖ South Kensington

Discreetly luxurious B&B in one of South Ken's prettiest white stucco terraces. All rooms are en suite and breakfast is served in the house's lovely conservatory. ❽.

The Gore

Map 3 B7. 189 Queen's Gate, SW7
Ⓣ 020/7584 6601
Ⓔ *sales@gorehotel.co.uk*
⊖ South Kensington, Gloucester Road or High Street Kensington

Popular, privately owned century-old hotel, awash with oriental rugs, rich mahogany, walnut panelling and other Victoriana. A pricey, but excellent bistro restaurant adds to its allure, and it's only a step away from Hyde Park. ❽.

The Hempel

Map 3, B5. 31–35 Craven Hill Gardens, W2
Ⓣ 020/7298 9000
Ⓦ *www.thehempelhotel.com*
⊖ Lancaster Gate or Queensway

Deeply fashionable minimalist

hotel, designed by the actress Anouska Hempel, with a huge and very empty atrium entrance. White-on-white rooms start around £290 a double, and there's an excellent postmodern Italian/Thai restaurant called *I-Thai*. ❾.

Hotel 167

Map 3, B8. 167 Old Brompton Rd, SW5
Ⓣ 020/7373 0672
Ⓦ *www.hotel167.com*
⊖ Gloucester Road
Small, stylishly furnished B&B with en-suite facilities, double glazing and a fridge in all rooms. Continental buffet-style breakfast is served in the attractive morning room/reception. ❻.

The Lanesborough

Map 3, E6. Hyde Park Corner, SW1
Ⓣ 020/7259 5599
Ⓦ *www.lanesborough.com*
⊖ Hyde Park Corner
A former hospital, this early nineteenth-century building has been meticulously restored in Regency style, with all mod cons discreetly hidden amid the ornate décor. Double rooms cost over £350, service is formal and the overall ambience conservative, in keeping with the tone of the diplomatic neighbourhood. ❾.

Vicarage Hotel

Map 3, A6. Vicarage Gate, W8
Ⓣ 020/7229 4030
Ⓦ *www.londonvicaragehotel.com*
⊖ High Street Kensington or Notting Hill
Ideally located B&B a step away from Hyde Park. Clean rooms with shared facilities and a full English breakfast. Cash/travellers' cheques only. ❹.

HAMPSTEAD

Hampstead Village Guesthouse

Map G3. 2 Kemplay Rd, NW3
Ⓣ 020/7435 8679
Ⓔ *hvguesthouse@dial.pipex.com*
⊖ Hampstead
Lovely B&B in an old house set in a quiet backstreet between Hampstead village and the Heath. Rooms (some

en suite, all non-smoking) have "lived-in" clutter, which makes a pleasant change from anodyne hotels and spartan B&Bs. Meals to order. ❺.

La Gaffe

Map 2, G2. 107–111 Heath St, NW3
Ⓣ 020/7435 4941
Ⓔ *la-gaffe@msn.com*
⊖ Hampstead
Small and warren-like but characterful hotel, situated over an Italian restaurant and bar in the heart of Hampstead village. All rooms are en suite and there's a roof terrace for use in fine weather. ❺.

EARL'S COURT

Philbeach Hotel

Map 3, A8. 30–31 Philbeach Gardens, SW5
Ⓣ 020/7373 1244
Ⓦ *www.philbeachhotel.freeserve.co.uk*
⊖ Earl's Court
Friendly, long-running gay/transvestite hotel, with basic and en-suite rooms, a pleasant TV lounge area, late bar and popular *Wilde About Oscar* garden restaurant. ❹.

Rushmore Hotel

Map 3, A8. 11 Trebovir Rd, SW5
Ⓣ 020/7370 3839
Ⓕ 020/7370 0274
⊖ Earl's Court
A cut above the average, with its colourful murals, imaginative Italianate room décor and conservatory in this often dreary area. The attic rooms are especially spacious and comfortable. Full continental breakfast is included in the rates. ❺.

York House Hotel

Map 3, A8. 28 Philbeach Gardens, SW5
Ⓣ 020/7373 7519
Ⓔ *yorkhh@aol.com*
⊖ Earl's Court
B&B in a quiet crescent right next to the Exhibition Centre; some en-suite rooms and more basic alternatives, all including English breakfast. Friendly service and a lovely garden. ❸.

Cafés and snacks

This chapter covers **cafés**, **coffee bars**, **ice-cream parlours** and **tearooms**, all of which you'll find open during the day for light snacks or just a drink. Some of them also provide full evening meals, and, as they make no pretence to being full-on restaurants, you can use them for an inexpensive or quick bite before going out to a theatre, cinema or club.

The listings here cover the full range, from unreconstructed workers cafés, where you can get traditional English breakfasts, fish and chips, pies and other calorific treats, to the refined salons of London's top hotels, where you can enjoy an Afternoon Tea blowout.

SNACKS, SANDWICHES, CAKES AND COFFEE

As well as the places we've listed below, there are several **London-wide chains** that are well worth checking out. **EAT** (Ⓦ *www.eatcafe.co.uk*) is a promising newcomer, and makes up excellent sandwiches on their own-baked bread; **Pret à Manger** also does ready-made sandwiches (though it helps if you like mayo), as well as hot stuffed croissants and sushi selections. **Caffè Nero** serves terrific coffee, a range of Italian cakes, and pasta, calzone and pizza. As far as other coffee chains go; there's **Costa Coffee**, the train station favourite, which serves some of the best coffee in town, as does **Starbucks** (Ⓦ *www.starbucks.com*), the infamous clean-cut Seattle coffee company – **Coffee Republic** is a slightly less memorable replica; the only drawback to **Aroma**, with its bright Aztec colours, designer sandwiches and Portuguese pastries, is that the whole chain is now owned by McDonalds. Also worth bearing in mind are the **Häagen-Dazs** outlets scattered around the capital, which offer cakes, sundaes, shakes and coffee alongside ice creams in a huge range of flavours.

MAYFAIR AND MARYLEBONE

La Madeleine

Map 4, C6. 5 Vigo St, W1 Ⓣ020/7734 8353. ⊖ Green Park or Piccadilly Circus. Mon–Sat 8am–8pm, Sun 11am–7pm.

An authentic French patisserie and café, with mountains of tempting pastries from which to indulge yourself while seated at the tables towards the front of the café; those at the back are for punters who want more substantial bistro fare.

Patisserie Valerie at Sagne

Map 3, E3. 105 Marylebone High St, W1 Ⓣ020/7935 6240; Ⓦ*www.patisserie-valerie.co.uk* ⊖ Bond Street or Baker Street. Mon–Fri 7.30am–7pm, Sat 8am–7pm, Sun 9am–6pm.

Founded as *Maison Sagne* in the 1920s, and preserving its wonderful décor from those days, the café is now run by Soho's fab patisserie makers, and is Marylebone's finest without doubt.

SOHO

Bar Italia

Map 4, H3. 22 Frith St, W1 Ⓣ020/7437 4520. ⊖ Leicester Square. Closed Mon–Thurs 5–7am.

A tiny café that's a Soho institution, serving coffee, croissants and sandwiches more or less around the clock

– as it has been since 1949. Popular with late-night clubbers and those here to watch the Italian-league soccer on the giant screen.

The Living Room

Map 4, G3. 3 Bateman St, W1 ⓣ020/7437 4827. ⊖ Tottenham Court Road. Mon–Sat 8am–10pm, Sun noon–10pm.

Hidden away in a Soho backstreet, this welcoming, laid-back café serves good sandwiches and cakes, and has groovy music as well as great armchairs and tatty sofas to chill out on.

Maison Bertaux

Map 4, H3. 28 Greek St, W1 ⓣ020/7437 6007. ⊖ Leicester Square. Mon–Sat 9am–8pm, Sun 9am–1pm & 3–8pm.

Long-standing, old-fashioned and downbeat Soho patisserie, with tables on two floors (and one or two outside) and a loyal clientele that keeps things busy. You'll be tempted in by the window full of elaborate cakes, but be warned: the service can be brusque and when it comes to coffee, they only do *café au lait*.

Patisserie Valerie

Map 4, H3. 44 Old Compton St, W1 ⓣ020/7437 3466; ⓦ*www.patisserie-valerie.co.uk* ⊖ Leicester Square or Piccadilly Circus. Mon–Fri 7.30am–10pm, Sat & Sun 9.30am–7pm.

Popular coffee, croissant and cake emporium dating from the 1920s and attracting a loud-talking, arty Soho crowd. The same outfit now have a branch at 8 Russell St, WC2, and also run *Patisserie Valerie at Sagne* in Marylebone (see opposite) and the café inside the RIBA building on Portland Place (see p.142).

COVENT GARDEN AND BLOOMSBURY

Coffee Gallery

Map 3, H3. 23 Museum St, WC1 ⓣ020/7436 0455. ⊖ Tottenham Court Road. Mon–Fri 8.30am–5.30pm, Sat 10.30am–5.30pm, Sun 12.30–6pm.

Excellent, if small, café close by the British Museum, serving mouthwatering Italian sandwiches and more substantial dishes at

INTERNET CAFÉS

If you just need to send a quick email to someone, or go online, head for a branch of *easyEverything* (Ⓦ *www.easyeverything.com*), the no-frills Internet café chain – there's a 24hr branch just up the Strand, off Trafalgar Square. Alternatively, the Internet cafés listed below are worth a visit in their own right.

Global Café
Map 4, D5. 15 Golden Square, W1 Ⓣ 020/7287 2242; Ⓦ *http://gold.globalcafe.co.uk.* Mon–Fri 9am–11pm, Sat 10am–11pm, Sun 11am–11pm. ⊖ Piccadilly Circus.
Pleasant, roomy Soho café, with helpful staff and a choice of bagels, double-decker sandwiches, coffee, tea and beer. Access to the terminals costs around £3 per half-hour; Saturday nights are women-only.

The Vibe Bar
Map 2, J4. Truman Brewery, 91 Brick Lane, E1 Ⓣ 020/7247 3479; Ⓦ *www.vibe-bar.co.uk*
⊖ Aldgate East. Mon–Sat 11am– 11pm. Head for "Room Service", a row of terminals in the corner of this trendy bar in a former East End brewery; Internet access is free of charge.

lunchtime. Get there early to grab a seat.

Mode

Map 4, K2. 57 Endell St, WC2 Ⓣ 020/7240 8085. ⊖ Covent Garden. Mon–Fri 8am–10pm, Sat 9am–9pm.
The best things about this stylish Covent Garden café are the Italian sandwiches, the cheeses from nearby Neal's Yard Dairy, and the laid-back, funky atmosphere.

Monmouth Coffee Company

Map 4, J3. 27 Monmouth St, WC2 Ⓣ 020/7836 5272. ⊖ Covent Garden or Leicester Square.

Mon–Sat 9am–6pm.
The marvellous aroma is the first thing you notice here, while the cramped wooden booths and daily newspapers on hand evoke an eighteenth-century coffee house atmosphere – pick and mix your coffee from a fine selection (or buy the beans to take home). No smoking.

CLERKENWELL, THE CITY AND THE EAST END

Brick Lane Beigel Bake

Map 2, J4. 159 Brick Lane, E1 ⓣ 020/7729 0616. ⊖ Shoreditch or Aldgate East. Daily 24hr.
The bagels at this no-frills takeaway in the heart of the East End are freshly made and unbelievably cheap, even when stuffed with smoked salmon and cream cheese.

Feast

Map 3, K3. 86 St John St, EC1 ⓣ 020/7253 7007. ⊖ Farringdon or Barbican. Mon–Fri 7.30am–4.30pm.
Delicious tortilla-wrapped sandwiches made to order; takeaway or eat in this small, trendy, designer Clerkenwell café.

LAMBETH AND SOUTHWARK

Konditor & Cook

Map 6, E5. Young Vic Theatre, 66 The Cut, E1 ⓣ 020/7729 0616. ⊖ Waterloo. Mon–Fri 8.30am–11pm, Sat 10.30am–11pm.
Cut above your average theatre café, this place gets its cakes and so forth made by the fabulous *Konditor & Cook* bakery, round the corner in Cornwall Road. You can also get snacks, organic ice creams and sorbets, and, of course, drinks at the bar.

KENSINGTON, CHELSEA AND NOTTING HILL

Books for Cooks

Map 2, F4. 4 Blenheim Crescent, W11 ⓣ 020/7221 1992; ⓦ *www.booksforcooks.com* ⊖ Ladbroke Grove or Notting Hill Gate. Mon–Sat

9.30am–6pm.
Tiny café/restaurant within London's top cookery bookshop. Conditions are cramped, but this is an experience not to be missed. Just wander in and have a coffee while browsing, or ring ahead to book a table for lunch. No smoking.

Lisboa Patisserie

Map 2, F4. 57 Golborne Rd, W10 ⓣ020/8968 5242. ⊖ Ladbroke Grove. Daily 8am–8pm.
Authentic and friendly Portuguese *pastelaria*, with coffee and cakes including the best custard tarts this side of Lisbon. The *Oporto*, at 62a Golborne Rd is a good fallback if this place is full.

Maison Blanc

Map 2, F5. 102 Holland Park Ave, W11 ⓣ020/7221 2494. ⊖ Holland Park. Mon–Sat 8am–7pm, Sun 8.30am–6pm.
French patisserie (with other branches in St John's Wood, Hampstead, Chelsea and Richmond) where you can guarantee you'll get the real thing when it comes to croissants and the like.

Raison d'Etre

Map 3, C7. 18 Bute St, SW7 ⓣ020/7584 5008. ⊖ South Kensington. Mon–Fri 8am–6pm, Sat 8am–4pm.
Smack in the middle of South Kensington's French quarter, this is a top-notch patisserie/boulangerie, serving excellent coffee.

NORTH LONDON

Café Delancy

Map 2, H3. 3 Delancy St, NW1 ⓣ020/7387 1985. ⊖ Camden Town or Mornington Crescent. Daily 9am–midnight.
Still probably the best French-style café in Camden, tucked away down a side road off Camden High Street; coffee, croissants, snacks and full meals.

Café Mozart

Map 2, H2. 17 Swains Lane, N6 ⓣ020/8348 1384. Gospel Oak train station, or bus #C2. Daily 9am–10pm.
Viennese café that's usefully close to the southeast side of

AFTERNOON TEA

The classic English **afternoon tea** – assorted sandwiches, scones and cream, cakes and tarts and, of course, lashings of tea – is available all over London. Best venues are the capital's top hotels and most fashionable department stores; a selection of the best is picked out below. To avoid disappointment it's best to book ahead. Expect to spend £15–20 a head, and leave your jeans and trainers at home – most hotels will expect men to wear a jacket of some sort, though only the *Ritz* insists on jacket and tie.

Brown's
Map 4, A7. 33–34 Albemarle St, W1 ⓣ 020/7493 6020; ⓦ *www.brownshotel.com* ⊖ Green Park. Daily 3–6pm.

Claridge's
Map 3, A5. Brook St, W1 ⓣ 020/7629 8860; ⓦ *www.savoy-group.co.uk* ⊖ Bond Street. Daily 3–5.30pm.

The Dorchester
Map 3, E5. 54 Park Lane, W1 ⓣ 020/7629 8888; ⓦ *www.dorchesterhotel.com* ⊖ Hyde Park Corner. Daily 3–6pm.

Lanesborough
Map 3, E6. Hyde Park Corner, SW1 ⓣ 020/7259 5599; ⓦ *www.lanesborough.com* ⊖ Green Park. Daily 3.30–6pm.

The Ritz
Map 4, A9. Piccadilly, W1 ⓣ 020/7493 8181; ⓦ *www.theritzhotel.co.uk* ⊖ Green Park. Daily 2–6pm.

The Savoy
Map 4, N6. Strand, WC2 ⓣ 020/7836 4343; ⓦ *www.savoy-group.co.uk* ⊖ Charing Cross tube. Daily 3–5.30pm.

The Waldorf
Map 5, A5. Aldwych, WC2 ⓣ 020/7836 2400; ⓦ *www.forte-hotels.com* ⊖ Holborn or Temple tube. Mon–Fri 3–5.30pm; tea dances Sat 2.30–5pm, Sun 4–6.30pm.

Hampstead Heath, and also serves a few hearty Austrian dishes.

Louis Patisserie

Map 2, G2. 32 Heath St, NW3 ⓣ020/7435 9908. ⊖ Hampstead. Daily 9am–6pm.
Popular central-European tearoom in Hampstead village serving sticky cakes to a mix of Heath-bound hordes and elderly locals.

Marine Ices

Map 2, G3. 8 Haverstock Hill, NW3 ⓣ020/7482 9003. ⊖ Chalk Farm. Mon–Sat 10am–11pm, Sun 10am–10pm.
Situated halfway between Camden and Hampstead, this is a splendid and justly famous old-fashioned Italian ice-cream parlour; pizza and pasta are served in the adjacent restaurant.

GREENWICH

Pistachio's Café

See p.145, B3. 15 Nelson Rd, SE10 ⓣ020/8853 0602. Cutty Sark DLR, or Greenwich DLR and train station. Daily 10am–6pm.
Just about the only good sandwich café in the centre of Greenwich, serving excellent coffee, and with a small garden out back.

BREAKFASTS, LUNCHES AND QUICK MEALS

There are cafés and small, basic restaurants all over London that can rustle up an inexpensive meal. You should be able to fill up at all of the places listed in this section for under £10, including tea or coffee.

Many of these cafés also feature big **English breakfasts** – fried egg, bacon, sausage and chips, usually available till 11am, but sometimes served all day and very filling. A huge number of London's cafés are run by Anglo-Italians, which means you're guaranteed good coffee and ciabatta sandwiches. Several of the places listed are also open in the evening, but the turnover is fast, so don't expect to linger;

they're best seen as fuel stops before – or in a few cases, after – a night out.

A few London-wide chains are worth checking out: the white-and-blue, Art Decoish **Café Flo** does decent French brasserie fare, as does the red-clad **Café Rouge**; **Crank's**, the original veggie café, is making a bid for world domination, losing its character and flavour en route; **Ed's Easy Diner** is a 1950s-theme fast-food joint dishing up some of the city's best burgers and fries; and **Stockpot**, which serve big portions at rock-bottom prices.

PICCADILLY, SOHO AND FITZROVIA

Bar du Marché

Map 4, E3. 19 Berwick St, W1 ⓣ 020/7734 4606. ⊖ Tottenham Court Road, Piccadilly Circus or Leicester Square. Mon–Sat noon–11pm.

A weird find in the middle of raucous Berwick Street market: a licensed French café serving quick snacks, brasserie staples, fried breakfasts and set meals for under £10.

Centrale

Map 4, I3. 16 Moor St, W1 ⓣ 020/7437 5513. ⊖ Leicester Square or Tottenham Court Road. Mon–Sat noon–9.45pm.

Tiny, friendly Italian café that serves up huge plates of steaming, garlicky pasta, as well as omelettes, chicken and chops for around £5. You'll almost certainly have to wait for – or share – a formica-topped table. Bring your own booze; there's a 50p–£1 corkage charge.

Indian YMCA

Map 3, G3. 41 Fitzroy Square, W1 ⓣ 020/7387 0411. ⊖ Warren Street. Mon–Fri 8–9.15am, 12.30–1.45pm & 8–9.15pm, Sat & Sun 8.30–9.30am, 12.30–1.45pm & 8–9.15pm.

Don't take any notice of the signs saying the canteen is only for students – this place is open to the public, just press the bell and pile in. The entire menu is portioned up into pretty little bowls; go and collect what you want and pay at the till. The food is great and the prices unbelievably low.

Lee Ho Fook

Map 4, H5. 4 Macclesfield St, W1 ⓣ020/7734 0782. ⊖ Leicester Square. Daily 11.30am–11pm.

A genuine Chinese barbecue house – small, spartan and cheap – that is very difficult to find. Firstly, it is not the larger, grander, more tourist-friendly *Lee Ho Fook* around the corner in Gerrard Street. Macclesfield Street runs from Shaftesbury Avenue to Gerrard Street; on the west side is Dansey Place, and on the corner with a red-and-gold sign in Chinese and a host of ducks hanging on a rack is this place.

Pollo

Map 4, H3. 20 Old Compton St, W1 ⓣ020/7734 5917. ⊖ Leicester Square. Daily noon–midnight.

You won't find much *haute cuisine* at *Pollo*, but you do get value for money. As at neighbouring *Centrale* (see overleaf), we're talking comfort food, Latin style. Devotees return time and again for the cheap platefuls of filling pasta dishes, and friendly prompt service. Alcohol is served.

Tokyo Diner

Map 4, I5. 2 Newport Place, WC2 ⓣ020/7287 8777. ⊖ Leicester Square. Daily noon–midnight.

Providing conclusive proof that you don't need to take out a second mortgage to enjoy Japanese food in London, this friendly eatery on the edge of Chinatown shuns elaboration for fast food, Tokyo style. Minimalist décor lets the sushi and sumo do the talking, which – if the number of Japanese who frequent the place is anything to go by – it does fluently.

COVENT GARDEN AND THE STRAND

Café in the Crypt

Map 4, K7. St Martin-in-the-Fields, Duncannon St, WC2 ⓣ020/7839 4342. ⊖ Charing Cross. Mon–Sat 10am–8pm, Sun noon–8pm.

The self-service buffet food is nothing special, but there are regular veggie dishes, and the handy location – below the church in the crypt – makes this an ideal spot to fill up before hitting the West End.

Food for Thought

Map 4, K2. 31 Neal St, WC2 ⓣ020/7836 0239. ⊖ Covent Garden. Mon–Sat 9.30am–8.30pm.

Long-established but minuscule bargain veggie restaurant and takeaway counter – the food is good, with the menu changing twice daily, plus regular vegan and wheat-free options. Expect to queue and don't expect to linger at peak times.

Frank's Cafe

Map 4, K2. 52 Neal St, WC2 ⓣ020/7836 6345. ⊖ Covent Garden tube. Mon–Sat 7.30am–8pm.

Classic Anglo-Italian café/sandwich bar with easy-going service. All-day breakfasts, plus plates of pasta and omelettes; come either side of lunch to make sure of a table.

Gaby's

Map 4, J6. 30 Charing Cross Rd, WC2 ⓣ020/7836 4233. ⊖ Leicester Square. Mon–Sat 9am–midnight, Sun 11am–9pm.

Busy café and takeaway joint serving a wide range of home-cooked veggie and Middle Eastern specialities. Hard to beat for value, choice, location or long hours – it's licensed, too, and the takeaway falafel are a central London bargain.

India Club

Map 5, A6. 143 Strand, WC2 ⓣ020/7836 0650. ⊖ Covent Garden or Temple. Mon–Sat noon–2.30pm & 6–10pm.

There's a faded period charm to this long-established, inexpensive Anglo-Indian eatery, sandwiched between floors of the cheap Strand *Continental Hotel* (see p.178). The "chillie bhajais" are to be taken very seriously.

Wagamama

Map 3, H4. 4 Streatham St, WC1 ⓣ020/7323 9223. ⊖ Tottenham Court Road. Mon–Sat noon–11pm, Sun 12.30–10pm.

Austere, minimalist canteen-style place where the waiters take your orders on hand-held computers. Diners share long benches and slurp huge bowls of noodle soup or stir-fried plates. You may have to queue, however, and the rapid turnover means it's not a place to consider for a long, romantic dinner.

CLERKENWELL, THE CITY AND EAST END

Arkansas Café

Map 3, N3. Unit 12, Old Spitalfields Market, E1 ⓣ020/7377 6999. ⊖ Liverpool Street. Daily except Sat noon–3pm.

American barbecue fuel stop, using only the very best ingredients. Try chef Bubb's own smoked beef brisket and ribs, and be sure to taste his home-made barbie sauce (made to a secret formula).

Clark & Sons

Map 3, K2. 46 Exmouth Market, EC1 ⓣ020/7837 1974. ⊖ Angel or Farringdon. Mon–Thurs 10.30am–4pm, Fri 10.30am–5.30pm, Sat 10.30am–5pm.

As Exmouth Market is currently undergoing something of a trendy transformation, it's all the more surprising to find a genuine eel and pie shop still going strong – this is the most central one in the capital.

Lunch

Map 3, K2. 60 Exmouth Market, EC1 ⓣ020/7278 2420. ⊖ Angel or Farringdon. Mon–Fri 8.30am–4pm, Sat 10am–4pm.

In style and ambience, the minimalist *Lunch* is typical of *nouveau* Clerkenwell. However, the food is good, salads fresh, the specials worth looking out for, and, in fine weather, there's often a barbie out the back.

The Place Below

Map 8, D4. St Mary-le-Bow, Cheapside, EC2 ⓣ 020/7329 0789. ⊖ St Paul's or Bank. Mon–Fri 7.30am–2.30pm.

Something of a find in the midst of the City – a café serving imaginative (albeit slightly pricey) vegetarian dishes. Added to that, the wonderful Norman crypt makes for a very pleasant place in which to dine.

Ponti's Polo Bar

Map 8, I1. 176 Bishopsgate, EC2 ⓣ 020/7283 4889. ⊖ Liverpool Street. Daily 24hr.

There's nothing in any way special about the *Ponti's* chain of cafés, but they're cheap, filling, vaguely Italian, and this particular branch is open round the clock.

KENSINGTON AND CHELSEA

Jenny Lo's Teahouse

Map 3, F7. 14 Ecclestone St, SW1 ⓣ 020/7259 0399. ⊖ Victoria. Mon–Fri 11.30am–3pm & 6–10pm, Sat opens noon.

Bright, bare and utilitarian yet somehow stylish and fashionable, too, *Jenny Lo's* serves good Chinese food at low prices. Be sure to check out the therapeutic teas.

New Culture Revolution

Map 3, D8. 305 King's Rd, SW3 ⓣ 020/7352 9281. ⊖ Sloane Square. Daily noon–11pm.

Great name, great concept – big bowls of freshly cooked noodles in sauce or soup or dumplings and rice dishes, all offering a one-stop meal at bargain prices in simple, minimalist surroundings. Not a place to linger.

GREENWICH

Tai Won Mein

See map on p.145, B2. 49 Greenwich Church St, SE10 ⓣ 020/8858 1668. Cutty Sark DLR or Greenwich DLR and train station. Daily 11.30am–11.30pm.

Good quality fast-food noodle bar that gets very busy at weekends. Décor is functional and minimalist; choose between rice, fried or soup noodles and *ho fun* (a flatter, softer, ribbon-like noodle).

Restaurants

London is a great place in which to **eat out**. You can sample more or less any kind of cuisine here, and, wherever you come from, you should find something new and quite possibly unique. Home to some of the best Cantonese restaurants in the whole of Europe, London is also a noted centre for Indian and Bangladeshi food, and has numerous French, Greek, Italian, Japanese, Spanish and Thai restaurants; and within all these cuisines, you can choose anything from simple meals to gourmet spreads. Traditional and modern British food is available all over town, and some of the best venues are reviewed below.

Another bonus is that there are plenty of places to eat around the main tourist drags of the West End: **Soho** has long been renowned for its eclectic and fashionable restaurants – and new eateries appear here every month – while **Chinatown**, on the other side of Shaftesbury Avenue, offers value-for-money eating right in the centre of town.

Many of the restaurants we've listed will be busy on most nights of the week, particularly on Thursday, Friday and Saturday, and you're best advised to **reserve a table** wherever you're headed. The majority of places take major credit cards, such as Visa, MasterCard and Amex; in the listings, we've simply noted those that don't.

As for **prices**, you can pay an awful lot for a meal in

London, and if you're used to North American portions, you're not going to be particularly impressed by the volume in most places. In the listings, we've quoted the minimum you can get away with spending (assuming you don't tip and don't drink) and the amount you can expect to pay for a full blowout. For really cheap eats, see the previous chapter.

Service is discretionary at most restaurants, but many tend to take no chances, emblazoning their bills with reminders that "Service is NOT included", or even including a ten to fifteen percent service charge on the bill (which they have to announce on the menu, by law). Normally you should, of course, pay service – it's how most of the staff make up their wages – but make sure you check you're not paying twice.

ST JAMES'S, MAYFAIR AND MARYLEBONE

Abu Ali

Map 3, D4. 136–138 George St, W1 ⓣ 020/7724 6338. ⊖ Marble Arch. Daily 9am–midnight. Cash/ cheques only. £7–25.

Spartan place that's the Lebanese equivalent to a northern working men's club, serving honest Lebanese fare that's terrific value for money, from the *tabbouleh* to the kebabs – wash it all down with fresh mint tea, and then have a go at a bubble pipe.

The Criterion

Map 4, F7. 224 Piccadilly, W1 ⓣ 020/7930 0488. ⊖ Piccadilly Circus. Mon–Sat noon–2.30pm & 6–11.30pm, Sun 6–10.30pm. £25–45.

One of the city's most beautiful restaurants, behind Eros on Piccadilly Circus. The high-vaulted gold mosaic ceiling sparkles, and the menu is courtesy of scourge of the faint-hearted, Marco Pierre White. The set menu lunch for under £20 a head is the best value and allows you to keep your table all afternoon.

La Spighetta

Map 3, E4. 43 Blandford St, W1 ⓣ 020/7486 7340. ⊖ Bond Street. Mon–Fri noon–2.15pm & 6.30–10.30pm, Sat closes 11pm, Sun 6.30–10.30pm. £10–25.

Not a spaghetti house – *spighetta* actually means wheat – but a large basement buzzing with activity and serving pizza, pasta and standard Italian main courses. The pizzas and pasta dishes are very good, as are the classic puddings.

Mandalay

Map 3, D4. 444 Edgware Rd, W2 ⓣ 020/7258 3696. ⊖ Edgware Road. Mon–Sat noon–2.30pm & 6–10.30pm. £6–16.

Small non-smoking restaurant that serves pure, freshly cooked and unexpurgated Burmese cuisine – a melange of Thai, Malaysian, a lot of Indian and a few things that are unique. The portions are huge, flavours hit the mark, the service friendly and the prices low.

Quaglino's

Map 4, C9. 16 Bury St, SW1 ⓣ 020/7930 6767; ⓦ *www.conran.com* ⊖ Green Park. Mon–Thurs noon–3pm & 5.30pm–midnight, Fri & Sat until 1am, Sun closes 11pm. £22–35.

Huge 1930s ballroom revived by Terence Conran as one of the capital's busiest and most glamorous eating spots, so you'll need to book well in advance. There's an unmistakeable buzz about the place, the surroundings are splendid, and the fish and seafood dishes are excellent – it's also open late.

Sea-Shell

Map 3, D3. 49–51 Lisson Grove, NW1 ⓣ 020/7224 9000. ⊖ Marylebone. Mon–Fri noon–2.30pm & 5–10.30pm, Sat noon–10.30pm, Sun noon–2.45pm. £12–20.

Top quality, no nonsense British fish and chips in the heart of Marylebone. The chips are done to a turn in quality groundnut oil, and the batter is just right. Takeaway or eat in.

SOHO

Aroma II

Map 4, H4. 118 Shaftesbury Ave, W1 ⓣ 020/7437 0370. ⊖ Leicester Square. Daily noon–11.30pm. £6–15.

Bright, modernist Chinese restaurant with an exhausting and exhaustive menu ranging from traditional hand-pulled noodles to braised sea slug or shark fin. This is one of the more serious but accessible gastronomic Chinatown places, so if you're stuck for what to choose, ask for advice.

Fung Shing

Map 4, H5. 15 Lisle St, W1 ⓣ 020/7437 1539. ⊖ Leicester Square. Daily noon–11.30pm. £15–40.

Bigger and brassier than ever, this is a Chinatown restaurant that takes its cooking and its service seriously. Prices are above average, but the portions are large, and the food has an earthy, robust quality redolent of a chef who is absolutely confident of his flavours and textures.

Kettner's

Map 4, H4. 29 Romilly St, W1 ⓣ 020/7734 6112. ⊖ Leicester Square. Daily noon–midnight. £12–30.

Despite the very handsome *belle époque* Baroque décor and the pianist, this place is by no means exclusive. In fact, it's modelled on the reliable *Pizza Express* restaurants, serving thin-base pizzas and the like. You can't book and might be forced to hang out a while in the noisy *Champagne Bar* – no great hardship.

Kulu Kulu

Map 4, D6. 76 Brewer St, W1 ⓣ 020/7734 7316. ⊖ Piccadilly Circus. Mon–Fri noon–2.30pm & 5–10pm, Sat noon–3.45pm & 5–10pm. £10–30.

Small, friendly *kaiten* (or conveyor belt) sushi restaurant which pulls off the unlikely trick of serving really good sushi without being impersonal or intimidating. Open your box containing a pair of disposable chopsticks, pickled ginger and soy sauce, grab one or two plates (they're priced/coded by design not colour here) and tuck in.

Mezzo

Map 4, F3. 100 Wardour St, W1 ⓣ 020/7314 4000; ⓦ *www.conran.com* ⊖ Piccadilly Circus or Tottenham Court Road. Mon–Thurs noon–3pm & 6pm–midnight, Fri until 3am, Sat until 1am, Sun 12.30–3pm & 6–11pm. £15–50.

Mezzo has remained popular ever since Terence Conran opened this 600-seater in 1995. There's a bar, an informal *Mezzonine* restaurant upstairs, and, down the sweeping staircase, the full-on *Mezzo* with a space for performers. This is not a place for a quiet night out. The tables are packed close, and there's a fashionable mayhem of noise, but considering the numbers served here, the French/Med food is pretty good. There's a £5 "music cover charge" after 8pm.

Mr Kong

Map 4, H5. 21 Lisle St, WC2 ⓣ 020/7437 7923. ⊖ Leicester Square. Daily noon–3am. £7–20.

One of Chinatown's finest, with a chef/owner who pioneered many of the modern Cantonese dishes now on menus all over town. To sample the restaurant's more unusual dishes – order from the "Today's" and "Chef's Specials" menu, and don't miss the mussels in black-bean sauce or the fresh razor clam with garlic.

New World

Map 4, H4. 1 Gerrard Place, W1 ⓣ 020/7734 0396. ⊖ Leicester Square. Daily 11am–midnight. £6–18.

Very probably the largest single restaurant in London, with over 500 seats. The menu is twelve pages long, but luckily you don't need it in order to enjoy the authentic *dim sum*, which is served from circulating "themed" trolleys, daily from 11am to 6pm.

Randall & Aubin

Map 4, F4. 16 Brewer St, W1 ⓣ 020/7287 4447. ⊖ Piccadilly Circus. Mon–Sat noon–11pm, Sun 4–10.30pm. £8–35.

Ex-butcher's shop that's now converted into a champagne and oyster bar, rotisserie, sandwich shop and charcuterie; in summer, it's a wonderfully airy place to eat, especially if you grab a seat by the window. Fish and seafood dominate the menu, but there are also hot-filled baguettes at lunchtime, and some adventurous puddings. Eat in or take away.

Soho Soho

Map 4, H3. 11–13 Frith St, W1 ⓣ 020/7437 3091. ⊖ Leicester Square or Tottenham Court Road. Mon–Fri noon–2.30pm & 5–11pm, Sat 6–11pm. £15–40.
Provençal restaurant with a lunchtime rotisserie on the ground floor, a more serious restaurant upstairs, and a cheaper brasserie in the basement. You won't be disappointed by whichever one you choose, but it's on the first floor that *Soho Soho* shows its full potential: good cooking with judicious use of spices and seasoning, and friendly service.

COVENT GARDEN

Belgo Centraal

Map 4, K3. 50 Earlham St, WC2 ⓣ 020/7813 2233; ⓦ *www.belgo-restaurants.com* ⊖ Covent Garden. Mon–Thurs noon–11.30pm, Fri & Sat noon–midnight, Sun noon–10.30pm. £5–30.
Massive metal-minimalist cavern off Neal Street, serving excellent kilo buckets of *moules marinière*, with frites and mayonnaise, a bewildering array of Belgian beers to choose from, and waffles for dessert. The £5 lunchtime specials are a bargain for central London.

The Ivy

Map 4, J4. 1 West St, WC2 ⓣ 020/7836 4751. ⊖ Leicester Square or Covent Garden. Daily noon–3pm & 5.30pm–midnight. £20–50.
Regency-style restaurant built in 1928 that's been a theatreland and society favourite throughout the last century – and never more so than today. The only problem is getting a table; either book

months ahead or try at very short notice, make do with a table in the bar area, or go for the bargain £15 three-course weekend lunch.

J. Sheekey

Map 4, J6. 28–32 St Martin's Court, WC2 ⓣ 020/7240 2565. ⊖ Leicester Square. Mon–Sat noon–3pm & 5.30pm–midnight, Sun noon–3.30pm & 5.30pm–midnight. £15–50.

J. Sheekey's pedigree goes back to World War I, but the place has recently been totally redesigned and refurbished. The menu is still focused on fish, but in addition to traditional fare such as grilled Dover sole, you're just as likely to find modernist dishes like grilled cuttlefish with creamed brandade. The weekend lunches at £10–15 are great value.

Livebait

Map 3, I4. 21 Wellington St, WC2 ⓣ 020/7836 7161. ⊖ Covent Garden. Mon–Sat noon–3pm & 5.30–11.30pm. £20–50.

Innovative, irrepressible restaurant with a large, bustling, black-and-white-tiled dining room. The emphasis is on fish so fresh you expect to see it flapping on the slab, and superb crustacea. The breads are still a feature and service is friendly.

Stephen Bull

Map 4, J4. 12 Upper St Martin's Lane, WC2 ⓣ 020/7379 7811. ⊖ Leicester Square. Mon–Fri noon–2.30pm & 5.45–11.30pm, Sat 5.45–11.30pm. £15–60.

The Bauhaus décor and "Modern British" food are a bold statement, but this restaurant has plenty of admirers – the dishes are genuinely innovative and desserts are equally experimental. A simple fixed-price system operates: lunch is £15 for two courses, or £19 for three, while the three-course dinner is around £30.

FITZROVIA AND BLOOMSBURY

Great Nepalese

Map 3, H2. 48 Eversholt St, NW1 ⓣ 020/7387 2789.

⊖ Euston or Mornington Crescent. Mon–Sat noon–2.45pm & 6–11.30pm, Sun noon–2.30pm & 6–11.15pm. £8–22.
Tucked round the back of Euston Station in a distinctly seedy area is this friendly, homely Nepalese restaurant. Don't bother with curry-house favourites like chicken tikka masala, but delve into the authentic Nepalese dishes, whose names you won't be familiar with, and only try the Coronation rum from Kathmandu if you know what you're doing.

Ikkyu

Map 3, G3. 67a Tottenham Court Rd, W1 ⓣ 020/7636 9280. ⊖ Goodge Street. Mon–Fri noon–2.30pm & 6–10.30pm, Sun 6–10.30pm. £10–40.
Busy, basic basement Japanese restaurant, good enough for a quick lunch or a more elaborate dinner. Either way, prices are infinitely more reasonable than elsewhere in the capital, and the food is tasty and authentic. Be warned, however: it's hard to find and, when you do, shockingly popular.

Malabar Junction

Map 3, H4. 107a Great Russell St, WC1 ⓣ 020/7580 5230. ⊖ Tottenham Court Road. Daily noon–3pm & 6–11.30pm. £12–25.
Inexpensive yet fully licensed, top-quality Keralan restaurant with two entirely (and religiously) separate kitchens: one serving mouthwatering, spicy and nutty veggie dishes, the other dishing out equally tasty meat and fish fare.

Rasa Samudra

Map 3, H4. 5 Charlotte St, W1 ⓣ 020/7637 0222. ⊖ Goodge Street. Mon–Sat noon–3pm & 6–11pm. £18–40.
Above average prices for exceptional South Indian fish dishes, which are freshly prepared using top-quality ingredients, and come complete with accompaniments. The cooking is well-judged and the spices well-balanced, but if you're still nervous of the bill, go for the fixed-price three-course lunch at £10 (vegetarian) or £15 (seafood).

R.K. Stanley

Map 3, G4. 6 Little Portland St, W1 ⓣ 020/7462 0099. ⊖ Oxford Circus. Mon–Sat noon–11.30pm. £10–25.

A highly successful celebration of British culinary strengths – sausages, whose inspiration is taken from all over the globe, and beer (ale, lager, stout or porter) – served in modern surroundings. Service is swift and friendly, and good-value pricing belies its location.

CLERKENWELL AND THE CITY

Cicada

Map 3, K3. 132 St John St, EC1 ⓣ 020/7608 1550. ⊖ Farringdon. Mon–Fri noon–11pm, Sat 6–11pm. £15–35.

Part bar, part restaurant, *Cicada* is set back from the street and, when the weather's fine, it's a great place for eating alfresco. The unusual Thai-based menu allows you to mix and match from small, large and side dishes ranging from hot, lemony, fishy tom yum soup, to sweet ginger noodles, fresh clams, white miso or kinome leaves.

St John

Map 3, K3. 26 St John St, EC1 ⓣ 020/7251 0848. ⊖Farringdon. Mon–Fri noon–3pm & 6–11pm, Sat 6–11pm. £20–35.

A genuinely English restaurant, only a stone's throw from Smithfield meat market and specializing in offal. All those strange and unfashionable cuts of meat that were once commonplace in rural England – brains, bone marrow, meat from a cow's sternum – are on offer at this white-painted former smokehouse.

Singapura

Map 5, G3. 1–2 Limeburner Lane, EC4 ⓣ 020/7329 1133. ⊖ Blackfriars or St Paul's. Mon–Fri 11.30am–3.30pm & 5.30–10pm, £20–40.

Beautiful, large, modern restaurant off Ludgate Hill that is one of the few places outside Singapore where you can sample *Nonya* cuisine – a fusion of Malayan and Chinese traditions and ingredients. The food is generally (but not always) spicy, and is characterized by a good deal of garlic, galangal, sweetness and lime leaves.

EAST END

Café Naz

Map 7, N1. 46–48 Brick Lane, E1 ☎ 020/7247 0234. ⊖ Aldgate East. Mon–Fri noon–midnight, Sat 6pm–midnight, Sun noon–3pm & 6pm–midnight. £8–20.

Self-proclaimed contemporary Bangladeshi restaurant that cuts an imposing modern figure on Brick Lane. The menu has all the standard Indian dishes plus a load of "baltis", the kitchen is open-plan, and the prices keen – as you'd expect in a street replete with rival curry houses.

Café Spice Namaste

Map 7, M5. 16 Prescot St, E1 ☎ 020/7488 9242. ⊖ Tower Hill or Tower Gateway DLR. Mon–Fri noon–3pm & 6.15–10.30pm, Sat 6.30–10.30pm. £12–30.

Very popular Indian on the fringe of the City that is definitely not your average curry house. Parsee delicacies rub shoulders with dishes from Goa, Hyderabad and Kashmir, and the tandoori specialities are awesome. Be sure to check out the speciality menu, which changes weekly.

Viet Hoa Café

Map 3, N2. 72 Kingsland Rd, E2 ☎ 020/7729 8293. ⊖ Old Street. Tues–Sun noon–3.30pm & 5.30–11.30pm. £8–18.

Large, light and airy Vietnamese café with a golden parquet floor, situated not far from the Geffrye Museum in Hoxton/ Shoreditch, and serving splendid "meals in a bowl" – soups and noodle dishes with everything from spring rolls to tofu. Be sure to try the *pho* soup, a Vietnamese staple that's eaten at any and every meal.

LAMBETH AND SOUTHWARK

Butlers Wharf Chop House

Map 7, L9. 36e Shad Thames,

SE1 ⓣ020/7403 3403; ⓦ *www.conran.com* ⊖ Tower Hill, London Bridge or Bermondsey. Mon–Fri & Sun noon–3pm & 6–11pm, Sat 6–11pm. £15–30.

Another Conran-owned restaurant, showcasing the best of British meat, fish and cheeses. Prices are high, but the *Chop House* tries to cater for all: you could enjoy a simple dish at the bar, a well-priced set lunch, or an extravagant dinner. You can't reserve the terrace tables, but try to book ahead for a window seat.

Fish!

Map 7, E8. Cathedral St, SE1 ⓣ020/7836 3236; ⓦ *www.fishdiner.co.uk* ⊖ London Bridge. Mon–Sat 11.30am–3pm & 5.30–11pm. £20–50.

Busy, buzzy, tank-like restaurant, with huge windows and a glass ceiling, right in the middle of Borough Market. Choose your fish, decide how you want it cooked, and with what sauce, and then sit back and wait. Portions are huge, and the fish is as good and fresh as you'd expect.

RSJ

Map 6, D3. 13a Coin St, SE1 ⓣ020/7928 4554. ⊖ Waterloo. Mon–Fri noon–2.30pm & 5.30–11pm, Sat 5.30–11pm. £18–45.

Those who know what an RSJ is won't be disappointed (there's one holding up the first floor) nor will those in search of high-standard Anglo-French cooking. Its position near the South Bank, makes it an excellent spot for a meal after or before a show or concert. The set meals for around £15 are particularly popular.

KENSINGTON AND CHELSEA

Bibendum Oyster House

Map 3, C8. Michelin House, 81 Fulham Rd, SW3 ⓣ020/7589 1480; ⓦ *www.conran.com* ⊖ South Kensington. Mon–Sat noon–11pm, Sun noon–10.30pm £12–30.

A glorious tiled affair built in 1911, this former garage is the best place to eat shellfish in London. There are three types of rock oysters, but if you're really hungry, try the "Plateau de Fruits De Mer", which also has crab, clams, langoustine, prawns, shrimps, whelks and winkles.

Boisdale

Map 3, F7. 15 Ecclestone St, SW1 ⓣ020/7730 6922. ⊖ Victoria. Mon–Sat noon–1am, Sun noon–11pm. £15–50.

Owned by Ranald MacDonald, son of the Chief of Clanranald, this is a very Scottish place, strong on hospitality, and with a befuddlingly large range of rare malt whiskies. Fresh Scottish produce rules wherever possible, including MacSween's haggis (sheep's innards and oatmeal), venison and salmon.

Hunan

Map 3, E8. 51 Pimlico Rd, SW1 ⓣ020/7730 5712. ⊖ Sloane Square. Mon–Sat noon–2.30pm & 6–11.30pm. £21.

Probably England's only restaurant serving Hunan food, a relative of Sichuan cuisine, with the same spicy kick to most dishes and a fair wallop of pepper in those that aren't actively riddled with chillis. Most people opt for the £23 "Hunan's special leave-it-to-us feast", a multi-course extravaganza which lets the maître d', Mr Peng, show what he can do.

Wódka

Map 3, A7. 12 St Alban's Grove, W8 ⓣ020/7937 6513. ⊖ High Street Kensington or Gloucester Road. Mon–Fri 12.30–2.45pm & 7–11pm, Sat & Sun 7–11pm. £14–35.

The food here is cooked with imagination, which makes the smart *Wódka* the place to go if you want to experience the best that Polish cuisine has to offer. It's not an expensive place to eat (especially if you go for the daily set-menu lunch), unless you start working your way through the large selection of flavoured vodkas.

NOTTING HILL

Alounak

Map 3, A4. 44 Westbourne

Grove, W2 ⓣ 020/7229 0416. ⊖ Queensway or Bayswater. Daily noon–midnight. £8–20.
Don't be put off by the dated sign outside – this place turns out really good, really cheap Iranian grub. The mixed starter is a fine sampler of all the usual dips, served with freshly-baked flat bread; lamb dishes feature heavily, but look out for the daily specials, and wash it all down with a pot of Iranian black tea.

The Mandola

Map 3, A4. 139 Westbourne Grove, W11 ⓣ 020/7229 4734. ⊖ Notting Hill Gate. Mon–Sat noon–10.30pm, sittings 7.30 & 9.30pm. Cash/cheque only. £12–22.
Small, seriously informal, unlicensed neighbourhood restaurant serving strikingly delicious "urban Sudanese" food at sensible prices. The place is so popular they've had to institute two sittings a night, yet the staff remain supremely laid-back. Be sure to check out the Sudanese spiced coffee at the end.

Rodizio Rico

Map 3, A4. 111 Westbourne Grove, W11 ⓣ 020/7792 4035. ⊖ Notting Hill Gate or Bayswater. Mon–Fri 6.30pm–midnight, Sat 12.30–4.30pm & 6.30pm–midnight. £18–25.
No menu, no prices, but no problem either, as this Brazilian *churrascarias* specializes in smoky, grilled meat. "*Rodizio*" means "rotating", and refers to the carvers who wander about and lop off chunks of freshly grilled meats, while you help yourself from the salad bar and hot buffet to prime your plate.

Rotisserie Jules

Map 3, A5. 133a Notting Hill Gate, W11 ⓣ 020/7221 3331. ⊖ Notting Hill Gate. Daily noon–11.30pm. £8–18.
One of three consistently sound restaurants – the other two are at 6 Bute St, SW7, and 338 King's Rd, SW3 – which excels in freshly roasted chicken hot off the spit at very reasonable prices. You can have a leg and thigh, a breast and wing, the whole chicken or even an entire leg

of lamb, which will feed three or four people.

NORTH LONDON

Cucina

Map 2, G3. 45a South End Rd, NW3 ⓣ020/7483 3765. ⊖ Belsize Park. Mon–Thurs noon–2.30pm & 7–10.30pm, Fri & Sat noon–2.30pm & 7–11pm. £16–35.

Brightly-painted, wooden-floored, roof-lit first-floor restaurant that's very contemporary, very fashionable and very Hampstead. The Modern British menu changes every two weeks or so and darts about a bit from cuisine to cuisine, but wherever you alight, each dish is well-presented, and the set lunch is a bargain at under £15.

Harry Morgan's

Map 3, C1. 245 Eversholt St, NW1 ⓣ020/7722 1869. ⊖ St John's Wood. Daily 11am–1pm. £7–20.

The salt beef on rye with horseradish is as good as it was when Harry Morgan first opened a restaurant on this site in 1962. Other Jewish medicines available at this newly revamped and airy eatery include chicken noodle soup, chopped liver and a whole range of pickled cucumbers.

Sauce barorganicdiner

Map 2, H3. 214 Camden High St, NW1 ⓣ020/7482 0777. ⊖ Camden Town. Mon–Sat noon–11pm, Sun noon–4.30pm. £15–30.

Sauce offers food free of chemicals, pesticides and preservatives in a bright, colourful diner, with a juice and cocktail bar attached. Burgers, sandwiches and wraps are on the menu, and it's also fine to go just for a coffee or a beer.

Wazobia

Map 2, H3. 257 Royal College St, NW1 ⓣ020/7284 1059. ⊖ Camden Town. Mon–Sat 4.30pm–midnight, Sun 4.30–10.30pm. £8–15.

This small, bright Nigerian restaurant runs on West African time, with service that is both unaffected and charming. The food is worth the wait, particularly the goat pepper soup, the prawn "doughnuts", and the wide range of rich stews.

GREENWICH

The North Pole

Map 2, L6. 131 Greenwich High Rd, SE10 ⓣ 020/8853 3020. Greenwich train station. Tues–Sun noon–2.30pm & 7–10.30pm. £15–30.

Downstairs is a vibrant bar full of the local hip young things; upstairs is a restaurant offering "East meets West" cuisine, combining Pacific Rim-style cooking with European ingredients. Eastern main courses such as pan-fired monkfish with a spicy galangal sauce share menu space with more European dishes like saffron *tagliolini*. Be sure to check out the goldfish-bowl lamps.

CHISWICK TO RICHMOND

Chez Lindsay

Map 2, C7. 11 Hill Rise, Richmond, Surrey ⓣ 020/8948 7473. ⊖ Richmond. Mon–Sat 11am–11pm, Sun noon–10pm. £8–25.

Small, bright, authentic Breton creperie, with a loyal local following, and fixed-price lunchtime menus for under £10. Choose between galettes, crepes or more formal French main courses, including lots of fresh fish and shellfish, and wash it all down with Breton cider in traditional earthenware *bolées*.

The Glasshouse

Map 2, D6. 14 Station Parade, Kew, Surrey ⓣ 020/8940 6777. ⊖ Kew Gardens. Mon–Sat noon–2.30pm & 7–10.30pm, Sun noon–3pm. £20–50.

Clean-cut, modern restaurant on the very doorstep of Kew Gardens tube, with blissfully comfortable chairs. The menu changes on a daily basis, with five or six choices for each course, and set-menu prices hovering around the £20 mark. The cooking is imaginative and straightforward, and owes much to genuine French food.

Springbok Café

Map 2, E5. 42 Devonshire Rd, W4 ⓣ020/8742 3149. ⊖ Turnham Green. Mon–Sat 6.30–11pm. £20–30.

Small, informal and ambitious South African restaurant, with an open-plan barbie-oriented kitchen. Many of the ingredients are imported, so there's plenty of biltong, game and fish from SA, plus smoked English ostrich to please expats.

Pubs and bars

Pubs are one of England's most enduring social institutions, and have outlived the church and marketplace as the focal points of communities, with London's fringe theatre, alternative comedy and live-music scenes still largely pub-based. At their best, pubs can be as welcoming as their full name, "public house", suggests, offering a fine range of drinks and filling food. At their worst, they're dismal rooms with surly bar staff and rotten snacks. One thing you can be sure of, however, is that most pubs and bars remain smoke-filled places where drinking alcohol is the prime activity.

London's great period of pub building took place in the Victorian era, to which many pubs still pay homage; genuine Victorian interiors, however, are increasingly difficult to find, as indeed are genuinely individual pubs. **Chain pubs** can now be found all over the capital: branches of All Bar One, Pitcher & Piano and the Slug & Lettuce are the most obvious, as they all share the chain name, whereas J.D. Wetherspoon pubs and the Firkin chain do at least vary theirs.

Pub food, on the whole, is a lunchtime affair, although "gastropubs", which put more effort into their cooking, are increasingly offering meals in the evening, too. The traditional image of London pub food is dire – a pseudo

ENGLISH BEER

Bitter, the classic **English beer**, is an uncarbonated and darkish beverage that should be pumped by hand from the cellar and served at room temperature. Some of the beer you'll see touted as good English ale is nothing of the sort (if the stuff comes out of an electric pump, it isn't the real thing), but these days even the big breweries distribute some very good brews – Directors, for example, produced by Courage, is a very classy strong bitter.

Smaller brewers whose beers are available across London include Young's and Fuller's – the two main London breweries – and Adnams, Greene King, Flowers and Samuel Smith's. Additionally, regional concoctions from other independent breweries are often available at free houses (pubs not tied to one particular brewery). London also has a number of **brewpubs**, which produce their own peculiar brand on the premises, the most famous being the one-joke Firkin chain, and the most recent being the Freedom Brewing Company.

Guinness, a very dark, creamy Irish stout, is also on sale virtually everywhere, and is an exception to the high-minded objection to electrically pumped beers.

"ploughman's lunch" of bread and cheese, or a murky-looking pie and chips – but the last couple of decades have seen plenty of improvements. You can get a palatable lunchtime meal at many of the pubs listed in this chapter, and at a few of them you're looking at cooking worthy of high restaurant-standard praise.

Standard pub opening hours are Mon–Sat 11am–11pm, Sun noon–10.30pm. Our listings only specify the exceptions.

Though pubs may be constantly changing hands (and names), the quickest turnover is in **bars**, which go in and out of fashion with incredible speed. These are very different places to your average pub, catering to a somewhat cliquey, often youngish crowd, with designer interiors and drinks; they also tend to be more expensive. We've listed a fair few, while leaving those more like (or in some cases attached to) clubs and dance places for the "Live Music and Clubs" chapter, which follows.

For pubs and bars that are music venues, see Chapter 18; for gay and lesbian pubs and bars, see Chapter 19.

England's **licensing laws** are likely to have changed by the time you read this, as after more than a century of draconian restrictions, the government has finally caved in and liberalized English opening hours. This should allow pubs and bars to stay open way beyond the standard 11pm last orders, so the times listed below may well have changed significantly since this book went to press.

WHITEHALL AND WESTMINSTER

Albert

Map 3, G7. 52 Victoria St, SW1 ⓣ 020/7222 5577. ⊖ St James's Park or Victoria.

Roomy High-Victorian pub, situated halfway between Parliament Square and Victoria, with big bay windows and glass partitions; good bar food, too, and an excellent carvery upstairs.

ICA Bar

Map 7, F3. 94 The Mall, SW1 ⓣ 020/7873 0057; ⓦ *www.ica.org.uk* ⊖ Piccadilly Circus or Charing Cross.

Mon–Sat noon–1am, Sun noon–10.30pm.

You have to be a member (or be visiting an exhibition or cinema/theatre/talk event) to drink here – but anyone can join on the door (Mon–Fri £1.50; Sat & Sun £2.50). It's a cool drinking venue, with a noir dress code observed by the arty crowd and staff.

Paviour's Arms

Map 3, H7. Page St, SW1 ⓣ020/7834 2150. ⊖ Pimlico, St James's Park or Westminster. Mon–Fri only.

A unique survivor, this large, stylish 1930s Art Deco pub, in the backstreets close to the Tate Gallery, has much of its original décor intact; you can also get decent Thai food with your beer. Be warned, though: the place is heaving with civil servants and locals at lunchtime, and much, much quieter in the evenings.

ST JAMES'S, MAYFAIR AND MARYLEBONE

Dover Castle

Map 3, F3. 21a Devonshire St, W1 ⓣ020/7935 8327. ⊖ Regent's Park. Mon–Fri 11.30am–11pm, Sat noon–11pm.

A really nice, traditional boozer down a quiet Marylebone mews. Restful, racing-green upholstery, dark wood, a nicotine-stained lincrusta ceiling and cheap Sam Smith's beer on tap.

Mulligans

Map 4, A6. 13–14 Cork St, W1 ⓣ020/7409 1370. ⊖ Green Park or Piccadilly. Mon–Sat 11am–11pm.

A fine and very smart Irish pub with an odd mix of clientele – Cork Street gallery staff and Irish lads – and some of the best Guinness in London. Also has a high-class restaurant downstairs, with fine Modern British/Irish cooking.

O'Conor Don

Map 3, F4. 88 Marylebone Lane, W1 ⓣ020/7935 9311. ⊖ Bond Street. Mon–Fri 11am–11pm, Sat noon–11pm.

A stripped bare, anti-theme Irish pub that's a cut above the average, with excellent Guinness, a pleasantly measured pace and Irish food on offer.

Red Lion

Map 7, D1. 2 Duke of York St, SW1 ⓣ020/7930 2030. ⊖ Piccadilly Circus. Mon–Sat 11.30am–11pm.

Popular little gin palace which has preserved its classic Victorian décor of dark wood and mirrors. The clientele are more often than not besuited, as you'd expect in St James's, and the malt whisky selection is impressive.

SOHO

Coach & Horses

Map 4, H3. 29 Greek St, W1 ⓣ020/7437 5920. ⊖ Leicester Square.

Long-standing – and, for once, little-changed – haunt of the ghosts of old Soho: *Private Eye*, nightclubbers, and art students from nearby St Martin's College. Fifties red-plastic stools and black formica tables make up the spartan, unchanging décor.

Dog & Duck

Map 4, G3. 18 Bateman St, W1 ⓣ020/7437 4447. ⊖ Leicester Square or Tottenham Court Road. Mon–Fri noon–11pm, Sat 6–11pm, Sun 7–10.30pm.

Tiny and very ancient Soho pub that retains much of its old character, a beautiful set of Victorian tiles and mosaics, and a loyal clientele that often includes jazz musicians from nearby *Ronnie Scott's* club.

French House

Map 4, G4. 49 Dean St, W1 ⓣ020/7437 2799. ⊖ Leicester Square. Mon–Sat noon–11pm, Sun noon–10.30pm.

This tiny French pub has been a Soho institution since before World War I, and boasts Free French and literary associations galore. Don't expect to get a seat, or order a pint (they only serve half pints and no real ale), or get into the fine little restaurant upstairs without booking ahead.

Two Floors

Map 4, C5. 3 Kingly St, W1 ⓣ020/7439 1007. ⊖ Oxford Circus or Piccadilly Circus. Mon–Sat 11am–11pm.

Relaxed, modernist Soho bar, laid out, unsurprisingly, on two floors, attracting a mixed gay/straight crowd, and pumping out drum'n'bass in the evenings – quite a find in an area short of decent drinking holes.

COVENT GARDEN

Denim

Map 4, J5. 4a Upper St Martin's Lane, WC2 ⓣ 020/7497 0376. ⊖ Leicester Square.
A sign that the style-conscious Soho bar scene has begun to drift over into Covent Garden. The retro Sixties red and pink décor goes down a treat with the young clubby punters, who don't seem to flinch at the outrageous bar prices.

Freedom Brewing Company

Map 4, K3. 41 Earlham St, WC2 ⓣ 020/7240 0606. ⊖ Covent Garden.
Busy, brick-vaulted basement brewery bar with wrought-iron pillars, lots of brushed steel and pricey, strong brews, made on the premises – in particular, there's a very fine organic honey wheat beer.

Lamb & Flag

Map 4, K5. 33 Rose St, WC2 ⓣ 020/7497 9504. ⊖ Leicester Square or Covent Garden.
Busy, tiny and highly atmospheric pub, well and truly hidden away down an alley between Garrick Street and Floral Street, where John Dryden was attacked in 1679 for writing scurrilous verses about one of Charles II's mistresses.

Punch & Judy

Map 4, M5. 40 The Market, WC2 ⓣ 020/7379 0923. ⊖ Covent Garden.
Horribly mobbed and loud, but this Covent Garden Market pub does boast an unbeatable location with a very popular balcony overlooking the Piazza – and a stone-flagged cellar.

Salisbury

Map 4, J6. 90 St Martin's Lane, WC2 ⓣ 020/7836 5863. ⊖ Leicester Square.
Easily one of the most beautifully preserved Victorian pubs in the capital – and certainly the most central – with cut, etched and engraved windows, bronze figures, red-velvet seating and a fine lincrusta ceiling.

BLOOMSBURY AND FITZROVIA

The Hope

Map 3, G3. 15 Tottenham St, W1 ⓣ 020/7637 0896. ⊖ Goodge Street.
Small Fitzrovia pub, chiefly remarkable for its superb meat and veggie sausages, supplied by Simply Sausages, served with beans and mash, and washed down with real ales.

The Lamb

Map 3, I3. 94 Lamb's Conduit St, WC1 ⓣ 020/7405 0713. ⊖ Russell Square.
Pleasant, traditional pub with a loyal clientele and a marvellously well-preserved Victorian interior of mirrors, leather seats, and old wood and "snob" screens.

Museum Tavern

Map 3, H3. 49 Great Russell St, WC1 ⓣ 020/7242 8987. ⊖ Tottenham Court Road or Russell Square.
Large and surprisingly characterful old pub, conveniently situated opposite the main entrance to the British Museum. The pub (though not the name), predates the BM, and it has the honour of being an erstwhile drinking hole of Karl Marx.

Newman Arms

Map 3, G3. 23 Rathbone St, W1 ⓣ 020/7636 1127. ⊖ Tottenham Court Road or Goodge Street. Mon–Fri 11.30am–11.30pm.
What *The Hope* is to sausages, the cosy *Newman Arms* is to home-made pies, with every sort, from gammon to steak-and-kidney, enjoyed by the suited office brigade.

THE STRAND, HOLBORN AND CLERKENWELL

Café Kick

Map 3, J2. 43 Exmouth Market, EC1 ⓣ 020/7837 8077. ⊖ Farringdon or Angel. Mon–Sat noon–11pm.
Stylish take on a smoky, local French-style café/bar in the heart of fashionable Exmouth Market, with three busy table-football games to complete the retro theme.

Clerkenwell House

Map 3, K3. 23–27 Hatton Wall, EC1 ☎020/7404 1113. ⊖ Farringdon. Mon–Sat 11am–2am, Sun noon–10.30pm.

One of a whole host of new bars to open on and off the Clerkenwell Road. The retro 1970s furniture includes some wickedly comfy semicircular sofas. The Med food is good if a tad pricey, and there are four American pool tables in the basement bar.

Eagle

Map 3, J3. 159 Farringdon Rd, EC1 ☎020/7837 1353. ⊖ Farringdon. Mon–Sat noon–11pm, Sun noon–5pm.

The first of London's pubs to go foody, this place is heaving and hearty at lunch and dinnertimes, as *Guardian* and *Observer* journos tuck into the excellent Mediterranean dishes, but you should be able to find a seat at other times.

Fox & Anchor

Map 3, K3. 115 Charterhouse St, EC1 ☎020/7253 4838. ⊖ Farringdon or Barbican. Mon–Fri 7am–11pm.

A handsome Smithfield market pub, complete with original Art Deco tiling, but most famous for its early opening hours and huge fried breakfasts, enjoyed by a strange mix of market workers and clubbers.

Jerusalem Tavern

Map 3, K3. 55 Britton St, EC1 ☎020/7490 4281. ⊖Farringdon. Mon–Fri 9am–11pm.

Cosy little converted Georgian parlour, stripped bare and slightly "distressed", serving tasty food at lunchtimes, along with an excellent range of draught beers from St Peter's Brewery in Suffolk.

Princess Louise

Map 3, I4. 208 High Holborn, WC1 ☎020/7405 8816. ⊖ Holborn. Mon–Fri 11am–11pm, Sat noon–11pm.

Incredibly busy after-work pub, with a superb, highly decorated ceiling, lots of glass, brass and mahogany, spectacular gents' porcelain urinals, and Sam Smith's bargain Yorkshire beer on tap.

THE CITY: FLEET STREET TO ST PAUL'S

The Black Friar

Map 5, G5. 174 Queen Victoria St, EC4 ⓣ020/7236 5650. ⊖ Blackfriars. Mon–Fri 11.30am–11pm, Sat noon–4.30pm.

A gorgeous, utterly original pub, with Art Nouveau marble friezes of boozy monks, cautionary homilies, and a wonderful, highly decorated alcove – all original fittings, dating back to 1905.

Old Bank of England

Map 5, E4. 194 Fleet St, EC4 ⓣ020/7430 2255. ⊖ Temple or Chancery Lane. Mon–Fri 11am–11pm.

Not the actual Bank of England, but the former Law Courts' branch, this imposing High Victorian banking hall is now a magnificently opulent Fuller's Ale & Pie House, serving decent standard pub fare and Fuller's beers.

Old Cheshire Cheese

Map 5, E4. Wine Office Court, 145 Fleet St, EC4 ⓣ020/7353 6170. ⊖ Temple or Blackfriars. Mon–Fri 11.30am–11pm, Sat noon–9.30pm, Sun noon–4pm.

A famous seventeenth-century watering hole, where Dickens and countless other journos once supped. The tiny, snug, dark-panelled front bar has a real fire and bags of atmosphere, but the rest simply packs in the tourists.

THE CITY: BANK TO BISHOPSGATE

The Counting House

Map 7, G4. 50 Cornhill St, EC3 ⓣ020/7283 7123. ⊖ Bank. Mon–Fri 11am–11pm.

Another ornate bank conversion, with fantastic high ceilings, a glass dome, chandeliers and a central oval bar. Naturally enough, given the location, it's wall-to-wall suits, but the space is great, the beer comes courtesy of Fuller's, and the food's not bad, either.

The George

Map 7, I2. Bishopsgate, EC2 ⓣ 020/7618 7310. ⊖ Liverpool Street.

The George – the pub on the corner of Liverpool Street – is a much more relaxing place to have a drink than the nearby *Hamilton Hall*. It's actually part of Conran's smoothly-run refurbished *Great Eastern Hotel*, and retains its wonderful original mock-Tudor décor.

Hamilton Hall

Map 7, I1. Liverpool Street Station, EC2 ⓣ 020/7247 3579. ⊖ Liverpool Street.

Cavernous, gilded former ballroom of the *Great Eastern* hotel, adorned with neo-Baroque nudes and chandeliers. Packed out with City commuters tanking up before the train home, but an awesome place nonetheless.

EAST END AND DOCKLANDS

Dickens Inn

Map 7, M7. St Katharine's Way, E1 ⓣ 020/7488 2208. ⊖ Tower Hill or Tower Gateway DLR.

Eighteenth-century timber-framed warehouse transported on wheels from its original site, and then much altered. Still, it's a remarkable building, with a great view, but very firmly on the tourist trail.

The Gun

Map 2, L5. 27 Cold Harbour, E14 ⓣ 020/7987 1692. South Quay or Blackwall DLR, or ⊖ Canary Wharf.

Inexpensive old dockers' pub with lots of maritime memorabilia, and – the chief attraction – an unrivalled view of the Millennium Dome from its riverside terrace.

Prospect of Whitby

Map 2, K4. 57 Wapping Wall, E1 ⓣ 020/7481 1095. ⊖ Wapping. Mon–Fri 11.30am–3pm & 5.30–11pm, Sat 11.30am–11pm, Sun noon–10.30pm.

London's most famous riverside pub has been here since 1520, and, with a flagstone floor, a cobbled courtyard and great views, it's still got bags of character and atmosphere. It's no secret, however, so expect to share the riverside terrace and balcony with others.

Town of Ramsgate

Map 2, K4. 62 Wapping High St, E1 ⓣ 020/7264 0001.
⊖ Wapping. Mon–Sat noon–11pm, Sun noon–10.30pm.

Dark, narrow medieval pub located by Wapping Old Stairs, which once led down to Execution Dock. Captain Blood was discovered here with the crown jewels under his cloak, and Admiral Bligh and Fletcher Christian were regular drinking partners in pre-mutiny days. Good draught beer and cheap pub grub available.

LAMBETH AND SOUTHWARK

Anchor Bankside

Map 7, C7. 34 Park St, SE1 ⓣ 020/7407 1577.
⊖ London Bridge, Southwark or Blackfriars.

While the rest of Bankside has changed almost beyond all recognition, this pub still looks much as it did when first built in 1770 (on the inside, at least). Probably the best – and most mobbed – spot for alfresco drinking by the river.

George Inn

Map 7, E9. 77 Borough High St, SE1 ⓣ 020/7407 2056.
⊖ Borough or London Bridge.

Tucked away off Borough High Street, this is London's only surviving coaching inn, with a rich historical pedigree stretching back to the seventeenth century, and now owned by the National Trust. The food isn't great, service can be slow, but it serves a good range of real ales.

Old Thameside Inn

Map 7, D7. 1 Clink St, SE1 ⓣ 020/7403 4243.
⊖ London Bridge. Mon–Fri 11am–11pm, Sat & Sun noon–4pm.

As so often with Thameside pubs, the main draw here is the popular riverside terrace, right by the *Golden Hinde*, though the converted warehouse interior is pleasant enough.

KENSINGTON, CHELSEA AND NOTTING HILL

Bunch of Grapes

Map 3, D7. 207 Brompton Rd, SW3 ⓣ020/7589 4944.
⊖ South Kensington.

This popular High-Victorian pub, complete with snob screens, is the perfect place for a post-V&A (or post-Harrods) pint, pie and chips.

The Cow

Map 3 A4. 89 Westbourne Park Rd, W2 ⓣ020/7221 5400.
⊖ Westbourne Park or Royal Oak.

Sort of vaguely Irish-themed pub owned by Tom Conran, son of gastro-magnate Terence, which pulls in the beautiful W11 types thanks to its spectacular food, including a daily supply of fresh oysters, and excellent Guinness.

Front Page

Map 3, C9. 35 Old Church St, SW3 ⓣ020/7352 2908.
⊖ Sloane Square, then buses #11, #19, #22, #211 or #319 along Kings Road.

Tucked away in the centre of villagey, boho Chelsea and infinitely preferable to anything on offer on the King's Road, the *Front Page* is small and snug, and serves very good Mediterranean food.

Market Bar

Map 2, F4. 240a Portobello Rd, W11 ⓣ020/7229 6472.
⊖ Ladbroke Grove. Mon–Fri noon–11pm,Sat noon–midnight, Sun noon–10.30pm.

Self-consciously bohemian pub divided by gilded mirrors and ruched curtains and scattered with weird *objets* – all very Portobello Road. Occasional live music and DJs.

Prince Bonaparte

Map 3, A4. 80 Chepstow Rd, W2 ⓣ020/7313 9491.
⊖ Notting Hill Gate or Royal Oak. Mon & Wed–Sat noon–11pm, Tues 5–11pm, Sun noon–10.30pm.

Very popular pared-down, trendy, minimalist pub, with

acres of space for sitting and supping while enjoying the bar snacks or the excellent Brit or Med food in the restaurant area.

ST JOHN'S WOOD AND MAIDA VALE

Prince Alfred

Map 3, B3. 9 Formosa St, W9 ⓣ020/7286 3027.
⊖ Warwick Avenue. Mon–Sat noon–11pm, Sun noon–10.30pm.

A fantastic period-piece Victorian pub with all its original 1862 fittings intact, right down to the glazed snob screens that divide the bar into a series of "snugs". The beer and food don't quite live up to the surroundings.

Warrington Hotel

Map 3, B2. 93 Warrington Crescent, W9 ⓣ020/7286 2929.
⊖ Maida Vale.

Yet another architectural gem – this time flamboyant Art Nouveau – in an area replete with them. The interior is rich and satisfying, as are the draught beers and the Thai restaurant upstairs. It is, however, incredibly, spilling-out-onto-the-street, popular.

CAMDEN TOWN

Crown & Goose

Map 2, H3. 100 Arlington St, NW1 ⓣ020/7485 2342.
⊖ Camden Town.

Lively pub/bar/restaurant, situated a block away from busy Camden High Street and not too badly mobbed until the evenings. The Modern British food is a bit special, too, and arrives in generous portions.

The Engineer

Map 2, H3. 65 Gloucester Ave, NW1 ⓣ020/7722 0950.
⊖ Chalk Farm.

One of a number of gastropubs in the much sought-after residential area of Primrose Hill, the *Engineer* is a smart, grandiose place which serves exceptional Modern Brit/Med food; it's pricey, though, and you're best off booking if you intend to nosh.

HAMPSTEAD AND HIGHGATE

The Flask

Map 2, G3. Flask Walk, NW3 ⓣ 020/7435 4580.
⊖ Hampstead.
Convivial Hampstead local, hidden away along the pedestrianized Flask Walk, which retains its original Victorian snob screen. The food is above-average pub fare, and the ales are supplied by Young's.

The Flask

Map 2, H2. 77 Highgate West Hill, N6 ⓣ 020/8340 7260.
⊖ Highgate.
Ideally situated at the heart of Highgate's village green, with a rambling low-ceilinged interior and a large, very popular summer terrace. The range of beers is good, but the food is nothing special.

Freemason's Arms

Map 2, G3. 32 Downshire Hill, NW3 ⓣ 020/7433 6811.
⊖ Hampstead.
Big, smart pub close to the Heath, popular on sunny days primarily for its large beer garden; also does comfort pub food, has a basement skittle alley, and an outdoor pell mell pitch.

Holly Bush

Map 2, G3. 22 Holly Mount, NW3 ⓣ 020/7435 2892.
⊖ Hampstead.
A lovely old wood-panelled, gas-lit pub, tucked away in the steep backstreets of Hampstead village. You can sup the excellent range of real ales in a calm and cosy atmosphere during the week, but the place can get mobbed at the weekends.

DULWICH AND GREENWICH

Crown & Greyhound

Map 2, J7. 73 Dulwich Village, SE21 ⓣ 020/8693 2466. North Dulwich or West Dulwich train stations.
Grand, spacious Victorian pub with an ornate plasterwork ceiling and a nice summer beer garden. Convenient for the Picture Gallery, but be prepared for

the Sunday lunchtime crowds.

Cutty Sark

Map 2, L5. Ballast Quay, off Lassell St, SE10 ⓣ 020/8858 3146. Cutty Sark DLR or Maze Hill train station.

The nicest riverside pub in Greenwich, spacious, more of a local and much less touristy than the more famous *Trafalgar Tavern* (it's a couple of minutes walk further east, following the river). The views are great, as is the draught beer, and the bar food is a cut above the norm.

Trafalgar Tavern

See map on p.145, E2. 5 Park Row, SE10 ⓣ 020/8858 2437. Cutty Sark DLR or Maze Hill train station.

A great riverside position and a mention in Dickens' *Our Mutual Friend* have made this Regency-style inn a firm tourist favourite, which is fair enough really, as it's a convivial period piece, and serves good food (including whitebait).

CHISWICK TO RICHMOND

The Dove

Map 2, E5. 19 Upper Mall, W6 ⓣ 020/8748 5405. ⊖ Ravenscourt Park.

Old, old riverside pub with literary associations, the smallest back bar in the UK (4ft by 7ft), and Thai food in the evening. Still by far the best of the Thameside inns within a short walk of Hammersmith, though you'll need to arrive early to get a seat on the tiny outdoor terrace.

White Cross Hotel

Map 2, C7. Water Lane, Richmond ⓣ 020/8940 6844. ⊖ Richmond.

With a longer pedigree and more character than its clinical chain rivals nearby, the *White Cross* is also much closer to the river (its front garden regularly gets flooded), and serves Young's beer and standard pub food.

White Swan

Map 2, C7. Riverside, Twickenham ⓣ 020/8892 2166.

Twickenham train station.

Filling pub food, draught beer and a quiet riverside location – with a beer pontoon overlooking Eel Pie Island if you want to get even closer to the water – make this a good halt on any towpath ramble.

Live music and clubs

Don't believe the Cool Britannia hype; London has had a bewilderingly large range of places to go after dark for the last twenty years. The **live music** scene remains extremely diverse, encompassing all variations of rock, blues, roots and world music; and although London's jazz clubs aren't on a par with those in the big American cities, there's a highly individual scene of home-based artists, supplemented by top-name visiting players.

If you're looking for **dance music**, then welcome to Europe's party capital. After dark, London is thriving, with diverse scenes championing everything from hip-hop to house, techno to trance, samba to soca and drum'n'bass to R&B on virtually any night of the week. Venues once used exclusively by performing bands now pepper the week with club nights, and you often find dance sessions starting as soon as a band has stopped playing. Bear in mind that there's sometimes an overlap between "live music venues" and "clubs" in the listings below; we've indicated which places serve a double function.

Proposed changes to England's licensing laws seem likely to finally take effect in 2000, so the already relaxed attitude to late night bars should become even more liberal in the near future. So far, though, the main consequence of the previously restrictions on late night drinking laws has been the rapid growth and diversity of **club-bars**, places which are essentially bars, but cater for a clubby crowd – funky décor, DJs, late opening hours and ridiculously overpriced foreign beers.

The dance and club scene is, of course, pretty much in constant flux, with the hottest items constantly moving location, losing the plot or just cooling off. Weekly listings magazines like *Time Out*, *DJ* and 7 give up-to-date details of prices and access, plus previews and reviews.

Exclusively gay clubs and discos are covered in Chapter 19.

LIVE MUSIC

London is hard to beat for its musical mix: whether you're into **jazz**, **indie**, **rock**, **R&B**, **blues** or **world music**, you'll find something worth hearing on almost any night of the week. **Entry prices** for gigs run from a couple of pounds for an unknown band thrashing it out in a pub to around £30 for the likes of U2, but you can reckon on around £10 for a good night out, not counting expenses at the bar. If you have a credit card, it's often cheaper to book tickets in advance via the Internet via sites such as Ⓦ *www.ticketweb.co.uk*, Ⓦ *www.tickets-online.co.uk* or Ⓦ *www.gigsandtours.com*. We've listed Web sites for all venues that have them.

ROCK AND BLUES

Astoria

Map 4, H1. 157 Charing Cross Rd, WC2 Ⓣ 020/7434 0403. ⊖ Tottenham Court Road.

One of London's best and most central medium-sized venues, this large, balconied one-time theatre tends to host slightly alternative bands, with club nights on Friday and Saturday. *LA2*, next door, is primarily a club (see p.245), but also attracts less well-known bands.

Borderline

Map 4, H2. Orange Yard, off Manette St, W1 ⓣ 020/7734 2095; ⓦ *www.borderline.co.uk* ⊖ Tottenham Court Road.

Intimate basement joint with diverse musical policy. Good place to catch new bands, although big names sometimes turn up under a pseudonym.

Brixton Academy

Map 2, I6. 211 Stockwell Rd, SW9 ⓣ 020/7771 2000. ⊖ Brixton.

This refurbished Victorian hall, complete with Roman decorations, can hold 4000 but still manages to seem small and friendly, probably because the audience isn't forced to sit down. Hosts mainly mid-league bands.

Fitz and Firkin

Map 3, G3. 240 Great Portland St, W1 ⓣ 020/7388 0588. ⊖ Great Portland Street.

A stone's throw from Regent's Park, this charismatic pub venue plays host to some of the best up-and-coming rock and indie bands.

Forum

Map 2, G3. 9–17 Highgate Rd, NW5 ⓣ 020/7344 0044; ⓦ *www.meanfiddler.com* ⊖ Kentish Town.

The Forum is perhaps the capital's best medium-sized venue, but is still a frequent stopoff point for established jazz-funk and rock bands. Great views and good bars.

The Mean Fiddler

Map 2, F4. 24–28a Harlesden High St, NW10 ⓣ 020/8961 5490; ⓦ *www.meanfiddler.com* ⊖ Willesden Junction.

An excellent – if inconveniently located – small venue with a main hall and smaller acoustic room. The bands veer from rock to world to folk.

The Orange

Map 2, F5. 3 North End Crescent, W14 ⓣ 020/7381 0444 (answerphone outside

office hours).
⊖ West Kensington.
Pub-like venue for serious-minded jazz-funkers. There are also varying club nights (call ahead).

Roadhouse

Map 4, M4. 35 The Piazza, WC2 Ⓣ 020/7240 6001;
Ⓦ *www.roadhouse.co.uk*
⊖ Covent Garden.
American food, 1950s US-style décor and a lineup of mainly blues and rock'n'roll bands performing to a mature, nostalgic crowd.

Rock Garden

Map 4, M4. 35 The Piazza, WC2 Ⓣ 020/7240 6001;
Ⓦ *www.rockgarden.co.uk*
⊖ Covent Garden.
Central, loud joint where you can get in free if you dine at the attached burger place first. Live music tends toward conventional rock, but the venue hosts a garage and R&B club night on Saturdays.

Station Tavern

Map 2, F5. 41 Bramley Rd, W10 Ⓣ 020/7727 4053.
⊖ Latimer Road.
Arguably London's best blues venue, with free – and occasionally great – blues six nights a week.

Subterania

Map 2, F5. 12 Acklam Rd, W10 Ⓣ 020/8960 4590;
Ⓦ *www.meanfiddler.com*
⊖ Ladbroke Grove.
One of the original live music/club crossover venues, set in an arch under a bridge. The crowd is as trendy as the music, which is often dance-oriented.

12 Bar Club

Map 4, I2. 22–23 Denmark Place, WC2 Ⓣ 020/7916 6989.
⊖ Tottenham Court Road.
A combination of live blues and contemporary country seven nights a week.

Underworld

Map 2, H3. 174 Camden High St, NW1 Ⓣ 020/7482 1932.
⊖ Camden Town.
Labyrinthine venue that's good for new bands, and has sporadic club nights.

JAZZ, WORLD MUSIC AND FOLK

Africa Centre

Map 4, L5. 38 King St, WC2 Ⓣ 020/7836 1973; Ⓦ *www.africacentre.org.uk* ⊖ Covent Garden.

The packed old hall was the venue that launched Soul II Soul; these days, it hosts African bands and nights like Saturday's P-funk-heavy *Funkin Pussy*, but still draws a vibrantly enthusiastic crowd.

Bull's Head Barnes

Map 2, E5. 373 Lonsdale Rd, Barnes SW13 Ⓣ 020/8876 5241. Bus #9 from ⊖ Hammersmith, or Barnes Bridge train station from Waterloo.

This riverside alehouse – with pub prices to boot – attracts Britain's finest jazz musicians, though it's now a little shabby round the edges.

Cecil Sharp House

Map 2, H3. 2 Regent's Park Rd, NW1 Ⓣ 020/7485 2206. ⊖ Camden Town.

A centre for British folk music: singing, dancing and a folk-music shop.

Dover Street

Map 8, B1. 8–9 Dover St, W1 Ⓣ 020/7629 9813. ⊖ Green Park.

London's largest jazz restaurant has music and dancing every night until 3am; the food is Modern British.

Jazz Café

Map 2, H3. 5 Parkway, NW1 Ⓣ 020/7916 6060; Ⓦ *www.jazzcafe.co.uk* ⊖ Camden Town.

Futuristic, white-walled venue with an adventurous booking policy exploring Latin, rap, funk, hip-hop and musical fusions. Diehard trad-jazz fans won't be happy, despite the fact that there's a rather good restaurant upstairs with a few prime-view tables overlooking the stage (book ahead if you want one).

100 Club

Map 2, G4. 100 Oxford St, W1 Ⓣ 020/7636 0933. ⊖ Tottenham Court Road.

After a brief spell as a stage for

punk bands, the *100 Club* is once again an unpretentious and inexpensive jazz venue – in a very central location.

Pizza Express

Map 4, F2. 10 Dean St, W1
☎ 020/7439 8722.
⊖ Oxford Street.
Enjoy a good pizza, then listen to the resident band or highly skilled guest players in this long-running basement venue. There's also a late-night session on Saturdays which starts at 9pm and finishes in the early hours of Sunday.

Ronnie Scott's

Map 4, H3. 47 Frith St, W1
☎ 020/7439 0747;
Ⓦ *www.ronniescotts.co.uk*
⊖ Leicester Square.
The most famous jazz club in London: small, smoky and still going strong, even though the great man himself has passed away. The place for top-line names, who play two sets – one at around 10pm, the other after midnight. Book a table, or you'll have to stand.

606 Club

Map 2, F6. 90 Lots Rd, SW10
☎ 020/7352 5953. ⊖ Fulham Broadway.
A rare all-jazz venue, located just off the less trendy end of King's Road. You can book a table, and the licensing laws dictate that you must eat if you want to drink, but there's no cover charge.

Union Chapel

Map 2, I3. Compton Ave, N1
☎ 020/7226 1686.
⊖ Highbury & Islington.
A wonderfully idiosyncratic old chapel that hosts an array of world fusion nights. Wrap up warm for winter gigs.

CLUBS

More than a decade after the explosion of acid-house, London remains *the* place to come if you want to party after dark. The sheer diversity of dance music has enabled the city to maintain its status as **Europe's dance capital** – and it's still a port of call for DJs from around the globe. The relaxation of late-night licensing has encouraged many venues to keep serving alcohol until 6am or even later, and the resurgence of alcohol in clubland (much to the relief of the breweries) has been echoed by the meteoric rise of the club-bar (see pp.248–250).

Nearly all of London's **dance clubs** open their doors between 10pm and midnight. Some are open six or seven nights a week, some keep irregular days, others just open at the weekend – and very often a venue will host a different club on each night of the week. Many of the best nights take place during the week, especially Wednesdays and Thursdays; for up-to-the-minute details of these, and of all the nights listed below, pop into one of Soho's many record shops (see p.310) to pick up flyers or check magazines like *7*, *DJ* or *Time Out* for details.

Admission charges vary enormously, with small midweek sessions starting at around £3 and large weekend events charging as much as £25; around £10 is the average for a Friday or Saturday night, but bear in mind that profit margins at the bar are often more outrageous than at live music venues.

CLUB VENUES

Annexe

Map 4, G3. 1 Dean St, W1
Ⓣ020/7287 9608.
⊖ Tottenham Court Road.
New, minimally chic, 400-capacity venue in the heart of the West End that plays host to some of London's best soulful house nights at weekends.

Aquarium

Map 3, M2. 256 Old St, EC1
Ⓣ020/7251 6136.
⊖ Old Street.
The place with the pool – when all the beautiful young things get hot and sweaty they can dive in and cool off.

The Arches

Map 3, L5. 53 Southwark St, SE1 Ⓣ020/7207 0707.
⊖ London Bridge.

A good place to head if you like your music retro. Soul, funk and disco from the Seventies and Eighties every weekend.

Bagley's

Map 3, I1. King's Cross Goods Yard, off York Way, N1 ⓣ020/7278 2171. ⊖ King's Cross.

Vast warehouse-style venue with a 2500-person capacity located in a post-apocalyptic industrial estate. The perfect place for enormous raves, with different music – normally including drum'n' bass, garage and old-school house in each of the three rooms, and a chill-out bar complete with sofas.

Bar Rumba

Map 4, G5. 36 Shaftesbury Ave, W1 ⓣ020/7287 2715; ⓦ*www.barrumba.co.uk* ⊖ Piccadilly Circus.

Fun, smallish West End venue with an adventurous mix of nights ranging from the future-jazz of *That's How It Is* on Mondays to the deep house vibes of *Space* on Wednesdays, and top-notch house and R&B at weekends. Pop in during the early evening (when it's free) to sample some cocktails on the cheap during happy hour.

Café de Paris

Map 3, H5. 3 Coventry St, W1 ⓣ020/7734 7700. ⊖ Leicester Square.

Elegantly restored ballroom that plays house, garage and disco to a smartly dressed crowd of wannabees – no jeans or trainers.

Camden Palace

Map 2, H3. 1 Camden High St, NW1 ⓣ020/7387 0428; ⓦ*www.camdenpalace.com* ⊖ Camden Town.

Home to popular Saturday garage nights with regular DJs such as Norris "Da Boss" Windross and Matt "Jam" Lamont; great lights, great sound, heaving crowds. Hard house dominates on Fridays at the long-running *Peach* club, hosted by DJ Graham Gold.

The Cross

Map 3, I1. Goods Way Depot, off York Way, N1 ⓣ020/7837 0828. ⊖ King's Cross.

Hidden underneath railway arches, the favourite flavours of this renowned club are hard house, house and garage. It's bigger than you imagine, but always crammed with glam clubby types, and there's a cool garden – perfect for those chill-out moments.

Cuba

Map 3, A6. 11–13 Kensington High St, W8 ⓣ 020/7938 4137. ⊖ Kensington High Street.
Grab a cocktail upstairs in the sociable bar before heading below for club nights that focus around Latin, salsa and Brazilian bossa-nova.

Electric Ballroom

Map 2, H3. 184 Camden High St, NW1 ⓣ 020/7485 9006; ⓦ *www.electricballroom.co.uk* ⊖ Camden Town.
Attracts a truly mixed crowd of Camden regulars from punks to b-boys who come for the wide range of sounds: rock, hip-hop, jazz and house.

The End

Map 3, I3. 18 West Central St, WC1 ⓣ 020/7419 9199; ⓦ *www.the-end.co.uk* ⊖ Holborn.
Designed for clubbers by clubbers, *The End* is large and spacious, with chrome minimalist décor and a devastating sound system. Well-known for its focus on tech-house and drum'n'bass at weekends, and well worth checking for monthly nights hosted by other clubs or record labels.

Fabric

Map 3, K3. 77a Charterhouse St, EC1 ⓣ 020/7490 0444; ⓦ *www.fabric-london.com* ⊖ Farringdon.
If you're a serious dance music fan then there really isn't a better weekend venue in London than the newly opened *Fabric*, a cavernous, underground brewery-like space with three rooms, holding 2500 people. Fridays alternate between hard house and hip-hop/drum'n'bass, while Saturdays concentrate on the most cutting-edge house sounds around, played by the best of the big-name DJs from around the globe. Get there early to avoid a night of queuing.

Fridge

Map 2, I6. Town Hall Parade, Brixton Hill, SW2 Ⓣ 020/7326 5100; Ⓦ *www.fridge.co.uk* ⊖ Brixton.

Weekends alternate between pumping mixed/gay nights, and trance favourites like the monthly *Escape from Samsara*, a Friday night with a psychedelic, trancey vibe, a hippy market and plenty of lightstick-waving action.

Gardening Club

Map 4, M4. 4 The Piazza, WC2 Ⓣ 020/497 3154. ⊖ Covent Garden.

A popular choice for house and garage, but be warned – you could well find yourself sharing the dancefloor with beer-boys and bemused tourists.

Gossips

Map 4, F2. 69 Dean St, W1 Ⓣ 020/7434 4480. ⊖ Tottenham Court Road.

Cave-like basement club that seems to have been around for aeons. Located deep in the heart of Soho, it's a popular stop for swing and hip-hop fans.

Hanover Grand

Map 3, G4. 6 Hanover St, W1 Ⓣ 020/7499 7977; Ⓦ *www.hanovergrand.com* ⊖ Oxford Circus.

A former Masonic hall that's now a cool and extravagant club, with a great light and sound system, a fine dancefloor, lots of alcoves – and air conditioning. Popular with a glammed-up, glittery and beautiful crew who like chart-bound house 'n' garage.

Home

Map 4, H6. 1 Leicester Square, WC2 Ⓣ 020/7909 0000; Ⓦ *www.homecorp.com* ⊖ Piccadilly Circus or Leicester Square.

The recently opened central London rival to *Fabric*, this multifloored superclub may often feel like a leisure complex, but with some of the best resident DJs in Britain and one of the finest sound systems around, it's hard to feel too depressed. The VIP bar on the sixth floor boasts spectacular panoramic views, but unless you're on the list you'll have to make do with the club rooms below.

HQs

Map 2, H3. West Yard, Camden Lock, NW1
Ⓣ 020/7485 6044.
⊖ Camden Town.
Smallish venue by the canal with a range of nights, though the emphasis is on hip-hop and jazz-fusion. Friendly vibe, good cocktails and free entry if you arrive early on weekdays.

ICA

Map 8, F3. The Mall, SW1
Ⓣ 020/7930 3647;
Ⓦ *www.ica.org.uk*
⊖ Piccadilly Circus.
The Institute of Contemporary Arts may not seem the perfect setting for a great club night, but weekends play host to some of the most cutting-edge audio-visual collaborations in town. If you're into Latin music, then the once a month, Friday night *Batmacumba*, with DJ Cliffy, is a must. There's also a great bar and excellent modern European food.

LA2

Map 4, H1. 157 Charing Cross Rd Ⓣ 020/7434 0403.
⊖ Tottenham Court Road.
Tacky but fun Nineties-house-meets-disco place with gay and straight nights. Come Saturday, it's home to the legendary 1970s disco night, *Carwash*.

The Leisure Lounge

Map 3, K4. 121 Holborn, EC1
Ⓣ 020/7242 1345.
⊖ Chancery Lane or Farringdon.
This sparsely decorated venue has had its share of the big name nights, and is always a good place to check out the latest grooves. Two dancefloors – one a full-on dance zone, the other a more relaxed bar area.

Ministry of Sound

Map 3, L7. 103 Gaunt St, SE1
Ⓣ 020/7378 6528;
Ⓦ *www.ministryofsound.co.uk*
⊖ Elephant & Castle.
A vast, state-of-the-art enterprise based on New York's legendary *Paradise Garage*, with an exceptional sound system and the pick of visiting US and Italian DJs. Corporate clubbing and full of tourists, but it still draws the top talent, especially on Saturdays. Look out for their excellent, hedonistic Bank

Holiday parties – go early to ensure you get in.

Notting Hill Arts Club

Map 3, A5. 21 Notting Hill Gate, W11 ⓣ 020/7460 4459. ⊖ Notting Hill Gate.
Basement club that's popular for everything from Latin inspired funk, jazz and disco through to soul, house and garage, and famed for Ben Watt's Sunday night deep house session, *Lazy Dog*.

Office

Map 3, G4. 3–5 Rathbone Place, W1 ⓣ 020/7636 1598. ⊖ Tottenham Court Road.
Various music styles, often focusing on swing and hip-hop, but best-known as home to a midweek session where you can play silly board games like Ker-Plunk. Booking a table in advance is advised.

Salsa!

Map 4, I3. 96 Charing Cross Rd, WC2 ⓣ 020/7379 3277. ⊖ Leicester Square.
Funky and fun salsa-based club-cum-restaurant that's a popular choice for group birthday bookings; you can book a table to eat as you mambo.

Scala

Map 3, J1. 278 Pentonville Rd, N1 ⓣ 020/7833 2022; ⓦ *www.scala-london.co.uk* ⊖ Kings Cross.
Once a cinema (it was forced to shut down after illegally showing Kubrick's *Clockwork Orange*), the *Scala* is now one of London's best clubs, holding unusual and multi-faceted nights that take in film, live bands and music ranging from quirky hip-hop to drum'n'bass and deep house. Club night *Sonic Mook Experiment*, which fuses genres as disparate as post-modern rock and leftfield dub, is a must for the open minded.

Subterania

Map 2, F5. 12 Acklam Rd, W10 ⓣ 020/7960 4590; ⓦ *www.meanfiddler.com* ⊖ Ladbroke Grove.
Just off Portobello Road, *Subterania* is worth a visit for its diverse club nights at weekends. The superior hip-hop- and R&B-heavy

Rotation is every Friday; also plays host to emerging hip-hop and R&B acts during club nights.

333

Map 3, N2. 333 Old St, EC1 ⓣ020/7630 5949.
⊖ Old Street.
One of London's best clubs for new dance music, in the heart of trendy-as-hell Hoxton. Three floors of drum'n'bass, twisted disco and breakbeat madness.

Turnmills

Map 3, K3. 63 Clerkenwell Rd, EC1 ⓣ020/7250 3409;
ⓦ*www.turnmills.com*
⊖ Farringdon.
The place to come if you want to sweat from dusk till dawn, with an alien-invasion-style bar and funky split-level dancefloor in the main room. Trance and house with top name guest DJs rule Fridays, but it's rightly famed for the awesomely glorious gay extravaganza, *Trade*, which begins on Sunday morning at 4am.

The Velvet Room

Map 3, H4. 143 Charing Cross Rd, WC2 ⓣ020/7439 4655.
⊖ Tottenham Court Road.
Very chic velvet-dripping interior, with house, techno and drum'n'bass nights. The ever-excellent Carl Cox resides at *Ultimate Base* on Thursdays.

The Wag Club

Map 4, G5. 35 Wardour St, W1 ⓣ020/7437 5534. ⊖ Leicester Square or Piccadilly Circus.
The rare-groove shrine of the 1980s, and now in need of an overhaul, though the two floors of sounds still pack 'em in on 1980s revival nights. The pick of the club nights, *Blow Up* (Saturday) offers a 1960s-schmooze meets jazz-funk-soundtrack flavour.

CLUB-BARS

The most notable event in the clubbing world in the past few years has been the rapid growth of **club-bars**: essentially bars with modern décor, dance music and a club clientele. Some of the places listed are more like regular bars, and not all of them have DJs, but all are more about socializing than dancing as there's no denying it gets tedious when you have to yell over the music.

AKA

Map 3, I3. 18 West Central St, WC1 ⓣ020/7836 0110; ⓦ*www.the-end.co.uk* ⊖ Tottenham Court Road.
Minimalist, twenty-first century-style bar next door to *The End*. A chrome balcony overlooks the main floor, which includes a well stocked bar and restaurant where you can partake of such delights as chive and butternut squash soup.

Alphabet

Map 4, D4. 61–63 Beak St, W1 ⓣ020/7439 2190. ⊖ Oxford Circus.
Upstairs is light and spacious, with decadent leather sofas, a great choice of European beers and mouthwatering food; downstairs, the dimmed coloured lights and car seats make for an altogether seedier atmosphere.

Bar Vinyl

Map 2, H3. 6 Inverness St, NW1 ⓣ020/7681 7898. ⊖ Camden Town.
Funky glass-bricked place with a record shop downstairs and a break-beat and trip-hop vibe.

Bug Bar

Map 2, I6. St Matthew's Church, Brixton Hill, SW2 ⓣ020/7738 3184. ⊖Brixton.
Set in a church crypt, this place certainly has character. A popular stopoff before the *Fridge*, playing reggae, drum'n'bass and house.

Detroit

Map 4, K3. 35 Earlham St, WC2 ⓣ020/7240 2662. ⊖ Covent Garden.

Cavernous underground venue with an open-plan bar area, secluded, Gaudíesque booths and a huge range of spirits. DJs take over at the weekends, with underground house on Saturdays.

Dog House

Map 4, F3. 187 Wardour St, W1 ⓣ020/7434 2118; ⓦ*www.doghouse.co.uk* ⊖ Leicester Square.

Colourful basement bar, popular for hip-hop, funk and acid-jazz, that draws a friendly mix of office types, students and film runners.

Embassy

Map 2, I3. 119 Essex Rd, N1 ⓣ020/7226 9849. ⊖ Angel or Highbury & Islington.

Art-school posturing meets pub debauchery in this charismatic, darkened bar just off Upper Street. Great music – deep house to drum'n'bass – from the resident DJs; the Sunday-night *They Do Play Records Don't They* is especially recommended.

Fridge Bar

Map 2, I6. 1 Town Hall Parade, Brixton Hill, SW2 ⓣ020/7326 5100; ⓦ*www.fridge.co.uk* ⊖ Brixton.

Packed at weekends (when there's free entry in the early evening), the two-floored *Fridge Bar* is a real melting pot, with a multitribal clientele grooving to R&B, house and drum'n'bass in the intimate, pitch-black downstairs club, or slamming shots in the bright upstairs bar. There are tables and chairs outside in the summer.

Hoxton Square Bar and Kitchen

Map 3, N2. 2–4 Hoxton Square, N1 ⓣ020/7613 0709. ⊖ Old Street.

Next door to the Lux cinema, this *Blade Runner*-esque concrete bar attracts the area's artists, writers and wannabees with its mix of modern European food, kitsch-to-club soundtracks, leather sofas and temporary painting and photography exhibitions. Best in the summer, though, when the drinking spills into the square in a carnival-like spirit.

Jerusalem

Map 3, G4. 33–34 Rathbone Place, W1 ⓣ 020/7255 1120. ⊖ Tottenham Court Road.
Décor is all chandeliers and velvet drapes; especially good music on Thursday nights, though it does attract a large proportion of office workers.

Lab

Map 4, I3. 12 Old Compton St, W1 ⓣ 020/7437 7820; ⓦ *www.lab-bar.co.uk* ⊖ Tottenham Court Road.
Chic, multicoloured former strip joint that stirs up some of the best cocktails in town to its style-conscious crowd of beautiful Soho-ites.

The Social

Map 3, G4. 5 Little Portland St, W1 ⓣ 020/7636 4992. ⊖ Oxford Circus.
Bacchanalian, industrial club-bar run by the Heavenly record label, with great DJs playing everything from rock to rap, a truly hedonistic-cum-alcoholic crowd and the ultimate snacks – beans on toast and cosy soup in a mug – for when you get an attack of the munchies. Fab music on the upstairs jukebox, too.

Lesbian and gay London

London's **lesbian and gay scene** is so huge, diverse and well-established that it's easy to forget just how much – and how fast – it has grown over the last few years. Pink power has given rise to the pink pound, gay liberation to gay lifestyle, and the ever-expanding gay village of Soho – now firmly established as the gay heart of the city – is vibrant, self-assured and unashamedly commercial. As a result of all this high-profile activity, straight Londoners tend to be a fairly homo-savvy bunch and, on the whole, happy to embrace and even dip into the city's queer offerings.

Soho is the obvious place to start exploring, with a mix of traditional gay pubs, trendy café/bars and a range of gay-run services. There are clubs to cater for just about every musical, sartorial and sexual taste, and while the bigger ones tend to cluster in the West End, there are equally well-established venues all over the city. Gay men still enjoy the best permanent facilities London-wide, but today's **lesbian scene** is bigger and more eclectic than it has ever been, and the cruisey girl bars which took up prize pitches on the boys' Soho turf a few years ago look like they're here to stay.

The two big **outdoor events** of the year are Mardi Gras and Summer Rites, in early July and early August respectively. A colourful, whistleblowing march through the city streets followed by a huge, ticketed party in Finsbury Park, **Mardi Gras** is the UK's biggest annual queer party, and attracts people from all over the country. For up-to-date information, festival plans and transport details, call Ⓣ020/7494 2225 or visit the Web site: Ⓦ*www.londonmardigras.com*. The ticketed **Summer Rites** in Brixton's Brockwell Park offers a similar menu of dance, music, performance and stalls, but has so far managed to remain a more laid-back and local affair. For more information on Summer Rites, check *Time Out* and the queer press (see below).

If you can't find it here, you can probably find it in the GAY to Z (Ⓦ*www.gaytoz.com*), a vast and comprehensive online directory of gay, lesbian, bisexual and TV/TS-friendly organizations and businesses. A 96-page print version is also available direct from Gay to Z Directories, 41 Cooks Rd, London SE17 3NG, priced £3 in the UK, and £10 outside the country.

London also boasts several queer-oriented annual arts events. In March, the National Film Theatre (see p.284) hosts the annual **Lesbian and Gay Film Festival**; in the last two weeks of June, the **Mardi Gras Arts Festival**, staged at venues throughout London, leads the run-up to Mardi Gras itself, and in mid-June, there's the unmissably camp **National Lesbian Beauty Contest**, currently held at the *Scala* in King's Cross; for information, call Ⓣ07932 046938; for tickets, call Ⓣ0870/606 0204.

Elsewhere, queer theatre and live art takes place all year

HELPLINES AND INFORMATION

All the following services provide information, advice and counselling, but the Lesbian & Gay Switchboard is the one to turn to first.

Bisexual Helpline ⓣ 0208/569 7500. Tues & Wed 7.30–9.30pm, Sat 10.30am–12.30pm. Advice, support and information for bisexuals.

Lesbian Line ⓣ 020/7251 6911, or minicom 020/7253 0924. Mon & Fri 2–10pm, Tues–Thurs 7–10pm. Advice, support and information for lesbians and those who think they might be, or who are questioning their sexuality.

London Friend ⓣ 020/7837 3337. Daily 7.30–10pm. Confidential information and support for lesbians and gay men. There's a women-only service on ⓣ 020/7837 2782, every evening except Fri & Sat.

London Lesbian & Gay Switchboard ⓣ 020/7837 7324. Huge, round-the-clock database on everything you might ever want to know, however trivial, plus legal advice, good counselling skills, and good humour. If you can't get through at first, keep trying.

National AIDS Helpline ⓣ 0800/567123. Freephone round-the-clock service for anyone worried about HIV and AIDS-related issues.

Project LSD at the Hungerford Drug Project ⓣ 020/7439 0717; ⓔ *projectlsd@hungerfordll.freeserve.co.uk.* Wed 6–9pm. The UK's only lesbian, gay and bisexual drugs project, offering information, advice and counselling on drug use.

Terrence Higgins Trust ⓣ 020/7242 1010. Daily noon–10pm. HIV and AIDS information and advice. For self-referrals to the counselling unit, call ⓣ 020/7835 1495.

round in the city's many fringe venues, arts centres, galleries and clubs. Details of most events appear in *Time Out* and in the many weekly, free gay papers and listings guides distributed in bars, clubs and bookshops. The most useful of these are *The Pink Paper* and *Axiom News*, which carry news and arts coverage as well as listings; *Boyz* and *qx* magazine are frothier and clubbier, with plenty of up-to-date scene information and gossip.

CAFÉS, BARS AND PUBS

There are loads of lesbian and gay **eating and watering holes** in London, many of them operating as cafés by day and transforming into **drinking dens** at night. Lots have **cabaret or disco nights** and are open until the early hours, making them a fine alternative to the more expensive clubs. The places listed here are merely a small selection of the most central, although almost every corner of London has its own gay local. Bear in mind that, as ever, "mixed" tends to mean mostly men.

Most of these cafés and bars have free admission, though a few levy a charge for the evening session (usually between £2 and £5) if there is music, cabaret or a disco.

MIXED CAFÉS, BARS AND PUBS

The Admiral Duncan

Map 4, G4. 54 Old Compton St, W1 ⓣ020/7437 5300. ⊖ Leicester Square. Mon–Sat noon–11pm, Sun noon–10.30pm.

Unpretentious, traditional-style gay bar in the heart of Soho, popular and busy with a post-work crowd, and now fully restored after the blast that ripped through it during a series of bomb attacks around London in 1999.

Balans

Map 4, G4. 60 Old Compton St, W1 ⓣ020/7437 5212. ⊖ Leicester Square. Mon–Thurs 8am–5am, Fri & Sat 8am–6am, Sun 8am–2am.

This relaxed, fashionable, but fairly pricey café-cum-bar-cum-brasserie is quintessential queer Soho, always packed, and often with a singer or cabaret after 11pm. *Balans*' breakfasts are an institution.

Bar Aquda

Map 4, M6. 13–14 Maiden Lane, WC2 ⓣ020/7557 9891. ⊖ Leicester Square or Covent Garden. Daily noon–11pm.

Bright, modern and fashionable café/bar with good food. Mixed, but mostly boys.

Bar Fusion

Map 2, I3. 45 Essex Rd, N1 ⓣ020/7688 2882. ⊖ Angel. Mon–Fri 3.30pm–midnight, Sat & Sun 2pm–midnight.

Friendly Islington café/bar with a pool table, comfy chairs at the back and a local, laid-back crowd.

The Black Cap

Map 2, H3. 171 Camden High St, NW1 ⓣ020/7428 2721. ⊖ Camden Town. Mon–Thurs noon–2am, Fri & Sat noon–3am, Sun noon–3pm & 7–10.30pm.

North London institution, offering drag and cabaret of wildly varying quality almost every night. *Mrs Shufflewick's Bar* upstairs is quieter, and opens onto a lush and lovely roof garden in the summer.

The Box

Map 4, J3. 32–34 Monmouth St, WC2 ⓣ020/7240 5828. ⊖ Covent Garden or Leicester Square. Mon–Sat 11am–11pm, Sun noon–10.30pm.

Popular café/bar serving good food for a mixed gay/straight crowd during the day, and becoming queerer as the night draws on.

The Edge

Map 4, G1. 11 Soho Square, W1 ⓣ020/7439 1313. ⊖ Tottenham Court Road. Mon–Sat noon–1am, Sun 1–10.30pm.

Busy, style-conscious and pricey Soho café/bar spread over several floors, although this doesn't seem to stop everyone ending up on the pavement, especially in summer.

First Out

Map 4, I1. 52 St Giles High St, WC2 ☎ 020/7240 8042. ⊖ Tottenham Court Road. Mon–Sat 10am–11pm, Sun 11am–10.30pm.

The West End's original gay café/bar, and still permanently packed, serving good veggie food at reasonable prices. Upstairs is airy and non-smoking, downstairs dark and foggy. *Girl Friday* is a busy Friday night pre-club session for grrrls; gay men are welcome as guests.

Freedom

Map 4, F4. 60–66 Wardour St, W1 ☎ 020/7734 0071. ⊖ Leicester Square or Piccadilly. Mon–Sat 11am–3am, Sun noon–midnight.

Hip, busy café/bar, popular with a mixed straight/gay Soho crowd. Great juices and healthy food in the daytime, cocktails and overpriced beer in the evening.

Fridge Café/Bar

Map 2, I6. 1 Town Hall Parade, SW2 ☎ 020/7326 5100. ⊖ Brixton. Mon–Wed 10am–11pm, Thurs 10am–2am, Fri & Sat 10am–4am; closed Sun.

Bang next door to the famous club of the same name, this hip café/bar lets you lurch from pint to party in one fell swoop and attracts a trendy straight/gay crowd.

The Gloucester

See map on p.145, B3. 1 King William Walk, SE10 ☎ 020/8293 6131. ⊖ Greenwich or train. Mon–Sat 11am–11pm, Sun noon–10.30pm.

Right at the gates of Greenwich Park and featured in the hit coming-out movie *Beautiful Thing*, this mixed, friendly local offers regular discos, cabaret and theme nights.

Ku Bar

Map 3, H4. 75 Charing Cross Rd, WC2 ☎ 020/7437 4303. ⊖ Leicester Square. Mon–Sat 4–11pm, Sun 4–10.30pm.

Trendy mixed bar serving a young, scene-conscious clientele. There's candlelight upstairs for those who want to canoodle.

Kudos

Map 4, K7. 10 Adelaide St, WC2 ⓣ 020/7379 4573. ⊖ Charing Cross. Mon–Sat 11am–11pm, Sun noon–10.30pm.

Busy venue, popular with smart besuited post-work boys, with a ground-floor café and a basement video bar.

The Oak

Map 2, I3. 79 Green Lanes, N16 ⓣ 020/7354 2791. ⊖ Manor House or buses #73 from Trafalgar Square, or #341 from Holborn or Angel ⊖. Mon–Thurs 5pm–midnight, Fri 5pm–2am, Sat 1pm–2am, Sun 1pm–midnight.

Friendly, spacious local pub with a dancefloor and pool table, recently refurbished and much improved. Hosts a range of mixed and women-only club nights and special events, including the wildly popular *Liberté*.

Old Compton Café

Map 4, H3. 34 Old Compton St, W1 ⓣ 020/7439 3309. ⊖ Tottenham Court Road or Leicester Square. Daily 24 hours.

This enduringly busy Soho institution never closes. Strong coffee and a cosmopolitan range of cakes and snacks make it the obvious solution to sudden mid- or post-party wooziness.

Popstarz Liquid Lounge

Map 3, I1. 275 Pentonville Rd, N1 (no phone). ⊖ Kings Cross. Thurs 5.30pm–2am, Fri 5.30pm–1am, Sat 5.30pm–3am.

Happy-go-lucky weekend dance bar popular with a young, indie-minded crowd. DJs and reliably cheap beer.

Retro Bar

Map 4, N7. 2 George Court, Adelphi Terrace (off the Strand), WC2 ⓣ 020/7321 2811. ⊖ Charing Cross. Mon–Sat noon–11pm, Sun noon–10.30pm.

Friendly indie/retro bar playing 70s, 80s, goth and alternative sounds, and featuring regular DJs and karaoke.

Rupert Street

Map 4, F5. 50 Rupert St, W1 ⓣ020/7734 5614. ⊖ Piccadilly Circus. Mon–Sat 11am–11pm, Sun noon–10.30pm.
Trendy, busy, glass-doored Soho bar; very boysy, very stylish.

Two Brewers

Map 2, H7. 114 Clapham High St, SW4 ⓣ020/7622 3621. ⊖ Clapham Common. Mon–Thurs noon–2am, Fri & Sat noon–3am, Sun noon–midnight.
Long-established and popular South London drag pub, with nightly cabaret in the front bar and a more cruisey dance-floor in the back.

Village Soho

Map 4, F4. 81 Wardour St, W1 ⓣ020/7434 2124. ⊖ Leicester Square or Piccadilly Circus. Mon–Sat 4pm–1am, Sun 4pm–10.30pm.
Elegant split-level café/bar attracting more pretty boys than girls.

The Yard

Map 4, G5. 57 Rupert St, W1 ⓣ020/7437 2652. ⊖ Piccadilly Circus. Mon–Sat 1–11pm, closed Sun.
Attractive café/bar with courtyard and loft areas. Good food, weekly cabaret and regular fortune tellers.

LESBIAN CAFÉS, BARS AND PUBS

Candy Bar

Map 4, F2. 4 Carlisle St, W1 ⓣ020/7494 4041. ⊖ Tottenham Court Road. Mon–Thurs 5pm–11.30pm, Fri 5pm–2am, Sat 4pm–2am, Sun 6–11pm.
Right in the heart of boys-land, the UK's first seven-day all-girl bar offers a retro-style cocktail bar-cum-pool room upstairs; a noisy, beery, long and narrow ground level cruising bar, and a range of club nights. Gay men welcome as guests.

The Drill Hall

Map 3, H3. 16 Chenies St, WC1 ⓣ020/7637 8270. ⊖ Goodge Street. Mon 6–11pm.
This lesbian-run arts centre offers good mixed queer and international theatre all year round, but has been opening

its bar, restaurant and workshops to women only on Monday nights since time began.

Due South

Map 2, J3. 35 Stoke Newington High St, N16 Ⓣ 020/7249 7543. Dalston or Stoke Newington train, or buses #73 from Trafalgar Square or #67, #76 and #149 from Angel ⊖. Thurs 5pm–midnight.

Hackney is the lesbian capital of London, and Thursday nights are a women-only fixture at this large, friendly mixed gay pub. Packed, beery, leery and fun, with a pool table, and a beer garden open in summer.

The Glass Bar

Map 3, H2. West Lodge, Euston Square Gardens, 190 Euston Rd, NW1 Ⓣ 020/7387 6184; Ⓦ *www.glassbar.ndo.co.uk* ⊖ Euston. Tues–Fri 5pm–late, Sat 6pm–late, Sun 2–7pm. No admission after 11.30pm.

This friendly and intimate women-only members bar (you become a member once you've found it) is housed in a listed building and features a wrought-iron spiral staircase which becomes increasingly perilous as the night goes on. Knock on the door to get in.

Vespa Lounge

Map 4, I1. Upstairs at The Conservatory, Centrepoint House, St. Giles High St, WC1 Ⓣ 020/7836 8956; Ⓔ *vespalounge@aol.com* ⊖ Tottenham Court Road. Thurs–Sat 6–11pm.

London's newest girl bar sets up shop in this prime location at weekends, and it gets busy. Pool table, video screen, cute bar staff and a mostly young crowd. Gay men welcome as guests.

GAY MEN'S CAFÉS, BARS AND PUBS

BarCode

Map 4, F5. 3–4 Archer St, W1 Ⓣ 020/7734 3342. ⊖ Piccadilly Circus. Daily noon–11pm.

Busy, stylish cruise and dance bar on two floors.

Brief Encounter

Map 4, J7. 41–43 St Martin's Lane, WC2 Ⓣ 020/7240 2221.

⊖ Leicester Square. Mon–Sat 11am–11pm, Sun noon–10.30pm.
One of the longest-running men's bars in London, recently given a facelift and still hard at it. A popular pre-*Heaven* or post-opera hang-out (it's next door to the *Coliseum*); the front bar is light, the back bar dark, and both are busy.

Brompton's

Map 3, A8. 294 Old Brompton Rd, SW5 ⓣ 020/7370 1344.
⊖ Earl's Court. Mon–Sat 4pm–2am, Sun 1pm–midnight.
Long-established bar-cum-club that's immensely popular, packed at weekends, and features regular cabarets and PAs.

Central Station

Map 3, I1. 37 Wharfdale Rd, N1 ⓣ 020/7278 3294.
⊖ King's Cross. Mon–Fri 5pm–2am, Sat noon–2am, Sun noon–midnight.
Award-winning community pub on three floors (one of them non-smoking), offering cabaret, cruisey club nights in the *Underground* basement area, and the UK's only gay sports bar. Not strictly male-only, but mostly so.

Chariots Café Bar

Map 3, N3. Chariots House, Fairchild St, EC2 ⓣ 020/7247 5222. ⊖ Liverpool Street. Mon–Sat 11am–11pm, Sun noon–10.30pm.
This large, stylish and friendly café/bar adjoins Chariots Sauna and offers regular late-licence extensions, cabaret and good-value food.

City of Quebec

Map 3, E4. 12 Old Quebec St, W1 ⓣ 020/7629 6159.
⊖ Marble Arch. Mon–Wed 11am–11pm, Thurs 11am–1am, Fri & Sat 11am–2am, Sun 11am–10.30pm.
Long-established and busy homo haunt with a downstairs disco. Especially popular with an older crowd.

The Coleherne

Map 3, A8. 261 Old Brompton Rd, SW5 ⓣ 020/7244 5951.
⊖ Earl's Court. Mon–Sat noon–11pm, Sun noon–10.30pm.
Famous, long-established and

permanently packed leather and denim bar, bristling with history, muscles and moustaches.

Compton's of Soho

Map 4, H4. 53 Old Compton St, W1 ⓣ 020/7479 7961. ⊖ Leicester Square. Mon–Sat noon–11pm, Sun noon–10.30pm.

This large, traditional-style pub is a Soho institution, always busy with a youngish crowd, but still a relaxed place to cruise or just hang out.

79CXR

Map 4, J5. 79 Charing Cross Rd, WC2 ⓣ 020/7734 0769. ⊖ Leicester Square. Mon–Thurs 1pm–2am, Fri & Sat 1pm–3am, Sun 1–10.30pm.

Busy, cruisey men's den on two floors, with industrial décor, late licence and a no-messing atmosphere.

Substation Soundshaft

Map 4, M8. Hungerford Lane (behind *Heaven*), WC2 ⓣ 020/7278 0995. ⊖ Charing Cross. Daily 10pm–5am.

The original late-night cruising pit. Steamy, cruisey and sleazy, offering a diverse seven-day menu of sartorial and musical preferences.

TEA DANCES

Somewhere between a café and a club is the institution of the **tea dance**, a fun and friendly place to try out good old-fashioned partner dancing. Traditionally, tea dancing happens on a Sunday, which means you're unlikely ever to get a serious tea dance habit – although be warned, it has happened. It's best to get there early, especially if you need a class: ring in advance for details.

Gay Tea Dance, *The Limelight*

Map 4, I4. 136 Shaftesbury Ave, W1 ⓣ 020/7439 0572. ⊖ Leicester Square. Sun 6–11pm.

A smorgasbord of 70s, 80s and 90s pop for gay boys and their

girlfriends, hosted by Miss Dusty O.

Original Sunday Tea Dance, *BJ's White Swan*

Map 2, K4. 556 Commercial Rd, E14 ⓣ020/7780 9870. ⊖ Aldgate East. Sun 5.30pm–midnight (tea and sandwiches until 7pm).

Hosted by the legendary tea dancing maestro Jo Purvis, and playing ballroom, cheesy disco and everything in between.

Pink Jukebox, *Warren Bar* at the *Grafton Hotel*

Map 3, G3. 130 Tottenham Court Rd, W1 ⓣ0374/443627. ⊖ Tottenham Court Road. Second and fourth Sun of each month, 6–11pm.

Lesbian and gay Latin and ballroom dancing club, with friendly classes for beginners and intermediates.

Ruby's Tea Dance, *Ruby's*

Map 4, C4. 49 Carnaby St, W1 ⓣ020/8302 6651. ⊖ Oxford Circus. Sun from 5.30pm (4.30pm for beginners).

Ballroom, Latin and line dancing, with free afternoon tea. Profits to Lesbian & Gay Switchboard.

Waltzing with Hilda, Jackson's Lane Community Centre

Map 2, H2. 269a Archway Rd, N6 ⓣ0793/907 2958. ⊖ Highgate. Monthly on varying Sat, 7.45pm–midnight.

Women-only Latin and ballroom dancing club – with a dash of country & western thrown in to keep you on your toes. Beer at pub prices and classes for beginners.

CLUBS

Clubs move, change and close down fast, so we've listed only the longest-running and most popular nights here – it's always a good idea to check the gay press, listings magazines and Web sites for up-to-date times and prices before you plan your night out.

Entry charges start at around £3 or £4, but are more often between £6 and £10. Some places offer concessions for students and those on benefits, and some extend **discounts** if you've managed to pick up the right flyer. Be aware of dress codes, especially in men's clubs; if in doubt, call ahead and check.

For a guaranteed harassment-free drive home, Freedom Cabs, next door to the *Rupert Street* bar, 50 Rupert St, W1 (Ⓣ 020/7734 1313), offers a conveniently located, reasonably priced, 24-hour gay cab service.

Most clubs kick off at around 10–11pm (although some don't get going until the small hours) and close between 3am and 5am, sometimes later. A fair few of London's gay bars and pubs can offer a good, cheap alternative to the fully fledged clubs, although they usually close earlier: check the listings above to see which have discos, DJs and dancing. Lastly, bear in mind again that "mixed" usually means mostly men.

MIXED CLUBS

Addiction to DTPM at *Fabric*

Map 3, K3. 77a Charterhouse St, EC1 Ⓣ 020/7251 8778. ⊖ Farringdon Road.

This long-running Sunday-nighter can now be found in *Fabric's* chic surroundings, with three dancefloors offering soul, jazz, funk, R&B, hip-hop, Latino house and progressive to hard house.

Club Kali at *The Dome*

Map 2, H3. 1 Dartmouth Park Hill, N19 (no phone). ⊖ Tufnell Park.

Held on the third Friday of every month, *Kali* is a huge multiethnic extravaganza offering bhangra, Bollywood, Arabic, swing, Hindi and house flavours for a friendly, attitude-free, mostly Asian mixed crowd.

Club V, upstairs at *The Garage*

Map 2, I3. 20–22 Highbury Corner, N5 ⓣ 020/7607 1818. ⊖ Highbury & Islington.

Every other Saturday, this mock-Tudor venue reverberates to the sounds of queercore and indie tunes spinning for a big, happy, well-lubricated crowd. Regular bands and cheap beer.

Crash

Map 3, I9. Arch 66, Goding St, SE11 ⓣ 020/7278 0995. ⊖ Vauxhall.

Four bars, two dancefloors, chill-out areas and plenty of hard bodies make this weekly Saturday-nighter busy, buzzy, sexy and mostly boysy.

Duckie at *The Royal Vauxhall Tavern*

Map 3, I9. 372 Kennington Lane, SE11 ⓣ 020/7737 4043; ⓦ *www.duckie.co.uk* ⊖ Vauxhall.

Modern rock-based hurdy gurdy for "homosexualists", their friends and fans. Regular live-art performances, occasional bouncy castles, and fabulously-titled theme nights.

Exilio Latino

Map 3, F3. 229 Great Portland St, W1 ⓣ 0956/983230 or 0793/137 4391; ⓔ *gexilio@aol.com* ⊖ Great Portland Street.

Every other Saturday night, *Exilio* erupts in a fabulous Latin frenzy, spinning salsa, cumbia and merengue, and featuring live acts.

Fist at *Imperial Gardens*

Map 3, J9. 299 Camberwell New Rd (entrance in Medlar St), SE5 (no phone). ⊖ Oval.

This famously depraved monthly Saturday sleaze pit offers a porn cinema, cruising gallery and chill-out area. Live action and strict leather/rubber/uniform/military/jock strap dress code.

G.A.Y. at *The Astoria (LA1 and LA2)*

Map 4, H1. *LA1*, 157 Charing Cross Rd ⓣ 020/7434 9592; *LA2*, 165 Charing Cross Rd ⓣ 020/7734 6963. ⊖ Tottenham Court Road.

Of the *Astoria*'s neighbouring venues, *LA1* hosts huge, unpretentious and fun-loving dance nights for a young crowd on Fridays and Saturdays, which are always packed and often feature big-name PAs. There are lots of cheap entry deals to be had at *LA2*, including the famous *G.A.Y. Pink Pounder* midweek trash bash – just £1 for a Wednesday night on the tiles.

Heaven

Map 4, M8. Under The Arches, Villiers St, WC2 ⓣ 020/7930 2020; ⓦ *www.heaven-london.com* ⊖ Charing Cross or Embankment.

Widely regarded as the UK's most popular gay club, this legendary, 2000-capacity club continues to reign supreme. Big nights are Mondays (*Popcorn*), Wednesdays (*Fruit Machine*) and Saturdays (*just Heaven*), all with big-name DJs, PAs and shows. More Muscle Mary than Diesel Doris.

Love Muscle at *The Fridge*

Map 2, I6. Town Hall Parade, Brixton Hill, SW2 ⓣ 020/7326 5100; ⓦ *www.fridge.co.uk* ⊖ Brixton.

A regular Saturday night workout for oiled torsos, disco dykes and fag hag friends, this sweaty, eight-year-old all-nighter offers everything from fluffy techno to hard house via Europop. Big stage shows, stunning lights, go-go dancers and a chill-out zone top off the party madness.

Popstarz at the *Scala*

Map 3, I1. 27 Pentonville Rd, N1 ⓣ 020/7738 2336. ⊖ King's Cross.

Ground-breaking Friday night indie club, now in its fifth year and its sixth venue, and with a consistently winning formula of indie and alternative tunes, 70s and 80s trash, cheap beer and no attitude.

Queer Nation at *Substation South*

Map 2, I6. 9 Brighton Terrace, SW9 ⓣ 020/7732 2095. ⊖ Brixton.

Long-running and popular New York-style house and garage night for funksters.

Trade at *Turnmills*

Map 3, K3. 63b Clerkenwell Rd, EC1 Ⓣ 020/7250 3409; Ⓦ *www.turnmills.com* ⊖ Farringdon.

This legendary Saturday all-nighter (business kicks off at 4am and will see you well through to Sunday lunchtime) is still going strong. Expect techno and hard house from some of the best DJs in the country, lots of lasers and special effects, and some very sweaty hard bodies – of all genders and flavours, but mostly boys.

LESBIAN CLUBS

Ace of Clubs

Map 3, G5. 52 Piccadilly, W1 Ⓣ 020/7408 4457. ⊖ Piccadilly Circus.

A veritable institution, this weekly Saturday night women-only club for all ages, styles and musical tastes has been packing 'em in for years, and shows no sign of losing its appeal.

Flirt! at the *Sauna Bar*

Map 4, L2. 29 Endell St, WC2 Ⓣ 020/7836 2236 or 7494 4041. ⊖ Covent Garden.

This'll get you sweating: the return of the lesbian sauna/club night from the successful *Candy Bar* crew, boasting a jacuzzi with room for 20. Mondays 6pm–midnight.

4 U Girl at *The Seen*

Map 4, F2. 93 Dean St, W1 Ⓣ 0956/514574; Ⓦ *www.wowbar.dircon.co.uk* ⊖ Tottenham Court Road.

A funky, glamour-dyke basement dive in the heart of Soho, playing house, soul and garage. Gay men welcome as guests.

Gia at *Shillibeers*

Map 2, H3. Carpenters Mews, North Rd, N7 Ⓣ 020/7607 0519. ⊖ Caledonian Road.

Monthly Saturday-nighter for North London grrrls and their gay male friends in a huge multilevel venue with a restaurant, cocktail and champagne lounge and a summer-only barbecue courtyard. Live PAs, celebrity guests, and a playlist of R&B, soul and NRG.

Liberté at *The Oak*

Map 2, I2. 79 Green Lanes, Newington Green, N16 ⓣ0956/673293. ⊖ Manor House or buses #73 from Trafalgar Square, or #341 from ⊖ Angel.

This hot, funky, friendly and wildly popular women-only night happens every last Saturday of the month, spinning soulful grooves, reggae and garage for girls who like to smile while they're swinging.

Loose at *Sunset Strip*

Map 4, G3. 30 Dean St, W1 ⓣ020/7494 4041. ⊖ Tottenham Court Road.

The only lesbian strip joint in the country, brought to you by the *Candy Bar* crew. Sit back, get a shot when the tequila girl comes round, order your dollars from the MC and tuck them in where you dare.

GAY MEN'S CLUBS

The Block

Map 2, L3. 28 Hancock Rd, Bow E3 ⓣ020/8983 4233. ⊖ Bromley-by-Bow.

Notorious late-night cruising haunt; think leather, rubber, uniform, skinhead, construction and industrial wear. Phone for membership details.

Chariots Roman Baths

Map 2, J4. 201–207 Shoreditch High St, EC1 ⓣ020/7247 5333. ⊖ Liverpool Street.

London's largest and most fabulous gay sauna features everything you could wish for in the way of clearing out your pores (and much else), and is open late all week and all night at weekends.

The Hoist

Map 3, I8. Railway Arch 47c, South Lambeth Rd, SW8 ⓣ020/7735 9972. ⊖ Vauxhall.

Weekend cruise bar with leather/rubber/industrial/uniform dress code. Hosts SM Gays every third Thursday.

Underground at *Central Station*

Map 3, I1. 37 Wharfdale Rd, N1 ⓣ020/7278 3294. ⊖ King's Cross.

The basement of this friendly, three-tiered pub offers sleazy late-night cruising seven nights a week, and is also host to *Gummi*, Europe's only rubber-only club, every second Sunday of the month. Equally picturesque theme nights take place on other nights: ring for details.

Classical music, opera and dance

With the South Bank, the Barbican and the Wigmore Hall offering year-round appearances by generally first-rank musicians and numerous smaller venues providing a stage for less established or more specialized performers, the capital should satisfy most devotees of **classical music**. What's more, in the annual Promenade Concerts at the Royal Albert Hall, London has one of Europe's greatest, most democratic music festivals – see p.272.

While the English National Opera quietly continues to try and demolish the elitist stereotypes of **opera**, the Royal Opera House continues to grab the headlines. After a long, costly and painful period of rebuilding and refurbishment, the ROH finally reopened at the end of 1999. Embarrassing technical hitches meant that part of the initial programme of events had to be cancelled, and ticket prices are still far too high, but the new Floral Hall development has generally been well-received.

The more modest economics of **dance** mean that you'll often find ambitious work on offer, with several adventurous companies appearing sporadically, while fans of classicism can revel in the Royal Ballet – as accomplished a company as any in Europe.

CLASSICAL MUSIC

London is spoilt for choice when it comes to **orchestras**. On most days you'll be able to catch a concert by either the London Symphony Orchestra, the London Philharmonic, the Royal Philharmonic, the Philharmonia or the BBC Symphony Orchestra, or a smaller-scale performance from the English Chamber Orchestra, London Sinfonietta or the Academy of St Martin-in-the-Fields. Unless a glamorous guest conductor is wielding the baton, or one of the world's high-profile orchestras is giving a performance, full houses are a rarity, so even at the biggest concert halls you should be able to pick up a ticket for around £12 (the usual range is about £8–20). During the week, there are also **free lunchtime concerts** by students or professionals in many of London's churches, particularly in the City; performances in the Royal College of Music and Royal Academy of Music are of an amazingly high standard, and the choice of work a lot riskier than the commercial venues can manage.

Barbican Centre

Map 7, D1. Silk St, EC2 Ⓣ020/7638 8891 or 7638 4141; Ⓦ*www.barbican.org.uk* ⊖ Barbican or Moorgate.
Home to the London Symphony Orchestra and the English Chamber Orchestra, and the regular haunt of big-name soloists, programming at the Barbican has become much more adventurous recently, and free music in the foyer is often very good. Unfortunately, however, it's a difficult place both to find and to find your way around.

BMIC (British Music Information Centre)

Map 3, F4. 10 Stratford Place, W1 Ⓣ020/7499 8567;

Ⓦ *www.bmic.co.uk*
⊖ Bond Street.
Low-price recitals most Tuesday and Thursday evenings, usually of freshly minted modern British music (good, bad and ugly).

Royal Academy of Music

Map 3, F3. Marylebone Rd, NW1 Ⓣ 020/7873 7373; Ⓦ *www.ram.ac.uk* ⊖ Regent's Park or Baker Street.
During term time, you can catch three free lunchtime concerts each week (days vary), and an early evening recital, for which there's sometimes an entry charge.

Royal College of Music

Map 3, C7. Prince Consort Rd, SW7 Ⓣ 020/7589 3643; Ⓦ *www.rcm.ac.uk* ⊖ South Kensington.
Concerts are staged at London's top music college (and occasionally at nearby St Mary Abbots church, Kensington High Street) every lunchtime at around 1pm during term time (free), as well as on occasional evenings (occasional entry charge).

St John's

Map 3, H7. Smith Square, SW1 Ⓣ 020/7222 1061; Ⓦ *www.sjss.org.uk*
⊖ Westminster.
This charming but empty deconsecrated Baroque church is situated behind Westminster Abbey, and presents a musical menu dominated by chamber music and solo recitals. The restaurant in the crypt is good for before or after.

St Martin-in-the-Fields

Map 4, K7. Trafalgar Square, WC2 Ⓣ 020/7839 8362; Ⓦ *www.stmartin-in-the-fields.org*
⊖ Charing Cross or Leicester Square.
Free lunchtime recitals on Mondays, Tuesdays and Fridays, plus a few fee-charging candlelit concerts in the evenings, sometimes featuring the top-notch orchestra of the Academy of St Martin-in-the-Fields.

South Bank Centre

Map 6, B3. South Bank Centre, SE1 Ⓣ 020/7960 4242; Ⓦ *www.sbc.org.uk*
⊖ Waterloo.

THE PROMS

The Royal Albert Hall's **BBC Henry Wood Promenade Concerts** – known to Brits as the "Proms" – tend to be associated primarily with the raucous "Last Night", when the flag-waving audience sings its patriotic heart out. This jingoistic nonsense completely misrepresents the Proms, however, which from July to September feature at least one concert daily in an exhilarating melange of favourites and new or recondite works. You can book a seat as you would for any other concert, but that would be to miss the essence of the Proms, for which the stalls are removed to create hundreds of standing places costing just £3. The upper gallery is similarly packed with people sitting on the floor or standing, and tickets there are even cheaper. The acoustics aren't the world's best, but the performers are usually outstanding, the atmosphere is great, and the hall is so vast that the likelihood of being turned away if you turn up on the night is slim. The annual *Proms Guide*, available at most bookshops from May, gives information on every concert; you can also call the Albert Hall direct on Ⓣ020/7589 8212, or visit the Web site: Ⓦ*www.royalalberthall.com*

The South Bank Centre has three concert venues: the Royal Festival Hall (RFH), is a gargantuan space, tailor-made for large-scale choral and orchestral works. It plays host to some soloists as well, though few can fill it nowadays; the Queen Elizabeth Hall (QEH) is the prime location for chamber orchestras and big-name soloists, but by no means an exclusively classical venue; the Purcell Room is the most intimate venue, excellent for chamber music and solo recitals by future star instrumentalists and singers. All concerts, other than the occasional performance in the foyer, are fee-paying.

Wigmore Hall

Map 3, F4. 36 Wigmore St, W1 Ⓣ020/7935 2141;

Ⓦ *www.wigmore-hall.org.uk*
⊖ Bond Street or Oxford Circus.
With its nigh-perfect acoustics, the Wigmore is a favourite with artists and audiences alike. An exceptional venue for chamber music, it is renowned for its song recitals and performances by rising young instrumentalists. Holds very popular, fee-paying mid-morning concerts on a Sunday.

OPERA

Despite enjoying an increase in popularity, opera remains an elitist genre and has had a bad press in London, largely owing to the travails of the **Royal Opera House**, which was expensively refurbished in 1999. In contrast to public perception of the ROH, the **English National Opera**, based at the London Coliseum, has worked hard to bring exciting, entertaining opera to the masses.

English National Opera

Map 4, K6. Coliseum, St Martin's Lane, WC2 Ⓣ 020/7632 8300; Ⓦ *www.eno.org*
⊖ Leicester Square or Charing Cross.
Home of the English National Opera, the Coliseum tends to employ more radical producers, put on a more ambitious and populist programme and offer way more democratic prices than its Royal Opera House rival. Ticket prices start at as little as £5, rising to just over £50; day seats are also available to personal callers after 10am on the day of the performance, with balcony seats going for just £2.50. Three hours before the performance, standbys go on sale (subject to availability) at a maximum price of £18 to students, senior citizens and the unemployed. All works are sung in English.

Royal Opera House

Map 4, M3. Bow St, WC2
Ⓣ 020/7304 4000;
Ⓦ *www.royaloperahouse.org*

⊖ Covent Garden.

The ROH is attempting to make itself more accessible – the new Floral Hall foyer is open to the public during the day, there's the odd free lunchtime recital, and a new studio theatre, tickets for which are more modestly priced. However, the ROH still has a deserved reputation for snobbery, conservative productions and ludicrous seat prices (over £100 for the best seats). A small number of day seats (for £30 or under) are put on sale from 10am on the day of a performance – these are restricted to one per person, and you need to get there by 8am for popular shows. Four hours before performances, low-price standbys (subject to availability) can be bought for around £15 by students, senior citizens, etc. In summer, some performances are occasionally relayed live to a large screen in Covent Garden Piazza. All operas are performed in the original language but are discreetly subtitled.

DANCE

From the time-honoured showpieces of the **Royal Ballet** to the offbeat acts of kinetic surrealism on show at the ICA, there's always a **dance performance** of some kind afoot in London, and the city also has a good reputation for international dance festivals showcasing the work of a spread of ensembles. The biggest of the annual events is the **Dance Umbrella** (Ⓣ020/8741 5881), a six-week season (Oct–Nov) of new work from bright young choreographers and performance artists at venues across the city.

ICA

Map 7, F3. Nash House, The Mall, SW1 Ⓣ020/7930 3647; Ⓦ*www.ica.org.uk*
⊖ Charing Cross.

Experimental performance-cum-dance shows dominate at the small-scale venue of the avant-garde Institute of Contemporary Arts.

London Coliseum

Map 4, K6. St Martin's Lane, WC2 ⓣ 020/7632 8300; ⓦ *www.eno.org* ⊖ Leicester Square or Charing Cross.

The English National Ballet performs on and off at this beautiful venue throughout the year (with regular spots in the summer and at Christmas), interspersed by occasional touring companies.

The Place

Map 3, H2. 17 Duke's Rd, WC1 ⓣ 020/7387 0031; ⓦ *www.theplace.org.uk* ⊖ Euston.

Home to the Richard Alston Dance Company, this small theatre also plays host to the finest in performance art and contemporary dance from across the globe.

Royal Ballet

Map 4 M3. Royal Opera House, Bow St, WC2 ⓣ 020/7304 4000; ⓦ *www.royaloperahouse.org* ⊖ Covent Garden.

The Royal Ballet is one of the world's finest classical companies, although its repertoire isn't all tutus and swans. Prices are considerably lower than for the opera – you should be able to get tickets for around £25 if you act quickly, though sell-outs are frequent (see Royal Opera House, opposite, for details of day tickets and standbys).

Sadler's Wells Theatre

Map 3, K2. Rosebery Ave, EC1. ⓣ 020/7863 8000; ⓦ *www.sadlers-wells.com* ⊖ Angel.

A diverse and exciting range of British and international dance goes on at the newly rebuilt Sadler's Wells in Islington, including productions from the Rambert Dance Company, which is usually resident here in spring and autumn. The Lilian Baylis theatre, tucked around the back, puts on smaller-scale shows, while Sadler's Wells continues to put on more populist dance at the Peacock Theatre in the West End.

South Bank Centre

Map 6, B3. South Bank, SE1 ⓣ 020/7960 4242; ⓦ *www.sbc.org.uk* ⊖ Waterloo.

The resident company here is the English National Ballet, which performs *The Nutcracker* to capacity audiences every winter and has a three- to six-week summer season in the Royal Festival Hall. The South Bank also regularly hosts dance performances by some of Europe's most adventurous groups.

Theatre, comedy and cinema

London has enjoyed a reputation for quality **theatre** since the time of Shakespeare, and despite the continuing prevalence of fail-safe blockbuster musicals and revenue-spinning star vehicles, the city still provides a platform for innovation. The **comedy** scene in London goes from strength to strength, so much so that the capital now boasts more comedy venues than any other city in the world, while comedians who have made the transition to television also stage shows in major theatres. **Cinema** is rather less healthy, for London's repertory film theatres are a dying breed, edged out by the multiscreen complexes which show mainstream Hollywood fare some months behind America. There are a few excellent independent cinemas, though, including the National Film Theatre, which is the focus of the richly varied **London Film Festival** in November.

Current details of **what's on** in all these areas can be found in a number of publications, the most comprehensive being the weekly *Time Out*. *The Guardian*'s "The Guide" section (free with the paper on Saturdays) and Friday's *Evening Standard* are other good sources.

THEATRE

At first glance, it might seem as though London's **theatreland** has become a province of the Andrew Lloyd Webber empire; however, few cities in the world can match the variety of the London scene. The state-funded **Royal Shakespeare Company** and the **National Theatre** often put on extremely original productions of mainstream masterpieces, while some of the most exciting work is performed in what have become known as the **Off West End** theatres, which consistently stage interesting and often challenging productions. Further still down the financial ladder are the **fringe theatres**, more often than not pub venues, where ticket prices are low, and quality variable.

Unfortunately, most theatre-going doesn't come particularly cheap. **Tickets** under £10 are very thin on the ground; the box-office average is closer to £15, with £30 the usual top whack. Tickets for the durable musicals and well-reviewed plays are like gold dust.

The Society of London Theatres (SOLT) **half-price ticket booth** in Leicester Square (Mon–Sat 2.30–6.30pm, Sun noon–3pm; noon–2.30pm for matinees only) sells tickets for that day's performances of all the West End shows, but they tend to be in the top end of the price range. Tickets here are sold for cash (or theatre tokens) only; they are restricted to four per person, and carry a service charge of up to £2 per ticket. If the SOLT booth has sold out, you could turn to reputable agencies such as Ticketmaster (Ⓣ020/7344 4444; Ⓦ*www.ticketmaster.co.uk*) or First Call (Ⓣ020/7497 9977; Ⓦ*www.firstcalltickets.com*), which can get seats for all West End shows, but add a ten percent mark-up on the ticket price. Bear in mind that if you buy from touts, there's no guarantee that the tickets are genuine.

Students, senior citizens and the unemployed can get **concessionary rates** on tickets for many shows, and nearly all theatres offer reductions on standby tickets to all these groups. The SOLT runs a very busy Student Theatre Line (Ⓣ 020/7379 8900) which lists all the student standby tickets available and their prices.

What follows is a list of those West End theatres that offer a changing roster of good plays, along with the most consistent of the Off West End and fringe venues. This by no means represents the full tally of London's stages, as there are scores of fringe places that present work on an intermittent basis – *Time Out* provides the most comprehensive and detailed up-to-the-minute survey.

Almeida

Map 2, I3. Almeida St, N1 Ⓣ 020/7359 4404; Ⓦ *www.almeida.co.uk* ⊖ Angel or Highbury & Islington.

A deservedly popular Off West End venue which premieres excellent new plays and excitingly reworked classics, and has attracted some big Hollywood names. The Almeida also puts on productions in other venues, including theatres in the West End.

Barbican Centre

Map 8, D1. Silk St, EC2 Ⓣ 020/7638 8891 or 7638 4141; Ⓦ *www.barbican.org.uk* ⊖ Barbican or Moorgate.

After a season in the company's HQ at Stratford, Royal Shakespeare Company productions move to one of the Barbican's two venues: the excellently designed Barbican Theatre and the much smaller Pit. A wide range of work is produced, though the writings of the Bard predominate.

Battersea Arts Centre

Map 2, H6. 176 Lavender Hill, SW11 Ⓣ 020/7223 2223; Ⓦ *www.bac.org.uk.* Clapham Junction train station from Victoria or Waterloo.

The BAC is a triple-stage building, housed in an old town hall in south London, and has acquired a reputation for excellent fringe productions, from straight theatre to comedy and cabaret.

Bush

Map 2, F5. Shepherd's Bush Green, W12 ⓣ 020/8743 3388. ⊖ Goldhawk Road or Shepherd's Bush.

This minuscule above-pub theatre is London's most reliable venue for new writing after the Royal Court, and its productions have turned up some real crackers.

Donmar Warehouse

Map 4, K3. Thomas Neal's, Earlham St, WC2 ⓣ 020/7369 1732; ⓦ *www.theambassadors.com* ⊖ Covent Garden.

A performance space that's noted for new plays and top-quality reappraisals of the classics, which has enticed several Hollywood stars – most notably Kevin Spacey and Nicole Kidman – to take to the stage. It's currently run by the young Oscar-winning director Sam Mendes.

Drill Hall

Map 3, H3. 16 Chenies St, WC1 ⓣ 020/7637 8270. ⊖ Goodge Street.

This studio-style venue off Tottenham Court Road specializes in gay, lesbian, feminist and politically correct new work. Monday evenings are women-only.

Hampstead Theatre

Map 2, G3. Swiss Cottage Centre, Avenue Rd, NW3 ⓣ 020/7722 9301; ⓦ *www.hampstead-theatre.co.uk* ⊖ Swiss Cottage.

A shed-like but comfortable theatre in Swiss Cottage (not in Hampstead proper) whose productions often move on to the West End. Such is its prestige that the likes of John Malkovitch have been seduced into performing here.

ICA

Map 7, F3. Nash House, The Mall, SW1 ⓣ 020/7930 3647; ⓦ *www.ica.org.uk* ⊖ Charing Cross.

The Institute of Contemporary Arts attracts the most innovative practitioners in all areas of performance. It also attracts a fair quantity of modish junk, but the hits outweigh the misses.

King's Head

Map 2, I3. 115 Upper St, N1 ⓣ 020/7226 1916. ⊖ Angel or Highbury & Islington.

The oldest and probably most famous of London's thriving pub theatres (with a useful late licence). Adventurous performances in a pint-sized room at lunchtimes and in the evenings.

National Theatre

Map 6, C2. South Bank Centre, South Bank, SE1 ⓣ 020/7452 3000; ⓦ *www.nt-online.org* ⊖ Waterloo.

The Royal National Theatre, as it's now officially known, consists of three separate theatres: the 1100-seater Olivier, the proscenium-arched Lyttelton and the experimental Cottesloe. Standards set by the late Lawrence Olivier, founding artistic director, are maintained by the country's top actors and directors in a programme ranging from *Wind in the Willows* to the work of Arthur Miller. Some productions sell out months in advance, but a few discounted tickets go on sale on the morning of each performance – get there by 8am for the popular shows.

Open Air Theatre

Map 3, E2. Regent's Park, Inner Circle, NW1 ⓣ 020/7486 2431. ⊖ Regent's Park or Baker Street.

If the weather's good, there's nothing quite like a dose of alfresco drama. This beautiful space in Regent's Park hosts a tourist-friendly summer programme of Shakespeare, musicals, plays and concerts.

Royal Court Theatre

Map 3, E8. Sloane Square, SW1 ⓣ 020/7565 5000; ⓦ *www.royalcourttheatre.com* ⊖ Sloane Square.

The Royal Court has recently undergone a massive refurbishment programme, but its long-standing tradition of presenting the finest in new writing looks set to continue. Smaller-scale and often more radical work gets its chance in the Theatre Upstairs studio space.

Shakespeare's Globe

Map 8, B7. New Globe Walk,

SE1 ⓣ020/7902 1500; ⓦ *www.shakespeares-globe.org* ⊖ London Bridge, Blackfriars or Southwark.

This thatch-roofed replica Elizabethan theatre uses only natural light and the minimum of scenery, and currently puts on solid, fun shows from mid-May to mid-September, with "groundling" tickets (standing-room only) for a mere £5. The new indoor Inigo Jones Theatre is set to continue the season throughout the winter months.

Tricycle Theatre & Cinema

Map 2, F3. 269 Kilburn High Rd, NW6 ⓣ020/7328 1000. ⊖ Kilburn.

One of London's most dynamic fringe venues, showcasing a mixed bag of new plays, with an emphasis on black and Irish issues, and international productions of the core repertoire.

Young Vic

Map 6, E5. 66 The Cut, SE1 ⓣ020/7928 6363; ⓦ *www.youngvic.org* ⊖ Waterloo.

A large, "in-the-round" space, perfect for Shakespeare, which is something of a speciality, as well as a studio for variable fringe productions. Big names have appeared at the main stage over the years – Vanessa Redgrave's version of Ibsen's *Ghosts* is near-legendary.

COMEDY AND CABARET

London's **comedy scene** continues to live up to its media-coined status as the new rock'n'roll with the leading fun-nypersons catapulted to unlikely stardom on both stage and screen. The Comedy Store is the best-known venue on the circuit, but even in the lowliest suburbs you can often find a local pub giving a platform to young hopefuls (again, *Time Out* gives full listings). Note that many venues operate only on Friday and Saturday nights, and that August is a lean month, as much of London's talent then heads north for the Edinburgh Festival. Tickets at smaller venues can be had for under £5, but in the more established places, you're looking at more like £12.

Backyard Comedy Club

Map 2, J4. 231 Cambridge Heath Rd, E2 ⓣ 020/7739 3122; ⓦ *www.leehurst.com* ⊖ Bethnal Green.

Purpose-built club in Bethnal Green established by comedian Lee Hurst, who has successfully managed to attract a consistently strong line-up. Fri & Sat.

Banana Cabaret

Map 2, H7. The Bedford, 77 Bedford Hill, SW12 ⓣ 020/8673 8904. ⊖ Balham.

This double-stage pub has become one of London's finest comedy venues – well worth the trip out from the centre of town. Fri & Sat from 9pm.

Canal Café Theatre

Map 3, B3. The Bridge House, Delamere Terrace, W2 ⓣ 020/7289 6054. ⊖ Warwick Avenue.

Perched on the water's edge in Little Venice, this venue is good for improvisation acts and is home to the "Newsrevue" team of topical gagsters; there's usually something going on from Thursday to Sunday.

Comedy Café

Map 3, M2. 66 Rivington St, EC2 ⓣ 020/7739 5706. ⊖ Old Street.

Long-established club on the edge of the City, often with impressive lineups, and free admission for the new-acts slot on Wednesday nights. Wed–Sat.

Comedy Store

Map 4, G6. Haymarket House, 1a Oxendon St, SW1 ⓣ 020/7344 0234; ⓦ *www.thecomedystore.co.uk* ⊖ Piccadilly Circus.

Widely regarded as the birthplace of alternative comedy, though no longer in its original venue, the Comedy Store has catapulted many a stand-up onto prime-time TV. Improvisation by in-house comics on Wednesdays and Sundays, in addition to a stand-up bill; Thursday night offers try-out spots for those brave enough to handle the hecklers, while Friday and Saturday are the busiest nights, with two shows, at 8pm and midnight – book ahead.

Jongleurs Camden Lock

Map 2, H3. Dingwalls Building, 36 Camden Lock Place, Chalk Farm Rd, NW1 ⓣ 020/7564 2500; ⓦ *www.jongleurs.com* ⊖ Camden Town.

Camden link in a top-ranking chain of venues, with a spot of post-revelry disco-dancing included in the ticket price on Fridays, and two shows on a Saturday. Book well in advance.

Meccano Club

Map 3, K1. Finnegan's Wake, 2 Essex Rd, N1 ⓣ 020/7813 4478. ⊖ Angel.

Popular, intimate, pub-based basement venue that features strong, and often Irish, line-ups. Fri & Sat.

CINEMA

There are an awful lot of **cinemas** in the West End, but only a very few places committed to non-mainstream movies, and even fewer repertory cinemas programming serious films from the back catalogue. November's **London Film Festival**, which occupies half a dozen West End cinemas, is now a huge event, and so popular that most of the films sell out a couple of days after publication of the festival's programme.

Tickets for regular showings tend to cost upwards of £7 at the major screens in the West End, although afternoon shows are usually discounted. The suburban screens run by the big companies (see *Time Out* for full listings) tend to be a couple of pounds cheaper, as do independent cinemas. Students, senior citizens and the unemployed can get concessionary rates for some shows at virtually all cinemas, usually all day Monday or at off-peak times on all weekdays.

BFI London Imax Centre

Map 6, C4. South Bank, SE1 Ⓣ 020/7902 1234; Ⓦ *www.bfi.org.uk* ⊖ Waterloo.

The British Film Institute's remarkable glazed drum sits in the middle of the roundabout at the end of Waterloo Bridge. It's stunning, state-of-the-art stuff alright, showing 2D and 3D films on a massive screen, but like all IMAX cinemas, it suffers from the paucity of good material that's been shot on the format.

Ciné Lumière

Map 3, C7. 17 Queensberry Place, SW7 Ⓣ 020/7838 2144. ⊖ South Kensington.

Predominantly – but by no means exclusively – French films both old and new (sometimes with subtitles), put on by the Institut Français.

Empire

Map 4, H6. Leicester Square, WC2; Ⓣ 0870/603 4567; Ⓦ *www.uci-cinemas.co.uk* ⊖ Leicester Square.

The huge, expensive, high-tech main auditorium here is London's second largest, and is the place where blockbusters tend to premiere, and royalty occasionally turn up.

ICA Cinema

Map 7, F3. Nash House, The Mall, SW1 Ⓣ 020/7930 3647; Ⓦ *www.ica.org.uk* ⊖ Piccadilly Circus or Charing Cross.

Vintage and underground movies shown on one of two tiny screens in the avant-garde HQ of the Institute of Contemporary Arts.

Lux Cinema

Map 3, M2. 2–4 Hoxton Square, N1 Ⓣ 020/7684 0201; Ⓦ *www.lux.org.uk* ⊖ Old Street.

Relatively new arts cinema in up-and-coming trendy Hoxton, showing an eclectic mix of films, and with an art gallery on the first floor.

National Film Theatre

Map 6, B2. South Bank, SE1 Ⓣ 020/7928 3232; Ⓦ *www.bfi.org.uk/nft*. ⊖ Waterloo.

Known for its attentive audiences and an exhaustive, eclectic programme that

includes directors' seasons and thematic series. Around six films daily are shown in the vast NFT1 and the smaller NFT2.

Odeon Leicester Square

Map 4, I6. 22–24 Leicester Square, WC2 ⓣ0870/505 0007; ⓦ*www.odeon.co.uk*
⊖ Leicester Square.
London's largest cinema, and another favourite for celeb-packed premieres. The adjacent Odeon Mezzanine crushes five screens into a far smaller space, and is one of London's least-loved cinemas.

Prince Charles

Map 4, H5. 2–7 Leicester Place, WC2 ⓣ020/7437 9127.
⊖ Leicester Square.
The bargain basement of London's cinemas (entry for most shows is just £2.50), with a programme of new movies, classics and cult favourites – the *Rocky Horror Picture Show* is a regular.

Galleries

The vast **permanent collections** of the National Gallery and the two Tates, the fascinating miscellanies of the Victoria and Albert Museum, and the select holdings of such institutions as the Courtauld and the Wallace Collection make London one of the world's great repositories of Western art. However, the city is also a dynamic creative centre, with young British artists such as Rachel Whiteread, Sarah Lucas and Steve McQueen maintaining the momentum established by the likes of Hockney, Caro, Auerbach and Freud.

In the environs of Cork Street, behind the Royal Academy, you'll find various **commercial galleries** showing the best of what's being produced in the studios of Britain and further afield, while numerous other private showcases are scattered all over London, from the superb Saatchi Gallery in St John's Wood to the consistently challenging space run by Flowers East over in the East End.

London fails to compete with Berlin, Paris and New York in only one respect – it doesn't have a designated **exhibition space** good enough to handle the blockbuster shows. Nevertheless, at any time of the year, London's public galleries will be offering at least one absorbing exhibition, on anything from the art of the apocalypse to Soviet supremacists.

Annual fixtures include the **Royal Academy's Summer Exhibition**, when hordes of amateur artists enter their efforts for sale, and November's controversial **Turner Prize**, devoted to new British work, which is preceded by a month-long display of work by the shortlisted artists at the Tate. More exciting than these, however, are the art school **degree shows** in late May and June, when the current crop of student talent puts its work on display. Pick up a copy of *Time Out* in mid-May for the times and locations of the student shows.

PERMANENT COLLECTIONS

Below is a list of London's principal permanent art collections, with a brief summary of their strengths, and, where relevant, a cross-reference to the page of the guide where you'll find more detailed coverage.

British Museum

Map 3, H3. Great Russell St, WC1 ⓣ 020/7636 1555; ⓦ *www.british-museum.ac.uk* ⊖ Russell Square or Tottenham Court Road. See p.58.
The BM owns a stupendous collection of drawings and prints, a small sample of which is always on show in room 90; it also stages excellent one-off exhibitions, sometimes with free entry.

Courtauld Institute

Map 5, A6. Somerset House, Strand, WC2 ⓣ 020/7848 2526; ⓦ *www.courtauld.ac.uk* ⊖ Covent Garden or Temple (Mon–Sat only). See p.67.
Excellent collection of Impressionists and post-Impressionists, with several masterpieces by Manet, Cézanne, Renoir, Gauguin and Van Gogh.

Dulwich Picture Gallery

Map 2, J7. College Rd, SE21 ⓣ 020/8693 5254; ⓦ *www.dulwichpicturegallery.org.uk*. West Dulwich train station from Victoria. See p.143.

London's oldest public art gallery has recently been refurbished, and houses a small but high-quality selection of work ranging from Poussin and Gainsborough to Rembrandt.

Estorick Collection

Map 2, I3. 39a Canonbury Square, N1 ⓣ 020/7704 9522; ⓦ *www.estorickcollection.com* ⊖ Highbury & Islington.

Georgian mansion with a small but interesting collection of twentieth-century Italian art, including Modigliani, di Chirico and the Futurists.

Guildhall Art Gallery

Map 7, D3. Gresham St, EC2. ⓣ 020/7332 1632; ⓦ *www.cityoflondon.gov.uk* ⊖ Bank or St Paul's. See p.85.

New purpose-built gallery housing the Corporation of London's collection, which contains one or two exceptional Pre-Raphaelite works by the likes of Rossetti and Holman Hunt.

Iveagh Bequest

Map 2, G2. Kenwood House, Hampstead Lane, NW3 ⓣ 020/8348 1286. Bus #210 from Archway ⊖ , or walk from Hampstead or Archway ⊖ . See p.138.

Stately home overlooking Hampstead Heath, that's best known for its pictures by Rembrandt, Gainsborough, Reynolds and Vermeer. Free entry.

Leighton House

Map 2, F5. 12 Holland Park Rd, W14 ⓣ 020/7602 3316. ⊖ High Street Kensington. See p.125.

The house itself is a work of art, but it also contains several works by Lord Leighton himself and his Pre-Raphaelite chums.

Lothbury

Map 7, F3. 41 Lothbury, EC2 ⓣ 020/7762 1642. ⊖ Bank.

Changing exhibitions from NatWest bank's vast art collection, which is especially strong on twentieth-century British art. Free entry.

National Gallery

Map 4, I8. Trafalgar Square, WC2 ⓣ 020/7306 0055;

Ⓦ *www.nationalgallery.org.uk*
⊖ Charing Cross or Leicester Square. See p.16.
The country's premier collection; it's difficult to think of a major artist born between 1300 and 1850 whose work isn't on show here.

National Portrait Gallery

Map 4, J7. 2 St Martin's Place, WC2 Ⓣ 020/7306 0055;
Ⓦ *www.npg.org.uk*
⊖ Leicester Square or Charing Cross. See p.18.
Interesting faces, but only a few works of art of a quality to match those on display in the neighbouring National Gallery, despite the NPGs snazzy redevelopment.

Tate Britain

Map 3, H8. Millbank, SW1
Ⓣ 020/7887 8000;
Ⓦ *www.tate.org.uk*
⊖ Pimlico. See p.30.
The old Tate is now devoted to British art from the sixteenth century onwards (the British tag is fairly loosely applied), with several galleries permanently given over to Turner.

Tate Modern

Map 6, H2. Bankside, SE1
Ⓣ 020/7887 8000;
Ⓦ *www.tate.org.uk*
⊖ Southwark. See p.109.
Housed in a spectacularly converted power station on the South Bank, the new Tate is the largest modern-art gallery in the world, and displays the cream of the international modern art collection.

Victoria and Albert Museum

Map 3, C7. Cromwell Rd, SW7
Ⓣ 020/7942 2000;
Ⓦ *www.vam.ac.uk* ⊖ South Kensington. See p.121.
The city's principal applied arts museum boasts a scattering of European painting and sculpture, a fine collection of English statuary, two remarkable rooms of casts, Raphael's famous tapestry cartoons, works by Constable, Turner and Rodin, and a photography gallery.

Wallace Collection

Map 3, E4. Hertford House, Manchester Square, W1
Ⓣ 020/7935 0687;

Ⓦ *www.wallace-collection.org.uk* ⊖ Bond Street.
See p.40.
A country mansion just off Oxford Street, with a small, eclectic collection, including fine paintings by Rembrandt, Velázquez, Hals, Gainsborough and Delacroix.

William Morris Gallery

Map 2, K1. Forest Rd, E17 Ⓣ 020/8527 3782; Ⓦ *www.lbwf.gov.uk/wmg* ⊖ Walthamstow Central.
Covers every aspect of Morris & Co's work, and there's a small gallery of Pre-Raphaelite work by Morris and his colleagues' upstairs.

MAJOR GALLERIES AND EXHIBITION SPACES

Expect to pay around £7 for entry to one of the big exhibitions at the Barbican or Hayward. Similar prices are charged for special shows at the National Gallery, the Tates and V&A (see above) and at the Royal Academy (see overleaf). Students, senior citizens and the unemployed are eligible for concessionary rates. Hours vary so it's always best to check *Time Out* or ring the gallery before setting off.

Barbican Art Gallery

Map 8, D1. Barbican Centre, Silk St, EC2 Ⓣ 020/7638 8891; Ⓦ *www.barbican.org.uk* ⊖ Barbican or Moorgate.
The Barbican's two-floor gallery is badly designed, but its thematic exhibitions – ranging from African bush art to the latest photography – are often well worth the entrance fee.

Hayward Gallery

Map 6, B3. South Bank Centre, Belvedere Rd, SE1 Ⓣ 020/7960 5226; Ⓦ *www.hayward-gallery.org.uk* ⊖ Waterloo.
Part of the huge South Bank arts complex, the Hayward is one of London's most prestigious venues for major touring exhibitions, with the bias towards twentieth-century work.

ICA Gallery

Map 8, F3. Nash House, The Mall, SW1 Ⓣ 020/7930 3647; Ⓦ *www.ica.org.uk* ⊖ Piccadilly Circus or Charing Cross.

The Institute of Contemporary Arts has two gallery spaces, in which it displays works that are invariably characterized as "challenging" or "provocative" – occasionally, they are. To visit, you must be a member of the ICA; a day's membership costs £1.50 (Mon–Fri) or £2.50 (Sat & Sun).

Royal Academy of Arts

Map 4, B7. Burlington House, Piccadilly, W1 Ⓣ 020/7300 8000; Ⓦ *www.royalacademy.org.uk*
⊖ Green Park or Piccadilly Circus. See p.37.

The Royal Academy is best known for its one-off exhibitions – its recent Monet extravaganza was the most popular art exhibition of all time. From early June to mid-August, the RA also stages its Summer Exhibition, when the public can submit work to be displayed (and sold) alongside the work of Academicians. Tasteful landscapes, interiors and nudes tend to predominate, but there's the odd splash of experimentation. For the most popular shows here, you're best advised to pre-book a ticket.

Royal Institute of British Architects (RIBA)

Map 3, F3. 66 Portland Place, W1 Ⓣ 020/7307 3770; Ⓦ *www.riba.net* ⊖ Oxford Circus. See p.42.

Regular architectural exhibitions by the leading lights, housed in a beautiful 1930s building, with an excellent café.

Saatchi

Map 2, G3. 98a Boundary Rd, NW8 Ⓣ 020/7624 8299.
⊖ Swiss Cottage.

First-rate exhibition space owned by Charles Saatchi, the Mr Big of Britain's art world who made his money in advertising. Shows change twice-yearly, and a couple of Saatchi's youngsters usually hit the headlines straight after the opening.

Serpentine Gallery

Map 3, C6. Kensington Gardens, Hyde Park, W2 ⓣ 020/7402 6075; ⓦ *www.serpentinegallery.org* ⊖ Lancaster Gate.

This fine gallery displays dynamic work by new and established modern artists, as well as hosting interesting Sunday afternoon lectures, and a performance-art festival in the summer. It's free, too.

Whitechapel Gallery

Map 7, M2. Whitechapel High St, E1 ⓣ 020/7522 7888. ⊖ Aldgate East.

The Whitechapel is a consistently excellent champion of contemporary art, housing major shows by living or not-long-dead artists. It's also the focal point of the Whitechapel Open, a biennial summer survey (the next one is in 2002) of the work of artists living in the vicinity of the gallery; the show spreads into several local studios too.

COMMERCIAL GALLERIES

The galleries listed below are at the hub of London's modern-art market. Most are open Monday to Friday 10am to 6pm, plus a few hours on Saturday morning, and many are closed throughout August, but you'd be best advised to ring to check the latest hours, as rehangings or private viewings often interrupt the normal pattern of business. Some of these places can seem as intimidating as designer clothes shops, but all at least are free.

Annely Juda

Map 3, F4. 23 Dering St, W1 ⓣ 020/7629 7578; ⓦ *www.annelyjudafineart.co.uk* ⊖ Oxford Circus or Bond Street.

One of the city's best modernist galleries; specializing in early twentieth-century avant-garde works, but equally strong on contemporary painting and sculpture.

Anthony d'Offay

Map 3, F4. Dering St and Haunch of Venison Yard, W1 ⓣ020/7499 4100; ⓦ*www.doffay.com* ⊖ Oxford Circus or Bond Street.

Several galleries on Dering Street, and a new one round the corner in the delightfully named Haunch of Venison Yard, all run by one of the real powerbrokers in the world of art politics. Works exhibited here range from recently dead greats of Pop Art, to pieces by leading contemporary artists such as Rachel Whiteread.

Entwistle

Map 4, A6. 6 Cork St, W1 ⓣ020/7734 6440. ⊖ Green Park.

Box-like space often featuring small shows by major figures in the contemporary British and American art scenes.

Flowers East

Map 2, J3. 199–205 and 282 Richmond Rd, E8 ⓣ020/8985 3333; ⓦ*www.flowerseast.com.* London Fields train station, from Liverpool Street.

This outstanding, ever-expanding East End gallery complex shows a huge variety of work, generally by young British artists.

Helly Nahmad

Map 4, A6. 2 Cork St, W1 ⓣ020/7494 3200. ⊖ Green Park.

A gallery where you're guaranteed a glimpse at some very expensive works by very famous artists, from Monet to Picasso.

Lisson

Map 3, C3. 52–54 Bell St, NW1 ⓣ020/7724 2739; ⓦ*www.lisson.co.uk* ⊖ Edgware Road.

An extremely important gallery whose regularly exhibited sculptors – among them Anish Kapoor and Richard Deacon – are hugely respected on the international circuit.

Marlborough Fine Art

Map 4, A6. 6 Albemarle St, W1 ⓣ020/7629 5161; ⓦ*www.marlboroughfineart.com* ⊖ Green Park.

This is where you'll find the latest work of many of

Britain's most celebrated artists, many in one-person shows. Essential viewing for anyone interested in modern British art.

Waddington's

Map 4, A6. 11, 12 and 34 Cork St, W1 ⓣ020/7437 8611; ⓦ*www.waddington-galleries.com* ⊖ Green Park.
No. 11 is the largest of three Cork Street premises owned by Leslie Waddington, and tends to concentrate on the established greats of the twentieth century. At the others you'll find newer international stars and younger upcoming artists.

White Cube

Map 4, C8. 44 Duke St, W1 ⓣ020/7930 5373; ⓦ*www.whitecube.com* ⊖ Green Park.
Open Friday and Saturday only, this is a gallery that likes to grab the headlines, with the latest YBAs (Young British Artists). Damien Hirst, Tracey Emin and various other Turner Prize artists display here.

PHOTOGRAPHY

The Barbican and the Hayward both host **photographic exhibitions** from time to time. The galleries listed below are places you can guarantee will always have photos on show. Apart from the V&A, entry is free.

Hamilton's

Map 3, F5. 13 Carlos Place, W1 ⓣ020/7499 9493; ⓦ*www.hamiltonsgallery.com* ⊖ Bond Street or Green Park.
Classy Mayfair exhibition space for the most famous and fashionable contemporary photographers. Loads of pricey prints for sale as well.

National Portrait Gallery

Map 4, J7. 2 St Martin's Place, WC2 ⓣ020/7306 0055; ⓦ*www.npg.org.uk* ⊖ Leicester Square or Charing Cross.
The NPG has lots of exceptional photos in its collection, with a fair sampling on permanent display; it also regularly holds

special (fee-charging) exhibitions on internationally famous photo-portraitists.

Photographers' Gallery

Map 4, J6. 5 and 8 Great Newport St, WC2 Ⓣ 020/7831 1772; Ⓦ *www.photonet.org.uk* ⊖ Leicester Square.

The capital's premier photography gallery shows work by new and established British and international photographers, often with a couple of exhibitions running concurrently. The prints are often for sale.

Victoria and Albert

Map 3, C7. Cromwell Rd, SW7 Ⓣ 020/7942 2000; Ⓦ *www.vam.ac.uk* ⊖ South Kensington.

The V&A now has a permanent gallery devoted to photography, though it's way too small to do justice to its vast collection. There's an admission charge for the museum.

Shops and markets

Whether it's time or money you've got to burn, London is one big shopper's playground. And although chains and superstores predominate along the high streets, you're still never too far from the kind of oddball, one-off establishment that makes shopping an adventure rather than a chore. From the *folie de grandeur* that is Harrods to the frantic street markets of the East End, there's nothing you can't find in some corner of the capital.

In the centre of town, **Oxford Street** is the city's most frantic chain store mecca, and together with **Regent Street**, which crosses it halfway, offers pretty much every mainstream clothing label you could wish for. Just off Oxford Street, high-end designer outlets line **St. Christopher's Place** and **South Molton Street**, and you'll find even pricier designers and jewellers along the very chic **Bond Street**.

Tottenham Court Road, which heads north from the east end of Oxford Street, is the place to go for electrical goods and furniture and design shops. **Charing Cross Road**, heading south, is the centre of London's book trade, both new and secondhand. At its north end, and particularly on **Denmark Street**, you can find music shops selling everything from instruments to sound equipment and sheet music. **Soho** offers an offbeat mix of sex boutiques, records

OPENING HOURS

Opening hours for central London shops are generally Monday to Saturday 9.30am to 6pm, although some stay open later, especially on Thursdays. Many are now open on Sundays, although hours tend to be shorter, from around noon to 5pm. The cheapest time to shop is during one of the two annual **sale seasons**, centred on January and July, when prices can be slashed by up to fifty percent. **Credit cards** are almost universally accepted by shops. Always keep your receipts: whatever the shop may tell you, the law allows a full refund or replacement on purchases which turn out to be faulty.

and silks, while the streets surrounding **Covent Garden** yield art and design shops, mainstream fashion stores and designer wear.

Just off Piccadilly, **St James's** is the natural habitat of the quintessential English gentleman, with **Jermyn Street** in particular harbouring shops dedicated to his grooming. **Knightsbridge**, further west, is home to Harrods, and the big-name fashion stores of **Sloane Street** and **Brompton Road**.

DEPARTMENT STORES

Fortnum & Mason

Map 4, C8. 181 Piccadilly, W1 ⓣ 020/7734 8040. ⊖ Green Park or Piccadilly Circus.

Beautiful and eccentric store featuring heavenly ceiling murals, gilded cherubs, chandeliers and fountains as a backdrop to its perfectly English offerings. Justly famed for its fabulous, gorgeously presented and pricey food, plus upmarket clothes, furniture and stationery.

Harrods

Map 3, D7. Knightsbridge, SW1 Ⓣ 020/7730 1234; Ⓦ *www.harrods.com* ⊖ Knightsbridge.

Put an afternoon aside to visit this enduring landmark of quirks and pretensions, most notable for its fantastic Art Nouveau tiled food hall, obscenely huge toy department, and supremely tasteless memorial to Diana and Dodi in the basement. Wear jeans and you may fail the rigorous dress code for entry.

Harvey Nichols

Map 3, E6. 109–125 Knightsbridge, SW1 Ⓣ 020/7235 5000. ⊖ Knightsbridge.

All the latest designer collections on the scarily fashionable first floor, where the shop assistants look better dressed than most of the customers. The cosmetics department is equally essential, while the food hall offers famously frivolous and pricey luxuries.

John Lewis

Map 3, F4. 278–306 Oxford St, W1 Ⓣ 020/7629 7711; Ⓦ *www.johnlewis.com* ⊖ Oxford Circus.

Famous for being "never knowingly undersold", this reliable institution can't be beaten for basics, from buttons to stockings to rugs, along with reasonably priced and well-made clothes, furniture and household goods. The staff are knowledgeable and friendly, too.

Liberty

Map 4, B3. 210–220 Regent St, W1 Ⓣ 020/7734 1234; Ⓦ *www.liberty-of-london.com* ⊖ Oxford Circus.

This fabulous and rather regal emporium of luxury is most famous for its fabrics and accessories, but is also building an excellent reputation for both mainstream and new fashion. The perfume, cosmetics and household departments are good, too.

Marks & Spencer

Map 3, E4. 458 Oxford St, W1 Ⓣ 020/7935 7954. ⊖ Marble Arch.

The flagship store of this

British institution offers a huge range of well-made own-brand clothes (the lingerie selection is fancier than in local branches), food, homeware and furnishings.

Selfridges

Map 3, F4. 400 Oxford St, W1 ⓣ 020/7629 1234.
⊖ Bond Street.
This huge, airy mecca of clothes, food and furnishings was London's first great department store, and remains one of its best, with a fashionable menswear department and a solid womenswear floor; the food hall is impressive, too.

CLOTHES AND ACCESSORIES

The listings below concentrate on the home-grown rather than the ubiquitous international names, but if you're after designer wear, bear in mind that nearly all of the department stores listed above stock lines from both major and up-and-coming designers. For designer-style fashion at lower prices, try the more upmarket high street chains: there are branches of Gap, French Connection, Karen Millen, Jigsaw, Monsoon, Kookai, Warehouse, Hobbs and Whistles all over the capital. Marks & Spencer and BHS are a good bet for even cheaper versions of the same styles. For street, clubwear, secondhand and vintage gear, London's markets also have plenty to offer.

DESIGNER

Amazon

Map 3, A6. Kensington Church St, W8 ⓣ 020/7937 4692.
⊖ High Street Kensington.
Several branches along the Kensington High Street end of Church Street, offering both designer and quality brand-name gear at huge discounts, with one stocking a great range of strictly designer labels.

Browns

Map 3, F4. 23–27 South Molton St, W1 ⓣ 020/7514 0016. ⊖ Bond Street.
Huge range of designer wear for men and women, with big international names under the same roof as the hip young things. Browns' **Labels for Less**, at 50 South Molton St, W1 (ⓣ 020/7514 0052) could save you precious pennies.

Burberry

Map 4, B5. 165 Regent St, W1 ⓣ 020/7734 4060.
⊖ Oxford Circus or Piccadilly.
The quintessential British outdoors label has hit the catwalk and relaunched itself as a fashion essential. Get the traditional stock at a huge discount from Burberry's Factory Shop, 29–53 Chatham Place, E9 (ⓣ 020/8985 3344; Hackney Central train).

Ghost

Map 2, F5. 36 Ledbury Rd, W11 ⓣ 020/7229 1057; ⓦ *www.ghost.co.uk*
⊖ Notting Hill Gate.
Romantic, floaty and hugely popular modern Victoriana in pastel shades.

Jean Paul Gaultier

Map 3, C7. Galerie Gaultier, 171–175 Draycott Ave, SW3 ⓣ 020/7584 4648.
⊖ South Kensington.
Outrageous, extravagant and fun, JPG's designs continue to raise a smile. Here you can get the mid-price (which still doesn't mean cheap) range, too.

Jones

Map 4, L4. 13 and 15 Floral St, WC2 ⓣ 020/7240 8312; ⓦ *www.jones-clothing.co.uk*
⊖ Covent Garden.
Formal, casual and street menswear from all the big names and some of the smaller ones. Sharp tailoring, jeans and everything in between.

Joseph

Map 3, G5. 23 Old Bond St, W1 ⓣ 020/7629 3713 (and many other branches).
⊖ Bond Street.
Offering classic cuts in imaginative styles, Joseph is the last word in luxury

fashion for men as well as women. The **Joseph Sale Shop** at 23 Avery Row, SW3 (Ⓣ 020/7730 7562; ⊖ Sloane Square) offers good discounts on womenswear.

Koh Samui

Map 4, J4. 65 Monmouth St, WC2 Ⓣ 020/7240 4280. ⊖ Leicester Square or Covent Garden.

The leading promoter of young British designers, stocking a highly selective range of womenswear with an elegant, eclectic and urban feel.

Nicole Farhi

Map 3, F4. 158 New Bond St, W1 Ⓣ 020/7499 8368 (and other branches). ⊖ Bond Street.

Classic designs and cuts for women, invariably in the shades of a chameleon resting on a sandy rock, but no less elegant and popular for that.

Paul Smith

Map 2, F5. Westbourne House, 122 Kensington Park Rd, W11 Ⓣ 020/7727 3553 (⊖ Notting Hill Gate); and 40–44 Floral St, WC2 Ⓣ 020/7379 7133 (⊖ Covent Garden); Ⓦ *www.paulsmith.co.uk*

The Covent Garden store is more accessible, but the Notting Hill shop-in-a-house is worth a visit, selling Smith's whole range of well-tailored, very English clothes for men, women and children. The Smith Sale Shop, at 53 Avery Row, W1 (Ⓣ 020/7493 1287; ⊖ Bond Street) offers huge discounts.

Vexed Generation

Map 4, F4. 3 Berwick St, W1 Ⓣ 020/7729 5669. ⊖ Piccadilly Circus.

Created in all kinds of new fabrics and coatings, the clothes here are so cool it hurts.

Vivienne Westwood

Map 3, F4. 6 Davies St, W1 Ⓣ 020/7629 3757 (and other branches). ⊖ Bond St.

Somewhat eccentric but revered by the international fashion pack, this quintessentially English maverick is still going strong.

STREET AND CLUBWEAR

AdHoc/Boy

Map 4, I3. 10–11 Moor St, W1 Ⓣ 020/7287 0911.
⊖ Leicester Square.
Party gear for exhibitionists: plenty of PVC, lycra, feathers and spangles, with fairy wings and magic wands to match your outfit, and a body-piercing studio downstairs.

Burro

Map 4, L4. 19a Floral St, WC2 Ⓣ 020/7240 5120.
⊖ Covent Garden.
Funky but with an air of studied nonchalance, this is for boys who want to look cool without looking like they want to look cool.

Cyberdog

Map 4, J3. 9 Earlham St, WC2 Ⓣ 020/7836 7855.
⊖ Covent Garden.
Club ambience for club gear, with a UV light showing off the goods to good effect: funky T-shirts, combat ski pants, and glowing accessories to show you the way home.

Diesel

Map 4, K3. 43 Earlham St, WC2 Ⓣ 020/7497 5543; Ⓦ *www.diesel.com*
⊖ Covent Garden.
Still cool despite the hype, this industrial-looking store for label-conscious men and women continues to offer that retro-denim look in a dazzling variety of colours and styles.

Duffer of St George

Map 4, K2. 29 Shorts Gardens, WC2 Ⓣ 020/7379 4660.
⊖ Covent Garden.
Covetable own-label boys' casuals and streetwear, plus a range of other hip labels in the land of jeans, shoes, jackets and so on.

Home

Map 4, L4. 28a Floral St, WC2 Ⓣ 020/7240 7077; Ⓦ *www.paulfrankisyourfriend.com* ⊖ Covent Garden.
The cheeky monkey featured on some of the capital's cooler streetwear accessories originated here. Jeans, shirts, trainers, shoes, bags, wallets and hats all serve to produce a one-stop, Paul Frank-style combo.

Mambo

Map 4, K3. 2–3 Thomas Neal Centre, 37 Earlham St, WC2 ⓣ 020/7379 6066; ⓦ *www.mambo.com.au* ⊖ Covent Garden.
Surf, skate and graffiti gear, including a range of books, mugs and hats.

Shop

Map 4, E5. 4 Brewer St, W1 ⓣ 020/7437 1259. ⊖ Piccadilly Circus.
Lots of cabinets stuffed with fashion accessories, some cushions and bedding, plus blaxploitation mugs and plates, and clothes: fleeces, jeans, T-shirts, slip dresses and more.

VINTAGE, SECOND-HAND AND ARMY SURPLUS

The Emporium

See map on p.145. A2. 330–332 Creek Rd, SE10 ⓣ 020/7305 1670. ⊖ Greenwich or train.
Elegant retro store specializing in 1940s to 1960s clothes for both men and women, and featuring kitsch displays in its beautiful glass-fronted cases. Well-kept bargains start at a tenner.

Laurence Corner

Map 2, H4. 62–64 Hampstead Road, NW1 ⓣ 020/7813 1010. ⊖ Warren Street.
London's oldest and most eccentric Army surplus shop, with lots of bargains and an extensive theatrical and fancy-dress hire section.

Oxfam Originals

Map 4, C4. 26 Ganton St, W1 ⓣ 020/7437 7338. ⊖ Oxford Circus.
Oxfam's well-kept retro branch offers cleaned-up clothes which appeal to hip, clubby bargain-hunters. There's another branch at 22 Earlham St, WC2 (ⓣ 020/7836 9666).

SHOES

Buffalo Boots

Map 4, K2. 47–49 Neal St, WC2 ⓣ 020/7379 1051; ⓦ *www.buffalo-boots.com* ⊖ Covent Garden.
Everything from the practical

to the clubby via spike-heeled boots and enormous platform shoes.

Dr Marten Department Store

Map 4, L5. 1–4 King St, WC2 ⓣ 020/7497 1460.
⊖ Covent Garden.
Five floors featuring every kind of Dr Marten for every kind of Doc-lover, from traditional black and oxblood to metallic, pastel or playground colours.

Office

Map 4, K2. 57 Neal St, WC2 ⓣ 020/7379 1896 (and many other branches).
⊖ Covent Garden.
Good, broad range of basics, including many own-label creations, at reasonable prices, plus some more frivolous fashion moments, too.

Pied à Terre

Map 3, G5. 31 Old Bond St, W1 ⓣ 020/7629 0686 (and many other branches).
⊖ Green Park.
Elegant but pricey women's footwear, with an interesting combination of classic and modern styles.

Shellys

Map 4, A2. 266–270 Regent St, W1 ⓣ 020/7287 0939 (and many other branches).
⊖ Oxford Circus.
Offering pretty much everything from the sensible to the silly and with a good deal in between, this always madly busy store has a huge range over several floors and at every price, for both men and women.

BOOKS

As well as the big-name **chain bookstores**, most of which have branches throughout the city, London is blessed with a wealth of **local, independent and specialist bookshops**, many of which are located on or around Charing Cross Road. They may not have everything stocked by the chains, but they will almost certainly be more interesting to browse around, and may well have some hidden jewels on their shelves.

Secondhand books are also sold at the Riverside Walk stalls, under Waterloo Bridge on the South Bank, SE1 (Sat & Sun 10am–5pm, and occasionally midweek); Waterloo ⊖ or train.

Any Amount of Books

Map 3, H4. 56 and 62 Charing Cross Rd, WC2 Ⓣ 020/7240 8140; Ⓦ *www.anyamountofbooks.com* ⊖ Leicester Square.

Sprawling secondhand bookshop spread over two neighbouring sites, stocking everything from obscure 50p bargains to rare and expensive first editions. Especially strong on fiction, the arts and literary biography.

Arthur Probsthain Oriental & African Bookseller

Map 3, H4. 41 Great Russell St, WC1 Ⓣ 020/7636 1096. ⊖ Tottenham Court Road.

Connected to the nearby School of Oriental and African Studies, this impressive academic store covers all relevant aspects of art, history, science and culture.

Atlantis Bookshop

Map 3, I3. 49a Museum St, WC1 Ⓣ 020/7405 2120; Ⓦ *www.atlantisbookshop.demon.co.uk* ⊖ Tottenham Court Road.

Splendid occult-oriented place with the perfect ambience for browsing through books and magazines covering spirituality, psychic phenomena, witchcraft and so on.

Blackwell's

Map 3, H4. 100 Charing Cross Road, WC2 Ⓣ 020/7292 5100 (and other branches); Ⓦ *www.bookshop.blackwell.co.uk* ⊖ Tottenham Court Road or Leicester Square.

The London flagship of Oxford's best academic bookshop has a wider range than you might expect; academic stock is unsurprisingly excellent, but so is the range of recent computing, travel and fiction titles.

Books for Cooks

Map 2, F5. 4 Blenheim Crescent, W11 ⓣ 020/7221 1992. ⊖ Ladbroke Grove.
Anything and everything to do with food can be found on the drooling shelves of this wonderful new and second-hand bookshop, which also has a tiny café (see p.193) offering cookery demonstrations, coffee for browsers, and lunch.

Books Etc

Map 3, H4. 120 Charing Cross Rd, WC2 ⓣ 020/7379 6838 (and other branches).
⊖ Tottenham Court Road.
Large, laid-back and user-friendly, with an on-site coffee shop and a wide and well-stocked range of mainstream and specialist titles, and especially good on contemporary fiction.

Borders Books & Music

Map 3, G4. 203–207 Oxford St, W1 (and other branches) ⓣ 020/7292 1600; ⓦ *www.borders.com*
⊖ Oxford Circus or Tottenham Court Road.
Enormous London flagship of the American import, boasting four floors of book, music and CD titles alongside a huge range of magazines and a coffee bar. Good range of titles, with staff recommendations and reviews, and a solid children's section.

Cinema Bookshop

Map 3, H4. 13–14 Great Russell St, WC1 ⓣ 020/7637 0206. ⊖ Tottenham Court Road.
Close to the British Museum and in the heart of Bloomsbury, this small outlet has every new and second-hand cinema title you might want somewhere on its towering shelves.

Daunt Books

Map 3, E3. 83 Marylebone High St, W1 ⓣ 020/7224 2295 (and other branches).
⊖ Bond Street or Baker Street.
Wide and varied range of travel literature as well as the usual guidebooks, presented by expert staff in the beautiful, galleried interior of this famous shop.

Forbidden Planet

Map 3, H4. 71–75 New Oxford St, WC1 ⓣ020/7836 4179. ⊖ Tottenham Court Road.
Two permanently-packed floors of all things science-fiction and fantasy-related, ranging from books and comics to games and ephemera.

Foyles

Map 3, H4. 113–119 Charing Cross Rd, WC2 ⓣ020/7437 5660. ⊖ Tottenham Court Road.
Endearingly (sometimes irritatingly) antiquated, this huge and famous London bookshop is best avoided if you're short of time. Pretty much everything you might want is here, but finding it is one adventure, and paying for it another; you queue once to part with your money, and again to pick up the book.

Gay's the Word

Map 3, H3. 66 Marchmont St, WC1 ⓣ020/7278 7654; ⓦ *www.gaystheword.co.uk* ⊖ Russell Square.
Extensive collection of lesbian and gay classics, pulps, contemporary fiction and non-fiction, plus cards, calendars, magazines and more. Known for the weekly lesbian discussion groups and readings held in the back of the shop.

Gosh!

Map 3, H4. 39 Great Russell St, WC1 ⓣ020/7636 1011. ⊖ Tottenham Court Road.
All kinds of comics for all kinds of readers, whether you're the casually curious or the serious collector. Check out the Cartoon Gallery in the basement.

Politico's

Map 3, G7. 8 Artillery Row, SW1 ⓣ020/7828 0010; ⓦ *www.politicos.co.uk* ⊖ St James's Park.
Mainstream political fare, new and secondhand, with plenty of big biographies. A cosy café, board games and irreverent window displays give it a more frivolous edge.

Silver Moon Women's Bookshop

Map 3, H4. 64–68 Charing Cross Rd, NW1 ⓣ020/7836 7906;

Ⓦ *www.silvermoonbookshop.co.uk* ⊖ Leicester Square.
Large, well-stocked and spread over two floors, boasting the biggest lesbian department in the country and knowledgeable staff. Good selection of magazines, periodicals, cards, T-shirts, etc too.

Souls of Black Folks

Map 2, I6. 407 Coldharbour Lane, SW9 Ⓣ020/7738 4141. ⊖ Brixton.
Dedicated black bookshop specializing in African, Caribbean and African-American literature, with regular readings, a buzzing café and late opening hours.

Stanford's Map and Travel Bookshop

Map 4, K4. 12–14 Long Acre, WC2 Ⓣ020/7836 1321. ⊖ Leicester Square or Charing Cross.
The world's largest specialist travel bookshop, this features pretty much any map of anywhere, plus a huge range of travel books and guides.

Unsworths Booksellers

Map 3, H3. 12 Bloomsbury St, WC1 Ⓣ020/7436 9836. ⊖ Tottenham Court Road.
Good for bargains, including recent and just-out-of-print novels and academic titles. Specializes in the humanities, and features an interesting antiquarian selection.

Waterstone's

Map 3, H4. 121–123 Charing Cross Rd, WC2, Ⓣ020/7434 4291 (and other branches). ⊖ Tottenham Court Road.
Flagship store of the huge, quality book chain, with technical and travel titles as well as fiction. The Waterstone's Arts store, at 8 Long Acre, WC2 (Ⓣ020/7836 1359; ⊖ Leicester Square or Covent Garden) covers all aspects of the graphic and fine arts, media and music.

Zwemmer Media Arts

Map 3, H4. 80 Charing Cross Rd, WC2 Ⓣ020/7240 4157 (and other branches); Ⓦ *www.zwemmer.com* ⊖ Leicester Square.

Specialist art bookstore with a fantastic and expert selection across several neighbouring branches. This branch specializes in film, design and photography.

MUSIC

MEGASTORES

HMV

Map 4, B2. 150 Oxford St, W1 ⓣ 020/7631 3423; ⓦ *www.hmv.co.uk* ⊖ Oxford Circus.
All the latest releases, as you'd expect, but also an impressive backlist, a reassuring amount of vinyl, and a good classical section downstairs. Dance music is also a strength.

Tower Records

Map 4, E7. 1 Piccadilly Circus, W1 ⓣ 020/7439 2500; ⓦ *www.towerrecords.co.uk* ⊖ Piccadilly Circus.
Fantastic range, although it's not always easy to find what you're looking for, and genre classifications sometimes seem a little random. The jazz, folk and world music department upstairs is especially impressive.

Virgin Megastore

Map 4, G1. 14–16 Oxford St, W1 ⓣ 020/7631 1234. ⊖ Tottenham Court Road.
The mainstream floor here is better stocked than the specialist sections: the bias is rock-heavy, but there's a little of everything else, and plenty of books, magazines, T-shirts and assorted music ephemera.

INDEPENDENT STORES

Caruso & Company

Map 3, G3. 10 Charlotte Place, W1 ⓣ 020/7636 6622. ⊖ Goodge Street.
Comfortable, well-stocked shop specializing in opera, but with much else besides.

Daddy Kool

Map 4, E2. 12 Berwick St, W1 ⓣ 020/7494 10181. ⊖ Oxford Circus or Tottenham Court Road.
Lots of collectable reggae

vinyl, most of it classic roots and Studio One, as well as the latest ragga and drum'n'bass.

Deal Real Records

Map 4, D2. 6a Noel St, W1 ⓣ 020/7734 8689. ⊖ Oxford Circus.
UK and US hip-hop specialist for those who know exactly what they're after.

Eukatech

Map 4, K2. 49 Endell St, WC2 ⓣ 020/7240 8060. ⊖ Covent Garden.
House, techno and trance on two floors, both vinyl and CD.

Gramex

Map 3, J6. 25 Lower Marsh, SE1 ⓣ 020/7401 3830. ⊖ Waterloo.
A splendid find for classical music lovers, this new and secondhand record store features both CDs and vinyl, and offers comfy leather armchairs to sample or discuss your finds at leisure.

Honest Jon's

Map 2, F5. 276 Portobello Rd, W10 ⓣ 020/8969 9822. ⊖ Ladbroke Grove.
Jazz, soul, funk, R&B, rare groove, dance and plenty more make this a browser's delight, with current releases, secondhand finds and reissues on vinyl and CD.

MDC Classic Music

Map 4, L7. 437 Strand, WC2 ⓣ 020/7240 2157 (and many other branches). ⊖ Charing Cross or Embankment.
Big and brassy, this central chain store has an impressive range of stock, but specializes in special offers and cut-price CDs.

Mr Bongo

Map 4, D3. 44 Poland St, WC1 ⓣ 020/7287 1887. ⊖ Oxford Circus.
Good on 12" singles, and equally reliable for hip-hop, jazz, funk, Latin American and Brazilian sounds.

Ray's Jazz Shop

Map 4, I4. 180 Shaftesbury Ave, WC2 ⓣ 020/7240 3969. ⊖ Leicester Square or Tottenham Court Road.
Essential jazz territory, lovingly curated and full of collectors

and browsers poring happily over its well-stocked bins. New and old releases on CD, plus an extensive vinyl collection, a good blues basement, some choice world and folk music, and expert staff.

Sister Ray

Map 4, E3. 94 Berwick St, W1 ⓣ020/7287 8385. ⊖ Oxford Circus or Piccadilly Circus.
Up-to-the minute indie sounds, with lots of electronica and some forays into the current dance scene, most on vinyl as well as CD.

Stern's African Record Centre

Map 3, G2. 293 Euston Rd, NW1 ⓣ020/7387 5550. ⊖ Euston Square.
World famous for its global specialisms, this knowledgeable store has an unrivalled stock of African music and excellent selections from pretty much everywhere else in the world.

MARKETS

Brick Lane, Columbia Road, Petticoat Lane and Spitalfields markets are reviewed on p.93.

Bermondsey (New Caledonian) Market

Map 3, N6. Bermondsey Square, SE1.
⊖ Borough or London Bridge.
Fri 5am–2pm.
Huge, unglamorous but highly regarded antique market offering everything from obscure nautical instruments to attractive but pricey furniture. As the real collectors arrive at dawn to pick up the bargains, you should get here before midday.

Camden

Map 2, H3. Camden High St to Chalk Farm Rd, NW1.
⊖ Camden Town. Mainly Thurs–Sun 9.30am–5.30pm.
On the high street, Camden Market (Thurs–Sun 9.30am–5.30pm) offers a good mix of new and second-

hand clothes and records, while the Electric Market (Sun 9am–5.30pm) and Camden Canal Market (Sat & Sun 10am–6pm) has cheap fashion, hippywear and souvenirs. Camden Lock, off Chalk Farm Road (Sat & Sun 10am–6pm) offers arts, crafts and clothes, with some shops (Wed–Sun, 10am–6pm) adding a few hip designers, antique dealers and booksellers to the mix. Leading off from Camden Lock, the Stables Yard (Sat & Sun 10am–6pm) is a sprawling adventure of clubwear, young designers, furniture, trinkets and antiques.

Covent Garden

Map 4, M4. Apple Market and Jubilee Market, off Southampton St, WC2. ⊖ Covent Garden. Daily 9am–5pm.

The Apple Market has rather twee handmade craft most days, while Jubilee offers endless cheap T-shirts, jewellery, souvenirs and so on – the Jubilee antiques market on a Monday is more enjoyable. Street performers are found in the piazza every day, and it's an amiable area to wander about in.

Greenwich

See map on p.145, B2. Greenwich High Rd, Stockwell St, and College Approach, SE10. ⊖ Greenwich or train, or Cutty Sark DLR. Mainly Thurs–Sun, 9.30am–5pm.

The covered College Approach section sells mostly twentieth-century antiques on a Thursday (7.30am–5pm), and handmade goods and clothes from Friday to Sunday (9.30am–5.30pm), while the Central Market off Stockwell Street has funky second-hand clothes, bric-a-brac and furniture. Shops inside the covered market and in the surrounding streets offer obscure maritime devices.

Portobello Road

Map 2, F5. Portobello Rd, W10, and Golborne Rd, W11. ⊖ Ladbroke Grove or Notting Hill Gate. Antique market Sat 7.30am–6.30pm; general market Mon–Wed 8am–6pm, Thurs 9am–1pm & Fri–Sat 7am–7pm;

organic market Thurs 11am–6pm. Golborne Rd market Mon–Sat 9am–5pm.
Start at the Notting Hill end and make your way through the antiques and bric-a-brac down to the fruit and veg stalls, and then under the Westway to the seriously hip new and secondhand clothes stalls and shops around which local style vultures circle and swoop. The Golborne Road market is cheaper and less crowded, with some very attractive antiques and retro furniture.

MISCELLANEOUS

Anything Left-Handed

Map 4, E5. 57 Brewer St, W1 ⓣ 020/7437 3910; ⓦ *www.anythingleft-handed.co.uk* ⊖ Piccadilly Circus.
The place to go for left-handed tools, implements and gifts.

Davenport's Magic Shop

Map 4, M8. 7 Charing Cross Tube Arcade, Strand WC2 ⓣ 020/7836 0408. ⊖ Charing Cross or Embankment.
The world's oldest family-run magic business, stocking marvellous tricks for both amateurs and professionals.

Flying Duck Enterprises

See map on p.145, A2. 320–322 Creek Rd, SE10 ⓣ 020/8858 1964. ⊖ Greenwich or train, or Cutty Sark DLR.
Kitsch aplenty, whether you're after tacky 1970s board games, Elvis soap or a 1950s polka-dotted dinner service.

Neal Street East

Map 4, L3. 5 Neal St, WC2 ⓣ 020/7240 0135. ⊖ Covent Garden.
Beautiful crafts, jewellery, books, clothes, puppets and knick-knacks from a loosely defined Orient.

Radio Days

Map 3, J6. 87 Lower Marsh, SE1 ⓣ 020/7928 0800. ⊖ Waterloo.
A fantastic collection of

memorabilia and accessories from the 1930s to the 1970s, including shoes, shot glasses, cosmetics and vintage magazines, plus a huge stock of well-kept ladies' and menswear from the same period.

Sport

As a quick glance at the national press will tell you, **sport** in Britain is a serious matter, with each international defeat being taken as an index of the country's slide down the scale of world powers. Many of the crucial domestic and international fixtures of the **football**, **rugby** and **cricket** seasons take place in the capital, and London also hosts one of the world's greatest tennis tournaments, the **Wimbledon** championships.

For **up-to-the-minute details** of sporting events in London, check the *Evening Standard* or *Time Out*, or ring the London Sportsline on ⓣ020/7222 8000.

FOOTBALL

English **football** (or soccer) is passionate, and if you have the slightest interest in the game, then catching a league or FA Cup fixture is a must. The season runs from mid-August to early May, when the **FA Cup Final** at Wembley rounds things off. There are four league divisions: one, two, three, and, at the top of the pyramid, the twenty-club **Premier League**. There are London clubs in every division, with around five or six in the Premiership at any one time.

The highlights of the day's best games are shown on BBC

TV's **Match of the Day**, on Saturday nights. Most Premiership fixtures kick off at 3pm on Saturday, though there are always a few midweek games (usually 7.30pm on Wednesday), and one or two each Sunday (kick-off between 2 and 4pm) and Monday (kick-off around 8pm), broadcast live on Sky TV.

London's top club at the moment is **Arsenal** (Ⓣ020/7704 4000; Ⓦ*www.arsenal.co.uk*), who won the double (league and FA Cup) in the 1997–98 season. Meanwhile, in west London, **Chelsea** (Ⓣ020/7386 7799; Ⓦ*www.chelseafc.co.uk*) waltzed away with the last-ever European Cup Winners' Cup. It's reasonably easy to get **tickets**, if booked in advance, for most London Premier League games, unless two London sides are playing each other. The biggest of these "derby" fixtures are the meetings of North London rivals Arsenal and Tottenham Hotspur (Ⓣ020/8365 5000; Ⓦ*www.spurs.co.uk*). Tickets for Premiership matches don't come cheap, however, with most charging a minimum of £15–20.

CRICKET

In the days of the Empire, the English took **cricket** to the colonies as a means of instilling the gentlemanly values of fair play while administering a sound thrashing to the natives. These days, the former colonies – such as Australia, the West Indies and India – all beat England on a regular basis, and to see the game at its best you should try to get into one of the **Test matches** between England and the summer's touring team. These international fixtures are played in the middle of the cricket season, which runs from April to September. Two of the matches are played in London: one at **Lord's** (Ⓣ020/7289 1611; Ⓦ*www.lords.org*), the home of English cricket, in St John's Wood, the other at **The Oval** (Ⓣ020/7582 6660; Ⓦ*www.surreyccc.co.uk*), in

Kennington. In tandem with the full-blown five-day Tests, there's also a series of one-day internationals, two of which are usually held in London.

Getting to see England play one of the big teams can be difficult unless you book months in advance. If you can't wangle your way into a Test, you could watch it live on television, or settle down to an inter-county match, either in the **county championship** (these are four-day games) or in one of the three fast and furious one-day competitions. Two county teams are based in London – **Middlesex**, who play at Lord's, and **Surrey**, who play at The Oval.

RUGBY

Rugby gets its name from Rugby public school, where the game mutated from football (soccer) in the nineteenth century. A rugby match may at times look like a bunch of weightlifters grappling each other in the mud – as the old joke goes, rugby is a hooligan's game played by gentlemen, while football is a gentleman's game played by hooligans – but it is in reality a highly tactical and athletic game. England's rugby team tends to represent the country with rather more success than the cricket squad, though they can't quite match the power and attacking panache of the sides from the Southern Hemisphere.

There are two types of rugby played in Britain: fifteen-a-side **Rugby Union**, which has upper-class associations (though the game is also very strong in working-class Wales) and only became a professional sport in 1995; and thirteen-a-side **Rugby League**, which has long been a professional game played almost exclusively in the north of England (though the final of one of its knock-out trophies is traditionally played at Wembley), and which has moved into a new era with the formation of Super League, featuring the big name northern clubs and one London club, the

London Broncos (Ⓣ020/8410 5000; Ⓦ*www.londonbroncos.co.uk*), which shares a ground with Charlton football club. Games traditionally take place on Sundays at 3pm, but there are also matches on Friday and Saturday nights. The season runs from March to September, thus enabling players to play Union in the winter.

In London, virtually all rugby clubs play Rugby Union, with the two biggest teams being **Harlequins** (Ⓣ020/8410 6000; Ⓦ*www.quins.co.uk*) and **London Wasps** (Ⓣ020/8902 4220; Ⓦ*www.wasps.co.uk*). The season runs from September until May, finishing off with the **Tetley Bitter Cup**, rugby's equivalent of the FA Cup. The cup final and international matches are played at **Twickenham** (Ⓣ020/8892 2000; Ⓦ*www.rfu.com*), in southwest London. Unless you are affiliated to one of the 2000 clubs of the Rugby Union, or willing to pay well over the odds at a ticket agency, it is tough to get a ticket for one of these big Twickenham games. A better bet is to go and see a Harlequins or Wasps league game, where there's bound to be an international player or two on display – you can usually get in for around £12.

TENNIS

Tennis in England is synonymous with **Wimbledon** (Ⓣ020/8946 2244; Ⓦ*www.wimbledon.com*), the only Grand Slam tournament in the world to be played on grass, and for many players the ultimate goal of their careers. The Wimbledon championships last a fortnight, and are always held during the last week of June and the first week of July. Most of the **tickets**, especially seats for the main show courts (Centre and No. 1), are allocated in advance to the Wimbledon tennis club's members, other clubs and corporate "sponsors" – as well as by public ballot – and once these have taken their slice there's not a lot left for the general public.

On tournament days, queues start to form around dawn – if you arrive by around 7am, you have a reasonable chance of securing one of the limited number of Centre and No. 1 court tickets held back for sale on the day. If you're there by around 9am, you should get admission to the outside courts (where you'll catch some top players in the first week of the tournament). Either way, you then have a long wait until play commences at noon – and if it rains you don't get your money back.

If you want to see big-name players in London, an easier opportunity is the Stella Artois men's championship at **Queen's Club** (Ⓣ020/7385 3421) in Hammersmith, which finishes a week before Wimbledon. Many of the male tennis stars use this tournament to acclimatize themselves to British grass-court conditions. As with Wimbledon, you have to apply for tickets in advance, although there is a limited number of returns on sale at 10am each day.

For the unlucky, there's the consolation of TV coverage, which is pretty all-consuming for Wimbledon.

HORSE RACING

There are five **horse racecourses** within easy reach of London: **Kempton Park** (Ⓣ01932/782292; Ⓦ*www.kempton.co.uk*), near Sunbury-on-Thames; **Sandown Park** (Ⓣ01372/463072; Ⓦ*www.sandown.co.uk*), near Esher in Surrey; and **Windsor** (Ⓣ01753/865234; Ⓦ*www.windsorracing.co.uk*), in Berkshire, which hold top-quality races on the flat (April–Sept) and over jumps (Aug–March). There's also **Ascot** (Ⓣ01344/622211; Ⓦ*www.ascot.co.uk*), in Berkshire, and **Epsom** (Ⓣ01372/726311; Ⓦ*www.epsomderby.co.uk*) in Surrey, which are the real glamour courses, hosting major races of the flat-racing season every June.

Thousands of Londoners have a day out at Epsom on Derby Day, which takes place on the first or second

Saturday in June. **The Derby**, a mile-and-a-half race for three-year-old thoroughbreds, is the most prestigious of the five classics of the April to September English flat season, and is preceded by another classic, **the Oaks**, which is for fillies only. The three-day Derby meeting is as much a social ritual as a sporting event, but for sheer snobbery, nothing can match the **Royal Ascot** week in mid-June, when the Queen and selected members of the royal family are in attendance, along with half the nation's bluebloods. The best seats are the preserve of the gentry, who get dressed up to the nines for the day; but, as is the case at most racecourses, the rabble are allowed into the public enclosure for a mere £5.

GREYHOUND RACING

A night out at the **dogs** is still a popular pursuit in London. It's an inexpensive, cheerful and comfortable spectacle: a grandstand seat costs less than £5 and all six London stadiums have one or more restaurants, some surprisingly good. Indeed, the sport has become so popular that you'd be best advised to book in advance if you want to watch the races from a restaurant table, particularly around Christmas. Meetings usually start around 7.30pm and finish at 10.30pm, and usually include around a dozen races. The two easiest stadiums to get to are in South London: **Catford** (Ⓣ 020/8690 8000; Ⓦ *www.thedogs.co.uk*) and **Wimbledon** (Ⓣ 020/8946 8000; Ⓦ *www.wimbledondogs.co.uk*).

ICE SKATING

London has just one centrally located indoor ice rink, plus the outdoor Broadgate rink – located in the heart of the City near Liverpool Street station. Session times tend to vary quite a lot, but generally last for around two to three hours.

Broadgate Ice Rink

Map 7, H1. Broadgate Circus, Eldon St, EC2 ⓣ020/7505 4068; ⓦ *www.broadgateestates.co.uk/ice/frameset.htm*
⊖ Liverpool Street.
A little circle of ice open from October to March. It's fun (in fine weather), but can get crowded during the weekend. Mon–Wed evenings are for "broomball" matches. Admission £5; skate rental £2.

Leisurebox

Map 3, A5. 17 Queensway, W2 ⓣ020/7229 0172.
⊖ Queensway or Bayswater.
The whole family can skate at this rink, which has ice-discos on Fri & Sat evenings. Admission £5; skate rental £1.

POOL AND SNOOKER

Pool has replaced darts as the most popular pub sport in London. There are scores of pubs offering small-scale pool tables, even in the centre of the city, where space is at a premium. Real **American pool**, played on a larger table than pub pool, is also moving into halls once dedicated to **snooker**, the equivalent British game.

Elbow Room

Map 3, A4. 103 Westbourne Grove, W2 ⓣ020/7221 5211; ⓦ *www.elbow-room.co.uk*
⊖ Bayswater or Notting Hill Gate. Mon–Sat noon–11pm, Sun noon–10.30pm.
The capital's trendiest pool club by far, with designer décor, purple-felt American pool tables, and better-than-average grilled fast-food and beer. No membership fee; you simply pay £6–9 per hour for use of the tables, depending on the time of day.

Ritzy's Pool Shack

Map 3, F8. 16 Semley House, Semley Place, SW1 ⓣ020/7823 5817. ⊖Victoria. Mon–Sat 11am–11pm, Sun noon–10.30pm.

Situated behind Victoria coach station, Ritzy's was exclusively a snooker hall but has now added 17 pool tables to its facilities. It's now another of the city's trendier pool clubs, with a cocktail bar and American-style diner. Day membership for the downstairs snooker club is £5; for pool you just pay the £6–9 fee per table per hour – the later the hour the pricier it gets.

SWIMMING, GYMS AND FITNESS CENTRES

Below is a selection of the best-equipped, most central of London's multipurpose **fitness centres**. We haven't given the addresses of the city's many council-run swimming pools, virtually all of which now have fitness classes and gyms. Wherever you go, however, a swim will usually cost you around £2.50.

If you fancy an alfresco dip, then the Serpentine Lido in Hyde Park (see p.119), or the **open-air pools** on Hampstead Heath are your best bet.

Ironmonger Row Baths

Map 3, M2. Ironmonger Row, EC1 ⓣ020/7253 4011. ⊖ Old Street. Men: Tues & Thurs 9am–9.30pm, Sat 9am–6pm. Women: Mon, Wed & Fri 9am–9.30pm, Sun 10am–6pm.

An old-fashioned kind of place that attracts all classes, with a steam room, sauna, small plunge pool, masseurs, a lounge area with beds, and a large pool. Admission for a three-hour session is a bargain at £10.

Oasis Sports Centre

Map 4, L3. 32 Endell St, WC2 ⓣ020/7831 1804. ⊖ Covent Garden. Indoor pool: Mon–Fri 6.30am–5pm, Sat & Sun 6.30am–4.30pm. Outdoor pool: Mon–Fri 7.30am–9pm, Sat & Sun 7.30am–4.30pm.

The Oasis has two pools, one of which is the only heated outdoor pool in central London. Other facilities include a gym, a health suite with sauna and sunbed, massage, and badminton and squash courts.

Porchester Spa

Map 3, A4. 225 Queensway, W2 ⓣ 020/7792 3980. ⊖ Bayswater or Queensway. Men: Mon, Wed & Sat 10am–10pm. Women: Tues, Thurs & Fri 10am–10pm, Sun 10am–4pm. Mixed: Sun 4–10pm.

Built in 1926, the Porchester is one of only two Turkish baths in central London, and is well worth a visit for the Art Deco tiling alone. Admission is around £20 and entitles you to use the saunas, steam rooms, plunge pool, jacuzzi and swimming pool.

The Sanctuary

Map 4, L4. 11–12 Floral St, WC2 ⓣ 08700/630300; ⓦ *www.thesanctuary.co.uk* ⊖ Covent Garden. Non-members: Mon, Tues & Sun 10am–6pm, Wed–Fri 9.30am–6pm, Sat 10am–8pm.

For a serious day of self-indulgence, this women-only club in Covent Garden is a real treat: the interior is filled with lush tropical plants and you can swim naked in the pool. It's a serious investment at around £50, but your money gets you unlimited use of the pool, jacuzzi, sauna and steam room, plus one sunbed session.

Festivals and special events

This chapter is simply a rundown of the principal **festivals and annual events** in the capital, ranging from the upper-caste rituals of Royal Ascot to the sassy street party of the Notting Hill Carnival, plus a few oddities like Horseman's Sunday. Our listings cover a pretty wide spread of interests, but they are by no means exhaustive; London has an almost endless roll-call of ceremonials and special shows, and for daily information, as always, it's well worth checking *Time Out* or the *Evening Standard*.

JANUARY 1

London Parade To kick off the new year, a procession of floats, marching bands, clowns, American cheerleaders and classic cars wends its way from Parliament Square at noon, through the centre of London, to Berkeley Square, collecting money for charity from around one million spectators en route. Information Ⓣ020/8566 8586; Ⓦ*www.london parade.co.uk*. Admission charge for grandstand seats in Piccadilly, otherwise free.

LATE JANUARY

London International Mime Festival Annual mime festival which takes place in the last two weeks of January on the South Bank, and in other funky venues throughout London. It pulls in some very big names in mime, animation and puppetry. Information Ⓣ020/7637 5661; Ⓦ*www.mimefest.co.uk*

LATE JANUARY/EARLY FEBRUARY

Chinese New Year Celebrations The streets of Soho's Chinatown explode in a riot of dancing dragons and firecrackers on the night of this vibrant annual celebration, and the streets and restaurants are packed to capacity.

MARCH

Head of the River Race Less well known than the Oxford and Cambridge race, but much more fun; there are over 400 crews setting off at ten-second intervals and chasing each other from Mortlake to Putney. Information Ⓣ01932/220401; Ⓦ*www.horr.co.uk*

LATE MARCH/EARLY APRIL

Oxford and Cambridge Boat Race Since 1845, the rowing teams of Oxford and Cambridge universities have battled it out on a four-mile, upstream course on the Thames from Putney to Mortlake. It's as much a social as sporting event, and the pubs at prime vantage points pack out early. Alternatively you can catch it on TV. Best source of information is the current sponsor's Web site: Ⓦ*www.aberdeen-asset.com*

THIRD SUNDAY IN APRIL

London Marathon The world's most popular city marathon, with some 35,000 runners sweating the 26.2 miles from Greenwich Park to Westminster Bridge. Only a handful of world-class athletes enter each year; most of the competitors are club runners or obsessive flab-fighters. There's always someone dressed up as a gorilla, and you can generally spot a fundraising celebrity or two. Information Ⓣ020/7620 4117; Ⓦ*www.london-marathon.co.uk*

MAY BANK HOLIDAY WEEKEND

IWA Canal Cavalcade Lively celebration of the city's inland waterways held at Little Venice (near ⊖Warwick Avenue), with scores of decorated narrowboats, Morris dancers and lots of children's activities. Information Ⓣ020/8874 2787.

SUNDAY NEAREST TO MAY 9

May Fayre and Puppet Festival The garden of St Paul's church in Covent Garden is taken over by puppet booths to commemorate the first recorded sighting of a Punch and Judy show, by diarist Samuel Pepys in 1662. Information Ⓣ020/7375 0441.

MID-MAY

FA Cup Final This is the culmination of the football (soccer) year: the premier domestic knock-out competition, played to a packed house at Wembley Stadium. Tickets are pretty much impossible to obtain if you're not an affiliated supporter of one of the two competing clubs, though they are often available at inflated prices on the black market.

The game is also shown live on television. Information ⓣ020/8902 0902.

THIRD OR FOURTH WEEK IN MAY

Chelsea Flower Show Run by the Royal Horticultural Society, the world's finest horticultural event transforms the normally tranquil grounds of the Royal Hospital in Chelsea for four days, with a daily inundation of up to 50,000 gardening gurus and amateurs (the general public are allowed in on the last two days only). It's a solidly bourgeois event, with the public admitted only for the closing stages, and charging an exorbitant fee for the privilege. Information ⓣ020/7834 4333; ⓦ*www.rhs.org.uk*

MAY 29

Oak Apple Day The Chelsea Pensioners of the Royal Hospital honour their founder, Charles II, by wearing their posh uniforms and decorating his statue with oak leaves, in memory of the oak tree in which the king hid after the Battle of Worcester in 1651. Information ⓣ020/7730 5282.

LATE MAY/EARLY JUNE

Beating of the Retreat This annual display takes place on Horse Guards' Parade over three evenings, and marks the old military custom of drumming the troops back to base at dusk. Soldiers on foot and horseback provide a colourful, very British ceremony which precedes a floodlit performance by the Massed Bands of the Queen's Household Cavalry. Information ⓣ020/7739 5323.

FIRST OR SECOND SATURDAY IN JUNE

Derby Day Run at the Epsom racecourse in Surrey, the Derby is the country's premier flat race – the beast that gets its snout over the line first is instantly worth millions. Admission prices reflect proximity to the horses and to the watching nobility. The race is always shown live on TV. Information ⓣ01372/726311; ⓦ*www.epsomderby.co.uk*

EARLY JUNE TO MID-AUGUST

Royal Academy Summer Exhibition Thousands of prints, paintings, sculptures and sketches, most by amateurs and nearly all of them for sale, are displayed at one of the city's finest galleries. See p.37. Information ⓣ020/7300 8000; ⓦ*www.royalacademy.org.uk*

JUNE

Fleadh Pronounced "flaa", this is a raucous (by no means exclusively) Irish music festival in Finsbury Park, North London. Van Morrison has pitched up here on more than a few occasions, but then so too have Bob Dylan and the briefly reformed Sex Pistols. Information ⓣ020/8963 0940; ⓦ*www.meanfiddler.com*

JUNE

Spitalfields Festival Classical music recitals in Hawksmoor's Christ Church, the parish church of Spitalfields, and other events in and around the old Spitalfields Market for a fortnight or so in June. Information ⓣ020/7377 0287; ⓦ*www.spitalfieldsfestival.org.uk*

SECOND SATURDAY IN JUNE

Trooping of the Colour This celebration of the Queen's official birthday (her real one is on April 21) features massed bands, gun salutes, fly-pasts and crowds of tourists and patriotic Britons paying homage. Tickets for the ceremony itself (limited to two per person) must be applied for well in advance; phone ⓣ020/7414 2479. Otherwise, the royal procession along the Mall lets you glimpse the nobility for free, and there are rehearsals (minus Her Majesty) on the two preceding Saturdays.

MID-JUNE

Royal Ascot A highlight of the society year, held at the Ascot racecourse in Berkshire, this high-profile meeting has the Queen and sundry royals completing a crowd-pleasing lap of the track in open carriages prior to the opening races. The event is otherwise famed for its fashion statements, and there's TV coverage of both the races and the more extravagant headgear of the female racegoers. Information ⓣ01344/622211; ⓦ*www.ascot.co.uk*

LAST WEEK OF JUNE AND FIRST WEEK OF JULY

Wimbledon Lawn Tennis Championships This Grand Slam tournament attracts the cream of the world's professionals and is one of the highlights of the sporting and social calendar. Tickets are hard to get hold of, but as they are valid for the whole day you could always hang around outside in the hope of gleaning an early leaver's cast-off. Don't buy from touts, even if you can afford to, as the tickets may well be fakes. Information ⓣ020/8946 2244; ⓦ*www.wimbledon.org*.

LATE JUNE TO MID-JULY

City of London Festival For nearly a month, churches (including St Paul's Cathedral), livery halls and corporate buildings around the City play host to classical and jazz musicians, theatre companies and other guest performers. Information ⓣ020/7377 0540; ⓦ*www.colf.org*

MID-JULY

Greenwich & Docklands Festival Ten-day festival of fireworks, music, dance, theatre, art and spectacles at venues on both sides of the river, plus a village fayre in neighbouring Blackheath. Information ⓣ020/8305 1818; ⓦ*www.festival.org*

MID-JULY TO MID-SEPTEMBER

BBC Henry Wood Promenade Concerts Commonly known as the Proms, this series of nightly classical concerts at the Royal Albert Hall is a well-loved British institution. See p.120. Information ⓣ020/7765 5575; ⓦ*www.bbc.co.uk/proms*

MID-JULY

Doggett's Coat and Badge Race The world's oldest rowing race, from London Bridge to Chelsea, established by Thomas Doggett, an eighteenth-century Irish comedian, to commemorate George I's accession to the throne. The winner receives a Hanoverian costume and silver badge. Information ⓣ020/7626 3531.

MID-JULY

Mardi Gras Gay and lesbian march through the city followed by a huge (ticketed) party in the park – for more details, see p.252.

THIRD WEEK OF JULY

Swan Upping Five-day scramble up the Thames, from Sunbury to Pangbourne, during which liveried rowers search for swans, marking them (on the bill) as belonging to either the Queen, the Dyers' or the Vintners' City liveries. At Windsor, all the oarsmen stand to attention in their boats and salute the Queen. Information Ⓣ020/7236 1863.

MID-AUGUST

Summer Rites Relaxed annual gay and lesbian festival – see p.252.

LAST BANK HOLIDAY WEEKEND IN AUGUST

Notting Hill Carnival The two-day free festival in Notting Hill Gate is the longest-running, best-known and biggest street party in Europe. Dating back 35 years, Carnival is a tumult of imaginatively decorated floats, eye-catching costumes, thumping sound systems, live bands, irresistible food and huge crowds. Information Ⓣ020/8964 0544; Ⓦ *www.nottinghillcarnival.net.uk*

SATURDAY IN EARLY SEPTEMBER

Great River Race Hundreds of boats are rowed or paddled from Ham House, Richmond, down to Island Gardens on the Isle of Dogs. Starts are staggered and there are any number of weird and wonderful vessels taking part. Information ⓣ020/8398 9057.

THIRD SUNDAY IN SEPTEMBER

Horseman's Sunday In an eccentric 11.30am ceremony at the Hyde Park church of St John & St Michael, a vicar on horseback blesses a hundred or so horses; the newly consecrated beasts then parade around the neighbourhood before galloping off through the park, and later taking part in show jumping. Information ⓣ020/7262 1732.

THIRD WEEKEND IN SEPTEMBER

Open House A once-a-year opportunity to peek inside over 400 buildings around London, many of which don't normally open their doors to the public. You'll need to book in advance for some of the more popular places. Information ⓣ0891/600061; ⓦ*www.londonopenhouse.org*

LATE SEPTEMBER/EARLY OCTOBER

Soho Jazz Festival Headed by *Ronnie Scott's*, this is a week-long celebration of one of Soho's most famous attributes – its jazz culture. Information ⓣ020/7437 6437.

FIRST SUNDAY IN OCTOBER

Costermongers' Pearly Harvest Festival Service Cockney fruit and vegetable festival at St Martin-in-the-Fields Church. Of most interest to the onlooker are the Pearly Kings and Queens who gather at around 3pm in their traditional pearl-button studded outfits. Information ⓣ020/7930 0089.

LATE OCTOBER/EARLY NOVEMBER

State Opening of Parliament The Queen arrives by coach at the Houses of Parliament at 11am accompanied by the Household Cavalry and gun salutes. The ceremony itself takes place inside the House of Lords and is televised; it also takes place whenever a new government is sworn in. Information Ⓣ 020/7219 3000; Ⓦ *www.parliament.uk*

NOVEMBER

London Film Festival A three-week cinematic season with scores of new international films screened at the National Film Theatre and some West End venues. Information Ⓣ 020/7928 3232; Ⓦ *www.bfi.org.uk* or (nearer the time) Ⓦ *www.lff.org.uk*

EARLY NOVEMBER

London Jazz Festival Big ten-day jazz fest held in all London's jazz venues, large and small. Information Ⓣ 020/7405 5974.

FIRST SUNDAY IN NOVEMBER

London to Brighton Veteran Car Run In 1896 Parliament abolished the Act that required all cars to crawl along at 2mph behind someone waving a red flag. Such was the euphoria in the motoring community that a rally was promptly set up to mark the occasion, and a century later it's still going strong. Classic cars built before 1905 set off from Hyde Park at 7.30am and travel the 58 miles to Brighton along the A23 at the heady maximum speed of 20mph. Information Ⓣ 01753/681736.

NOVEMBER 5

Bonfire Night In memory of Guy Fawkes – executed for his role in the 1605 Gunpowder Plot to blow up King James I and the Houses of Parliament – effigies of the hapless Mr Fawkes are burned on bonfires all over Britain. There are also council-run fires and fireworks displays right across the capital; Parliament Hill in Hampstead provides a good vantage point from which to take in several displays at once. Information ⓣ020/7971 0026.

SECOND SATURDAY IN NOVEMBER

Lord Mayor's Show The newly appointed Lord Mayor begins his or her day of investiture at Westminster, leaving there at around 9am for Guildhall. At 11.10am, the vast ceremonial procession, headed by the 1756 State Coach, begins its journey from Guildhall to the Law Courts in the Strand, where the oath of office is taken at 11.50am. From there the coach and its train of 140-odd floats make their way back towards Guildhall, arriving at 2.20pm. Later in the day there's a fireworks display from a barge tethered between Waterloo and Blackfriars bridges, and a small funfair on Paternoster Square, by St Paul's Cathedral. Information ⓣ020/7606 3030; ⓦ *www.corpoflondon.gov.uk*

NEAREST SUNDAY TO NOVEMBER 11

Remembrance Sunday A day of nationwide commemorative ceremonies for the dead and wounded of the two world wars and other conflicts. The principal ceremony, attended by the Queen, various other royals and the Prime Minister, takes place at the Cenotaph in Whitehall, beginning with a march-past of veterans and building to a one-minute silence at the stroke of 11am.

CHRISTMAS

Each year since the end of World War II, Norway has acknowledged its gratitude to the country that helped liberate it from the Nazis with the gift of a mighty spruce tree that appears in Trafalgar Square in early December. Decorated with lights, it becomes the focus for carol singing versus traffic noise each evening until Christmas Eve.

NEW YEAR'S EVE

The New Year is welcomed en masse in Trafalgar Square as thousands of inebriated revellers stagger about and slur to Auld Lang Syne at midnight. For the millennium, there was a big firework display along the Thames, and it remains to be seen whether the show will be repeated or if the crowds will once more return to their traditional haunt. Whatever happens, London Transport runs free public transport all night, sponsored by various public-spirited breweries.

Kids' London

On first sight London seems a hostile place for children, with its crowds, incessant noise and intimidating traffic. English attitudes can be discouraging as well, particularly if you've experienced the more indulgent approach of the French or Italians – London's restaurateurs, for example, tend to regard children and eating out as mutually exclusive concepts. Yet if you pick your place carefully, even central London can be a delight for the pint-sized, and it needn't overly strain the parental pocket.

Covent Garden's buskers and jugglers provide no-cost entertainment in a car-free setting, and there's always the chance of being plucked from the crowd to help out with a trick. Don't underestimate the value of London's **public transport** as a source of fun, either. The #11 double-decker from Victoria, for instance, will trundle you past the Houses of Parliament, Trafalgar Square and the Strand on its way to St Paul's Cathedral for 40p per child. The driverless Docklands Light Railway is another guaranteed source of amusement – grab a seat at the front of the train and pretend to be driver, then take a boat back to the centre of town from Greenwich.

MUSEUMS

Lots of London's **museums** will appeal to children. Below are those that are primarily geared towards entertaining and/or educating children – some are covered in the main part of our guide, and are cross-referenced accordingly. Most offer child-oriented programmes of workshops, educational story trails, special shows and suchlike during the school holidays. *Time Out* has listings of kids' events, and also produces *Kids Out*, a monthly listings magazine for those with children.

Bethnal Green Museum of Childhood

Map 2, J4. Cambridge Heath Rd, E2 ⓣ 020/8983 5200; ⓦ *www.vam.ac.uk* ⊖ Bethnal Green. Daily except Fri 10am–5.50pm; free. See p.97.
Best known for its collection of historic dolls' houses, the museum also has a few buttons to press, and lots of weekend/holiday events and activities.

Horniman Museum

Map 2, J7. London Rd, SE23 ⓣ 020/8699 1872; ⓦ *www.horniman.ac.uk.* Forest Hill train station, from Victoria or London Bridge. Mon–Sat 10.30am–5.30pm, Sun 2–5.30pm; free. See p.143.
An ethnographic museum, but with lots to interest kids, including an aquarium, a natural history section and lovely grounds.

Kew Bridge Steam Museum

Map 2, D5. Green Dragon Lane, Brentford, TW8. ⓣ 020/8568 4757; ⓦ *www.kbsm.org.uk.* Kew Bridge train station from Waterloo, or bus #237 or #267 from Gunnersbury ⊖ . Daily 11am–5pm; Mon–Fri adults £3, children £1; Sat & Sun adults £4, children £2. See p.155.
Best visited at weekends, when the beam engines are in steam and the miniature steam railway is in operation.

Legoland

Windsor, Berkshire ⓣ 0870/504 0404;

Ⓦ *www.legoland.co.uk.* Windsor & Eton Central, from Paddington (change at Slough), or Windsor & Eton Riverside, from Waterloo. Daily 10am–6pm or dusk; adults £17.50. children £14.50.

Very expensive but enjoyable and relatively tasteful theme park with gentle rides – perfect for five- to eight-year-olds.

London Aquarium

Map 6, A6. County Hall, SE1 Ⓣ 020/7967 8000; Ⓦ *www.londonaquarium.co.uk* ⊖ Westminster or Waterloo. Daily 10am–6pm or later; adults £8.50, children £5. See p.105.

London's largest aquarium is situated on the South Bank, and is very popular with kids, especially the bit where they get to stroke the (non-sting) rays.

London Zoo

Map 3, E1. Regent's Park, NW1 Ⓣ 020/7722 3333; Ⓦ *www.londonzoo.co.uk.* Bus #274 from ⊖ Camden Town or Baker Street. Daily: March–Oct 10am–5.30pm; Nov–Feb 10am–4pm; adults £9, children £7. See p.133.

Architecturally interesting inner-city zoo which has recently opened its new Web of Life building, as part of a drive to redefine itself as eco-conscious.

Natural History Museum

Map 3, C7. Cromwell Rd, SW7 Ⓣ 020/7942 5000; Ⓦ *www.nhm.ac.uk* ⊖ South Kensington. Mon–Sat 10am–5.50pm, Sun 11am–5.50pm; adults £7.50, children: Mon–Fri all free after 4.30pm, Sat & Sun all free after 5pm. See p.124.

Dinosaurs, stuffed animals, live ants, a "rainforest", an earthquake simulator and lots of rocks, fossils, crystals and gems.

Pollock's Toy Museum

Map 3, G3. 1 Scala St, W1 Ⓣ 020/7636 3452; Ⓦ *www.pollocks.cwc.net* ⊖ Goodge Street. Mon–Sat 10am–5pm; adults £3, children £1.50.

Housed above a toy shop, the museum's impressive toy collection includes a fine example of the Victorian

paper theatres sold by Benjamin Pollock.

Ragged School Museum

Map 2, K4. Copperfield Rd, E3
Ⓣ 020/8980 6405; Ⓦ *www.ics-london.co.uk/rsm*
⊖ Mile End. Wed & Thurs 10am–5pm, first Sun in month 2–5pm; free.

The reconstructed Victorian schoolroom here makes kids realize what an easy life they have these days.

Science Museum

Map 3, C7. Exhibition Rd, SW7
Ⓣ 020/7942 4455;
Ⓦ *www.nmsi.ac.uk*
⊖ South Kensington. Daily 10am–6pm; adults £6.95, children free; all free after 4.30pm. See p.123.

More and more hands-on galleries aimed at kids are being introduced, and there are excellent daily demonstrations, plus a totally revamped transport wing.

Syon

Map 2, C6. Syon Park, Brentford, Middlesex
Ⓣ 020/8560 7272. Bus #237 or #267 from Gunnersbury ⊖.
See p.156.

Good place for a day out, with the Butterfly House, an Aquatic House full of fish, reptiles and amphibians, plus a miniature steam railway in the house's lovely gardens. Snakes and Ladders, an indoor childrens' play area with impressive apparatus, is also in the park (Ⓣ 020/8847 0946; daily 10am–6pm; adults free, under 5's £3.55, over 5's £4.65, with reductions on weekdays.

PARKS AND CITY FARMS

Central London has plenty of **green spaces**, such as Hyde Park, which has playgrounds and ample room for general mayhem, as well as a diverting array of city wildlife. If you want something more unusual than ducks and squirrels, though, head for one of London's **city farms**.

Battersea Park

Map 2, G6. Albert Bridge Rd, SW11 ⓣ 020/8871 7540 (zoo) or 8871 6374 (playground). Battersea Park or Queenstown Road train station, from Victoria. Zoo: Easter–Sept daily 10am–5pm; Oct–Easter Sat & Sun 11am–3pm; adults £1.80, children 90p. Adventure playground: term time Tues–Fri 3.30–7pm; holidays & weekends 11am–6pm; free.

A children's zoo with monkeys, reptiles, birds, otters and mongooses; challenging adventure playground and lots of open space. Every August, the free "Teddy Bears' Picnic" draws thousands of children and their plush pals.

Coram's Fields

Map 3, I2. 93 Guilford St, WC1 ⓣ 020/7837 6138. ⊖ Russell Square. Daily 9am–dusk/8pm; free.

Ducks, sheep, pigs, rabbits, goats and chickens, plus a large free playground with slides and swings. Adults admitted only if accompanied by a child.

Hampstead Heath

Map 2, G2. Info centre by Lido, NW3. Wed–Fri 1–5pm Sat & Sun 10am–5pm; ⓣ 020/7485 4491. ⊖ Hampstead, or Gospel Oak or Hampstead Heath train stations. Open daily 24hr. See p.138.

Nine hundred acres of grassland and woodland, with superb views of the city. Excellent kite-flying, birdwatching and swimming potential too.

Hyde Park/Kensington Gardens

Map 3, D5. W8 ⓣ 020/7298 2100; ⓦ *www.royalparks.co.uk* ⊖ High Street Kensington or Lancaster Gate. Daily dawn–dusk. See p.117.

Hyde Park is central London's main open space; in Kensington Gardens, adjoining its western side, you can find the famous Peter Pan statue (near the Long Water), a playground and a pond that's perfect for toy boat sailing.

Kew Gardens

Map 2, C6. Richmond, Surrey ⓣ 020/8332 5000; ⓦ *www.kew.org*

⊖ Kew Gardens. Daily 9.30am to 7.30pm or dusk; adults £5, children £2.50. See p.159.
You have to pay a hefty entry fee to get into the Royal Botanical Gardens, but they are fun for kids and adults. There's lots of green space, wildfowl, and some great glasshouses, one of which has an aquarium.

Mudchute City Farm

Map 2, L5. Pier St, E14 ⓣ 020/7515 5901. Mudchute or Island Gardens DLR. Daily 9am–5pm; free.
Covering some 35 acres, this is London's largest city farm, with barnyard animals, llamas, a pets' corner and a café.

Richmond Park

Map 2, D7. Richmond, Surrey ⓣ 020/8948 3209; ⓦ *www.royalparks.co.uk* ⊖ Richmond, or Richmond train station from Waterloo. Daily 8am–dusk; free. See p.161.
A fabulous stretch of countryside, with opportunities for duck-feeding, deer-spotting, mushroom hunting and cycling.

THEATRE

Numerous London theatres put on **kids' shows** at the weekend – for full listings, see *Time Out* – but there are one or two venues that are almost entirely child-centred. Ticket prices hover around the £5 mark for children and adults alike, unless the show is at a West End theatre, in which case you're looking at more like £15 and upwards.

Little Angel Theatre

Map 2, I3. 14 Dagmar Passage, off Cross St, N1 ⓣ 020/7226 1787. ⊖ Angel or Highbury & Islington.
London's only permanent puppet theatre, with shows on Saturdays and Sundays at 11am and 3pm; the mornings are for three- to six-year-olds, the afternoons for older kids. Additional shows during the holidays and occasionally in the evenings.

Polka Theatre

Map 2, F8. 240 The Broadway, SW19 Ⓣ 020/8543 4888; Ⓦ *www.polkatheatre.com* ⊖ Wimbledon or South Wimbledon.

A specially designed junior arts centre aimed at kids aged up to around twelve, with two theatres, a playground, a café and a toy shop. Storytellers, puppeteers and mimes make regular appearances.

Puppet Theatre Barge

Map 3, B3. Little Venice, Blomfield Rd, W9 Ⓣ 020/7249 6876 or 0836/202745; Ⓦ *www.movingstage.co.uk* ⊖ Warwick Avenue.

Wonderfully imaginative marionette shows on a fifty-seater barge moored in Little Venice from November to May, then at various points along the Thames (including Richmond). Shows usually start at 3pm at weekends and in the holidays.

Unicorn Theatre

Ⓣ 020/7700 0702; Ⓦ *www.unicorntheatre.com*

The Unicorn is the oldest professional children's theatre in London, and is currently performing in several venues across the capital, including the Pleasance Theatre, off the Caledonian Road, N1. Shows run the gamut from mime and puppetry to traditional plays.

SHOPS

Benjamin Pollock's Toy Shop

Map 4, M4. 44 Covent Garden Apple Market, WC2 Ⓣ 020/7379 7866; Ⓦ *www.pollocks.cwc.net* ⊖ Covent Garden. Mon–Sat 10.30am–6pm.

An old-fashioned outlet selling puppets, traditional teddies and dolls, as well as charming model theatres complete with cut-out sets, props and tiny actors.

Children's Book Centre

Map 2, F5. 237 Kensington High St, W8 Ⓣ 020/7937 7497; Ⓦ *www.childrensbookcentre.co.uk* ⊖ Kensington High Street. Mon, Wed, Fri & Sat

9.30am–6.30pm, Tues 9.30am–6pm, Thurs 9.30am–7pm, Sun noon–6pm.
Immense bookshop just for kids, where classic yarns nestle with the best in contemporary adolescent fiction.

Davenport's Magic Shop

Map 4, K8. Charing Cross Shopping Arcade, WC2 ⓣ 020/7836 0408. ⊖ Charing Cross or Embankment. Mon–Fri 9.30am–5.30pm, Sat 10.15am–4.30pm.
London's oldest magic shop sells tricks for the professional and the infant amateur.

Electronics Boutique

Map 4, E1. 100 Oxford St, W1 ⓣ 020/7637 7911. ⊖ Tottenham Court Road. Mon–Sat 9.30am–9pm, Sun noon–6pm.
All the latest computer games to excite the goggle-eyed enthusiast, plus more traditional board games.

Eric Snook's Toyshop

Map 4, M4. 32 Covent Garden Market, WC2 ⓣ 020/7379 7681. ⊖ Covent Garden. Mon–Sat 10am–7pm, Sun 11am–6pm.
Eschewing movie merchandise and cheap tat, this shop sells only the most tasteful, meticulously crafted playthings.

Hamleys

Map 4, B4. 188 Regent St, W1 ⓣ 020/7494 2000; ⓦ *www.hamleys.com* ⊖ Oxford Circus. Mon–Fri 10am–8pm, Sat 9.30am–8pm, Sun noon–6pm.
The most celebrated toy shop on the planet, multistorey Hamleys is bursting with childish delights – from the humble Slinky to scaled-down petrol-driven Porsches. A smaller branch in Covent Garden Piazza gives a taste of what's on offer at the real thing.

Skate Attack

Map 2, H3. 95 Highgate Rd, NW5 ⓣ 020/7267 6961; ⓦ *www.skateattack.com* ⊖ Tufnell Park. Mon–Fri 9.30am–6pm, Sat 9am–6pm, Sun 10am–1.30pm.
Europe's largest retailer of roller skates, rollerblades and equipment. Roller rental, with protective equipment, is £10 a day, £15 a weekend or £20 a week, plus £100 deposit.

Directory

AIDS HELPLINE ⓣ 0800/567123.

AIRLINES Aer Lingus ⓣ 0645/737747 (ⓦ *www.aerlingus.ie*); Aeroflot ⓣ 020/7355 2233 (ⓦ *www.aeroflot.co.uk*); Air France ⓣ 0845/084 5111 (ⓦ *www.airfrance.com*); Alitalia ⓣ 0870/544 8259 (ⓦ *www.alitalia.co.uk*); American Airlines ⓣ 08457/789789 (ⓦ *www.aa.com*); British Airways ⓣ 08457/222111 (ⓦ *www.britishairways.com*); Buzz ⓣ 0870/240 7070 (ⓦ *www.buzzaway.com*); Canadian Airlines ⓣ 020/8577 7722 (ⓦ *www.cdnair.ca*); Delta ⓣ 0800/414767 (ⓦ *www.delta-air.com*); EasyJet ⓣ 0870/600 0000 (ⓦ *www.easyjet.com*); Go ⓣ 0845/605 4321 (ⓦ *www.go-fly.com*); KLM ⓣ 0870/575 0900 (ⓦ *www.klm.com*); Lufthansa ⓣ 08457/737747 (ⓦ *www.lufthansa.co.uk*); Qantas ⓣ 08457/747767 (ⓦ *www.qantas.com*); Ryanair ⓣ 0541/569569 (ⓦ *www.ryanair.com*); United Airlines ⓣ 0845/844 4777 (ⓦ *www.ual.com*); Virgin ⓣ 01293/747747 (ⓦ *www.fly.virgin.com*).

AIRPORT ENQUIRIES Gatwick ⓣ 01293/535353 (ⓦ *www.baa.co.uk*); Heathrow ⓣ 0870/000 0123 (ⓦ *www.baa.co.uk*); London City Airport ⓣ 020/7646 0000 (ⓦ *www.londoncityairport.com*); Luton ⓣ 01582/405100 (ⓦ *www.london-luton.com*); Stansted ⓣ 01279/680500 (ⓦ *www.baa.co.uk*).

AMERICAN EXPRESS 30–31 Haymarket, SW1 ⓣ 020/7484 9600;

Ⓦ *www.americanexpress.com*. Mon–Sat 9am–6.30pm, Sun 10am–5pm. ⊖ Piccadilly Circus.

BANKS Opening hours for most banks are Mon–Fri 9.30am–4.30pm, with some staying open half an hour later, and some high street branches opening on Saturday mornings.

BIKE RENTAL Bikepark, 14 Stukeley St Ⓣ 020/7430 0083; Ⓦ *www.bikepark.co.uk*. Mon–Fri 8.30am–7pm, Sat 10am–6pm ⊖ Covent Garden. There's also a branch at 151 Sydney St, SW3 (Ⓣ 020/7565 0777), which is open on Sundays.

CAR RENTAL Avis Ⓣ 0870/606 0100 (Ⓦ *www.avis.com*); Global Leisure Cars Ⓣ 0870/241 1986 (Ⓦ *www.globalleisurecars.com*); Hertz Ⓣ 0870/599 6699 (Ⓦ *www.hertz.com*); Holiday Autos Ⓣ 0870/530 0400 (Ⓦ *www.holidayautos.com*).

CONSULATES AND EMBASSIES Australia, Australia House, Strand, WC2 Ⓣ 020/7379 4334 (Ⓦ *www.australia.org.uk*); Canada, MacDonald House, 1 Grosvenor Square, W1 Ⓣ 020/7258 6600 (Ⓦ *www.canada.org.uk*); Ireland, 17 Grosvenor Place, SW1 Ⓣ 020/7235 2171; New Zealand, New Zealand House, 80 Haymarket, SW1 Ⓣ 020/7930 8422 (Ⓦ *www.newzealandhc.org.uk*); South Africa, South Africa House, Trafalgar Square, WC2 Ⓣ 020/7451 7299 (Ⓦ *www.southafricahouse.com*); USA, 24 Grosvenor Square, W1 Ⓣ 020/7499 9000 (Ⓦ *www.usembassy.org.uk*).

CULTURAL INSTITUTES French Institute, 17 Queensberry Place, SW7 Ⓣ 020/7838 2144 (Ⓦ *www.institut.ambafrance.org.uk*); Goethe Institute, Princes Gate, Exhibition Rd, SW7 Ⓣ 020/7596 4000 (Ⓦ *www.goethe.de/london*); Italian Cultural Institute, 39 Belgrave Square, SW1 Ⓣ 020/7235 1461 (Ⓦ *www.italcultur.org.uk*).

DENTISTS Emergency treatment: Guy's Hospital, St Thomas St, SE1 Ⓣ 020/7955 4317 (Mon–Fri 8.45am–3.30pm).

ELECTRICITY Electricity supply in London conforms to the EU standard of approximately 230V.

EMERGENCIES For police, fire and ambulance services, call ☎ 999.

HOSPITALS For 24hr accident and emergency: Charing Cross Hospital, Fulham Palace Rd, W6 ☎ 020/8846 1234; Chelsea & Westminster Hospital, 369 Fulham Rd, SW10 ☎ 020/8746 8000; Royal Free Hospital, Pond St, NW3 ☎ 020/7794 0500; Royal London Hospital, Whitechapel Rd, E1 ☎ 020/7377 7000; St Mary's Hospital, Praed St, W2 ☎ 020/7886 6666; University College Hospital, Grafton Way, WC1 ☎ 020/7387 9300; Whittington Hospital, Highgate Hill, N19 ☎ 020/7272 3070.

LAUNDRY There are self-service launderettes all over London. Duds'n'Suds is a good central outfit with TV, pool and pinball: 49–51 Brunswick Shopping Centre, WC1 ☎ 020/7837 1122 (Mon–Fri 8am–9pm, Sat & Sun 8am–8pm; ⊖ Russell Square).

LEFT LUGGAGE AIRPORTS Gatwick: North Terminal ☎ 01293/502013 (daily 6am–10pm); South Terminal ☎ 01293/502014 (24hr). Heathrow: Terminal 1 ☎ 020/8745 5301 (daily 6am–11pm); Terminal 2 ☎ 020/8745 4599 (daily 6am–10.30pm); Terminal 3 ☎ 020/8759 3344 (daily 5.30am–10.30pm); Terminal 4 ☎ 020/8745 7460 (daily 5.30am–11pm). London City Airport ☎ 020/7646 0000 (daily 6.30am–10pm). Stansted Airport ☎ 01279/680500 (24hr). TRAIN STATIONS Charing Cross ☎ 020/7839 4282 (daily 7am–11pm); Euston ☎ 020/7320 0528 (Mon–Sat 6.45am–11.15pm, Sun 7.15am–11pm); Victoria ☎ 020/7928 5151 ext 27523 (daily 7am–10.15pm, plus lockers); Waterloo International ☎ 020/7928 5151 (Mon–Fri 4am–11pm, Sat & Sun 6am–11pm).

LOST PROPERTY AIRPORTS Gatwick ☎ 01293/503162 (daily 7.30am–5.30pm); Heathrow ☎ 020/8745 7727 (Mon–Fri 8am–5pm, Sat & Sun 8am–4pm); London City Airport ☎ 020/7646 0000

(Mon–Fri 6am–9.30pm, Sat 6am–1am, Sun 10.30am–9.30pm); Stansted ⓣ 01279/680500 (daily 5.30am–11pm).
BUSES ⓣ 020/7222 1234.
HEATHROW EXPRESS ⓣ 020/8745 7727.
TAXIS (black cabs only) ⓣ 020/7833 0996.
TRAIN STATIONS Euston ⓣ 020/7922 6477 (Mon–Sat 6.45am–11pm, Sun 7.15am–11pm); King's Cross ⓣ 020/7922 9081 (daily 8am–7.45pm); Liverpool Street ⓣ 020/7928 9158 (Mon–Fri 7am–7pm, Sat & Sun 7am–2pm); Paddington ⓣ 020/7313 1514 (Mon–Fri 9am–5.30pm); Victoria ⓣ 020/7922 9887 (Mon–Fri 7.30am–10pm); Waterloo ⓣ 020/7401 7861 (Mon–Fri 7.30am–8pm).
TUBE TRAINS London Regional Transport ⓣ 020/7486 2496.

MOTORBIKE RENTAL Scootabout, 1–3 Leeke St, WC1 ⓣ 020/7833 4607; ⓦ *www.hgbmotorcycles.co.uk.* Mon–Fri 9am–6pm, Sat 9am–1pm.

POLICE Central police stations include: Charing Cross, Agar St, WC2 ⓣ 020/7240 1212; Holborn, 70 Theobalds Rd, WC1 ⓣ 020/7404 1212; King's Cross, 76 King's Cross Rd, WC1 ⓣ 020/7704 1212; Tottenham Court Road, 56 Tottenham Court Rd, W1 ⓣ 020/7637 1212; West End Central, 10 Vine St, W1 ⓣ 020/7437 1212. City of London Police, Bishopsgate, EC2 ⓣ 020/7601 2222.

POSTAL SERVICES The only late-opening post office is the Trafalgar Square branch at 24–28 William IV St, WC2 4DL ⓣ 020/7484 9304 (Mon–Fri 8am–8pm, Sat 9am–8pm); it's also the city's poste restante collection point. For general postal enquiries phone ⓣ 08457/740740, or visit the Web site: ⓦ *www.royalmail.co.uk*

PUBLIC HOLIDAYS January 1, Good Friday, Easter Monday, First Monday in May, Last Monday in May, Last Monday in August, December 25, December 26; if January 1, December 25 or 26 fall on a Saturday or Sunday, the holiday falls on the following weekday.

TELEPHONES A variety of companies have public payphones on the street, the largest one being British Telecom (BT). Most phones take all coins from 10p upwards, though some only take phonecards, available from post offices and newsagents, and/or credit cards. International calls can be made from any phonebox, by dialling 00, then the country code; to reach the operator, phone ⓣ 100, or for the international operator phone ⓣ 155. London phone codes changed in 2000, and all London numbers are now prefixed by the new area code ⓣ 020. The old ⓣ 0171 numbers are now prefixed with a 7, while ⓣ 0181 numbers have an 8 in front of them.

TIME Greenwich Mean Time (GMT) is used from October to March; for the rest of the year the country switches to British Summer Time (BST), one hour ahead of GMT.

TRAIN ENQUIRIES For national train enquiries, call ⓣ 08457/484950.

TRAVEL AGENTS Campus Travel, 52 Grosvenor Gardens, SW1 ⓣ 0870/240 1010 (ⓦ *www.usitcampus.co.uk*); Council Travel, 28a Poland St, W1 ⓣ 020/7437 7767 (ⓦ *www.destination-group.com*); STA Travel, 86 Old Brompton Rd, SW7 ⓣ 020/7361 6161 (ⓦ *www.statravel.co.uk*); Trailfinders, 42–50 Earl's Court Rd, SW5 ⓣ 020/7938 3366 (ⓦ *www.trailfinders.co.uk*).

CONTEXTS

A brief history of London

Roman Londinium

There is evidence of scattered **Celtic settlements** along the Thames, but no firm proof that central London was permanently settled by the Celts before the arrival of the **Romans** in 43 AD. Although the Romans' principal settlement was at **Camulodunum** (Colchester) to the northeast, **Londinium** (London) was established as a permanent military camp, and became an important hub of the Roman road system.

In 60 AD, when the Iceni tribe rose up against the invaders under their queen **Boudicca** (or Boadicea), Londinium was burned to the ground, along with Camulodunum. According to the Roman historian, Tacitus, the inhabitants were "massacred, hanged, burned and crucified", but the Iceni were eventually defeated and Boudicca committed suicide. In the aftermath, Londinium emerged as the new commercial and administrative (though not military) capital of **Britannia**, and was endowed with an imposing basilica and forum, a governor's palace, temples, bathhouses and an amphitheatre. To protect against further attacks, fortifications were built, three miles long, fifteen feet high and eight feet thick.

Saxon Lundenwic and the Danes

By the fourth century, the Roman Empire was on its last legs, and the Romans officially abandoned the city in 410 AD (when Rome was sacked by the Visigoths), leaving the country – and Londinium – at the mercy of marauding Saxon pirates. The **Saxon** invaders, who controlled most of southern England by the sixth century, appear to have settled, initially at least, to the west of the Roman city.

In 841 and 851 London suffered Danish Viking attacks, and it may have been in response to these raids that the Anglo-Saxons decided to reoccupy the walled Roman city. After numerous sporadic attacks, and the odd extended sojourn, the Danish leader Cnut (or Canute), became King of All England in 1016, and made London the national capital, a position it has held ever since.

Danish rule only lasted 26 years, and with the accession of **Edward the Confessor** (1042–66), the court and church moved upstream to Thorney Island. Here Edward built a splendid new palace so that he could oversee construction of his "West Minster" (later to become Westminster Abbey). Thus it was Edward who was responsible for the geographical separation of power, with royal government based in **Westminster**, and commerce centred upstream in the **City of London**.

From 1066 to the Black Death

On his deathbed, the celibate Edward appointed Harold, Earl of Wessex, as his successor. Having crowned himself in the new Abbey – establishing a tradition that continues to this day – Harold was defeated by **William of Normandy** (William the Conqueror) and his invading army at the Battle of Hastings. On Christmas Day, 1066, William crowned himself king in Westminster Abbey. The new king granted the City numerous privileges, and, as an insurance policy, also constructed three defensive towers, one of which survives as the nucleus of the Tower of London.

Over the next few centuries, the City waged a continuous struggle with the monarchy for a degree of self-government and independence. In the Magna Carta of 1215, for instance, London was granted the right to elect its own sheriff, or **Lord Mayor**. However, in 1348, the city was hit by the worst natural disaster in its entire history – the arrival of the Europe-wide bubonic plague outbreak known as the **Black Death**. This disease, carried by black rats, and transmitted to humans by flea bites, wiped out something like half the capital's population in the space of two years.

Tudor London

Under the **Tudor royal family**, London's population, which had remained constant at around 50,000 since the Black Death, increased dramatically, trebling in size during the course of the century.

The most crucial development of the sixteenth century was the English **Reformation**, the separation of the English Church from Rome. A far-reaching consequence of this split was Henry's **Dissolution of the Monasteries**, begun in 1536 in order to bump up the royal coffers. The Dissolution changed the entire fabric of the city: previously dominated by its religious institutions, London's property market was suddenly flooded with confiscated estates, which were quickly snapped up and redeveloped by the Tudor nobility.

Henry VIII may have kickstarted the English Reformation, but he was a religious conservative, and in the last ten years of his reign he executed as many Protestants as Catholics. Henry's sickly son, **Edward VI** (1547–53), however, pursued an even more staunchly anti-Catholic policy. By the end of his reign, London's churches had lost their altars, their paintings, their relics and virtually all their statuary. Following Edward's death, the religious pendulum swung the other way with the accession of "**Bloody Mary**" (1553–58). This time, it was Protestants who were martyred with abandon at Tyburn and Smithfield.

Despite all the religious strife, the Tudor economy remained in good health, reaching its height in the reign of **Elizabeth I** (1558–1603). London's commercial success was epitomized by the millionaire merchant Thomas Gresham, who erected the **Royal Exchange** in 1572, establishing London as the premier world trade market. The 45 years of Elizabeth's reign also witnessed the efflorescence of a specifically **English Renaissance**, especially in the field of literature, which reached its apogee in the brilliant careers of **Christopher Marlowe**, **Ben Jonson** and **William Shakespeare**, whose plays were performed in the theatres of Southwark, the city's entertainment district.

Stuart London

In 1603, James VI of Scotland became **James I** of England (1603–25), thereby uniting the two crowns and marking the beginning of the **Stuart dynasty**. His intention of exercising religious tolerance was thwarted by the public outrage that followed the **Gunpowder Plot** of 1605, when Guy Fawkes, in cahoots with a group of Catholic conspirators, was discovered attempting to blow up the king at the state opening of Parliament.

Under James's successor, **Charles I** (1625–49), the animosity between Crown and Parliament culminated in full-blown **Civil War**. London was the key to victory for both sides, and as a Parliamentarian stronghold it came under attack from Royalist forces almost immediately. However, having defeated the Parliamentary forces to the west of London in 1642, Charles hesitated and withdrew to Reading, thus missing his greatest chance of victory. After a series of defeats in 1645, Charles surrendered to the Scots, who handed him over to Parliament. Eventually, in January 1649, the king was tried and executed in Whitehall, and England became a **Commonwealth** under Oliver Cromwell. London found itself in the grip of the Puritans' zealous laws, which closed down all theatres, enforced observance of the Sabbath, and banned the celebration of Christmas, which was considered a papist superstition.

In 1660, the city gave an ecstatic reception to **Charles II** (1660–85) when he arrived in the capital to announce the **Restoration** of the monarchy, and the "Merry Monarch" immediately caught the mood of the public by opening up the theatres and concert halls. However, the good times that rolled came to an abrupt end with the onset of the **Great Plague** of 1665, which claimed 100,000 lives. The following year, London had to contend with yet another disaster, the **Great Fire** (see p.88). Some eighty percent of the City was razed to the ground; the death toll didn't reach double figures, but more than 100,000 were left homeless.

Within five years, 9000 houses had been rebuilt with bricks and mortar (timber was banned), and fifty years later, **Christopher Wren** had almost single-handedly rebuilt all the City churches and completed the world's first Protestant cathedral, **St Paul's**. The **Great Rebuilding**, as it was known, was one of London's remarkable achievements, and extinguished virtually all traces of the medieval city.

Georgian London

With the accession of **George I** (1714–27), the first of the Hanoverian dynasty, London's expansion continued unabated. The shops of the newly developed **West End** stocked the most fashionable goods in the country, the volume of trade more than tripled, and London's growing population – it was by now the world's largest city, with a population approaching one million – created a huge market, as well as fuelling a building boom.

Wealthy though London was, it was also experiencing the worst mortality rates since records began. Disease was rife, but the real killer was **gin**. It's difficult to exaggerate the effects of the gin-drinking orgy which took place among the poor between 1720 and 1751. At its height, gin consumption was averaging two pints a week, and the burial rate exceeded the baptism rate by more than two to one. Eventually, in the face of huge vested interests, the government passed an act that restricted gin retailing and halted the epidemic.

Policing the metropolis was also an increasing preoccupation for the government, who introduced **capital punishment** for the most minor misdemeanours. Nevertheless, crime continued unabated throughout the eighteenth century, the prison population swelled, transportations to the colonies began, and 1200 Londoners were hanged at Tyburn's gallows. Rioting became an ever-more popular form of protest among the poorer classes in London, the most serious insurrection being the **Gordon Riots** of 1780, when up to 50,000 Londoners went on a five-day rampage through the city.

The nineteenth century

The **nineteenth century** witnessed the emergence of London as the capital of an empire that stretched across the globe. The city's population grew from just over one million in 1801 to nearly seven million by 1901. The world's largest enclosed **dock system** was built in the marshes to the east of the City, and the world's first public transport network was created, with horse-buses, trains, trams and an underground railway. **Industrialization**, however, brought pollution and overcrowding, especially in the slums of the East End; smallpox, measles, scarlet fever and cholera killed thousands of working-class families. It is this era of slum-life, and huge social divides, that Dickens evoked in his novels.

The accession of **Queen Victoria** (1837–1901) coincided with a period in which the country's international standing reached unprecedented heights, and as a result Victoria became as much a national icon as Elizabeth I had been. The spirit of the era was perhaps best embodied by the **Great Exhibition** of 1851, a display of manufacturing achievements from all over the world, which took place in the Crystal Palace erected in Hyde Park.

Local government arrived in 1855 with the establishment of the **Metropolitan Board of Works** (MBW), followed in 1888 by the directly-elected **London County Council** (LCC). The achievements of the MBW and the LCC were immense, in particular those of its chief engineer, Joseph Bazalgette, who helped create an underground sewer system (much of it still in use), and greatly improved transport routes.

While half of London struggled to make ends meet, the other half enjoyed the fruits of the richest nation in the world. Luxury establishments such as the *Ritz* and Harrods belong to this period, personified by the dissolute Prince of

Wales, later **Edward VII** (1901–10). For the masses, too, there were new entertainments to be enjoyed: music halls boomed and public houses prospered. The first "Test" cricket match between England and Australia took place in 1880 at the Kennington Oval, and during the following 25 years, nearly all of London's professional football clubs were founded.

From World War I to World War II

During **World War I** (1914–18), London experienced its first aerial attacks, with Zeppelin raids leaving some 650 dead, but these were minor casualties in the context of a war that destroyed millions of lives and eradicated whatever remained of the majority's respect for the ruling classes.

Between the wars, London's population increased further still, reaching close to nine million by 1939. In contrast to the nineteenth century, however, there was a marked shift in population out into the **suburbs**. After the boom of the "Swinging Twenties", the economy collapsed with the crash of the New York Stock Exchange in 1929. The arrival of the Jarrow Hunger March, the most famous protest of the Depression years, shocked London in 1936, the year in which thousands of British fascists tried to march through the predominantly Jewish East End, only to be stopped in the so-called **Battle of Cable Street**.

London was more or less unprepared for the aerial bombardments of **World War II** (1939–45). The bombing campaign, known as the **Blitz** (see p.80), began on September 7, 1940, and continued for 57 consecutive nights. Further carnage was caused towards the end of the war by the pilotless V1 "doodlebugs" and V2 rockets, which caused another 20,000 casualties. In total, 30,000 civilians lost their lives in the bombing of London, with 50,000 injured and some 130,000 houses destroyed.

Postwar London

To lift the country out of its postwar gloom, the **Festival of Britain** was staged in 1951 on derelict land on the south bank of the Thames, a site that was eventually transformed into the **South Bank Arts Centre**. Londoners turned up at this technological funfair in their thousands, but at the same time, many were abandoning the city for good, starting a slow process of population decline that has continued ever since. The consequent labour shortage was made good by mass **immigration** from the former colonies, in particular the Indian subcontinent and the West Indies. The newcomers, a large percentage of whom settled in London, were given small welcome, and within ten years were subjected to race riots, which broke out in Notting Hill in 1958.

The riots are thought to have been carried out, for the most part, by **Teddy Boys**, working-class lads from London's slum areas and new housing estates, who formed the city's first postwar youth cult. Subsequent cults, and their accompanying music, helped turn London into the epicentre of the so-called **Swinging Sixties**, the Teddy Boys being usurped in the early 1960s by the **Mods**, whose sharp suits came from London's Carnaby Street. Fashion hit London in a big way, and – thanks to the likes of the Beatles, the Rolling Stones and Twiggy – London was proclaimed the hippest city on the planet on the front pages of *Time* magazine.

Thatcherite London

In 1979, **Margaret Thatcher** won the general election for the Conservative Party, and the country and the capital would never be quite the same again. The Conservatives were to remain in power for seventeen years, steering the country into a period of ever-greater social polarization.

While taxation policies and easy credit fuelled a consumer boom for the professional classes (the "yuppies" of the 1980s), a calamitous number of people ended up trapped in long-term unemployment. The Brixton riots of 1981 and 1985, and the Tottenham riot of 1985, were reminders of the price of such divisive policies, and of the feeling of social exclusion rife among the city's black youth.

Nationally, the opposition Labour Party went into sharp decline, but in the GLC (successor to the LCC), the party won a narrow victory, led by the **radical Ken Livingstone**, or "Red Ken" as the tabloids dubbed him. Under Livingstone, the GLC poured money into projects among London's ethnic minorities, into the arts, and most famously into a subsidized fares policy for public transport. Such schemes endeared Livingstone to the hearts of many Londoners, but it was too much for Thatcher, who abolished the GLC in 1986, leaving London as the only European capital without a citywide elected body.

Abolition exacerbated tensions between the poorer and richer boroughs of the city. For the first time since the Victorian era, **homelessness** returned to London in a big way, with the underside of Waterloo Bridge transformed into a "Cardboard City" sheltering up to 2000 vagrants. At the same time, the so-called "**Big Bang**" took place, abolishing a whole range of restrictive practices on the Stock Exchange and fuelling the building boom in the reclaimed Docklands, the most visible legacy of Thatcherism. Stocks and shares headed into the stratosphere, and shortly after, they inevitably crashed, ushering in a recession that dragged on for the best part of the next ten years.

Millennium London

On the surface at least, twenty-first century London has come a long way since the bleak Thatcher years. Redevelopment has begun again apace, partly fuelled by money from the National Lottery, which has funded a series of prestigious new **millennium projects** that have changed the face of the city. A new pedestrian bridge now spans the Thames, leading to the new Tate Modern gallery, spectacularly housed in a converted power station. Numerous other national institutions have transformed themselves, too; among them the British Museum, the Royal Opera House, the Science Museum, the National Portrait Gallery and the National Maritime Museum. And last, but not least, there's the controversial Millennium Dome, built and stuffed full of gadgetry for £750 million, but which has yet to achieve the sort of success predicted by its backers.

The most significant political development for London has been the creation of the new **Greater London Assembly** (GLA), along with an American-style **Mayor of London**, both elected by popular mandate. The New Labour government, which came to power on a wave of enthusiasm in 1997, did everything they could to prevent the election of the former GLC leader Ken Livingstone. Yet despite being forced to leave the Labour Party and run as an independent, Livingstone won a resounding victory in the elections of May 2000. It remains to be seen whether Ken can make any impact on the biggest problems facing the capital: transport, crime and racism within the Metropolitan Police Force.

Books

Given the enormous number of books on London, the list below is necessarily a very selective one. The recommendations we've made are in print and in paperback. Publishers are detailed with the British publisher first, separated by an oblique slash from the US publisher, in cases where both exist. Where books are published in only one of these countries, UK or US follows the publisher's name; where the book is published by the same company in both countries, the name of the company appears just once. UP designates University Press. If you want to find the cheapest copy to buy online, try Ⓦ *www.bookbrain.co.uk*.

Travel, journals and memoirs

James Boswell, *London Journal* (Edinburgh UP). Boswell's diary, written in 1762–3 when he was lodging in Downing Street, is remarkably candid about his frequent dealings with the city's prostitutes, and a fascinating insight into eighteenth-century life.

John Evelyn, *The Diary of John Evelyn* (Oxford UP/Boydell & Brewer). In contrast to his contemporary, Pepys, Evelyn gives away very little of his personal life, but his diaries cover a much greater period of English history and a much wider range of topics.

George Orwell, *Down and Out in Paris and London* (Penguin). Orwell's tramp's-eye view of the

1930s, written from first-hand experience. The London section is particularly harrowing.

Samuel Pepys, *The Shorter Pepys* (Penguin); *The Illustrated Pepys* (Unwin/University of California). Pepys kept a voluminous diary while he was living in London from 1660 until 1669, recording the fall of the Commonwealth, the Restoration, the Great Plague and the Great Fire, as well as describing the daily life of the nation's capital. The unabridged version is published in eleven volumes; Penguin's *Shorter Pepys* is abridged though still massive; Unwin's is made up of just the choicest extracts accompanied by contemporary illustrations.

Iain Sinclair, *Lights Out for the Territory* (Granta). Sinclair is one of the most original London writers of his generation. *Lights Out* – a series of ramblings across London starting in Hackney – is his most accessible yet.

History, society and politics

Angus Calder, *The Myth of the Blitz* (Pimlico, UK). A timely antidote to the backs-against-the-wall, "London can take it" tone of most books on this period. Calder dwells instead on the capital's internees – Communists, conscientious objectors and "enemy aliens" – and the myth-making processes of the media of the day.

Roy Porter, *London: A Social History* (Penguin/Harvard UP). This immensely readable history is one of the best books on London published since the war. It's particularly strong on the continuing saga of London's local government, and includes an impassioned critique of the damage done by Mrs Thatcher's administration.

Ben Weinreb and Christopher Hibbert, *The London Encyclopaedia* (Papermac/St Martin's Press). More than 1000 pages of concisely presented information on London past and present, accompanied by the odd illustration. The most fascinating book on the capital.

Art, architecture and archeology

Felix Barker and Ralph Hyde, *London As It Might Have Been* (John Murray). A richly illustrated book on the weird and wonderful plans that never quite made it from the drawing board.

Samantha Hardingham, *London: A Guide to Recent Architecture* (Ellipsis/ Knickerbocker Press). Wonderful pocket guide to the architecture of the last ten years or so, with a knowledgeable, critical text and plenty of black-and-white photos.

Niklaus Pevsner and others, *The Buildings of England* (Penguin). Magisterial series, started by Pevsner to which others have added, inserting newer buildings but generally respecting the founder's personal tone. The latest of the London volumes (there are now five in the series) is a paperback edition devoted to London Docklands.

Richard Trench and Ellis Hillman, *London under London* (John Murray). Fascinating book revealing the secrets of every aspect of the capital's subterranean history, from the lost rivers of the underground to the gas and water systems.

London in fiction

Peter Ackroyd, *English Music* (Penguin, UK); *Hawksmoor* (Penguin, UK); *The House of Doctor Dee* (Penguin, UK); *The Great Fire of London* (Penguin, UK); *Dan Leno and the Limehouse Golem* (Minerva, UK). Ackroyd's novels are all based on arcane aspects of London, wrapped into thriller-like narratives, and conjuring up kaleidoscopic visions of various ages of English culture. *Hawskmoor*, about the great church architect, is the most popular and enjoyable.

Martin Amis, *London Fields* (Vintage/Random House). "Ferociously witty, scabrously scatological and balefully satirical", it says on the back cover, though many regard Amis Jnr's observation of lowlife London as pretentious drivel, written by a man who lives in comfortable Notting Hill.

Anthony Burgess, *A Dead Man in Deptford* (Vintage, UK). Playwright Christopher Marlowe's unexplained murder in a tavern in Deptford provides the background for this historical novel, which brims over with Elizabethan life.

Angela Carter, *The Magic Toyshop* (Virago, UK). Carter's most celebrated novel, about a provincial woman moving to London.

G.K. Chesterton, *The Napoleon of Notting Hill* (Wordsworth). Written in 1904 but set eighty years in the future, in a London divided into squabbling independent boroughs – something prophetic there – and ruled by royalty selected on a rotational basis.

Liza Cody, *Bucket Nut*; *Monkey Wrench*; *Musclebound* (all Bloomsbury, UK). Feisty, would-be female wrestler of uncertain sexuality, with a big mouth, in thrillers set in lowlife London.

Joseph Conrad, *The Secret Agent* (Penguin). Conrad's wonderful spy story based on the botched anarchist bombing of Greenwich Observatory in 1894, exposing the hypocrisies of both the police and the anarchists.

Charles Dickens, *Bleak House*; *A Christmas Tale*; *Little Dorritt*; *Oliver Twist* (all Penguin). The descriptions in Dickens' London-based novels have become the clichés of the Victorian city: the fog, the slums and the stinking river. *Little Dorritt* is set mostly in the Borough and contains some of his most trenchant pieces of social analysis; much of *Bleak House* is set around the Inns of Court that Dickens knew so well.

Arthur Conan Doyle, *The Complete Sherlock Holmes* (Penguin). Deer-stalkered sleuth Sherlock Holmes and dependable sidekick Dr Watson penetrate all levels of Victorian London, from Limehouse opium dens to millionaires' pads. *A Study in Scarlet* and *The Sign of Four* are set entirely in the capital.

Graham Greene, *The Human Factor*; *It's a Battlefield*; *The Ministry of Fear*; *The End of the Affair* (all Penguin). Greene's London novels are all fairly bleak, ranging from *The Human*

Factor, which probes the underworld of the city's spies, to *The Ministry of Fear*, which is set during the Blitz.

Nick Hornby, *High Fidelity* (Indigo/Riverhead). Hornby's extraordinarily successful second book focuses on the loves and life of a thirty-something bloke who lives near the Arsenal . . . rather like Hornby himself.

Hanif Kureishi, *The Buddha of Suburbia*; *The Black Album*; *Love in a Blue Time* (all Faber & Faber). *The Buddha of Suburbia* is a raunchy account of life as an Anglo-Asian in late 1960s suburbia, and the art scene of the 70s. *The Black Album* is a thriller set in London in 1989, while *Love in a Blue Time* is a set of short stories set in 1990s London.

Jack London, *The People of the Abyss* (Pluto Press). London's classic London novel.

Timothy Mo, *Sour Sweet* (Vintage). Very funny and very sad story of a newly arrived Chinese family struggling to understand the English way of life in the Sixties, written with great insight by Mo, who is himself of mixed parentage.

Iris Murdoch, *Under the Net*; *The Black Prince*; *An Accidental Man*; *Bruno's Dream*; *The Green Knight* (all Penguin). *Under the Net* was Murdoch's first, funniest, and arguably her best novel, centred on a hack writer living in London. Many of her subsequent novels are set in various parts of middle-class London and span several decades of the second half of the twentieth century. *The Green Knight*, her last novel, is a strange fable mixing medieval and modern London, with lashings of the Bible and attempted fratricide.

George Orwell, *Keep the Aspidistra Flying* (Penguin). Orwell's 1930s critique of Mammon is equally critical of its chief protagonist, whose attempt to rebel against the system only condemns him to poverty, working in a London bookshop and freezing his evenings away in a miserable rented room.

Edward Rutherford, *London* (Arrow/Fawcett). A big, big novel which stretches from Roman times to the present and deals with the most dramatic moments of London's history.

Masses of historical detail woven in with the story of several families.

Iain Sinclair, *White Chappell, Scarlet Tracings* (Granta, UK); *Downriver* (Vintage, UK); *Radon Daughters* (Granta, UK). Sinclair's idiosyncratic and richly textured novels are a strange mix of Hogarthian caricature, New Age mysticism and conspiracy-theory rant. Deeply offensive and highly recommended.

P.G. Wodehouse, *Jeeves Omnibus* (Hutchinson, UK). Bertie Wooster and his stalwart butler, Jeeves, were based in Mayfair, and many of their exploits take place with London showgirls, and in the Drones gentlemen's club.

Virginia Woolf, *Mrs Dalloway* (Penguin). Woolf's novel relates the thoughts of a London society hostess and a shell-shocked war veteran, with her "stream of consciousness" style in full flow.

INDEX

A

B

I

J

K

L

Q

R

S

T

I would like to receive ROUGHNEWS: please put me on your free mailing list.

NAME . . . .

ADDRESS . . . .

Please clip or photocopy and send to: Rough Guides, 62-70 Shorts Gardens, London WC2H 9AH, England

or Rough Guides, 375 Hudson Street, New York, NY 10014, USA.

1. THE LONDON UNDERGROUND

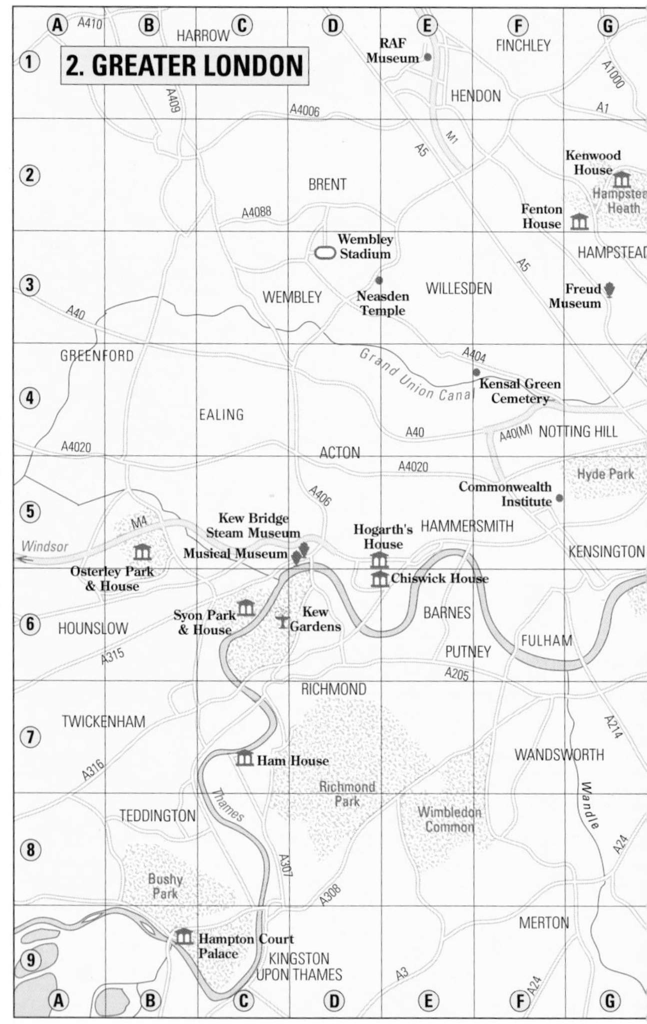
2. GREATER LONDON
HARROW
RAF Museum
FINCHLEY
HENDON
A410
A409
A4006
A1000
A1
M1
A5
BRENT
Kenwood House
Hampstead Heath
Fenton House
HAMPSTEAD
A4088
Wembley Stadium
A5
WEMBLEY
Neasden Temple
WILLESDEN
Freud Museum
A40
GREENFORD
Grand Union Canal
A404
Kensal Green Cemetery
EALING
A40
A40(M)
NOTTING HILL
A4020
ACTON
A4020
Hyde Park
Commonwealth Institute
A406
M4
Kew Bridge Steam Museum
Hogarth's House
HAMMERSMITH
Windsor
Musical Museum
KENSINGTON
Osterley Park & House
Chiswick House
Syon Park & House
Kew Gardens
BARNES
HOUNSLOW
FULHAM
A315
PUTNEY
A205
RICHMOND
TWICKENHAM
A214
WANDSWORTH
Ham House
A316
Richmond Park
Wandle
Thames
Wimbledon Common
TEDDINGTON
A24
A307
Bushy Park
A308
MERTON
Hampton Court Palace
KINGSTON UPON THAMES
A3
A24

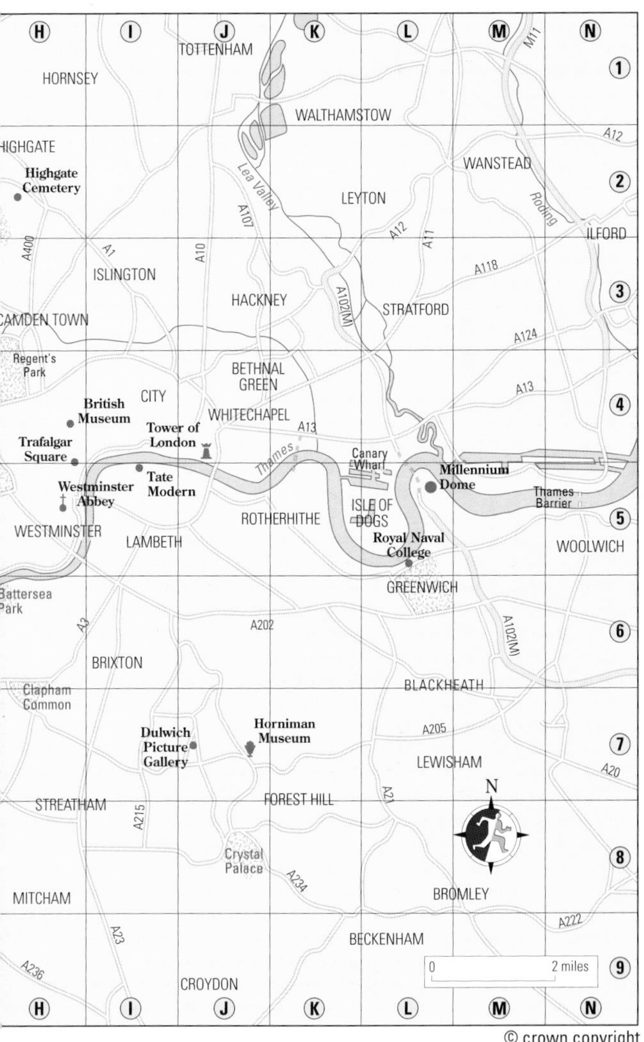

© crown copyright

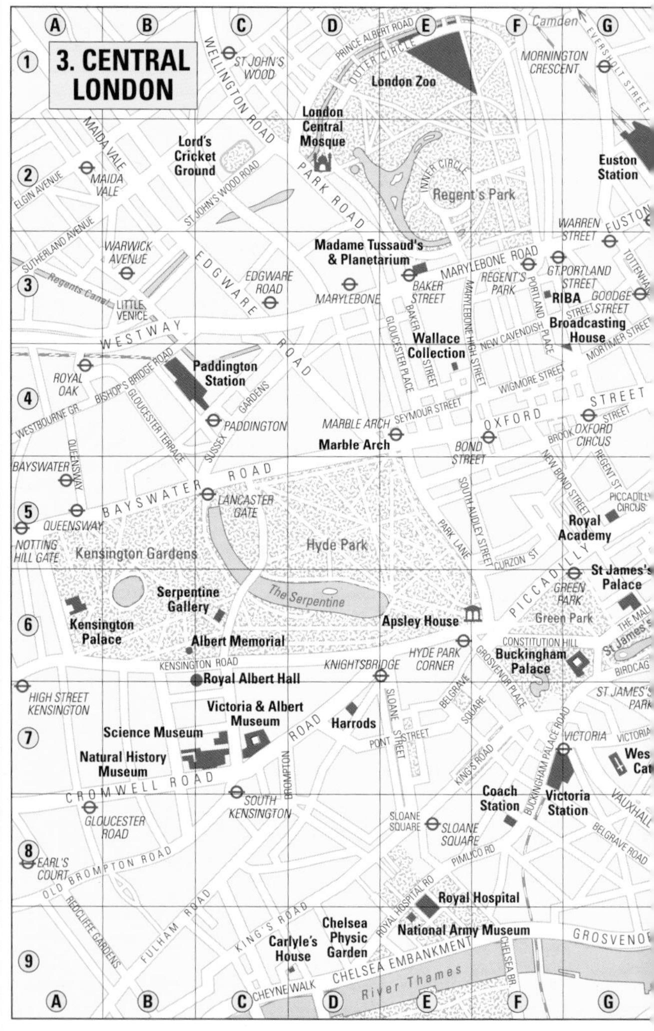

3. CENTRAL LONDON
London Zoo
London Central Mosque
Lord's Cricket Ground
Regent's Park
Euston Station
Madame Tussaud's & Planetarium
RIBA
Broadcasting House
Wallace Collection
Paddington Station
Marble Arch
Hyde Park
Kensington Gardens
The Serpentine
Serpentine Gallery
Kensington Palace
Albert Memorial
Apsley House
Royal Academy
St James's Palace
Green Park
Buckingham Palace
Royal Albert Hall
Victoria & Albert Museum
Harrods
Science Museum
Natural History Museum
Coach Station
Victoria Station
Royal Hospital
National Army Museum
Chelsea Physic Garden
Carlyle's House
River Thames

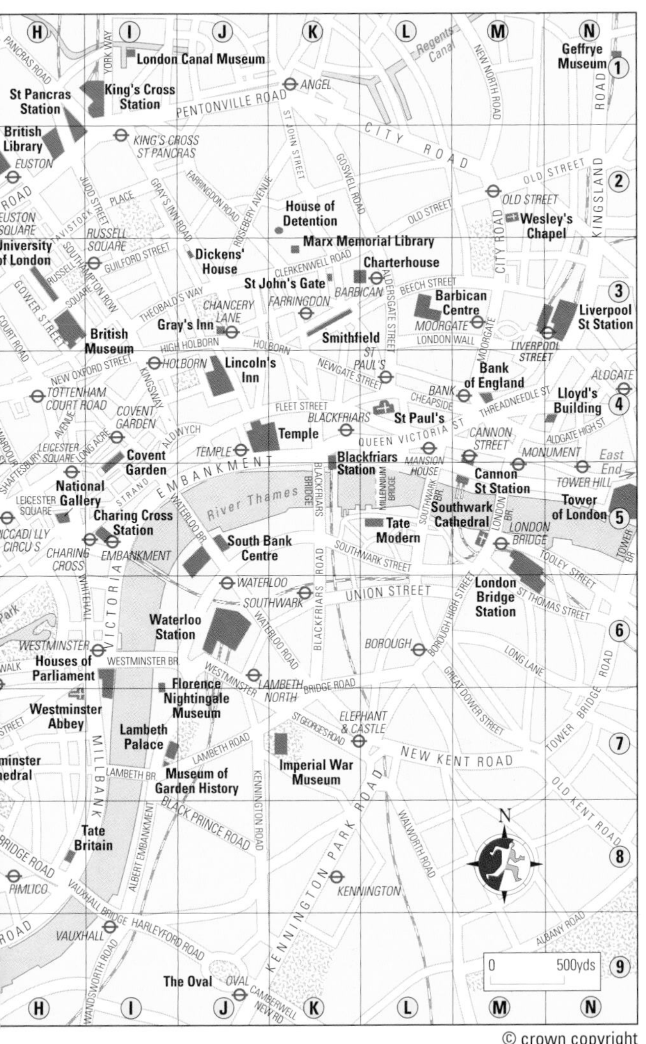

© crown copyright

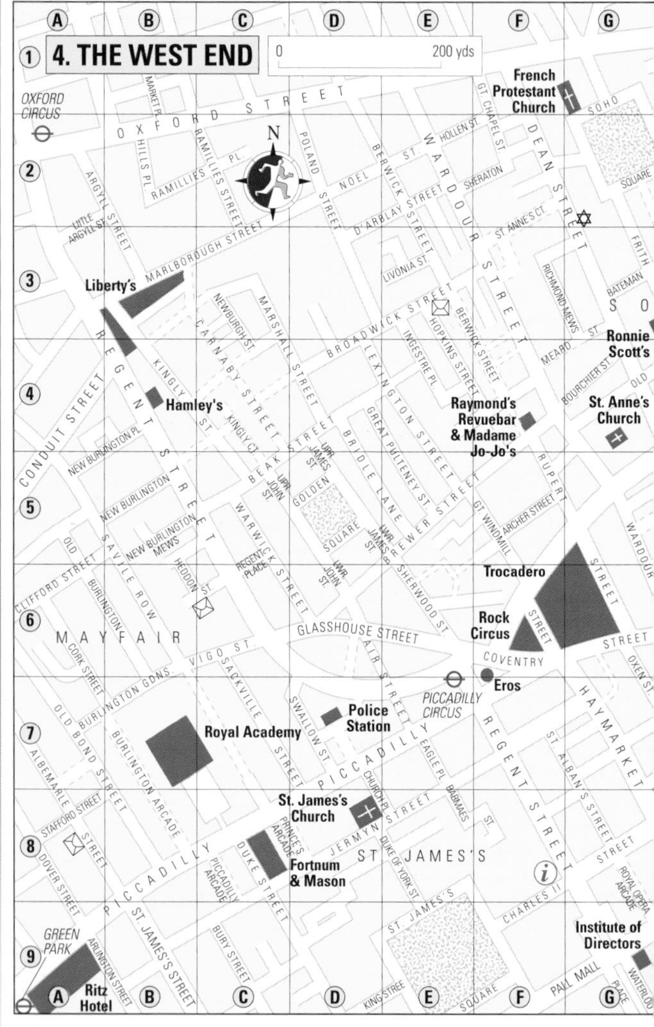

4. THE WEST END
0
200 yds
OXFORD CIRCUS
OXFORD STREET
French Protestant Church
SOHO SQUARE
Liberty's
Hamley's
Ronnie Scott's
St. Anne's Church
Raymond's Revuebar & Madame Jo-Jo's
GOLDEN SQUARE
Trocadero
Rock Circus
Eros
PICCADILLY CIRCUS
MAYFAIR
Police Station
Royal Academy
St. James's Church
Fortnum & Mason
ST. JAMES'S
ST. JAMES'S SQUARE
Institute of Directors
GREEN PARK
Ritz Hotel
REGENT STREET
CARNABY STREET
WARDOUR STREET
PICCADILLY
HAYMARKET
PALL MALL
GLASSHOUSE STREET
COVENTRY STREET
BROADWICK STREET
MARLBOROUGH STREET
CONDUIT STREET
SAVILE ROW
JERMYN STREET
DEAN STREET

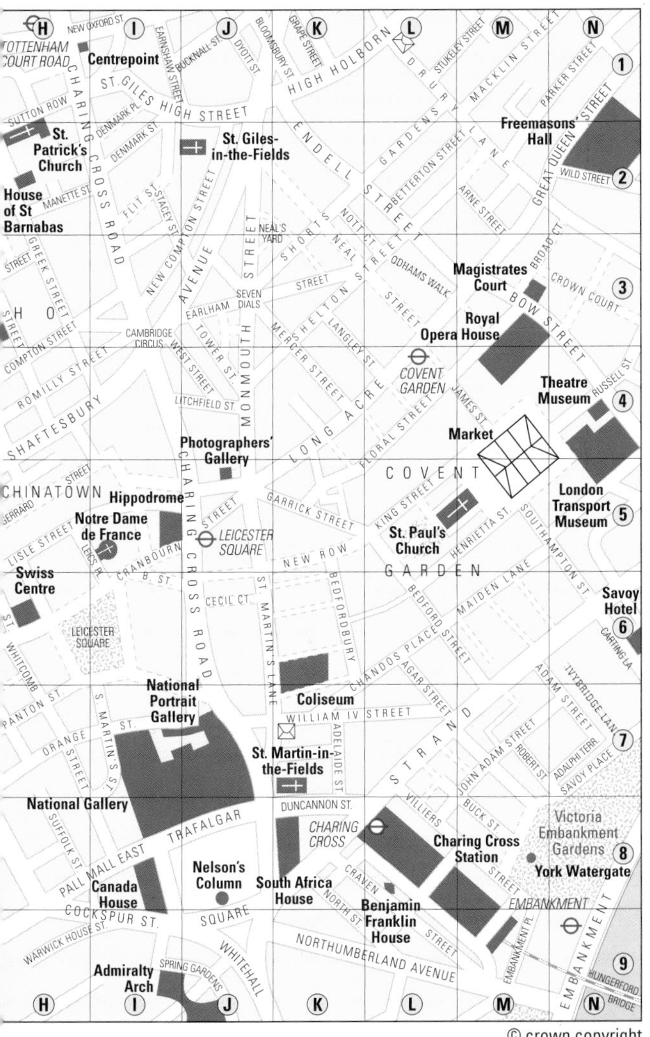
H
I
J
K
L
M
N
1
2
3
4
5
6
7
8
9
NEW OXFORD ST.
TOTTENHAM COURT ROAD
Centrepoint
EARNSHAW STREET
BUCKNALL ST.
DYOTT ST.
BLOOMSBURY ST.
GRAPE STREET
HIGH HOLBORN
DRURY LANE
STUKELEY STREET
MACKLIN STREET
PARKER STREET
ST. GILES HIGH STREET
SUTTON ROW
DENMARK PL.
DENMARK ST.
CHARING CROSS ROAD
St. Patrick's Church
St. Giles-in-the-Fields
ENDELL STREET
GARDENS
BETTERTON STREET
GREAT QUEEN STREET
Freemasons' Hall
WILD STREET
House of St Barnabas
MANETTE ST.
FLIT ST.
STACEY ST.
NEW COMPTON STREET
NEAL'S YARD
SHORTS GARDENS
NOTT CT.
NEAL STREET
ARNE STREET
BROAD CT.
GREEK STREET
AVENUE
STREET
ODHAMS WALK
Magistrates Court
CROWN COURT
BOW STREET
SEVEN DIALS
EARLHAM STREET
SHELTON STREET
SOHO
Royal Opera House
CAMBRIDGE CIRCUS
COMPTON STREET
TOWER ST.
MONMOUTH STREET
MERCER STREET
LANGLEY ST.
COVENT GARDEN
ROMILLY STREET
WEST STREET
LONG ACRE
Theatre Museum
RUSSELL ST.
JAMES ST.
LITCHFIELD ST.
SHAFTESBURY AVENUE
FLORAL STREET
Market
Photographers' Gallery
COVENT GARDEN
CHINATOWN
GERRARD STREET
Hippodrome
GARRICK STREET
KING STREET
London Transport Museum
Notre Dame de France
LISLE STREET
LEICESTER SQUARE
HENRIETTA ST.
SOUTHAMPTON ST.
St. Paul's Church
LEICS PL.
CRANBOURN STREET
NEW ROW
Swiss Centre
B. ST.
CECIL CT.
ST. MARTIN'S LANE
BEDFORDBURY
BEDFORD STREET
MAIDEN LANE
Savoy Hotel
LEICESTER SQUARE
CARTING LA.
CHANDOS PLACE
AGAR STREET
ADAM STREET
IVYBRIDGE LANE
WHITCOMB ST.
National Portrait Gallery
Coliseum
PANTON ST.
WILLIAM IV STREET
ORANGE STREET
ADELAIDE ST.
STRAND
JOHN ADAM STREET
ROBERT ST.
ADALPHI TERR.
SAVOY PLACE
St. Martin-in-the-Fields
National Gallery
DUNCANNON ST.
VILLIERS STREET
BUCK ST.
Victoria Embankment Gardens
SUFFOLK ST.
TRAFALGAR SQUARE
CHARING CROSS
Charing Cross Station
York Watergate
PALL MALL EAST
Nelson's Column
South Africa House
CRAVEN STREET
Canada House
Benjamin Franklin House
EMBANKMENT
COCKSPUR ST.
NORTH ST.
EMBANKMENT PL.
WARWICK HOUSE ST.
WHITEHALL
NORTHUMBERLAND AVENUE
Admiralty Arch
SPRING GARDENS
HUNGERFORD BRIDGE

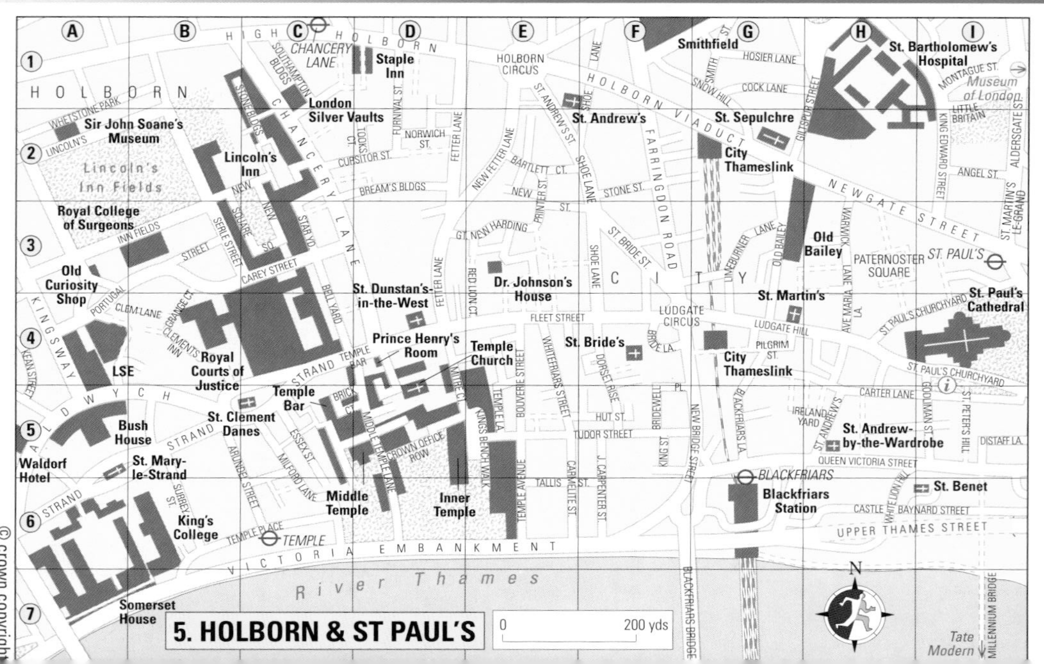

5. HOLBORN & ST PAUL'S
0
200 yds
N
Smithfield
St. Bartholomew's Hospital
Museum of London
Staple Inn
London Silver Vaults
Sir John Soane's Museum
Lincoln's Inn
Lincoln's Inn Fields
Royal College of Surgeons
Old Curiosity Shop
LSE
Royal Courts of Justice
St. Dunstan's-in-the-West
Prince Henry's Room
Temple Church
Dr. Johnson's House
St. Andrew's
St. Sepulchre
City Thameslink
Old Bailey
Paternoster Square
St. Paul's Cathedral
St. Martin's
St. Bride's
Temple Bar
St. Clement Danes
Bush House
Waldorf Hotel
St. Mary-le-Strand
King's College
Somerset House
Middle Temple
Inner Temple
Blackfriars Station
St. Andrew-by-the-Wardrobe
St. Benet
Tate Modern
River Thames
HIGH HOLBORN
HOLBORN
CHANCERY LANE
HOLBORN CIRCUS
HOLBORN VIADUCT
FARRINGDON ROAD
NEWGATE STREET
ST. PAUL'S
LUDGATE CIRCUS
FLEET STREET
LUDGATE HILL
CITY
STRAND
ALDWYCH
KINGSWAY
VICTORIA EMBANKMENT
TEMPLE
BLACKFRIARS
NEW BRIDGE STREET
BLACKFRIARS BRIDGE
MILLENNIUM BRIDGE
UPPER THAMES STREET
QUEEN VICTORIA STREET
KING EDWARD STREET
ALDERSGATE ST.
ST. MARTIN'S LE-GRAND
MONTAGUE ST.
LITTLE BRITAIN
ANGEL ST.
HOSIER LANE
COCK LANE
SNOW HILL
SMITH ST.
GILTSPUR STREET
WARWICK LANE
AVE MARIA LA.
ST. PAUL'S CHURCHYARD
CARTER LANE
GODLIMAN ST.
ST. PETER'S HILL
DISTAFF LA.
IRELAND YARD
ST. ANDREW'S
WHITE LION HILL
CASTLE BAYNARD STREET
OLD BAILEY
LIMEBURNER LANE
PILGRIM ST.
BLACKFRIARS LA.
BRIDE LA.
BRIDEWELL PL.
KING ST.
ST. BRIDE ST.
SHOE LANE
STONE ST.
DORSET RISE
HUT ST.
TUDOR STREET
J. CARPENTER ST.
CARMELITE ST.
TALLIS ST.
WHITEFRIARS STREET
BOUVERIE STREET
TEMPLE AVENUE
TEMPLE LA.
KINGS BENCH WALK
MITRE CT.
NEW FETTER LANE
BARTLETT CT.
PRINTER ST.
NEW ST.
GT. NEW HARDING
RED LION CT.
FETTER LANE
ST. ANDREW'S ST.
NORWICH ST.
FURNIVAL ST.
TOOKS CT.
CURSITOR ST.
BREAM'S BLDGS
SOUTHAMPTON BLDGS
STONE BLDGS
NEW SQUARE
STAR YD
BELL YARD
CAREY STREET
SERLE STREET
INN FIELDS STREET
WHETSTONE PARK
LINCOLN'S
PORTUGAL
CLEM LANE
GRANGE CT.
CLEMENTS INN
TEMPLE BAR
BRICK CT.
MIDDLE TEMPLE LANE
CROWN OFFICE ROW
ESSEX ST.
MILFORD LANE
ARUNDEL STREET
TEMPLE PLACE
SURREY ST.
KEAN STREET

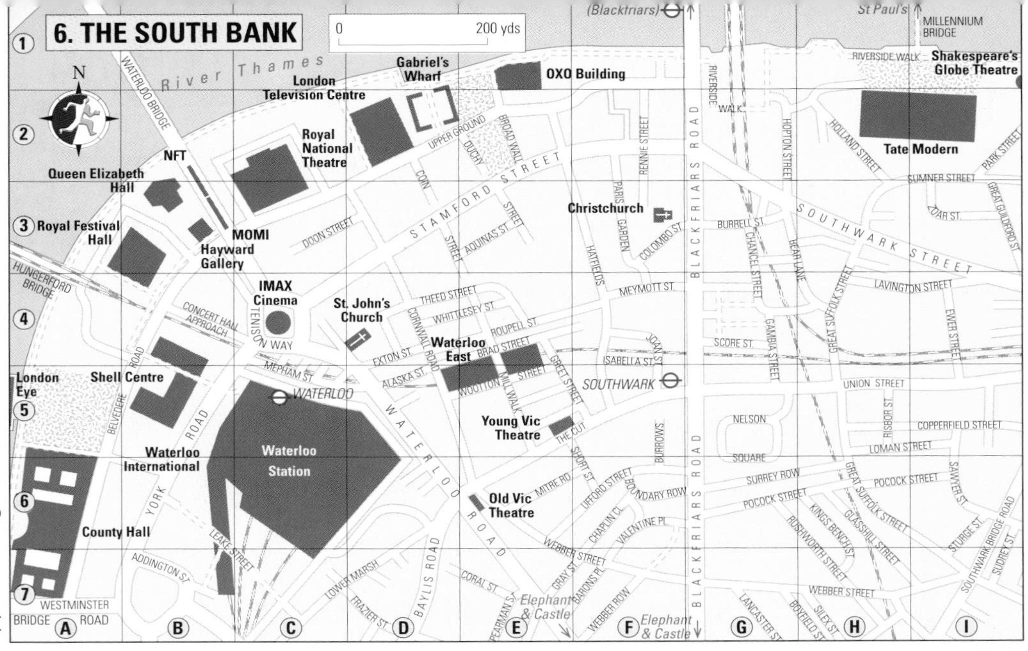
6. THE SOUTH BANK
0
200 yds
N
River Thames
(Blackfriars)
St Paul's
MILLENNIUM BRIDGE
Shakespeare's Globe Theatre
RIVERSIDE WALK
Tate Modern
OXO Building
Gabriel's Wharf
London Television Centre
Royal National Theatre
NFT
Queen Elizabeth Hall
Royal Festival Hall
MOMI
Hayward Gallery
IMAX Cinema
St. John's Church
Christchurch
Waterloo East
Young Vic Theatre
Old Vic Theatre
London Eye
Shell Centre
Waterloo International
Waterloo Station
County Hall
WATERLOO BRIDGE
HUNGERFORD BRIDGE
UPPER GROUND
DUCHY
BROAD WALL
COIN
STAMFORD STREET
DOON STREET
AQUINAS ST.
STREET
CONCERT HALL APPROACH
TENISON WAY
MEPHAM ST.
WATERLOO
THEED STREET
WHITTLESEY ST.
ROUPELL ST.
CORNWALL ROAD
EXTON ST.
ALASKA ST.
BRAD STREET
WOOTTON
MILL WALK
GREET STREET
THE CUT
SHORT ST.
MITRE RD.
UFFORD STREET
BOUNDARY ROW
CHAPLIN CL.
VALENTINE PL.
WEBBER STREET
GRAY ST.
BARONS PL.
WEBBER ROW
PEARMAN ST.
CORAL ST.
BAYLIS ROAD
LOWER MARSH
FRAZIER ST.
LEAKE STREET
ADDINGTON ST.
YORK ROAD
BELVEDERE ROAD
WESTMINSTER BRIDGE ROAD
WATERLOO ROAD
Elephant & Castle
RENNIE STREET
PARIS GARDEN
HATFIELDS
COLOMBO ST.
MEYMOTT ST.
JOAN ST.
ISABELLA ST.
SOUTHWARK
BURROWS
BLACKFRIARS ROAD
RIVERSIDE WALK
HOPTON STREET
HOLLAND STREET
PARK STREET
SUMNER STREET
GREAT GUILDFORD ST.
ZOAR ST.
SOUTHWARK STREET
BURRELL ST.
CHANCEL STREET
BEAR LANE
GREAT SUFFOLK STREET
LAVINGTON STREET
EWER STREET
SCORE ST.
GAMBIA STREET
UNION STREET
RISBOR ST.
COPPERFIELD STREET
LOMAN STREET
NELSON SQUARE
SURREY ROW
POCOCK STREET
SAWYER ST.
KINGS BENCH ST.
GLASSHILL STREET
RUSHWORTH STREET
WEBBER STREET
LANCASTER ST.
BOYFIELD ST.
SILEX ST.
STURGE ST.
SOUTHWARK BRIDGE ROAD
SUDREY ST.
1
2
3
4
5
6
7
A
B
C
D
E
F
G
H
I

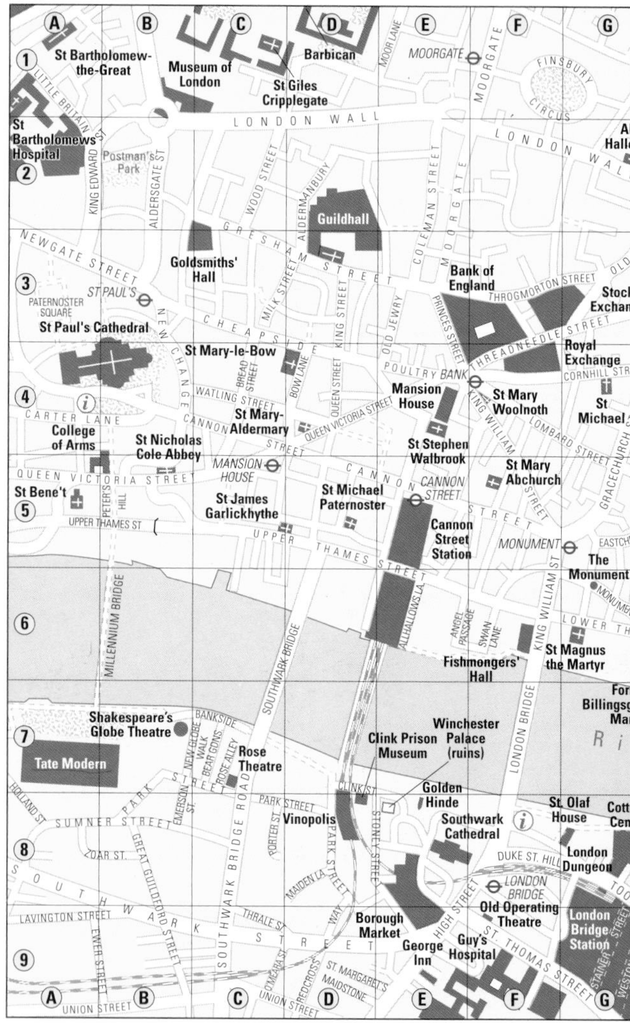
St Bartholomew-the-Great
Museum of London
Barbican
St Giles Cripplegate
MOORGATE
FINSBURY CIRCUS
LITTLE BRITAIN
St Bartholomews Hospital
Postman's Park
LONDON WALL
All Hallows
KING EDWARD ST
ALDERSGATE ST
WOOD STREET
ALDERMANBURY
Guildhall
COLEMAN STREET
MOORGATE
NEWGATE STREET
Goldsmiths' Hall
GRESHAM STREET
Bank of England
THROGMORTON STREET
OLD BROAD
Stock Exchange
ST PAUL'S
PATERNOSTER SQUARE
St Paul's Cathedral
MILK STREET
KING STREET
OLD JEWRY
PRINCES STREET
CHEAPSIDE
NEW CHANGE
St Mary-le-Bow
BREAD STREET
BOW LANE
QUEEN STREET
POULTRY
BANK
THREADNEEDLE STREET
Royal Exchange
CORNHILL STREET
WATLING STREET
Mansion House
St Mary Woolnoth
St Michael
CARTER LANE
CANNON STREET
St Mary-Aldermary
QUEEN VICTORIA STREET
KING WILLIAM STREET
LOMBARD STREET
GRACECHURCH STREET
College of Arms
St Nicholas Cole Abbey
St Stephen Walbrook
MANSION HOUSE
St Mary Abchurch
QUEEN VICTORIA STREET
CANNON STREET
St Bene't
PETER'S HILL
St James Garlickhythe
St Michael Paternoster
UPPER THAMES ST
Cannon Street Station
MONUMENT
EASTCHEAP
UPPER THAMES STREET
The Monument
MONUMENT ST
MILLENNIUM BRIDGE
SOUTHWARK BRIDGE
ALLHALLOWS LA.
ANGEL PASSAGE
SWAN LANE
KING WILLIAM ST
LOWER THAMES
St Magnus the Martyr
Fishmongers' Hall
Former Billingsgate Market
River
Shakespeare's Globe Theatre
BANKSIDE
Winchester Palace (ruins)
Clink Prison Museum
LONDON BRIDGE
NEW GLOBE WALK
BEAR GDNS
ROSE ALLEY
Rose Theatre
Tate Modern
CLINK ST
Golden Hinde
HOLLAND ST
PARK STREET
EMERSON ST.
SOUTHWARK BRIDGE ROAD
PARK STREET
Vinopolis
STONEY STREET
Southwark Cathedral
St. Olaf House
Cottons Centre
SUMNER STREET
PORTER ST.
ZOAR ST.
GREAT GUILDFORD STREET
DUKE ST. HILL
London Dungeon
MAIDEN LA.
LONDON BRIDGE
TOOLEY
SOUTHWARK STREET
LAVINGTON STREET
THRALE ST.
WAY
Borough Market
HIGH STREET
Old Operating Theatre
London Bridge Station
EWER STREET
George Inn
Guy's Hospital
ST. THOMAS STREET
STAINER STREET
WESTON STREET
O'MEARA ST
REDCROSS
ST. MARGARET'S
MAIDSTONE
UNION STREET
UNION STREET
A
B
C
D
E
F
G
1
2
3
4
5
6
7
8
9

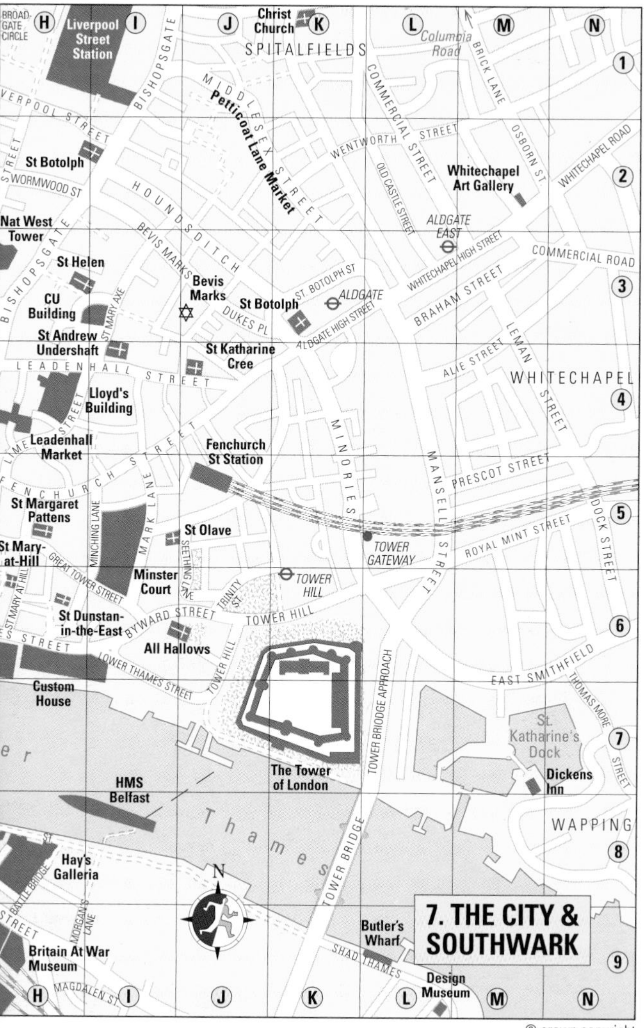
7. THE CITY & SOUTHWARK
Liverpool Street Station
Christ Church
SPITALFIELDS
Columbia Road
BRICK LANE
BISHOPSGATE
MIDDLESEX STREET
Petticoat Lane Market
COMMERCIAL STREET
LIVERPOOL STREET
St Botolph
WORMWOOD ST
HOUNDSDITCH
WENTWORTH STREET
OSBORN ST
WHITECHAPEL ROAD
Whitechapel Art Gallery
OLD CASTLE STREET
ALDGATE EAST
Nat West Tower
BEVIS MARKS
St Helen
Bevis Marks
ST. BOTOLPH ST
ALDGATE
WHITECHAPEL HIGH STREET
COMMERCIAL ROAD
BRAHAM STREET
CU Building
ST MARY AXE
St Botolph
DUKES PL
ALDGATE HIGH STREET
St Andrew Undershaft
St Katharine Cree
LEMAN STREET
ALIE STREET
LEADENHALL STREET
WHITECHAPEL
Lloyd's Building
LIME STREET
Leadenhall Market
Fenchurch St Station
MINORIES
MANSELL STREET
FENCHURCH STREET
PRESCOT STREET
St Margaret Pattens
MINCHING LANE
MARK LANE
St Olave
DOCK STREET
TOWER GATEWAY
ROYAL MINT STREET
St Mary-at-Hill
GREAT TOWER STREET
SEETHING LANE
Minster Court
TOWER HILL
TRINITY ST.
ST MARY AT HILL
St Dunstan-in-the-East
BYWARD STREET
TOWER HILL
All Hallows
LOWER THAMES STREET
TOWER BRIDGE APPROACH
EAST SMITHFIELD
THOMAS MORE STREET
Custom House
St. Katharine's Dock
Dickens Inn
The Tower of London
HMS Belfast
Thames
WAPPING
TOWER BRIDGE
Hay's Galleria
BATTLE BRIDGE
MORGAN'S LANE
N
Butler's Wharf
SHAD THAMES
Britain At War Museum
Design Museum
MAGDALEN ST
BROAD-GATE CIRCLE
H I J K L M N
1 2 3 4 5 6 7 8 9

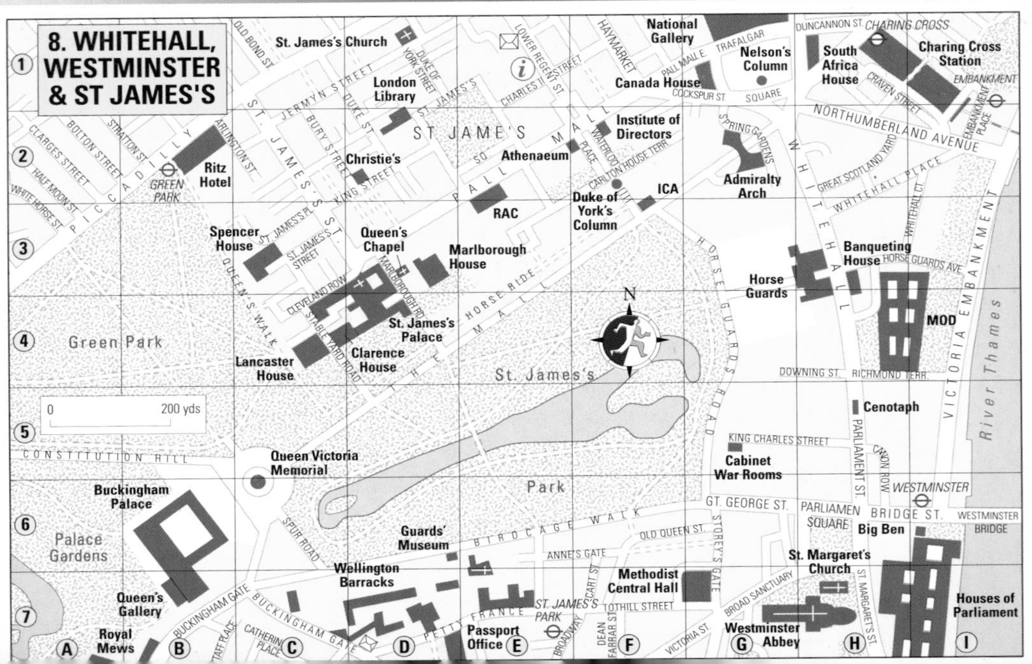
8. WHITEHALL, WESTMINSTER & ST JAMES'S
St. James's Church
London Library
National Gallery
Nelson's Column
South Africa House
Charing Cross Station
Canada House
Institute of Directors
Admiralty Arch
Ritz Hotel
Christie's
Athenaeum
RAC
Duke of York's Column
ICA
Spencer House
Queen's Chapel
Marlborough House
Horse Guards
Banqueting House
MOD
St. James's Palace
Clarence House
Lancaster House
Green Park
St. James's
Park
Cenotaph
Cabinet War Rooms
Queen Victoria Memorial
Buckingham Palace
Palace Gardens
Guards' Museum
Wellington Barracks
Queen's Gallery
Royal Mews
Passport Office
Methodist Central Hall
St. Margaret's Church
Big Ben
Westminster Abbey
Houses of Parliament
River Thames
VICTORIA EMBANKMENT
NORTHUMBERLAND AVENUE
WHITEHALL
PARLIAMENT ST.
HORSE GUARDS ROAD
THE MALL
PALL MALL
PICCADILLY
CONSTITUTION HILL
BIRDCAGE WALK
HAYMARKET
TRAFALGAR SQUARE
0
200 yds